PRAISE FOR *NISEI RESISTANCE AND RESILIENCE*

"This powerful biography of Dr. Maruyama comes when we most desperately need a reminder of the dark history and continuing legacy of Asian American racism in the United States. Purvis-Smith has written a meticulously researched and entertainingly crafted story of a beautiful soul whose resistance and resilience are inspirational. Through Purvis-Smith's captivating retelling, we witness Maruyama's struggles against discrimination and other challenges to live an authentic life of service while in search of eternal truths."

—ALITHEA DANIELSKI, WORCESTER POLYTECHNIC INSTITUTE

"In this moment, with our country riven by centuries of division, we must find stories to help us understand our common humanity. Purvis-Smith has found the perfect grain of sand in which we can see our world. Her compassionate, unflinching interpretation of the story of one man, Allen Maruyama, allows us to understand the forces that have divided us and, even more importantly, the ties and commonalities that unite us in our diversity."

—CHARLES SICHEL-OUTCALT, SOUTHERN NEW HAMPSHIRE UNIVERSITY

"This book is an insightful exploration of one Japanese American man's journey from his youth in rural Colorado, overcoming the overt and subtle discrimination in mid-century America, to become a gifted and sought-after pastor in the Presbyterian Church, and his attempts to scale the heights of its leadership. Purvis-Smith's thorough and sensitive depiction of Allen Maruyama's life reveals the struggles and triumphs he experienced as he sought and succeeded to serve those in need and to address many of society's ills and challenges, including racism, penal reform, homelessness and disengaged youth. His admirable personal traits and inspiring journey of resistance and resilience are comprehensively, carefully, and elegantly showcased in these pages."

—ANNE PATTERSON FINN, CRIMINAL JUSTICE ATTORNEY

"Allen Maruyama, the son of Japanese, Buddhist sharecroppers, is embraced by Colorado neighbors and a small-town Presbyterian church. However, he confronts the racism of the surrounding community following Pearl Harbor and struggles with internalized self-hatred. His spiritual journey takes him on a 'trail of discrimination,' but he experiences his own healing as he ministers to others. Purvis-Smith does a beautiful job of describing his complicated, inspiring, and compassionate life."

—BETH BURBANK, ACPE CLINICAL PASTORAL EDUCATOR

"Rep. John Lewis suggests we cause 'good trouble' in seeking social justice. Purvis-Smith writes 'good history' because she invites the reader to look in a mirror and ask the visualized image, 'What lies are you telling yourself?' 'If only I had lived in Las Animus when the Japanese Americans were being incarcerated, ridiculed, and persecuted I would have been an advocate for justice and kindness to Japanese American citizens facing such painful circumstances.' 'If only' is a lie we tell ourselves. Healing begins when we personally commit to 'next time.' 'Good history' says, 'Next time is here in our present culture.' The author invited me to see myself therein reflected in the white space between the words. *Love* is a verb calling for action now. Love reveals our identity, which requires an active itinerary that writes our legacy. Purvis-Smith writes 'good history' that challenges the reader to invest in a new legacy now!"

—JOHN ROSS, RETIRED SENIOR PASTOR OF FIRST PRESBYTERIAN CHURCH, PUEBLO, COLORADO

Nisei Resistance and Resilience

Nisei Resistance and Resilience

A Japanese-American Life

V. L. PURVIS-SMITH

Foreword by Grace Kaori Suzuki

RESOURCE *Publications* · Eugene, Oregon

NISEI RESISTANCE AND RESILIENCE
A Japanese-American Life

Resource Publications
An Imprint of Wipf and Stock Publishers
199 W. 8th Ave., Suite 3
Eugene, OR 97401

www.wipfandstock.com

PAPERBACK ISBN: 978-1-7252-9547-6
HARDCOVER ISBN: 978-1-7252-9546-9
EBOOK ISBN: 978-1-7252-9548-3

07/28/21

Nisei Resistance and Resilience: A Japanese-American Life is dedicated to Umeyo Amino and Masakuni Maruyama, Allen's parents, and Anne Campbell and George Purvis, the author's grandparents, in gratitude that their neighborliness contributed to building community on the High Plains of Colorado.

Contents

PART II: WITHOUT A DREAM, THE PEOPLE PERISH

Foreword

AS THE PASTOR OF the oldest Japanese and Japanese-American Christian church in Northern America, it is not uncommon for me to receive emails or phone calls regarding the history of our church and the many members and friends who have been through its doors. Founded in 1885, Christ United Presbyterian Church in San Francisco holds a rich history and heritage in the Japanese and Japanese-American religious communities in the United States and beyond. Typically, such interactions result in a brief and amicable exchange, whether it is for me to offer any information that our church may (or may not) have or refer them to another source that is able to assist them further.

However, the email that I received from Rev. V. L. Purvis-Smith, PhD, back in December 2018 was anything but typical. Not only was she informing me that she was writing a book about Allen Maruyama, PhD, whose close friends were from our congregation (Rev. Minoru and Mrs. June Mochizuki), she was also asking if someone from our church would be able to read the manuscript to "give feedback about places where [her] perspective as a white (clergy)woman may compromise Dr. Maruyama's story and its accuracy." Although I had not heard of Dr. Maruyama at that time (I was familiar with the Mochizukis, if only by name), I was intrigued by her request and deeply impressed with her humility for allowing such feedback. Thus, my relationship with Ginny and *Nisei Resistance and Resilience: A Japanese-American Life* began.

In the following pages, you will find the biography of an amazing Japanese-American man who has lived while trying to be faithful to God's calling and navigating his life between his "Japanese-ness" and "American-ness." Although there are times when the distinctions between these two realities blur, Dr. Maruyama, as have many Japanese Americans, still had to carve out a sense of identity in the midst of differing (and sometimes clashing) cultures, religions, and expectations. His story is somewhat unique among Japanese Americans of his generation because he did not experience the Japanese concentration (internment) camps that so many others did. Regardless, his struggles were similar: the struggle to "belong" in places where he was not always welcomed; the struggle to somehow resist being assimilated into the dominant culture (with the irony that assimilation was seen as a way to survive, particularly given the circumstances during World War II); and the struggle to be resilient despite both overt and subtle discrimination.

In addition to a straight telling of the facts and events of his life, Ginny surrounds them with thorough and thoughtful explanations and insights. These mini history lessons help the reader understand the depth and complexity of the Japanese-American experience as well as the polity and politics of the Presbyterian Church in which Dr. Maruyama served. Although I have been engaged in ministry with the Japanese-American community as a Presbyterian pastor since 2004, there were quite a few things that I learned, or learned more about, from reading this biography.

Per Ginny's request, I read the draft editions and offered feedback using my "Asian lenses"—as a native Japanese woman who has lived in the US for much of my adult life and currently serves as pastor of a Japanese/Japanese-American Presbyterian congregation. I appreciated the level of cultural care and sensitivity that she had already incorporated into her writing, both in describing events (especially as they pertained to the experiences of the Japanese and Japanese Americans) and interpreting them. In addition, she was very gracious and open to the feedback I gave, which added to my awe of her passion and her wanting Dr. Maruyama's story to be told in a way that did him (and other Japanese Americans) justice.

In my current ministry context, I am honored to have heard many stories of the *Nisei* (second-generation Japanese). Some are about *resistance*, such as being one of the "No-No Boys," or sneaking out of Camp Topaz and running toward the hills in Utah just to get exercise! Some are about their *resilience*, such as withstanding the major sandstorms, or making beautiful artwork from seeds, shells, and scrap wood. When they are asked about these experiences, I am certain they would not claim that their stories of resistance or resilience were extraordinary, by any means.

In the same way, in the beginning chapters of the book, Dr. Maruyama's wife Rose asks, "Why do you want to write Allen's biography? His life is ordinary, and our life together isn't remarkable." To this, Ginny responds, "For many of us our lives seem ordinary until they're examined, and what seems ordinary might be instructive and inspiring to someone else. . . .

[People] might think their lives are ordinary, but how they are living that
life is extraordinary."[1]

Nisei Resistance and Resilience depicts the life of Dr. Allen Maruyama
and his particular story of resistance and resilience. Even if Rose (and
maybe even Dr. Maruyama himself) may not see their lives as anything but
ordinary, I believe that Ginny has done a skillful job of doing justice in telling his story—his extraordinary story.

Rev. Dr. Grace Kaori Suzuki
Pastor, Christ United Presbyterian Church, San Francisco
November 2020

Preface

THE STORIES OF OUR individual lives begin well before birth, because we enter physical, cultural, and historical spaces already assembled. We become aware of some of their aspects as we mature; some layers are invisible to us but affect us nonetheless, what Richard Frishman calls the testimonies of our landscapes.[2]

On its surface, Allen Maruyama's life is that of an all-American who is a high school athlete and World War II veteran making use of the GI Bill to achieve professional success. However, taking his particular physical, cultural, and historical matrix into account discloses another narrative.

Allen and I share much of that matrix. Although born almost two decades apart, we are both members of the "Silent Generation." We grew up on the High Plains of Southeastern Colorado, are descendants of immigrants, attended the same elementary school in our early years, were members of the same small-town church, attended the same seminary, and both of us were ordained as ministers in the Presbyterian Church in the United States of America—the PC(USA).

Not until my friendship with Allen began in 2007, though, did I begin to understand how differently we occupied the shared layers of our respective histories. He is the son of Japanese immigrants and was a teenager at the time of the Pearl Harbor attack. I am the granddaughter of a Scottish Canadian immigrant, and I was born two months after the end of World War II in the Pacific.

Our shared histories diverge most sharply consequent to that attack, with Allen as one of thousands of Japanese/Japanese Americans in the United States who were assaulted by varied expressions of anti-Japanese sentiment. The forced relocation of almost one hundred twenty thousand West Coast Japanese/Japanese Americans and their incarceration at ten sites in the US interior was perhaps the most unjust, illegal, and destructive expression of that hostility and suspicion.

One of those sites was Southeastern Colorado's Camp Amache. Allen knew all about it. He and his family visited there, the Maruyamas on one side of the barbed wire fence and guard tower, and, on the other, family friends who had relocated to the West Coast but were forcibly returned and incarcerated. Allen was not confined, but as a Japanese American living in the interior, he regularly suffered verbal racist attacks and shunning.

I only learned about Camp Amache, formally known as the Granada War Relocation Center, in my forties, when my aunt, Pauline Reyher, mailed me a clipping about restoration work being done there. Almost eight thousand Japanese/Japanese Americans were incarcerated at Amache from 1942 to 1945, only sixteen miles from the town where I was born. Shortly after my birth in October 1945, the camp was almost completely dismantled, which concealed an entire physical layer of the area's history but not its existence in the memories of those incarcerated and their descendants.

The name itself, Camp Amache, reveals another cruel layer of Southeastern Colorado's history, this one little-known to both Allen and me as we were growing up. As the area that would become the state took its current shape in the mid-nineteenth century, Colorado coalesced into seventeen counties. One of them, located to the east, was the Cheyenne and Arapaho Indian Reservation, established in 1861.

However, subsequent to increasing tension resulting from the influx of settlers on Cheyenne and Arapaho lands, US Army troops under the command of Colonel John Chivington massacred a group of mostly women, children, and the elderly at Sand Creek in 1864. Among those killed included a chief who had been negotiating for peace by the name of Ochinee. He was the father of an eighteen-year-old named Amache. Just three years prior to the massacre, Amache had married John Prowers, an early settler and cattleman.

In 1869, the remaining Cheyenne and Arapaho were forcibly removed to Indian Territory in Oklahoma, and the next year, most of the southeast quadrant of the state became Bent County. The reservation was renamed Greenwood County, only to be dissolved in 1874, as reservation and county were erased and divided between Bent and Elbert counties. In 1888, the quadrant itself was divided into six counties. One was called Prowers, its name derived from John Prowers, the county in which Camp Amache was eventually located.

The county that retained the Bent name memorialized the brothers William and Charles Bent, who had established a trading post on the

Arkansas River in the 1830s. At the time, the land south of the river was part of Mexico.[3]

In 1892, George Purvis, a Scottish Presbyterian, immigrated from Canada to teach at Boggsville, a settlement south of the river but, subsequent to 1848, part of the United States. It was founded by an employee of the Bents, Thomas Boggs. John Prowers, who had also worked for the Bents, and Amache lived at Boggsville for a number of years before moving to the town of Las Animas. Purvis settled in the area, married, and early in the 1900s, moved his family to a farm east of what had by then become a thriving town.

Las Animas owed its growth to its location on the river and the railroad. One young railroad worker was Masakuni Maruyama, a Japanese Buddhist immigrant. Attracted by the fertile river-bottom soil, as were other Japanese families, Maruyama stayed and initially sharecropped for Purvis.

Scottish Presbyterian and Japanese Buddhist families occupied land relatively recently layered with the histories of inhabitants from numerous other nations and cultures. None of this history is immediately visible. Newcomers are struck by the area's seeming desolation—flat, arid, a thin line of cottonwood trees tracing the flow of the Arkansas River and would not think that the place had hosted such complexity. In fact, Cheyenne, Arapaho, Comanche, Apache, Sioux, and other nations left evidence of their histories in the "Indian writings" on the arroyo cliffs scattered throughout the area and the thousands of arrowheads embedded in the soil.

Perhaps a local will take the newly arrived to see the "writings" south of the river, on the land formerly part of Mexico, and to walk in parallel ruts that are faintly visible north of it, out on the "dryland." The ruts are vestiges of wagon wheel tracks left by settlers slogging along the Santa Fe Trail. There might be enough daylight remaining to visit Fort Lyon, used by Chivington as a staging post for his attack at Sand Creek.

Fort Lyon is now a complex of buildings resembling a college campus and currently run by the Colorado Coalition for the Homeless as a supportive residential community. Allen has been an advocate of this program, primarily through his contacts with the Colorado Council of Churches and the Denver and Pueblo presbyteries.

The Purvis and Maruyama stories again converged when I collaborated with Allen on my historical novel, *Greenwood Riven*, whose setting is our shared locale at the time of the Pearl Harbor attack. In the process of my research, Allen introduced me to his friend, Rev. Minoru Mochizuki, and his wife, June. June and her family were incarcerated at Amache. Min's, June's, and Allen's stories gave rise to several of the characters in the novel.

A novel alone does not do justice to Allen's story, though. A biography was necessary to tell of his negotiations through Southeastern Colorado's matrix of history and culture and beyond, from his position as a Japanese-American Presbyterian. The biography is not only an accounting of the facts of his life but an excavation of layers: of historical events and theological disputes in the life the PC(USA); discussions of neo-orthodoxy, liberation theology, and the Civil Rights Movement; a recounting of the 1980 and 1990 PC(USA) General Assemblies, when Allen ran as the first Asian American candidate for moderator of the national church; an exploration of Asian American history; a comparison and contrast of Allen's experiences with those of Min and June; an examination of his dissertation and his report on his sabbatical in Japan; and descriptions of his vocation as a massage therapist and Reiki master.

This is Allen's story, primarily as he told it in my thirty-plus transcribed interviews with him and Rose, his wife of sixty-three years. It is also based on numerous conversations with him starting in 2007. I interviewed his two children Sarah and John, his brother Joe, and his sister Virginia. I spoke with thirteen of his colleagues or their survivors and seven members of congregations in Iowa and Colorado, where he served as pastor prior to his 1992 retirement from Montview Boulevard Presbyterian Church, Denver.

Everyone I interviewed was generous and expansive in our conversations, as were the members of the Montview Heritage Committee and personnel at the Presbyterian Historical Society in Philadelphia. Doug Kurtz, my writing coach, and Rev. Dr. Grace Kaori Suzuki combed through early iterations of the manuscript with diligence and did not hesitate to give necessary and welcome feedback.

My investment in Allen's story is not mine alone. It began well over a century ago with my Scottish Presbyterian immigrant grandfather, who died before both Allen's birth and mine, and his friendship with Allen's father. I am not a neutral narrator, so I make my perspective explicitly known in the prologue and epilogue, but in chapters one through thirty-five, I attempt distance to respect Allen's telling of his own story.

I am grateful that the chronicle of Allen's life continues in my family, now a century after Purvises and Maruyamas farmed together in Colorado. My husband Terry, also a Presbyterian minister, is one of Allen's friends and colleagues and a close reader of early drafts of this biography. My daughter Julie, yet another critical reader, consulted about technical matters. She and her family, my son Steven and his family, and my sister-in-law Patricia Eichenlaub and her husband Frank have provided constant support and motivation with their curiosity and suggestions.

Katheryn Reyher, Aunt Pauline's daughter-in-law, recently sent me a newspaper clipping, "Could Amache Become a National Park?" The commissioners in a neighboring county, Otero, are supporting the efforts of their Prowers County counterparts to move the camp's status as a National Historic Landmark to that of a new unit of the National Park System.

Thankfully, many individuals and organizations are insuring that Camp Amache's ignoble history is not forgotten and that the valor of its residents is remembered and honored. To mention some of their accomplishments, those incarcerated at Camp Amache had the highest rate of military service of all ten camps, and any number of individuals who passed by its guard tower achieved notable success.[4]

Denver University's Department of Anthropology has developed an ongoing excavation project, and the Amache Preservation Society, under the direction of Granada High School teacher and principal John Hopper, continues the maintenance and education efforts it began in 1993.[5] The guard and water towers and a barrack have been rebuilt. All these efforts unearth the testimony of past layers of history in order to inform the present.

Dr. Allen Maruyama's story is similarly instructive. His "go, go, go" personality, aptly described by a Japanese expression, *issho kenmei*, "all in, full throttle and nonstop," means that he is thoroughly and thoughtfully engaged in whatever cultural milieu he finds himself. Such engagement reveals his personal history but also illuminates the history of the times and places he inhabits.

REV. V. L. PURVIS-SMITH, PHD
December 2020

Prologue

"How long since you've seen him? How will we recognize them?"

I had no ready answers to my husband's questions. I might have last seen Allen over fifty years prior, when he married Rose in 1954 and brought her home to Colorado for introductions. His brother Ted had hosted a reception for them in the living room of his farmhouse across the highway from our place. As an eight-year-old, I had sat across from Rose and stole an occasional glance at her, thinking she must be quite special to be Allen's bride. His popularity had only been magnified by the authority everyone ceded him due to his ordination as a Presbyterian minister in our Las Animas church the previous year.

"How many elderly Japanese-American men with European-American wives do you think will be arriving on this flight into Nassau?" I teased.

My husband and I had established contact with Allen several months earlier when we had visited family in Colorado. We had had opportunity to worship at Denver's Montview Boulevard Presbyterian Church, where Allen had served for twenty years. Montview was of interest to us because, as Presbyterian ministers, we were familiar with its reputation: its cathedral-like sanctuary, imposing choir, and community outreach.

We had also hoped to see Allen. He had retired in 1992, but he still occasionally worshipped there. He, too, was well regarded in the denomination, not only as the first Asian American to stand for its highest elected position but also for his many national leadership roles.

He was apparently not in attendance that Sunday, so we asked an usher if she would pass along our contact information. Not long afterward, we received an email from him, and several exchanges later, we invited him and Rose to visit us in The Bahamas.

They accepted! Even though he and I were from the same small Arkansas Valley town and had both attended McCormick Theological Seminary,

I was nervous about the visit. How would we entertain this celebrity, a nationally recognized elder statesman of the church, the hometown boy made good?

When they emerged from customs, we were quickly caught up in Allen's energy, spontaneity, and candor.

"They've lost my luggage!" he said, accompanying the words with a handshake. "We're going to be here for a week, and I won't even have a change of clothes!"

Rose steered the conversation back to customary greetings. "It's so nice of you to invite us. I can't believe we're in The Bahamas. Our first time. And we hardly know you. Maybe his bag will come on a later flight." (It was never recovered.)

By the time we exited the airport parking lot, I was at ease. They seemed as pleased to be with us as we were to be with them. As Allen and I shared stories about growing up in Southeastern Colorado, though, I was confronted with my naïveté. Not only did he know my Purvis family in ways I had not imagined, I had wrongly assumed a comfortable correspondence between his childhood and mine. As a Japanese American teenager in Las Animas, he had grown up in World War II Colorado, a place unfamiliar to me—a contradictory and cruel blend of exclusion and acceptance.

Even so, the Maruyama and Purvis stories intertwined. Allen's father, Masakuni Maruyama, arrived in Colorado in the early 1900s. Mr. Maruyama came from an area southwest of Tokyo, near Mt. Fujiyama in Yamanashi Prefecture, where his family were farmers.[6] He initially sharecropped for my grandfather, George Purvis, who had immigrated to Colorado in 1892 from the Canadian province of Ontario, where his Scottish parents had settled. As the decades went by, Mr. Maruyama sometimes also sharecropped for or rented from other Scottish Presbyterian families in the area. The various arrangements Japanese immigrant farmers made in the Arkansas Valley were probably similar to those made in Colorado's Platte River Valley farther north, where the farmer agreed either to rent for cash or for a share of the crop. If the latter, the farmer generally paid the landowner twenty-five or thirty percent of the gross proceeds.[7]

Allen's mother, Umeyo Amino, came to the United States as a "picture bride," a common method that families used to arrange marriages for Japanese men living overseas. The marriage was arranged by the families in Japan and registered there, so the couple would already be husband and wife when the bride arrived stateside.[8] The Aminos farmed in the same area in Japan as the Maruyama family, and Joe, one of Allen's older brothers, said Mr. Maruyama had last seen their mother when she was twelve.[9]

Virginia Maruyama Chapman, Allen's younger and only sister, remembers that their mother sailed alone to Seattle in 1916 or 1917. The voyage took thirty days, and she was sick most of the time. Mr. Maruyama traveled from Colorado by train to meet her, and, with the combination of the sea voyage and long train ride, she arrived in Las Animas exhausted.[10]

Some of my cousins recall that my grandmother, Anne Campbell Purvis, taught Mrs. Maruyama some basics about local food and its preparation. Anne was herself a migrant from Natural Bridge, Virginia, uprooted after the devastation of the Civil War as a young teen. She arrived in Colorado in 1888.

Allen's sister more specifically refers to the Purvis family as the Maruyamas' sponsors. She describes how her mother felt warmly welcomed by my grandmother and other neighbor women who helped her organize the household and garden.

My grandfather died in 1917, leaving my grandmother with six children. One of my cousins remembers that, during the Depression, Mr. Maruyama leased land from my grandmother, which probably saved her financially and allowed her to keep the farm.[11]

Wanting their children to have what they considered to be American names, Mr. and Mrs. Maruyama chose Purvis ones for their children. George was their first child, born in 1918, named after my grandfather and father; Theodore was the second, named after a Purvis son-in-law; Joseph came next, named after another of George and Anne's sons; fourth was Allen, born in 1926 and named after a Purvis cousin; and last born was Virginia. Both she and I are named after my father's twin sister, the name that memorializes my grandmother's home state.

Allen emphasizes the rarity of this relationship between the Purvises and Maruyamas, symbiotic in ways he did not see taking place between other European Americans and the fifteen or so Japanese families in the area.[12] For decades, children from the two families attended the same schools, the same church, and shared the vagaries of farming the arid land of the Arkansas Valley.

Allen recalls that various Purvis family members took their own children and those of the Maruyamas who were not working in the fields on a Sunday morning to the First Presbyterian Church. This arrangement was not a problem for, as Allen sometimes refers to him, his "liberal Buddhist father."

Bonds formed between early settler families figure prominently in the memories of both Maruyama and Purvis children. In his May 19, 1978, congratulatory letter to Allen on the occasion of the twenty-fifth anniversary of Allen's ordination, Joseph W. Purvis writes, "I shall never forget one day, many, many years ago, your dad drove into our yard and told my mother that they had a new baby boy at his house, and, with her permission, they would like to name him George, honoring my father. Of course, Mother was thrilled no end. Then after more boys and finally Virginia and always the same procedure, little wonder your family became more endeared to us all the time . . . . He was one of the best farmers I ever knew and certainly helped me a lot, as I grew up without a father."

As established as the Maruyamas and other Japanese families were in the community, the protection provided by their reputation went only so far after the Pearl Harbor attack. Allen emphasizes that all the movies, magazines, and newspapers "were just full of hate for the Japanese." The hostility penetrated his fifteen-year-old self-image. As a player on the basketball and football teams, he was exposed to the chants of opposing fans: "Kill that goddamn J*p! Kill that goddamn J*p!" He could not understand why none of the parents or school personnel restrained those kids from using such "foul, hateful language."[13]

He blamed all the hostility on Japan and "developed a violent hatred for anything Japanese, including myself." Every time he looked in the mirror he saw the enemy. "I wanted to commit suicide, but I wanted to do it for the honor of my country." His plan was to join a certain US "suicide battalion" that he heard had a casualty rate approaching ninety-eight percent.[14]

When my husband and I moved to Denver in 2007, following Rose and Allen's visit to Nassau, we visited often with them. Distressed by Allen's vulnerability as a Japanese-American teen during World War II and its profound effect on him, I read books and local newspapers about those years in Southeastern Colorado and spoke with some of Allen's contemporaries. The research grew into a historical novel about ethnic antagonism exacerbated by the war, but I had not solved the underlying puzzle.[15]

How, given the hatred heaped on him after the Pearl Harbor attack, had he summoned the inner resources to live, and to live what is, by all appearances, an extraordinarily successful life? He became a man comfortable enough with himself and his Japanese heritage that he displays souvenirs from his 1986 sabbatical in Japan in his home. He was a beloved pastor. He was a national leader in the Presbyterian Church (USA). He immersed himself in major social and religious movements that shape, and continue into the present, commitments that still play out in the context of conservative-liberal battles in his mainline Protestant denomination. Now in his nineties, what does he make of his life's journey on, as he calls it, a "trail of discrimination"?[16]

He attributes his resilience over the decades to multiple and complicated factors, which makes his biography instructive and worthy of telling.

Yet more nuance emerges from my research and interviews with his colleagues, friends, and family. Often Allen himself circles back to the same stories and retells them with other details and different conclusions. His biography is many-layered, and, while each layer hints at insights, readers will extract their own meaning from it.[17]

When he gave me permission for the project, Allen stipulated that his biography be "kept short." That could be heard as "Keep it real. No ostentation. No embellishment."

Rose, also down-to-earth, asked a more pointed question. "Why do you want to write Allen's biography? His life is ordinary, and our life together isn't remarkable."

"You might see it that way," I answered her, "but for many of us our lives seem ordinary until they're examined, and what seems ordinary might be instructive and inspiring to someone else."

We were eating lunch in one of the dining areas at the retirement complex where she and Allen lived, and she looked around the room. "You mean, a biography of any one of the people sitting at these tables would be interesting?"

"Well, depending on how it's told, but, yes, I imagine each person here has lived through and gained wisdom from relationships, conflict, joy, sorrow, disappointment, and achievement that others would benefit from knowing. They might think their lives are ordinary, but how they are living that life is extraordinary."

"So, I'm forgetting to look at Allen as anything more than what I see in him as the person I live with day to day."[18]

Surely a story of his immigrant roots, of his family not only surviving the Depression but emerging successfully from it; of his adolescence as a member of a despised minority during World War II when persons of Japanese ancestry living on the West Coast, the majority of those in the United States, were forcibly removed and incarcerated; and of his spiritual healing would be compelling. That he took public, principled stances during times of social, religious, and cultural upheaval would be inspiring.

When Rose raised her question on another occasion about the worth of writing Allen's biography, I did not respond with those arguments. Rather, I said, "Others might look at the two of you and note yours is an interracial marriage. When you married in 1954, just nine years after the war, did that take courage? How do you think other people saw the two of you?"

"I don't know very many interracial marriages. I don't even think of mine as being that way. . . . I never felt that [racial contrast] with Allen. We're not that different in our features.

"Maybe when I went to the [Maruyama] farm the first few times I might have wondered if I belonged there." Still, that did not ring true to her. "But I don't recall thinking that." He was simply her husband "who happened to be a different nationality."

The connections Rose felt with Allen went well beyond similarities she perceived in physical appearance. They shared their Presbyterian heritage, as well as other cultural "languages" of rural communities and working-class backgrounds. They both embarked into larger worlds via their educations. Neither her parents nor Allen's attended college, but both sets "wanted us to have a college education." Rose said her mother and father saved so they could give each of their three daughters two years of higher education because "you could get a teaching license with two years."[19]

"And the two of you are so fully your own people," I added.

Rose came back to the topic of mixed marriages and how theirs did not make Allen's story unusual. "Being the wife of a Japanese man did not come first in my thinking of who I am." She made this comment in the context of describing an article in the Dubuque newspaper, in a city where they had lived for a decade. The paper reported an achievement of her high school students and their Future Business Leaders of America club activities, but it identified her only by noting that she was Dr. Maruyama's wife.

"He was the important person [in Dubuque]. Not me." She wrote the editor, saying she was proud to be married to Allen Maruyama, but her role in the students' accomplishments was not based on her status as his wife. They printed an apology and acknowledged she was a person in her own right.[20]

In an early conversation about Allen's biography, Rose laughingly admitted that she had contributed to Allen's success. She commented that maybe she "should get at least a chapter in this book!"[21]

On his part, Allen says of Rose, quoting a friend of theirs, "He thought what I became was because of Rose. He had more admiration for Rose than any person I ever knew."[22]

As she debated the merits of an Allen biography, Rose finally came to a positive verdict, but her conclusion came up obliquely. The two of them were speculating why a Japanese-American acquaintance of theirs had never married.

"She would have been a wonderful wife for somebody," Rose said. "And then here I am with Allen. I never could have imagined myself being with anyone like Allen because I didn't know anybody like him. They simply didn't exist."[23]

Her enthusiasm about his unique personality as unimaginable and irreproducible came as a surprise. Characteristically measured in her comments, on this topic, she expressed no doubt that Allen was special, at least to her.

Her story extends far more than one chapter. It runs throughout: Rose, the consummate entertainer always looking for an occasion to organize a party; the faithful church choir member; a stalwart leader in the League of Women Voters; the voracious reader; and unyielding in the pride she took in her own vocation, that of teacher.

Friends envied how articulate she was and that she actually read all the magazines to which she subscribed.[24] A former colleague at Gateway High School in Aurora, Colorado, says, "She was the only one in the teacher's lounge who didn't stare stupidly when I told my quirky jokes. She got them—and laughed!"[25]

Others remember Rose as "quite a lady, respected, enthusiastic, visible, well-liked." She was straightforward and spoke her mind, but judiciously. Allen agrees. When she gave an opinion, she could be trusted to mean what she said.[26]

On the cover of the four-inch thick album Rose assembled on the occasion of Allen's twenty-fifth anniversary of his ordination (1978), she wrote, "From Rose, Your Devoted Wife of Twenty-Four Years." The album was many months in the making, as indicated by the quantity of material: photos, news releases, and correspondence she had solicited from colleagues and church members from every aspect of Allen's professional life, beginning with tributes from his Las Animas home church, continuing through the "student charge" congregation in Girard, Illinois, and the co-pastorate at Montview. Rose's thoroughness and the fact that she and Allen maintained contact with so many people over the years is noteworthy.

Rose participated in the majority of the interviews with Allen. Sadly, she died December 6, 2017, a week short of her ninety-first birthday. They were married sixty-three years.

Rev. Dr. Cynthia Cearley, one of Allen's former colleagues at Montview, said of Rose's claim to an ordinary life in her eulogy, "but it was *beautifully ordinary*—a life with ordinary gifts becomes a life with *extraordinary* love and happiness."[27]

Front Matter Endnotes

1. Allen and Rose Maruyama, interview with author, Aurora, CO, Oct. 12, 2016.
2. Frishman, "Hidden in Plain Sight."
3. History Colorado, "One Hundred Sixty-Seven Years Ago"; Amache, "Amache and Japanese American Timeline"; and Bent County Historical Society, "Boggsville."
4. Burney, "Could Amache."
5. Amache Preservation Society.
6. Allen Maruyama, interview with author, Aurora, CO, May 30, 2019.
7. Lebra, *We Chose Colorado*, 15.
8. Minoru and June Mochizuki, Interview with author, Denver, Apr. 25, 2017.
9. Joe, as athletic and active, or more, than Allen, skied and played golf well into his 90s. In the fall of 2019, he fell while volunteering at his golf course. The fall led to a series of health problems, and Joe died in the winter of 2020. I am grateful for his energetic participation in writing Allen's biography. Joseph Maruyama, interview with author, Broomfield, CO, Nov. 28, 2016.
10. Virginia Maruyama Chapman, conversation with author, Denver, Jan. 6, 2018, and letter to author, Jan. 26, 2018.
11. Joseph B. Mahaney, various conversations with author over the years.
12. Allen Maruyama, interview with author, Aurora, CO, Nov. 13, 2017.
13. Allen Maruyama, interview with author, Aurora, CO, Nov. 13, 2016.
14. Allen and Rose Maruyama, interview with author, Aurora, CO, Jan. 3, 2017.
15. Purvis-Smith, *Greenwood River.*
16. Allen Maruyama, interview with author, Aurora, CO, Apr. 3, 2018.
17. Paul Ricoeur, French philosopher, is one of many who assert that personal identity can be thought of in terms of narrative identity, that is, the story people tell about their lives. Ricoeur elaborates by saying that identity is also comprised of the network of stories others tell about the person. One of many resources for Ricoeur's thought is *A Ricoeur Reader.*
18. Allen and Rose Maruyama, interview with author, Aurora, CO, Oct. 12, 2016.
19. Appiah observes that "what actually matters to us about other people depends on connections that pass through language and culture, as well as through our physical bodies" (*Lies that Bind,* 121).
20. Allen and Rose Maruyama, interview with author, Aurora, CO, Apr. 17, 2017.
21. Allen and Rose Maruyama, interview with author, Aurora, CO, Oct. 12, 2016.
22. Allen and Rose Maruyama, interview with author, Aurora, CO, Apr. 17, 2017.
23. Allen and Rose Maruyama, interview with author, Aurora, CO, Oct. 12, 2016.

24. Ruth Hart, interview with author, Denver, Dec. 10, 2018.

25. Vince Nicoletti, conversation with author, Golden, CO, Apr. 13, 2019.

26. Shirley Burkhart, interview with author, Denver, Mar. 20, 2017; and Allen and Rose Maruyama, interview with author, Aurora, CO, Mar. 22, 2017.

27. Cearley, "Homily."

PART I

A Nisei Childhood Inspires a Vocation

Chapter 1

Shock

ALLEN IS A KIND, gregarious gentleman, but that outcome could not have been anticipated at the time of the Pearl Harbor attack, weeks after his fifteenth birthday.

Until then, Allen "didn't realize Japanese and Asians generally were that badly discriminated against." He thought of himself as a "normal person. Being Asian, Japanese American, didn't bother me. I felt like people accepted me for who I was."[1]

By his middle and high school years, most of his friends were European American. Only in his early elementary grades at rural Rixey School east of Las Animas does he remember that he and other Japanese-American children tended to play exclusively with one another. He attributes this to how close the several Japanese families in the community were with one another. They celebrated most holidays and special occasions together, so naturally the children congregated at school.

His more significant experience at that young age happened when he was five and began first grade. Rixey School did not have a kindergarten class. As one of the younger first graders, he says, "They've told me I cried all the time. The teachers said I was not ready for school and finally sent me home." He began first grade the following year, "and that's why I was always the oldest one in the class, due to my November birthday."[2]

The Maruyamas moved from the Rixey community to a farm nearer Las Animas, so his later elementary and middle school years were spent in town at Columbian. He received the American Legion award upon his eighth-grade graduation, and the principal of the school "liked me enough to make me the captain of patrol. I was so proud of that."[3] Community newspapers of the time list his name and Virginia's on the honor roll almost every marking period.[4] By most measures of school success—academic and leadership abilities—Allen was an all-American boy.

Imperial Japan attacked Pearl Harbor only months after he received the American Legion award and began his freshman year. Suddenly, some of the people he considered friends did not want anything to do with him. Others in the community immediately thought they had a "whole group of enemies living in their midst," and the barbershop where he got his hair cut displayed a big sign in its window reading "25 cents for a J*p ear." It seemed the attitude of the proprietors toward him had not changed, though, and when he visited the shop, they apparently thought the sign was funny, if they applied its message to him at all. However, the hostility it displayed reinforced for Allen the ubiquitous message of hatred toward all Japanese.[5]

"World War II was a shocking, shocking experience to me" is a phrase he often repeats. Not only was he shocked by the reversal of community sentiment toward him, but he was shocked that his family's bank account and those of the neighboring Japanese families were frozen early in 1942. His dad did not even have cash available to buy groceries.

He was shocked that almost one hundred twenty thousand people of Japanese ancestry were forcibly removed from the West Coast and shipped inland to internment camps during the summer and fall of 1942. One of those ten incarceration sites was located less than fifty miles east of Las Animas. With its population of over seven thousand, Camp Amache became the tenth largest city in Colorado almost overnight, and it was the smallest of the ten sites. Tule Lake, California, was the largest at almost nineteen thousand.[6]

Camp Amache was also known as the Granada War Relocation Center. Apparently the name "Amache" was assigned to it to prevent confusion on the part of the postal service with the nearby town of Granada. The irony of the name is not lost on those who know the history of the region. Amache was a Cheyenne Indian princess who married John Prowers, an early white settler in the area for whom the county in which the camp was located was named. Amache's father, Chief Ochinee, had promoted peace between the Cheyenne and the European-American settlers, but was murdered by U.S. Army soldiers at the Sand Creek Massacre in 1864. The site of the massacre is less than one hundred miles north of Camp Amache's location. The forcibly relocated Japanese and Japanese Americans (sometimes shortened to JaJAs) were incarcerated on land that had belonged to other nations, including the Cheyenne and Arapaho, also forcibly removed, only half a century prior to the camp's construction. Two other incarceration sites were actually located on Indian reservations.[7]

Allen was shocked that a Japanese family from the area who had moved to the West Coast was among those incarcerated at Amache. When he went with his parents to visit them, he was confused that his friends were confined and under guard, but he lived outside the barbed wire fence. He speculated that they must have done something wrong to deserve imprisonment.

He saw some redheads and blonds behind the barbed wire and asked why they were confined. His parents explained that maybe a grandparent was Japanese, or one parent was half Japanese, but that everyone in the camp had been uprooted from their homes.

"I thought, 'Japan has done all this.'"

The JaJA emotional response to the Pearl Harbor attack and its aftermath is uniquely traumatic for each individual, family, and community. For Allen, Pearl Harbor triggered a personal, interior transformation. He "developed a violent hatred for Japan and anything Japanese," including himself. His anger and loathing reached such a pitch that he asked his parents to sign a form that would, he thought, allow him to enlist in a suicide battalion about which he had heard. Signing would have implicated his parents in a lie about his age.

"I wanted to kill as many Japanese people as I could before I died. I hated myself, hated my parents. I was just full of hate, and the only way I could resolve it was to go out and kill the enemy that was causing all the problems."

He says he sees why "crazies" in terrorist groups are willing to strap a bomb on their bodies and enter a crowded group and kill as many people as they can. "That's the kind of mentality I had."

His parents refused to sign the form.[8]

After turning seventeen, he tried to enlist again because he wanted to be in the military service rather than attend school. The papers his parents had to sign this time did not entail deception but simply gave permission because he was not yet eighteen. Allen volunteered for the Marines first, because he had the "greatest admiration for them," but was rejected, followed by the same result with his application to other branches of military service. His attempts ended with the Merchant Marines. "They all said to me that as of Pearl Harbor, we will not accept anyone of Japanese ancestry."

Mildred Scott advocated on his behalf. An active member of the Presbyterian church and remembered as the postmistress, she sometimes gave Allen rides home when football practice ran late. She was a daughter of Alex Scott, for whom Mr. Maruyama was a sharecropper at the time. She wrote letters to "the senator and congressperson," who, in turn, vouched for the

Maruyama family. They said, "This young man is a real American, and you don't have to worry," and they contacted certain military personnel on Allen's behalf. The War Department eventually sent Allen a letter that echoed the responses of the several military services. Allen remembers it saying, "We appreciate you wanting to go into the service to defend our country, but we're sorry. The law says we cannot accept anyone of Japanese ancestry."[9]

Allen's expectation that he could enlist was understandable. That he could not might have had to do with his age and his timing. Before the Pearl Harbor attack, his oldest brother George had been drafted after graduating from Colorado Western State (now Colorado Western University), Gunnison. Joe, the brother nearest Allen in age, enlisted in 1942, also assisted by Mildred Scott, and went into the Military Intelligence Service as a translator.

Eventually the participation of American men of Japanese ancestry was not only allowed but required. Allen welcomed this outcome, but other Nisei (second-generation American citizens) resisted, particularly those incarcerated in the camps. They could not reconcile fighting for a country that had imprisoned them and their families, thereby violating their constitutional rights. These Nisei resistors, as well as the "No-No Boys" who had responded in the negative to two questions on a loyalty questionnaire required of people in the camps, were ostracized by many JaJAs who criticized their lack of patriotism. Resistors and "No-No Boys" were sent to Tule Lake, which became a segregation center for "troublemakers."[10]

As a measure of the intensity of JaJA feelings swirling around the proper response to the war, disagreements between these various groups remain raw to this day. At its August 2019 national convention, the Japanese American Citizens League (JACL) discussed a resolution at length that was intended to reconcile its "hyperpatriotic" stance during the war with the resulting ostracism of the resistors and "No-No Boys." The Japanese American Veterans Association (JAVA) denounced JACL's resolution "as a shameful and unwarranted demeaning of the legacy forged by the valor and loyalty of the Japanese Americans who served in the US military during WWII."[11]

The Nisei who eventually did serve were put in the all-Japanese-American 100th Battalion/442nd Regimental Combat Team (RCT), organized in 1943. It is the most decorated military unit for its size and length of service in American military history. After Allen completed basic training in 1945, he would have been sent overseas as part of this unit, were it not for a health problem that prevented his deployment.

Another division in the JaJA experience during the war is between those who were incarcerated, that is, those who lived on the West Coast and constituted the majority of people of Japanese ancestry in the United States, and families such as Allen's who lived in the interior. While the trauma of racism was experienced differently by those in the camps and those not, by those who served and those who did not, the shock for everyone was consequential and enduring.

Chapter 2

The 1980 Detroit General Assembly

To HONOR ALLEN'S REQUEST and keep short the story of his ninety-plus years of life with its many transitions is no small task. Skipping ahead to Allen's 1980 candidate's speech for moderator of the 192nd General Assembly of the United Presbyterian Church in the United States of America (UPCUSA) suggests a workaround. Detroit hosted that year's assembly.[12]

General Assembly gatherings from those years, the annual national expression of the denomination, were not routinely recorded, but these audio tapes exist. They bring the assembly to life.[13]

The speech gives space for historical context and the perspectives of Allen's contemporaries. It structures, in his words, his journey on that "trail of discrimination" in the decades following World War II, and it offers some answers to the question of how the adolescent Allen, so filled with hate, survived the war and became an admired leader in the denomination.

Candidacy for moderator of the General Assembly is a rare honor granted to few ministers and elected church officers of local congregations (teaching and ruling elders, respectively).[14] Allen had been nominated by the Denver Presbytery, the regional body encompassing the United Presbyterian churches in that area and the presbytery in which he was a member. In Allen's case, the honor is magnified because he was the first Asian American to be nominated in the history of the 192-year-old denomination.

Allen is one of five candidates and fourth to speak, the order determined by lot. Gathered before him are the 617 ruling and teaching elders, in equal numbers, elected by the various presbyteries that comprise the

UPCUSA. Also in the audience are family members of various commissioners, miscellaneous observers, representatives from other religious bodies, staff members from the New York national office, members of the General Assembly Council and of the numerous committees and commissions scheduled to give their reports, and media personnel, but only the 617 commissioners elected by their presbyteries are eligible to vote.

Members of his family—Rose and their children, Sarah and John; his brothers, save for Ted, who died in 1975; their spouses and some of their children; cousins; and his mother—are there. Allen's father died in 1949, while Allen was a student at the University of Colorado, and Virginia, married to a career army sergeant and leading a peripatetic life of her own, was unable to attend. Rose's parents and her two sisters and their husbands are there.

Many of Allen's close friends, acquaintances, and colleagues are scattered throughout the hall. Among them is Rev. Dr. C. Samuel Calian, a friend from the decade Allen spent in Dubuque, member of the General Assembly Program Agency Board, and soon-to-be president of Pittsburgh Theological Seminary. Rev. Dr. Arthur L. Miller, former pastor of Montview Boulevard Presbyterian Church and moderator of the 1959 General Assembly, is watching to see if this successor, Allen himself, will be elected moderator. Allen's close friend, Rev. Larry Angus from the Wheat Ridge Presbyterian Church in the Denver Presbytery, his campaign manager and the one who persuaded him to stand for moderator, is there.

"Persuaded" might understate Angus's influence. Allen regards him highly, as always having been an inspiration, "partly because he had a strong vision of me, better than I even thought about myself. He pushed and pushed. I don't think I would have ever run for moderator of General Assembly were it not for Larry Angus. He really believed in me." He was the friend who also believed in the strength Allen derived from Rose. Angus "thought what I became was because of Rose."[15]

Allen's family and friends would have known some of the details and emotion implied but not articulated in his speech, if they had been able to concentrate. For several days before the nominations and that morning, they had run Allen's campaign booth, visiting with commissioners passing by, pressing Allen's brochure into their hands, and distributing badges supporting his campaign—as had the boosters for the other four nominees. As brother Joe said, "[General Assembly] is a big production, . . . a big event. There's housing to worry about, events to be worried about. Everybody's there from all the states, and their families. It's a lot of fun!"[16]

Allen had spent several days before the assembly in meetings with various committees, as had the other four candidates, where "they interrogate you and you have to answer their questions." Committee members, if they had taken the time, had available to them the candidates' biographies and position statements about various theological, ecclesiastical, and social issues, which had been circulated in national publications of the denomination.[17]

In spite of Allen's attendance at those committee meetings, his prior visits to some of the Presbyterian seminaries, and appearances at yet other seminaries on the part of members of his campaign committee, Allen, Angus, and Calian emphasize that winning the election hinges on the candidate's speech to the assembly.[18] The speeches and the follow-up period of questions and answers are judged to best reveal the candidates' mettle, charisma, and ability to represent the denomination in the coming year. On the tape, the current moderator is heard introducing the speeches by specifying that the candidates will be "expressing the concerns [each feels] to be most important for the church in this General Assembly and the ensuing year."

The election of the moderator is the first item on the assembly agenda, which indirectly speaks to the esteem in which the position is held. Even a brief description of the expectations fails to convey the position's prestige. The moderator is seen as leading and guiding the witness of the whole church. Tasks include running the General Assembly meetings; traveling to member synods, presbyteries, and churches throughout the country; frequently speaking and/or preaching at meetings and worship services in those settings; and representing the denomination at any number of public events such as ecumenical gatherings, local and worldwide.

When Allen takes the stage, after the five nominating speeches and three of the candidates' speeches, he has five minutes to convince the commissioners he is the person for the job. He keeps it within the five-minute limitation while encapsulating his life experience, values, and theology, an achievement that may not have been immediately apparent to his audience.

What is known about him before he stands to speak is this, for those who studied the May 26 publication of the nationally syndicated *Presbyterian Outlook* that introduced the candidates and provided summaries of their positions. He just completed his term as moderator of the Presbytery of Denver and is now chairperson of its General Council. He was a member of the General Assembly Special Committee on the Theology of Liberation and Renewal (1975–1977) and the General Assembly Sub-Committee on Judicatory Relations (1977–1979). He is a visiting lecturer at the Iliff School of Theology in Denver and served in a similar capacity at the University of Dubuque Theological Seminary.[19]

The speech has to animate these abstract facts with vitality and credibility. Even Angus did not read between the lines of Allen's speech and missed much of the underlying drama, although he forthrightly admits that Allen is a good preacher, straightforward and with good material. But Angus describes Allen as "no great orator." Angus and others worked with Allen on the speech and videotaped him while he practiced. In frustration, they would say, "Allen, get on fire!"

Allen would retort, "I am on fire!"[20]

"He's so humble," Angus says. "I really think he felt that being Japanese would help because the church was becoming more accepting. They'd had a black person as moderator, but not a Japanese."[21]

Chapter 3

My Little Stand

ALLEN'S FIRST WORDS ON the recording are, "Mr. Moderator, commissioners, and friends of the 192nd General Assembly, as I was bringing my little stand up, I noticed some of the commissioners looked kind of worried." The audience can be heard responding with chuckles.[22]

If Allen's internal fire is burning in this initial sentence before the General Assembly, Angus is correct about its invisibility because it is cloaked in understatement. Allen starts off with the standard, polite address to the current moderator and commissioners but immediately inserts his characteristic gesture of establishing rapport with humility and humor by means of the extemporaneous comment about the footstool he is carrying onto the stage.

In the expanse of Detroit's Cobo Hall, he would be nearly invisible without the stand. However, his use of the word "worry" is more clever than he might have intended. He does not remember the specifics of the speech, and the sentence probably came as a spontaneous, self-deprecating way to connect with his audience in the moment, but attributing "worry" to those present could be interpreted in several ways. It could evoke concern on their part that he might drop the stand or fall. However, "worry" also could be heard as an indirect challenge to the unconscious bias in favor of height that Americans tend to associate with leadership. This "worry" hints at another probable underlying prejudice, a veiled dare that the assembly see and then set aside the assumption that an Asian man barely five feet two inches can lead a denomination of three million.

Calling attention to his height is not unusual for Allen. It says, in effect, "Yes, I'm short, but don't underestimate me—neither my strength nor my will." When he was a high school senior in 1944, the Las Animas football team made the state semifinals. The team, representing a high school of several hundred, was up against Pueblo Central, a city school many times larger. The Pueblo newspapers made a great show of the contest with photos of five-feet-two-inches Allen Maruyama lined up against the Central six-feet-three-inches or six-feet-four-inches end—this in the context of headlines in editions of *The Pueblo Chieftain* at the time that customarily included news of the war in the Pacific using terms like "J*ps" and "N*ps." As a 1994 Pueblo sports writer reflected on this particular game, he noted that the "CF&I [Colorado Fuel and Iron] Corporation ran full out those days." Working there were "real men, their sons [those on Central's team] hard-nosed replicas of the old man."[23]

The Las Animas Trojan team was undefeated, 8–0, going into the game, so folks thought they had a chance against the Central Wildcats. On their part, the Wildcats had defeated some of their opponents by scores of 45–6 and 40–0. That 40–0 score was against crosstown rival Pueblo Centennial. Centennial was to be the state champion runner-up the following year and came out on top in 1946. The Central Wildcats were a formidable team.

Even though Allen's team lost 33–0 to Pueblo, the Las Animas team, from a small-town school largely comprised of the children of farmers, small business owners, and professionals serving a rural community, held its own fairly well. Allen says that each time that tall end caught the ball, all he could do was hit the guy as hard as he could. He learned that "when you tackle someone that tall, they fall HARD. It was fun!"[24]

Allen and his Trojans competed in the "big league." They stood up to the tough city school and the Wildcat team, which was comprised of a number of those sons of steel workers, many of them also children of immigrants with names like Gurovich and Vaccaro. The Trojan team competed against Central during its football "golden era." Central recaptured the state title in 1947, for the second time in the decade.[25]

Another public event that spotlighted Allen's stature occurred in the 1950s, when his friend Dorothy Rawlings asked him to be a groomsman at her wedding in the Las Animas church. She was the daughter of the town's bank president, and she and the groom, Richard (Dick) Nelson, were Allen's classmates at McCormick Theological Seminary. The family were all tall and slender; evidently so was the groom and the other five or so groomsmen.

"So, I got my monkey suit rented, and rehearsal night I went to meet the wedding party. . . . Here I was five feet two, and all the wedding party were at least six feet. It was the funniest thing. I'm sure they had a big joke about it."[26]

That banker father, John W. Rawlings, an elder in the Las Animas Presbyterian Church, had visited each Japanese family in the area a decade prior to the wedding, after their accounts had been frozen in 1942 by order of the Treasury Department. That the families did not have access to their money had been shocking, but Mr. Rawlings' generosity was equally remarkable—and unexpected. Allen and his brother Joe tell and retell the story of Mr. Rawlings's visits to each farmhouse. He assured the families that, although he had no choice but to enforce the order, he would personally lend them the money they needed to meet operating expenses as well as for immediate necessities.

When he visited the Maruyama home, Mr. Rawlings gave Allen's father cash on the spot for buying groceries. "My dad was just shocked because he didn't know the president that well, just to say 'hello' to him when he went into the bank." The Japanese farmer's son and the banker's daughter, who had grown up in the church's youth programs together, remained friends and colleagues throughout their lives.

The Las Animas football players stood their ground against the Central boys, a game that Allen remembers as "fun." The son of the Japanese farmer and the daughter of the banker to whom that farmer was temporarily indebted shared the intimate family moment of a wedding as equals, which Allen remembers with amusement. In his high school and young adult years, his race was the source of hurt; his hometown church friends and class origins were not. By 1980, the only boost he needed from the "little stand" was literal, to guarantee his visibility.

Chapter 4

The Threat

WHEN ALLEN BEGINS HIS speech, a dozen or so conservative pastors sitting in the audience may be particularly "worried." They had invited him to their caucus breakfast and confronted him just hours earlier. They had abruptly informed him that, were he to be elected moderator, they would walk out of the assembly. As a measure of how shocked Allen was by their rejection, Rose did not remember hearing about the confrontation until the 2017 interview, thirty-seven years later.

Allen characterized it this way: "Evidently I didn't talk about it. Because it's embarrassing to talk about that."[27]

It would be difficult to tell if the confrontation with the conservative pastors, which Allen characterizes as "violent," dampened Allen's internal fire as he began his speech and made him less confident at that crucial moment. Certainly, it was significant enough that he was still "embarrassed" about it almost four decades later. The only person he told at the time was Angus.

Allen's discomfort in speaking about the confrontation, while certainly secondary to his outrage during World War II, carried a similar emotional tone: shock that others saw him as someone other than he knew himself to be.

His reactions as an adolescent—hatred of anything Japanese after the Pearl Harbor attack, even hating his parents and seeing his own face in the mirror as one belonging to the enemy—are expressions of shame as reflected in textbook definitions: "Shame is the intensely painful feeling or

experience of believing we are flawed and, therefore, unworthy of acceptance and belonging. . . . It's when your very own body makes you sick."[28]
More intensely, when one identifies with a devalued group and struggles
to disassociate from it, "such rejection of one's own heritage [becomes]
self-hatred."[29]

We are shamed for who we are, something we cannot change. Overwhelmed by powerlessness, we react irrationally with flight, fight, and freeze
responses. Self-loathing is lashing out at ourselves, or we might externalize
our reaction and strike out at others.[30] With his desire to enlist in a suicide
battalion, Allen's reaction was to fight on both the internal and external
fronts. Thankfully, his parents refused to sign the form that would have allowed him to enlist.

Feeling shamed subsequent to Pearl Harbor was not a response unique
to Allen. It was expressed personally and communally and dealt with in
any number of ways on the part of people in the United States who were
of Japanese ancestry. It appears in written materials and countless personal
testimonies—shame at being associated with Imperial Japan and the attack; shame on the part of those living on the West Coast at being forcibly torn away from homes, schools, churches, and temples as if they had
done something horribly wrong; shame upon being stripped of possessions
and dignity; shame at being accused of sabotage; shame at being denied
constitutional rights (two-thirds of those removed from the West Coast
were American citizens); and shame at being transported in trains with the
shades pulled to isolated concentration camps. All of it was an incalculable
affront. To underscore the force and the ubiquity of shame, then and now,
"the fierce need to bring no shame to one's family and community" is a
powerful social dynamic in Japanese-American culture.[31]

While shame is a commonly voiced response to their World War II
experiences, the way individual JaJAs lived through it depended on any
number of factors: age, location, family circumstance. Rev. Dr. Grace Kaori
Suzuki, pastor at Christ United Presbyterian Church in San Francisco, observes that shame is definitely prevalent in all the voices she has heard regarding the aftermath of Pearl Harbor, but it did not necessarily lead to the
reaction Allen had.[32]

An example of the way other Japanese Americans speak of this shame
emerges in Jeanne Wakatsuki Houston and James D. Houston's *Farewell
to Manzanar*, published in 1973. Jeanne Houston describes the agony she
experienced in the process of revisiting her family's years of incarceration
at Manzanar. Emotions surfaced that she had suppressed for decades. She
says: "[my feeling was] one of deep humiliation, like a person who had been

raped. You are the victim, yet you are sullied by the experience, ashamed to draw attention to it."[33]

Allen's parents were also subjected to a very public shaming during the war's early years. Mr. Maruyama was a member of the Japanese Farmers' Association of the Arkansas Valley, and he and two other Japanese farmers were the ones who presented their Japanese school building, unused since 1936, to the Las Animas Veterans of Foreign Wars and the Boy Scouts in 1942 as an act of patriotic solidarity. The local newspaper's account of the donation had included the three farmers' names.

When the structure was moved, an undersheriff discovered a Japanese naval map of the Pacific crumpled behind a desk drawer. The FBI was called in, and the outcome made the front page of the hometown newspaper. A picture of Congressman Martin Dies Jr. of Texas, the chairman of the House Committee on Un-American Activities, shows him standing in front of the large map, which is pinned to the office wall behind him. Although the map had served as a simple instructional tool in the classroom, Dies declared it to be evidence of Japanese belligerence before the war.

Allen says his father was mortified. The gift of the building, which even the local reporter understood as being "a gesture toward the war effort," implicated Mr. Maruyama as a saboteur.[34]

Although Allen says he was only "embarrassed" by the 1980 confrontation with the conservative pastors, the scene implies stronger elements reminiscent of the shame of those war years, especially his inclination not to discuss the pastors' rejection for decades and his use of the word "violent" to describe it. When asked to clarify why he describes their threat as "violent," he says, "Well, to leave the assembly, that's pretty violently opposed."[35]

Allen's self-assessment as being simply "embarrassed" by the confrontation should be respected, but "embarrassment" implies a feeling that is "fleeting or innocuous," something normal that will go away.[36] That his reaction endured seems to give it a different quality, one which emerges in an expanded vocabulary of feelings used to express degrees of shame—feeling mortified, mocked, scorned, humiliated, and, yes, simply embarrassed.

Assigning a more apt descriptive word than embarrassment to his feeling requires knowing the context for the conservative pastors' reaction. Their primary issue was the withdrawal of several churches in the Denver Presbytery from the denomination the prior year. Allen's term as presbytery moderator had coincided with their withdrawal.

Even before his confrontation with the pastors that morning, the timing of these withdrawals had also influenced the attitude of students and faculty at the University of Dubuque Theological Seminary, where Allen had studied and received his master's in sacred theology, cum laude, in 1966.

They had declined to endorse Allen's candidacy when he visited the campus. Allen describes their reaction to him as "hostile." Clearly, they blamed him for the churches' withdrawal.[37]

He told the conservative pastors that morning he was sorry the churches wanted to leave but, "there's nothing I can do about all that [discord in Denver Presbytery]. I've tried to explain to you who I am and what happened. I didn't instigate that." His reaction to their accusations seems less embarrassment than humiliation, that is, we do not believe we deserve what is attributed to us.[38]

A quick review of Presbyterian church government and some of the issues prompting those churches to withdraw sheds light on Allen's explanation to the conservative pastors and the significance of the confrontation for Allen's candidacy. One of the pastors of the withdrawing Denver churches disagreed with the denomination's stance on the ordination of women. The denomination, through action of a prior General Assembly and ratification by a majority of the presbyteries, had voted that women could be ordained as ruling and teaching elders. The pastor of the withdrawing church refused to ordain a woman elected by the congregation to serve as a ruling elder. The eventual outcome would have been for the Denver presbytery to take away his ordination, to "defrock" him. Rumor spread that if the pastor were defrocked, the congregation would also be kicked out of the presbytery, which was not true.[39] In any event, the pastor convinced his church to pull out of the denomination (ironic in that the congregation had initially elected the woman).

Another of the withdrawing churches had asked the Denver Presbytery to approve a loan for their building needs. A presbytery owns the church properties in its area and must approve decisions related to purchase, sale, remodeling, and so forth. The presbytery commissioners, comprised of ordained ruling and teaching elders, refused to approve the loan, because the congregation gave most of its mission money to its own outreach projects and only minimal funds to the mission of the larger church, that is, to the presbytery, synod, and to the national expression of the church—the General Assembly.

The PC(USA) is a "connectional church" that follows a representative form of government in which local congregations are expressions of the larger church, comprised of the regional bodies of presbyteries, synods, and the General Assembly. Particular congregations are not independent. The member churches are responsible for providing financial support for mission at all levels of the church to facilitate the functioning of the whole. This particular church also chose to withdraw from the denomination rather than to reach an agreement on an appropriate fund reallocation that would take into account their responsibility for the mission of the larger church.

Complicating matters, when a church votes to withdraw, and the presbytery agrees with the decision—that the differences, in spite of numerous attempts to resolve them, are so great that reconciliation is not possible—the church property reverts to the presbytery. The hostility on the part of one of the withdrawing churches had reached the point that some of its members threatened to enter the building and strip it. Consequently, an unarmed, retired policeman was posted before the locked doors the night after the presbytery concurred with the congregation's decision to withdraw. If the church members attempted a break-in, the person on guard was to immediately notify presbytery officials, which included Allen. There was no such attempt, but the drama reached the pages of *The Denver Post* and eventually the whole denomination.

The fallout from the national publicity was reminiscent of the hysteria reflected in the coverage about the naval map of the Pacific discovered in the donated schoolhouse—a public humiliation tied to the Maruyama name. That the student body at the Dubuque seminary was hostile to Allen when he visited was a measure of the extent of the damage to Allen's reputation. Allen tried to explain to them that the dispute had its source in the condition the Denver Presbytery placed on the loan the church had requested, not on any action he had taken. The church had refused, left the denomination, and consequently lost its building. Allen's explanation had no ameliorating effect.[40]

The equally hostile pastors who confronted Allen before his speech laid the blame for the Denver churches leaving the denomination the prior year at his feet, even though the issues about the ordination of women and the disposition of a church's property when it withdraws were not unique to Denver. Any number of Presbyterian churches were disputing these very issues at that time throughout the country. In fact, the national nature of those disputes is implied throughout contemporaneous denominational publications.

Allen does not say that the conservative pastors or students and faculty at Dubuque ever openly referenced their feelings about the fact that he is Asian American. However, one wonders if any of them would have taken the license to be so summarily dismissive of a European-American candidate. It might have been an underlying factor they did not express, given that Allen made his race one of the distinguishing marks of his candidacy.

Chapter 5

Who I Am

ACTUALLY, ALLEN HAD "WORKED to try to reconcile" the presbytery and the departing churches. He had met with their pastors, one of whom had been a friend at McCormick Theological Seminary. "But they wouldn't even listen. Their hostility toward presbytery was so great that even if presbytery had changed its mind, the churches would have left."[41]

A dominant characteristic of Allen's leadership is this priority on working through conflict, which he attempts by building relationships. When he was associate pastor at the Westminster Presbyterian Church in Dubuque, Iowa (1962–1972), the front lawn of the church, located across the street from the University of Dubuque, became a gathering spot for students. Their growing numbers developed into a matter of contention between the students, church members, neighborhood residents, and city officials.

Allen says, "It was a perfect place [for them to gather] because the streets came together at a junction with a lot of traffic." The university bookstore was on one corner, and stores and houses on another. Rose more specifically described the church lawn as large and triangular, located in the middle of a residential neighborhood.[42]

The number of students hanging out on the lawn grew. Their behaviors, some based on rumor, some not (using the church bathrooms—or the bushes—leaving a stray condom or two on church pews, staying on the lawn overnight, smoking pot, using LSD) incited disgust on the part of church members and residents.[43]

Employees from the Dubuque John Deere plant threatened to bring shotguns and "cut all those hippies' hair." On one occasion, a group did come with guns, and Allen confronted them, saying something to the effect that what the kids did on the church lawn was not their business. It was church property. On another occasion, a man brought his shotgun, and the kids welcomed him. Allen speculates that the kids gave him pot, but in any case, they got him to sit down and chat. By the time the police (and some John Deere people) came, he was docile. They avoided a bad scene.

As the associate pastor, one of Allen's responsibilities was youth ministry, but coincident with the students gathering on the lawn, he was the acting pastor. The senior pastor had recently taken another position, so for a period, all the responsibilities rested on Allen.

The youth representatives on session, the governing body of the church, tried to explain the dilemma from the students' point of view, that they simply needed a gathering place. "No home is big enough to have many kids, and this is just a group of them hanging out together. They're not doing anything wrong. They're orderly. They're good kids."

Session had "knock-down, drag-out debates" about it, but the youth representatives pleaded for the church not to oust the students, that they were not hurting anyone. Allen didn't "usually argue with people, but I'd ask, 'What if your own kid was out there? What would you do? They're sitting and talking and singing. We've got to provide a place where they can go and not be a problem.'"[44]

Eventually students from the University of Iowa (Iowa City) campus and the University of Wisconsin-Platteville joined the conclave on the lawn. At times the kids numbered two to four hundred. "Those numbers lasted only two or three weekends because it got to be a real traffic problem. That's when the city came in, cleaned off the lawn, and made their nearby park the center for the kids to gather."[45]

Allen became somewhat of a hero to the young people due to his advocacy for their cause, but even more of a hero to his son, John. His memories of those incidents have their source in the impressions of a preteen boy who saw his dad "on TV all the time, . . . interviewed at the church with his collar on." Over time, John began to look back on those weeks through the prism of the needs of the homeless, police harassment, and the civil rights and anti-war movements, so he tells the story with more drama than Allen does.

As John remembers, it was not just "hippies" hanging out there that upset the town; those who gathered included "a real diverse group of folks." The neighborhood people hated what was happening and "called the cops." His dad got in the middle of it and told the cops to get lost, that "these are children of God and they have every right to be on our church property. You can't touch them."[46]

John thinks Allen had good support from the church, but the community gave Allen "a lot of flack. It got to be a huge controversy in town. . . . The City Council got involved. . . . He's just this little four foot eleven [not the height Allen claims!] guy who is standing up for these kids. . . . My seeing Martin Luther King Jr. get shot and all that. . . . It obviously stuck with me that my dad was standing up for something really, really important."[47]

Allen tends to downplay his personal impact, and John's memory might conflate various historical events, but, in any event, the incidents around the students on the church lawn figure prominently in Allen's ministry in Dubuque. In spite of, or perhaps because of, his public role and principled stance, he was appointed to the mayor's Youth Commission and the City Council Human Rights Commission. He continued to work with the city to establish more suitable places for young people to gather.

He also convinced the church to sponsor a coffeehouse. Rose described opening night. "They called it the Milk House because the store [where they opened it] had sold bottled, fresh milk. Allen called me. He was so excited and said, 'You've got to come over here.' I left our kids at home. They were old enough to take care of themselves. The older kids were just teeming inside and out of the Milk House. The police could have shut it down that night. But it calmed down after that. The kids knew they were welcome; they really came and engaged in lots of conversation. It was a place to go, to be together. They did not have planned programs."[48]

Yet again, Allen's emphasis on building relationships emerges in the way members and staff at the Montview Boulevard church in Denver describe him. He is characterized as the "pastoral" member of the three-person co-pastorate. Members were likely to call him in times of crisis, and, after session meetings, he would reserve a corner in a nearby bar on Colfax Avenue where many of the elders would convene to debrief and enjoy one another's company.[49]

Allen says he does not argue with people he does not know. When there is disagreement, he tries to understand the background and ideas of the other person, his or her personality. If there is no chance of reaching agreement or compromise, he at least tries to bring people to the point of accepting that "the other person is a human being and [should not] be treated as an enemy. . . . To think of opposing groups as enemies and [those agreeing with us] as friends distorts the truth. . . . I try to become a friend and see if they are willing to be friends, to have lunch together, to go to a party together. . . . Once you establish the friendship, a little bit of trust, you can begin to work toward blending your ideas, grappling with the differences. . . . In the end, your friendship and trust have been strong enough that you can live together and work together. That is a victory." Certainly this was the eventual outcome in Dubuque with the dispute over the students on the lawn.[50]

Perhaps Allen's approach to handling disagreement is most poignantly visible in his relationship with his oldest brother, George. Allen characterizes George and Joe as the "most religious" of the family, even though Allen was the one who spent almost seven decades of his life as an ordained minister. George was an ardent Goldwater champion in the 1964 presidential campaign, a position Allen would, most emphatically, not have shared. Allen suspects their positions in regard to the 2016 election were similarly at odds. In the 1960s, Allen was fully engaged in the civil rights movement as an associate pastor of the Dubuque Westminster church where George was on the session. But Allen says, "We loved each other because we were brothers!"[51]

The conservative pastors that morning in 1980 were not interested in conversation or relationship. They delivered an ultimatum. Perhaps they also associated Allen with some of his other work in the denomination, for example, his role on a committee on mass communication that was to report later in the meeting, certainly a cutting-edge issue at that time in the denomination.

Allen had also served as one of only several pastors on the General Assembly special committee tasked with studying and reporting on the church's response to liberation theology, another cutting-edge debate. The committee had issued its report in 1977, just three years prior.[52] The committee included feminist theologians and academicians and had met for five to six years. Allen even developed a study guide for local congregations that he used at the Montview Boulevard church, which was included in the report. He also authored another section of the report and co-authored two others.

For whatever reason, in the eyes of those pastors who evidently imagined a sort of liberal-conservative continuum, Allen represented a position that was decidedly not theirs. Whereas Allen would have gotten together over a cup of coffee to get better acquainted and talk through differences, they staged an ambush. Their agenda was intimidation.

Their strategy worked in one sense because Allen was still "embarrassed" about the confrontation thirty-seven years later. In another sense, it did not work. Although humiliated, Allen was well beyond the shame of his adolescence, in part because, as he and Joe describe it, he had come into his own and matured as a pastor, particularly during those years in Dubuque. Indeed, the conservative pastors confronting him in 1980 were not reacting to who he was or what he believed.

Chapter 6

Adopted

ALLEN CONTINUES HIS CANDIDATING speech by musing about a question, to which he offers an answer: "I've asked myself this morning, as I stand here before this assembly, what it is that has brought me here.

"I'm here because I'm a child of mission, and I'm a product of your evangelism. You see, my parents are immigrants who came from Japan; they were Buddhists. They sharecropped for some Scottish Presbyterians, and these Scottish Presbyterians kind of adopted us, and my parents named all the children's first names after their children's first names. The Purvis family adopted us. And all the children were taken to Sunday church school by them, after they got the consent of my parents."[53]

In calling attention to his stature with the "little stand" comment, he has indirectly challenged stereotypes about his race, but now he tackles it head-on. He explicitly names his parents' country and religion of origin. By doing so, he implicitly identifies with many of those seated in Cobo Hall, also immigrants and children of immigrants.

For those who might harbor doubts about the legitimacy of his candidacy as a Japanese American, though, he positions himself as embraced by the church through its own evangelism. Not only that, he proceeds to claim the heritage of Scottish Presbyterians, the ultimate pedigree for that particular gathering, a denomination that traces its ancestry through the reformer John Knox, founder of the Kirk of Scotland in the sixteenth century, a protegé of John Calvin. Calvin was a leading figure in the Protestant Reformation, sometimes characterized as the leader of the second generation of reformers following Martin Luther. Calvin became part of the Reformation as a French law student and eventually settled in Geneva, Switzerland, where, in 1555, he became its religious and political leader. In 1536, he wrote the first edition of his *Institutes of the Christian Religion*, an early summary of Reformed theology, which he periodically updated and expanded.

Knox joined a company of theologians, clergy, and other reformers in their journeys to Geneva to consult and study with Calvin. They carried Calvin's ideas not only to Scotland, but throughout Europe, to the Netherlands (the Reformed Church), England (the Puritan movement), and Hungary. Church officials in these locations incorporated Calvin's theology in a number of church confessions, or statements of belief unique to their context: the *Second Helvetic Confession*, adopted by the Hungarian Reformed Church in 1567; the *Heidelberg Catechism*, Germany, 1563, adopted by the Dutch Reformed Church in 1571; and the *Westminster Confession*, England, 1646.[54]

When Allen reminisces, he describes his faith in the early years of his ministry in the context of these and the church's later confessions. By claiming a Scottish Presbyterian heritage, Allen is establishing himself as a bona fide member of the assembly gathered before him, orthodox in his theology. Certainly the majority there would know to associate Scottish Presbyterian with the name John Knox, and many of them would have memorized at least segments of particularly well-known confessions during their confirmation process to become members of the Presbyterian Church. Also, it would be rare for any Presbyterian seminary graduate not to have at least passing familiarity with Calvin's *Institutes*.

In these opening sentences, Allen Maruyama, the first Asian American to stand for moderator of the General Assembly, establishes himself not as the suspect other, but as adopted into its household of faith. He even names a Scottish Presbyterian family, the Purvises, as being the instrument for that adoption, adding specificity to his claim. He and his siblings are adoptees to the extent that they even carry that family's first names.

Allen is giving substance to what the assembly heard earlier, in Rev. Vernon Foresberg's speech that placed his name in nomination. Representing John Knox Presbytery where Allen served churches from 1953 to 1962, Foresberg had also taken on the possibility of Allen's suspect "otherness."

Foresberg begins his speech by helping the assembly become comfortable with the Maruyama name. He says it is not difficult to pronounce. It comes easily because it represents Presbyterian mission, and Foresberg reinforces the pronunciation by saying "Maruyama" several times. He also sets the stage for other remarks Allen will make in his own speech, such as mentioning how Allen's local church of his childhood offered caring and compassion when Allen's ethnic group experienced injustice and intolerance during World War II.

With this emphasis on the church's caring and compassion, Foresberg stresses the critical role the church played in Allen's life, but also notes the faithfulness Allen reciprocates in his ministry. He quotes a colleague of Allen's that Allen always asks these two questions in deliberations and decisions affecting the life of the church: "Is this biblically grounded?" and "What is its theological purpose?"[55]

Foresberg has shifted from highlighting Allen's ethnicity to his theology. By doing so, he indirectly addresses what will emerge in all the speeches that morning as the tension between conservative and liberal factions throughout the assembly, one so dramatically demonstrated by the manner in which the conservative pastors confronted Allen at breakfast. Each speech will signal at some point how the nominee will bring unity between the factions and/or that the candidate is theologically "safe."

Quotations from *The Presbyterian Layman*, a publication generally identified with a conservative position, of the prior year underscore the ubiquity of this tension and its intensity. Its December 1978–January 1979 issue contains two articles of note. In "Evangelicals and Pluralism," Richard F. Lovelace acknowledges that some approaches used by theological conservatives are "wrong" and not "biblical." Those engaging these strategies attempt to disrupt mainline congregations in two ways: to drive out all leadership that is not conservative and to lead congregations out of the denomination when this is not possible.[56]

Allen had been the target of both tactics. In an attempt to drive him from leadership, the conservative pastors had threatened him point-blank that were he to be elected, they would walk out. It was either they or he. In the Denver Presbytery, conservative factions had resorted to the second tactic with their uncompromising stance and had led their churches out of the denomination the prior year, coincidently during Allen's term as moderator.

Rather, Lovelace's counsel to conservatives is to speak out, boldly and often, against important deviations from sound teaching, as the apostle Paul did, and to speak and vote against candidates who diverge so far from important doctrines that their ministry would harm the church. However, conservatives should rule out those two "unbiblical" strategies: persecution and separation.

While Lovelace urges less confrontational approaches, in the same issue, Stephen Chapman expresses his opinion with stridency. His argument concerns a grant from the World Council of Churches and its Programme to Combat Racism. The Council had awarded it to the Patriotic Front in

Zimbabwe. In the prior decade, the United Presbyterian Church had made continuous contributions to the World Council program.

In his piece "Killing for Christ," Chapman writes that the program grew out of the "theologies of liberation," which he says appeared in the 1960s and "inventively portray Jesus of Nazareth as hardly more than an early-day Che Guevara."

However, Chapman saves his most damning criticism for "fashionably liberal denominations" and "aggressively radical third-world Protestants, mostly from Africa and Asia." The money comes from "affluent whites, but its spending is controlled by poor non-whites."[57]

From this historical distance, Chapman's piece screams white privilege, if not white supremacy. In his view, whites have relinquished their power and money to undeserving non-whites.

It is difficult to determine the impact such opinions had on the majority of commissioners to the 1980 General Assembly, given that prior assemblies had demonstrated support of liberation theology, the World Council of Churches, and anti-racism efforts in a number of prior decisions. Chapman's may have been an extreme expression of the "conservative" position, whereas Lovelace's preference for less strident methods was more generally accepted by the majority of people sympathetic to a conservative stance.

However, Allen's candidacy had proven to be more than questionable from the conservative pastors' perspective at their early morning caucus. Perhaps, as emphatically, Allen was Japanese American, suspect by guilt through association as one of those "aggressively radical third-world Protestants, mostly from Africa and Asia"; he was a primary figure on the General Assembly committee to study liberation theology; and he was intricately involved in the civil rights movement during his Dubuque years.

Foresberg's approach in his nominating speech to skirt the duality of the conservative versus liberal debates and issues circling civil rights was perhaps well advised. Instead, he emphasizes and expands on Allen's faithfulness to the church that offered him caring and compassion during those difficult war years and, in particular, Allen's "pastoral service in areas of great human need."

To underscore the significance of Allen's ministry to the Dubuque youth who gathered on the church lawn, Foresberg gives details. He characterizes it as ministry to alienated youth and uses it as an example of Allen's energy, imagination, and empathy. Foresberg emphasizes Allen's key leadership in developing the coffeehouse ministry to college-age students and in establishing an ecumenical crisis center serving primarily youth with drug-related problems.

To make the point that youth ministry represents Allen's commitment to the church's mission is wise, but he also describes the effectiveness of the collegial staff model of Montview Boulevard Presbyterian Church (Denver), where Allen is serving. Three pastors share responsibilities equally. Foresberg offers Montview's model as an example of how to accomplish mission and do ministry in cooperative ways heretofore thought "inconceivable." Although he does not elaborate on the collegial pastor model or why he thinks it is so extraordinary, the course of Montview's careful implementation of it in the mid-1970s and Foresberg's comments in 1980 imply that the model of ministers functioning collaboratively is unusual. Many churches were following authoritarian patterns in which the senior pastor was in charge of everything.

Building on his representation of Allen as a biblically and theologically grounded collaborator, Foresberg creates an image of him as a leader of the present and the future but with an orientation built on orthodox biblical and theological foundations. He shapes an image of Allen as compassionate and a team player, one practiced and effective at bridging differences between people to reach the church's goals.

However, Foresberg might not have won over those conservative pastors with his insertion of this bit of humor. He had said that the Dubuque youth loved Allen so much they called him Pastor Marijuana!

Foresberg's little joke about the students' affection is another example of the importance Allen places on building relationships. Allen tells an anecdote that also reveals how comfortable he and the students were with each other. Several of them came to his office and advised that he would be even more popular if he were to try LSD and marijuana. He had answered, "Are you guys out of your minds? I'd lose my job. The fact that I know you use it is bad enough!"[58]

Foresberg's nominating speech and Allen's candidating speech synchronize to present the impression of a person so firmly grounded in Presbyterian tradition and theology that he considers himself an adoptee. The two speeches also build positively on Allen's Asian lineage by casting him as an exemplar of Presbyterian mission and a recipient of its care who has reciprocated throughout his ministry.

Chapter 7

The Japanese-American Story

ALLEN FOLLOWS THE LENGTHY statement about his Presbyterian pedigree with this brief observation: "The Japanese-American story is unique in American history."[59]

Although Allen begins by establishing commonality with the audience through his and his family's adoption by Scottish Presbyterians, how can he not reference the unique experience of Japanese Americans, particularly during World War II, if only by means of this short sentence?

This mention in passing might have been sufficient to evoke memories of that Japanese-American experience and of decades of discrimination before it for many in that audience. In 1980, people who had lost family and friends in combat would have been in attendance, along with a number of veterans, Allen and two of his older brothers among them. Joe served in the Military Intelligence Service, George in the U.S. Army Coast Artillery Corps in the Caribbean, and Allen served stateside, beginning in the war's final months.

Fewer in the audience would have known about the forced relocation and incarceration of West Coast persons of Japanese ancestry in the ten concentration camps in the interior, or about the restrictions placed on Japanese Americans not living on the West Coast who were not forcibly removed. The few who were aware of this history would have included Presbyterians on the West Coast who had helped evacuees store possessions they had to leave behind and those who assisted people incarcerated in the camps to find sponsors outside, resulting in their release.[60]

However, the majority in the audience would not know many details at all about the longer history of discrimination against Asians in the United States. Although Allen left unsaid specifics of its history extending back into the 1800s and the first half of the twentieth century, discrimination's historical weight still hovered over Cobo Hall. Only in 1953 was his immigrant mother able to become a US citizen, subsequent to the Immigration and Nationality Act of 1952.

The history of discrimination against Asians starts with the California Gold Rush in 1848, when Chinese laborers began to immigrate to the United States in appreciable numbers to work in the mines, also one of the originating industries in Colorado. In addition, they were a significant labor supply for railroad construction in the West and worked in agriculture and factories. When many became successful entrepreneurs, anti-Chinese sentiment grew, based on ethnic discrimination and perceived economic competition. Rumors spread that where Chinese laborers gathered, there were dens of prostitution, gambling, and opium use. As Japanese immigrants arrived, they were not distinguished in the popular American mind from the Chinese.

In 1875, the Page Act was passed, the first restrictive federal immigration law, which marked the end of open borders. The Page Act outlawed the importation of East Asian prostitutes, and it was applied without distinction to the majority of Chinese women attempting to immigrate. It also prohibited the immigration of felons and all East Asian contract laborers, referred to as "coolies," who were generally assumed to be brought to the United States for a term of service, that is, as forced labor.[61]

By 1882, anti-immigrant pressure grew to the extent that Congress passed the Chinese Exclusion Act, which "suspended the immigration of Chinese laborers (skilled or unskilled)" for ten years. It was renewed in 1892 and made permanent in 1902.[62]

These legislative acts and others set "a precedent for the establishment of discriminatory race and class based immigration laws in the United States. . . . [They were examples] of government-mandated racism. . . . [They] served as the foundation for the racialization of Asian immigrants, including the Japanese, as inassimilable 'aliens.'"[63]

Hostile and violent incidents directed toward East Asians occurred throughout the West, including Denver. For example, in 1880, a white mob invaded Chinatown and destroyed property, beat the residents, and killed one person, Luck Young.[64] The heritage of hatred toward the "outsider" continued in the twentieth century with the Ku Klux Klan coming to dominate Denver's political life. In the 1920s, the Denver mayor, police chief, and Colorado's governor openly counted themselves as members.[65] This history continues to be re-examined, with consideration being given to renaming the Stapleton area of Denver because Mayor Benjamin F. Stapleton (1869–1950), after whom it is named, was one of those KKK members.

Another example of violent incidents targeting East Asians took place in Wyoming in 1885. Anti-Chinese rioters burned Chinatown in Rock Springs, killing twenty-eight miners and wounding fifteen. All sixteen white suspects were acquitted.[66]

The cumulative effect of the antipathy and the various laws was to bar Chinese immigrants from most civic participation. Restrictions were not loosened until 1943, when, during World War II, China was suffering under the Japanese invasion, Japan had attacked Pearl Harbor, and the United States government turned to target the Japanese. Denying "civil rights for Japanese Americans during World War II occurred simultaneously with the expansion of immigration rights for the Chinese." Lest one think this was a magnanimous gesture toward the Chinese, the yearly immigration quota was established at 105.[67]

There were some voices of inclusion. For example, Central Presbyterian Church ran the Chinese School in Denver from 1877 to 1919 and gave workers educational and spiritual support.[68]

Although initially directed against Chinese and Japanese contract laborers, this early history of discrimination against East Asians seamlessly enveloped Korean and Japanese immigrants when they started arriving in greater numbers to meet the growing need for cheap labor in the United States. Japanese contract laborers had arrived in Hawaii in the late 1860s to work "in the sugar and pineapple fields in a plantation economy."[69] Starting in 1885, and propelled by a famine in Japan, the first Japanese immigrants arrived on the US mainland, also as agricultural workers.[70] As their population increased and they became successful, they experienced discrimination at levels similar to those directed toward the Chinese. By 1906, the San Francisco Board of Education voted to send Japanese, Chinese, and Korean children to separate schools.

However, because of the rising prestige and political power of Imperial Japan at that time, President Theodore Roosevelt reached a "Gentlemen's Agreement" in 1907 with the Japanese government that, in exchange for the desegregation of schools, while Japanese laborers would be denied entry, Japanese wives and children of men already in residence would be admitted. In 1910, the ratio of Japanese men to women in the United States was seven to one; by 1920, it was less than two to one. The "Gentlemen's Agreement" was the provision allowing Mr. Maruyama to bring his bride to the United States.

Nevertheless, citizenship was not an option for any Asian immigrant. In 1790, the United States enacted the provision that "any alien, being a free white person . . . may be admitted to become a citizen."[71] Asian immigrants were not counted as white and could not attain citizenship until the Immigration and Nationality Act (McCarran-Walter Act) of 1952, under which Allen's mother became a US citizen—less than thirty years prior to Allen's speech in Cobo Hall.[72]

To give perspective, only in 1870 had the Naturalization Act opened citizenship for African Americans. Not until the Immigration and Nationality Act (Hart-Celler Act) of 1965, which amended the 1952 act, was there to be no discrimination based on race, sex, nationality, birthplace, or residence.[73]

As if all the to and fro of immigration prohibitions of the prior century were not confusing enough, other repressive legislation had grown out of who could and could not be citizens. In 1913, California passed the Alien Land Law, which forbade "all aliens ineligible for citizenship" from owning land and, later, from leasing it.[74] Variations of restrictive laws regarding land ownership existed in fifteen western and southern states. Colorado was not one of them.[75]

Allen's brother Joe implied their father was a sharecropper because he arrived destitute, with no connections, but Allen conflates his father's circumstances with these restrictive laws against land ownership.[76] (Perhaps Allen's perception of the laws was prompted by state-wide discussion in 1944 to "specifically bar alien Japanese,"[77] which did not happen.) Despite these barriers, by 1920, Japanese-American farmers produced more than 10 percent of California's total crop value,[78] a level of industriousness replicated in Colorado's Arkansas Valley, Allen's home.

Perhaps because of their more limited numbers in the valley, the fifteen or so Japanese families around Las Animas during Allen's childhood enjoyed success and relative acceptance. He says that when he entered junior high, he began to understand that he "lived in a Caucasian society," but his awareness was not yet of discrimination toward Japanese Americans. Rather, his parents and the larger community had "real racial prejudice, . . . [but it was] against the Mexicans."

In the context of contrasting the harsh discrimination directed at Mexican migrant workers with the treatment of Japanese families, Allen's perception is that the European-American farm owners' access to the large Japanese families with a number of children provided laborers who turned European-American farms on Colorado's arid High Plains into profitable businesses. "Who else is willing to take that kind of land and irrigate it and do all the hard work but these Japanese farmers? So [the farm owners] appreciated them so much that they really took care of the Japanese farmers."[79]

The families lived in relatively nice homes and were treated respectfully. Joe thought the Japanese-American farmers around Las Animas were protected during the war because they had lived and farmed there all their

lives. All the European-American farmers knew them, and the school teachers knew the children well.[80] There was a Japanese store in Las Animas, as
well as the Japanese school near the Fort Lyon veterans hospital's gate, east
of Las Animas, the donation of which became a source of shame for Mr. and
Mrs. Maruyama in 1942. Virginia, Allen's younger sister, corroborates that
before the Pearl Harbor attack the "Las Animas population was very fair
and good to the [Japanese] farmers."[81]

In contrast, the Mexicans lived in what Allen describes as "huts." They
could not eat in the restaurants or get their haircuts "north of the tracks."
Often as a child he wanted to play with the Mexican children of the laborers
who worked on the Maruyama farm, and their mothers would bring out
tortillas and other Mexican foods at lunch. One time, Allen came in at midday but told his mother he was not hungry. When she asked why, he said he
had eaten with the Mexican kids. She scolded him and said, "Don't eat their
food!" She insisted they were dirty and their food was "no good for you."[82]

The Mexican laborers were most numerous from July to October,
when the younger children might attend school. Allen remembers Mexican
children in the elementary school, but not in the middle or high school. The
older children were expected to work in the fields.[83]

The discrimination he saw operating against Mexicans in the Arkansas
Valley might have heightened Allen's attentiveness and sensitivity to mar-
ginalized populations. In any event, over the years Allen invested himself
professionally in liberation theology, jail reform, civil rights, and justice for
sex workers, to name just a few of his concerns relating to people forced to
society's margins.

Also, perhaps the pointed discrimination against Mexican migrant
workers in the Arkansas Valley somewhat shielded the Japanese families.
Allen's experience was that when the Japanese-American children went to
school, they were respected by the townspeople. He knows he was something of a teacher's pet, and that made some of the other children jealous.
Several bullies hounded him in junior high, and when he won the American
Legion Award, it got a little worse. Allen discovered that "you do not want
to accept recognition from the principal or from the teachers." The bullies
called him "Goochie," a name that stuck through high school. However, by
then, his friends outnumbered the bullies, and the nickname did not bother
him as much.[84]

Allen's simple sentence alluding to the uniqueness of the Japanese-
American story contains none of these details. Perhaps its vagueness reflects
this lesson learned, that calling attention to oneself, even for achievement,
can result in a negative outcome. Alternatively, it might simply have served
as prelude to his next assertion.

Chapter 8

Befriended

ALLEN MOVES AWAY QUICKLY from the cryptic reference to the "unique" experiences of JaJAs in the United States to a positive statement about his adopted family. "During World War II, my little church in Las Animas was so helpful to me. While the community around me looked with suspicion and distrust, those Presbyterians befriended me."[85]

Having a safe community in which he felt "befriended" was crucial for teenage Allen as he tried to negotiate his place in a country that regarded him and his family as "enemy aliens." Although he attributes his decision to stay somewhat invisible to his embarrassment at being called "Goochie," his conclusion is reinforced by traditional Japanese culture. It places a high value on humility and maintaining a low profile. This value can have both positive and negative effects. Adhering to these Issei (first-generation) codes of behavior was an especially effective strategy for West Coast JaJAs having to find ways to survive the forcible removal and incarceration experience of World War II. However, many contemporary Japanese Americans feel tension between this posture of humility with its accompanying preference for understatement and the American bias toward visibility, self-promotion, and directness. These are the sorts of behaviors that encourage a public speaker to "get on fire," as Allen's coaches for his candidating speech urged him to do.

At the same time, many members of the majority culture suspect members of minorities who are perceived as being too outspoken. As Allen stood before the General Assembly, he might have been working to achieve a balance between these behaviors of humility and directness, a dynamic invisible to Angus, but perhaps a factor inhibiting Allen from getting "on fire."

Achieving this balance was especially critical during the war years. Yoshimi Hasui Watada, born in 1935, spent her elementary and high school years in the Arkansas Valley. She reports that during the war she "avoided spending time with other Japanese Americans in school, but we did things together on the week-ends. It was our arrangement." The inference is that Japanese-American children knew not to draw attention to themselves, even by congregating at school.[86]

Another Japanese-American Colorado resident, Dr. Seichi Otsuka, also speaks about the difficulty of finding a balance between a humble or a direct approach. He grew up in the northeastern part of the state on his family's farm, located several hundred miles north of Camp Amache. Unlike Allen, who is second-generation (Nisei), Otsuka is third-generation (Sansei), his grandparents having immigrated to the area. He is at least a decade younger than Allen, so does not personally carry the burden of wartime ostracism.

Because the Otsukas also lived in the interior of the United States, they were not incarcerated, but Otsuka does describe wartime suspicion directed toward Japanese Americans as having a covert effect. They "had to be quiet, not make waves, and their activities were restricted and monitored by the FBI." Home became "like a large [incarceration] camp that extended miles and miles without physical borders."[87]

In the years following the war, his parents tried to teach him to be "invisible and indirect." They counseled that if he did well in school, he should avoid becoming the teacher's pet and bragging about his accomplishments. Compete, but do not let it be known that you are competent. His father evidently walked this line successfully, because he was a spokesman for farmers in the area and would travel periodically to Washington, D.C., to testify about farmers' needs and viewpoints.[88]

In spite of their counsel, Otsuka grew up thinking of himself as part of white culture. He describes his habits of thought and approach to work as those of a white male—a direct, assertive manner. The realization that he had to be unobtrusive as a smart and capable Asian man evolved in his professional life. Because colleagues did not see him as part of the majority culture, he came to understand that the way he was presenting himself and his ideas was not effective. He changed tactics to accomplish his goals. He more purposefully built alliances with white male colleagues, emphasizing their needs and interests. He characterizes these tactics, in light of his emerging acceptance of his Japanese heritage and minority status, as feeling somewhat manipulative, but the indirect approach better achieved his ends.[89]

In this portion of his speech, Allen articulates his preferred approach for balancing the expectation of invisibility as a member of a minority in American culture with exerting effective leadership: establish relationships, similar to Otsuka's realization. In these two sentences, Allen only briefly conjures the "suspicion and distrust" directed toward people of Japanese lineage in the United States during the war years, while emphasizing that his little Presbyterian church ameliorated the hostility by "befriending" him.

Perhaps his disposition toward friendship grows out of Allen's gregarious personality, but over time, his strategy of developing relationships and trust as foundational to cooperation and overcoming difference has been effective, as seen by his professional success and the testimony of those who know him. Even today, in the setting of the retirement community where he lives, other residents can be heard commenting, "I like Allen. He's so outgoing!"[90]

In contrast to Otsuka, though, the Maruyama siblings had a more sustained exposure to their cultural heritage. They and many of the other Japanese-American children growing up in the 1920s and 1930s around Las Animas attended the Japanese school on Saturdays, and, during the summer, they went half days, Monday through Friday. The instructor, a Buddhist priest brought down from Denver, who was from Japan, lived in a small apartment at the back of the facility, which was built by the families. The school provided parking spaces and a playground. The curriculum included culture study and Japanese speaking, reading, and writing.[91]

Allen remembers speaking Japanese at home as a preschooler and mixing Japanese and English at meals. Joe said eventually the Maruyama kids spoke English so their parents could learn it. When Virginia, the youngest sibling, recalls those years, she remembers that while the children spoke English, their parents conversed with each other and the children in Japanese and English.

"Speaking English" and "speaking Japanese" can be thought of as inclusive not only of vocabulary but also of culture. Allen's was a "bilingual" childhood in this broader sense. For him and his siblings, public education seems to have been as important an integrating factor into the larger culture as the church. He says that the significant gift his parents gave them was the counsel that to get ahead, you must have education, an especially effective bridge for entry.[92] Their reasoning was that education did not belong only to the white culture but "was something that belonged equally to you, and you could succeed in it."[93]

Mr. and Mrs. Maruyama were both literate in Japanese, not surprising in that, starting in the 1860s, the Meiji government required at least four years of schooling.[94] All the Maruyama children attended college and enjoyed successful careers, as have their children. As one example, George had a graduate degree in biochemistry, and one of George's children is a professor at the University of Minnesota.[95] Education seems to have been a particularly important measure of the competency that was also of such value to the Otsuka family.

Rose and Allen so "drummed" the importance of education into their kids' heads that daughter Sarah's decision to quit college and get married was distressing, both to her and her parents. Sarah recalls, "My parents were really upset with me. They said, 'If you quit college, we're not going to pay later if you want to go back.' Still, I decided to do it and started having health problems. We were seeing a doctor who was a parishioner at Montview. He was just the coolest family doctor, like Dr. Welby [of the 1969–1976 television series *Marcus Welby, M.D.*]. I went in and had an upper and lower GI series. He sat me down and said, 'There's nothing physically wrong. What's going on?' I said, 'Well, I want to quit college and get married in June and my parents aren't very happy about it.'

"He called my dad and advised he sit down and talk to me. 'She's physically ill because she's so upset about this.' With HIPAA [the Health Insurance Portability and Accountability Act], they can't do that today. It wasn't because my parents were being so difficult. I just didn't want to disappoint them. I knew it was totally against their wishes for me. They sat me down and said, 'We don't want you to be sick. If this is upsetting you that much, we want you to know it's okay.' And it did work out okay. I got my bachelor's degree and my MBA at night when I was working at General Electric, and they paid for my education. My parents were happy, and I felt good about it, but I believe you follow a certain path in life. If you try to keep in the right direction, it will come out okay."[96]

Allen says that he "really appreciated" that eventually she completed college (after putting her husband through) and got her master's degree while she was working.[97] Not only did Sarah fully understand the value her parents placed on education, but she also showed a determination reminiscent of her father's.

Even though Allen might have rightly concluded that recognition by his teachers set him up as a target for his peers, he achieved public success as a scholar and an athlete. Nor were his brothers discouraged from such accomplishments. George, older than Allen by about eight years; Ted, the next oldest; and Joe, two years older than Allen, were all athletic, and probably also consistently made the honor roll. Virginia fondly remembers Allen and Ted, in particular, helping her with her homework.[98]

Allen lettered each of his four years in high school in track (hurdles, the 100-yard dash and the 220-yard relay), football, and basketball. He remembers Ted played football and pole vaulted, and George, Ted, and Joe all played basketball. George was taller and liked basketball best. George was also the Presbyterian church's softball team's pitcher, known, as Allen says, for his "spin on the ball."

If newspaper accounts reflect community interest, the summer softball leagues were standout events in Las Animas, and the Presbyterian minister, Rev. Jason T. Harbert, was the broadcaster at the park before leaving early in the war to serve as an army chaplain.[99] Allen's dad "used to not miss a game. He was so great when his sons played."[100]

The Maruyama boys' athletic capabilities and competitiveness were perhaps not entirely American-born. Mr. Maruyama might have brought those skills and interest with him from his Japanese boyhood, a heritage that became part of his children's lives. As early as 1915, high school baseball was so well established in Japan that national baseball championship games began.[101]

Joe was quick to note that he knows very little of what Allen went through in high school during the war. Joe had already left the Arkansas Valley by the time of the Pearl Harbor attack, so his memories of that area were largely positive ones of the community's support of Japanese farmers before the war. He observed that the age differences between the siblings and having different friends meant "I never saw the rest of my brothers."[102]

Although this might have been the case socially, the brothers played and worked together on the farm. Allen remembers Ted built a pole vaulting apparatus in the yard so he could practice. Jack Crompton, Joe's best friend and Mildred Scott's only child who lived up the road, would often walk to the Maruyama place to play various sports with them.[103]

The boys worked in the fields from the age they demonstrated they had the physical strength to handle it. "I would say eight or nine years old, we were out doing work." Allen describes his negotiations with his father about the inequity between their "wages" because Mr. Maruyama based each boy's hourly pay on their age, with the oldest getting the highest amount. As the youngest boy, Allen chafed under the arrangement, not so much the pay differential between himself and George and Ted, the two oldest brothers, but between himself and Joe, as Joe was only two years older.

"By the time we were teenagers, we were all doing an equal amount of work. . . . By then we had tractors. One memory I cherish is that when we had lots of land on alfalfa, we used an older method of stacking the hay all in one big pile, maybe twenty or thirty feet high and twenty to twenty-five feet wide. A big stack. You form the foundation and keep throwing on more hay.

"When I was just barely able to get my feet down on the pedals, I had the job of driving the truck attached to the big fork that people would put the hay on. The truck would pull a wire that pulled that hay fork up and into the stack. That was really fun. I used to look forward to it because you've got the rack up there, dump the hay, and then it automatically comes back down. The poor two people up on top had to arrange that hay so it would stack up. They had the hard job, especially when it was hot.

"When we still had horses, . . . at least eight or ten of them and a pony, whoever was taking care of irrigation rode the pony around to do it all. . . . I never did drive the team of horses. They hauled the fertilizer. [That equipment] had a propeller on the back that threw the fertilizer—manure from all the cattle, horses, and the half dozen pigs we had. The first tractor we had was an old John Deere that did nothing but plow up the ground. It pulled those big plows to till the soil.

"Every spring we had a big butcher and killed a hog. We had a lot of chickens. I'm at a loss how my mother cooked, washed clothes, took care of getting the eggs, feeding all those chickens, and still farmed that big garden."

From his perspective, Virginia, as the pampered baby sister who never worked in the fields, got by with minimal work in that acre-sized garden and with household chores. As Allen described Virginia's easy childhood, Rose was quick to interject, "I bet she has a different story!"[104]

Before the war, the Maruyama children enjoyed academic success and athletics and were part of a typical, hard-working farm family. They were welcomed by their church community. Farm work only intensified during the war, as laborers, including George and Joe and eventually Allen, left to join the military service. Japanese farmers, as did their neighbors, dealt with increased production demands due to the war effort but with fewer resources, given the scarcity of replacement parts, tires, fuel, and labor.

While they shared many of the demands of the wartime economy with their neighbors, the Maruyamas faced additional hardship due to the restrictions placed on them as "enemy aliens." As a high school student, Allen encountered any number of microaggressions in the town and at school. It is an understatement when Allen asserts that the friendship of "those Presbyterians" in that "little church in Las Animas" was "so helpful" for him in that atmosphere of "suspicion and distrust." Going to church was one community activity in which he was relatively safe and welcome.

Chapter 9

Becoming Christian

ALLEN OBSERVES TO THOSE gathered at General Assembly that "all my brothers and sister and I have become Christians, as well as my parents."[105]

In addition to sharing in the work on the farm, the church has been a unifying thread for the Maruyama family. The ages of the five Maruyama siblings spanned ten years, with the Pearl Harbor attack punctuating their adolescence and young adulthood. Naturally, each had his and her own experiences, but their early years were spent in a majority European-American community that was generally supportive, particularly the congregation of the Las Animas Presbyterian church.

At the time of the attack, Joe and George had already left Las Animas. Ted was absorbed with helping Mr. Maruyama on the farm. Virginia was still in elementary school and seems not to have been aware of many of the changes in the public attitude toward JaJAs. Allen was in a different situation as a high school freshman, particularly exposed during football and basketball games as one of only several Japanese-American athletes. Many of his experiences belie the feeling of some of his other siblings that the community remained generally supportive of the Japanese families.

Although the Maruyamas and other Arkansas Valley Japanese Americans were not incarcerated, some of them have vivid memories of microaggressions. Even those who were quite young at the time remember these experiences. Yoshimi Hasui Watada can recall such a painful moment. Her second grade teacher took the class to an ice cream store with a "No

J*ps Allowed" sign in the window. The teacher made her eat her ice cream alone, outside.[106]

In this unstable environment, "becoming Christian" could have offered more than just a welcoming community to the Maruyamas. Possibly neither Allen nor most in the assembly audience before him fully appreciated that membership in a Presbyterian church might have given the Maruyamas a protective cover.

The majority of persons of Japanese ancestry on the West Coast were Buddhist. Because they embraced a faith with Asian origins, their religious and racial difference became a "multiplier of suspiciousness." Could one be American in a nation that conflated race (white) and religion (Christian) as a prerequisite for belonging? Some US officials did not think so. Even prior to Pearl Harbor, the US government had created registries of individuals on the West Coast deemed to be dangerous. Among the groups repeatedly mentioned as suspect were Buddhist (and Shinto) priests.[107]

Within hours after the attack, nearly two hundred West Coast Buddhist priests were rounded up and confined, but only a handful of JaJA Christian ministers were. Eventually, almost three quarters of the Buddhist leadership was detained, and all Shinto priests, but just 17 percent of Christian ministers were. Of the latter, many were released and allowed to rejoin their families.[108]

Once in the ten concentration camps, JaJA Christians were given preferential treatment. The authorities believed that being an American "required abandoning anything linked to Japan and its religion or culture." Buddhists were even sometimes urged to convert by other incarcerated people because becoming Christian was seen as a positive step toward assimilation.[109]

From a young age, church membership and participation were central commitments throughout each of the Maruyama siblings' lives. Additionally, during their youth, the closest friends of various Maruyama children were also members of the Presbyterian church. Joe's best friend was Jack Crompton. Jack's mother, Mildred Scott, was quite active in the Presbyterian church. Allen's closest friend was Jim Petersen, whose parents were the Sunday school teachers and youth advisors.

Ted died suddenly in his fifties, after open-heart surgery, but as an adult had been ordained as a ruling elder in the Las Animas church. George, who died only eight months shy of his hundredth birthday, was also an ordained ruling elder and member for fifty years in the Westminster Presbyterian Church in Dubuque.

Doris Calian, a member of that congregation and Dr. Calian's spouse, knew George as a fellow elder and Allen as the associate pastor. She says

George was well accepted in the community, and she admired him and Allen. George was a biochemist, as was she, and for nearly four decades he directed a clinic owned by a group of physicians, after he completed his master's degree upon return from the service.[110]

Joe graduated from high school in the spring of 1941 and from the University of Colorado after the war with a degree in business management. He worked his entire career for International Harvester in Chicago, primarily in labor relations. He and his wife were active in Presbyterian churches in Chicago, and when he retired, he assumed leadership roles in his United Church of Christ congregation in Genesee, Colorado.

Virginia sang in the church choir and, as late as 2018, still taught Sunday school in her church in Topeka, Kansas. She was also working part-time as a substitute for the Topeka Public Schools Special Education Department (in her upper eighties!), after years with the civil service in the General Services Administration. In her life as an army wife, she lived in Japan following the Korean War, on Okinawa, and on various bases in the United States, fulfilling her church commitments in various locations as she was able.

Not only did "becoming Christian" possibly offer a subtle form of protective cover during the war, but it was also the source of advocates for the Maruyama children. In the fall of 1941, Jack Crompton and Joe had enrolled together at the University of New Mexico in Albuquerque. After the attack, Crompton enlisted in the Air Force, and Joe completed his freshman year. He transferred to the University of Colorado his sophomore year, and, when he tried to enlist, Crompton's mother, Mildred Scott, advocated on his behalf, as she would try to do for Allen.

As Joe described it, he could select which branch of the service he wanted to enter, but Scott's advocacy and his bilingual ability enabled him to get a special assignment in military intelligence (G-2) as a linguist. He was sent to Japanese language school at Fort Snelling, Minnesota, after basic training in Alabama.[111]

These Military Intelligence Service (MIS) language training programs produced between four thousand and six thousand Nisei graduates, a figure represented variously in different sources. They are sometimes credited with shortening the war, perhaps by several years, and served in every major battle and campaign in the Pacific theater of war.[112]

When Joe's group graduated from language school, they were shipped out to the Pacific right away and assigned as individuals to various units. He described his interrogations and interpretations for Japanese prisoners of war as a process of asking basic questions about their military service. The prisoners "conversed freely" because the questions were not personally threatening. "They felt safe with us. We never tortured our prisoners!" After the armistice, he went to Okinawa, and as soon as they "got that settled," they went on to Tokyo to assist with "billeting for the army" and to establish the military government. The task became "setting up democracy" in Japan. For one year, they worked on "setting up voting places and making sure everyone got to vote." Once that task was completed, as Joe put it, they had served their time and came home.

George served in the Caribbean and was stationed on the island of Antigua. He regularly played bridge with a British government official—and his daughter Helen. She became George's wife.[113]

Ted was in a unique position. He had some college education, but either due to a farm accident that impaired their father's sight, and/or because two brothers were already serving, Ted did not enlist. He had to stay home to help Mr. Maruyama and meet wartime farming production goals.

Allen says, "My dad was pretty desperate when the war broke out because he knew he couldn't take care of the farm. His physical strength and abilities were diminished. But it was nice that Ted took care of my father as long as he did." Ted eventually married Florence, a young Japanese-American woman from Oklahoma, and had four daughters.[114] Virginia says staying home during the war was hard on Ted, but he maintained a good attitude.[115]

The wartime experience of each of the Maruyama children, most of whom were in Cobo Hall for Allen's speech, was distinct, and each probably read their own meanings into Allen's words about the unique Japanese-American history in the United States, becoming Christian, and their experiences during World War II. The stories of other Japanese-American Presbyterians in the audience, who had lived along the West Coast and to whom their churches also gave significant emotional support, were even more varied.

The history of discrimination toward them in the decades leading up to Pearl Harbor was pronounced, unlike the Maruyama children's experiences. The 1924 Immigration Act shut the doors to Japanese immigration. Previously, Japanese entry was regulated by non-legislative measures, but California officials pressured Congress continuously to curb Japanese rights. V.C. McClatchy, the newspaper publisher, put opposition to Japanese immigration in especially florid terms, claiming that the Japanese "astronomical birth rates" and their increased landholding "menaced California's Anglo-Saxon civilization."

The U.S. Department of State and the Japanese Ministry of Foreign Affairs warned that setting aside the 1907 "Gentlemen's Agreement" would have negative repercussions. Indeed, that the 1924 act singled out the Japanese provoked militarists to pursue a more aggressive stance against the

United States and "pushed the Japanese public to oppose further diplomatic cooperation with the West in China."

The cascading effects of the 1924 Immigration Act prevented many relatives from joining their families in the United States and contributed to the growing tension between the Issei (immigrants), who could not attain citizenship, and their American Nisei children. More significantly, it ensured the concentration of persons of Japanese ancestry on the West Coast.[116]

If this were the extent of the troubled treatment of Japanese immigrants in the United States, it might have somewhat faded by the time Allen carried his "little stand" onto the Cobo Hall stage in 1980. However, the Pearl Harbor attack, December 7, 1941, changed everything for all persons of Japanese ancestry in the United States.

At least three people in the audience that morning knew both the longer record of discrimination against Asians and the World War II incarceration experience full well: Rev. Minoru Mochizuki, his wife June, and Allen's sister-in-law Dorothy Maruyama, Joe's wife. Unlike Allen and Joe who grew up in the interior of the United States, these three lived in ethnic enclaves on the West Coast, had attended ethnic churches, and were incarcerated. June and her family were forcibly removed to Amache, Min and his family to Tule Lake in California, and Dorothy and her family to Rohwer in Arkansas. In contrast, Allen is standing at the podium and claiming his unique Japanese heritage while simultaneously presenting himself as assimilated from a young age.

In 1980, Min was attending as a member of the General Assembly Mission Council and the Advisory Council on Discipleship and Worship. June was there as a member of the Council on Church and Race. June would soon emerge as a leader of workshops for women's groups in churches throughout the nation on "assertiveness training, conflict resolution, and women's liberation." The Mochizukis lived in Kalamazoo, Michigan, where Min began as a campus minister in the late 1950s at Western Michigan University and by 1980 was on the faculty. June also worked at the university, in the counseling office.[117]

They grew up in that more dense population of West Coast Japanese immigrant families and could have added whole chapters to Allen's two sentences about being viewed with suspicion and mistrust during World War II, as well as to his gratitude for the church's friendship during those difficult years. Although no single story can be said to be representative of JaJA individuals in those coastal states, the Mochizukis' experiences offer a sample of the disparity between the majority who lived there and the Japanese families, such as the Maruyamas, who lived inland.

This disparity manifested itself in any number of ways, including in the perspectives of those who grew up in ethnic churches and Allen's experience as a member of a minority within a majority white congregation. The differences, perhaps invisible and unspoken, could have diminished Allen's claim to be representative of JaJA experiences specifically and Asian American experiences generally, as lived by the attendees with those heritages.

Descriptions of Min and June's personal histories highlight these differences. June's parents had met and married in Japan, the connection established because her father's sisters attended the same high school as her mother. She describes girls attending high school at that time as the equivalent of sending them to college today. Her mother had studied English and "wrote it beautifully," but she had just a basic grasp of its use. June was born in the United States and grew up on her family's farm outside the town of Livingston, in Merced County, between San Jose and Fresno.

Her Japanese enclave has a distinctive history. The editor of a Japanese newspaper in San Francisco wanted to start a Christian community and recruited young Japanese families to the place he located, Livingston—if they became Christian. June's parents, the Suzukis, accepted the offer. The close-knit community consisted of about sixty families working on small farms. The local Methodist church, an ethnic congregation, played a large role in helping these Japanese immigrants adjust and study English.

After the birth of their first child, June's parents formed a corporation, named their American-born son president, and bought the land they farmed in his name. Her parents were officers of the corporation. By the time all the children went to college, the family owned quite a bit of land under this arrangement.[118]

They also had a close working relationship with the Ortiz family, who agreed to move into their home and maintain the land during the Suzukis' World War II incarceration. This proved crucial because June's family had a place to return to after their release. Many families who were forcibly relocated retained only the minimal possessions they could carry, and, if they had property and businesses, they had no choice but to sell them in haste, at well below their value, if they could find buyers. The haste and indiscriminate manner of the forced relocations penetrated all levels of JaJA communities on the West Coast. Even children of Japanese ancestry in orphanages were relocated.

After the Suzukis returned from camp, the Ortizes continued to work for them. June describes the relationship between the families as close and warm. The Suzukis would bring their Japanese food into the fields midday, because the Ortizes loved it, and the Ortizes would bring their Mexican food, which the Suzukis loved—a relationship between immigrant families that benefitted both (reminiscent of that between the Maruyama and Purvis immigrant families).

A month before June's high school graduation, May 1942, all the Livingston Japanese families had been removed to the assembly center at the Merced County fairgrounds. The principal showed up there, located each graduate, and unceremoniously handed them their diplomas.

Although awkwardly executed, at least the principal saw to it that June and her classmates received their diplomas. Some schools refused to grant them to graduating Japanese-American seniors. For example, a Los Angeles high school principal "vowed that Aika Herzig-Yoshinaga and her Japanese-American schoolmates would be denied their diplomas because 'your people bombed Pearl Harbor.'"[119]

June's family did not live in the fairground's cattle and horse barns, as some did, but in hastily erected barracks. The grass grew up between the floor boards. They would laugh about how easy it was to sweep because the dirt simply disappeared down the cracks. The tarpaper roofs offered little protection during the hot months of summer when the temperature would rise to 110—on a cool day! In August, they boarded the train for Camp Amache, the one known to Allen, located east of Lamar and just fifty miles from the Maruyama farm.[120]

None of the camps was ready for the arrivals. Their deficiencies varied from location to location, but a typical example was the lack of suitable toilet facilities at Minidoka (Idaho). Those who were incarcerated were forced to use open-pit latrines for the first six months while the sewage treatment plant was installed, a hardship which would have carried into cold and snowy winter months. "Once lavatory facilities were built, they still afforded no privacy as there were no partitions between the toilets." This lack of privacy in toilets was a ubiquitous feature in the camps, and some chose to avoid them until late night hours in order to recover what privacy they could.[121]

Apparently the government anticipated that the forced removal of persons of Japanese ancestry to the interior would be temporary. They would vacate the West Coast, but "eventually, according to the government plan, loyal internees and their families would leave the camps for jobs in the interior. . . . The WRA [War Relocation Authority] was the government entity charged with moving Japanese Americans from the camp back into America's mainstream."[122]

How widely this objective was shared or communicated is another question. Even if it was known, the barriers to leaving the camps were considerable. From the viewpoint of those incarcerated, leaving camp might expose them to hostile, if not violent, encounters; furthermore, how would they find the required sponsor, where would they go, where would they work, and how would they find housing?

Not until 1943 were men in camp allowed (required) to enlist, and, although college in the interior was an option for the younger people, some colleges and universities might delay or refuse admittance. "Only 25 percent of colleges admitted Japanese Americans during World War II." Even among those who were admitted, "some were unable to secure military permission" to enroll.[123]

June applied to Colorado schools and was accepted at Fort Collins, the agricultural college. She thought it would have a good home economics department, appropriate for her interest in dietetics, perhaps not fully aware that admittance to colleges and universities was not something to be taken for granted for the majority of Japanese-American young people in the camps. In December, she requested leave from Amache to visit her sister, who was working as a "house girl" in Denver. June's sister's experience is not typical, either, in that positions were not easy to find in Colorado, and some were treated poorly on the "outside."[124]

In letters exchanged between the wife of a farmer who owned land about twenty-five miles from Camp Amache and her brother, who had enlisted, the brother asks how hiring a J*p from the camp has worked out. He reports to her that their sister had written that several of the neighbors were "trying to make trouble. What was the outcome? Why don't you tell them off? I don't particularly like J*ps myself but labor is hard to get and most of the J*ps are good Americans anyway." She answers that the arrangement fell apart due to their neighbors' hostile reactions, and they sent the worker back to Amache.[125]

In comparison, June and her sister were fortunate. They both simply left Denver, headed directly to Colorado State College of Education in Greeley, enrolled, and did not return to Amache, effectively AWOL. She entered as a freshman, and her sister transferred in as a junior, having attended college in California. June marveled that no one ever came after them.[126]

During their first quarter, the vice president called the dozen or so Japanese-American students together and asked what they were doing at Greeley. It was a teacher's college, after all, and who would want to hire J*ps to teach their children?[127]

Consequently, June transferred to Fort Collins, where she originally had been accepted, and pursued her interest in becoming a dietitian. June's older sister stayed at Greeley, graduated, went back to Amache, and taught music there.[128]

The constancy of the church is a major theme in Min's story also, and his early experiences, like June's, took place in the context of ethnic congregations. However, being Christian was not a conduit to majority culture for Min and June as it was for Allen. Min's father was baptized as a Christian in Kobe, Japan, before coming to the United States at a young age as an importer for a large Seattle department store. Min's mother arrived in 1917, roughly the same time as Allen's mother, also as a "picture bride." His father eventually established his own import business in San Francisco. Min, the second son, grew up in San Francisco's Japantown and, with his family, attended the Japanese Church of Christ, Presbyterian (Christ United Presbyterian Church). After public school each afternoon, he attended Japanese school. Japanese was spoken at home, and, in 1929, the family spent six months back in Japan. Min's mother hoped they would return permanently one day, a hope Min did not understand or ever share.

Even before Pearl Harbor, Min's family had undergone dramatic changes. In 1938, his older brother Shigeaki ("Shig") had been accepted at the University of California, Berkeley, but decided to attend university in Japan. The family, experiencing "deep discrimination" toward the Japanese, knew there was no future at American companies for college-educated Nisei young men. In any case, from Min's mother's point-of-view, the family would be reuniting in Japan.

In 1940, the import business shriveled due to the US embargo against Japanese goods and banking. Min's father sold his inventory for the meager sum of $250 and was out of business the whole year before Pearl Harbor. He worked as a laborer at a rice farm, and his mother worked as a domestic.[129]

After Pearl Harbor, Min's junior year in high school, his father moved the family to what he thought would be the safety of a location further east, to Sacramento, having heard rumors about "evacuation." The move tore Min from his school, his friends, and his closely-knit community. The Japanese-American church in Sacramento was not welcoming. "That's typical Japanese-American," says Min. "I was just an outsider."

His isolation continued when they were forcibly relocated in May 1942 to the Walerga Assembly Center (Camp Kohler) with a duffel bag and suitcase apiece. He knew none of the other Japanese Americans his age because the San Francisco families had been sent to different locations. In July, the Mochizukis were confined at Tule Lake, the largest of the incarceration sites. Min spent his senior year there, pursuing his athletic interest by playing on the championship basketball team and contributing his musical talent in a double quartet.

Following graduation and for the next year, Min shuttled from place to place after being thwarted in his attempt to attend Gustavus Adolphus College in Minnesota. He had understood that his admission to the college had released him from Tule Lake permanently. He arrived in Minneapolis but worked as a busboy for several months while he waited for approval to enroll, only to receive news from the registrar that he "had been removed from Nisei enrollment." He was told he would have to gain approval from the provost marshal's office in Washington, D.C., an approval that did not materialize. He never understood why he was denied nor the mechanism for it.[130]

His sense of betrayal (of the promise that he had been released permanently from Tule Lake) led him to think that "Mom was right. The US government will trick you at every turn."[131]

He returned "home" to Tule Lake, unlike June, who simply went AWOL, and unlike those who did receive military permission to enroll in college. He took a circuitous route back to California, visiting friends in Columbus, Ohio, and Chicago. He traveled to the Amache (Colorado), Topaz (Utah), and Minidoka (Idaho) incarceration sites and had no trouble entering or leaving any of them. From Boise, Idaho, he wired Tule Lake administrators he was returning.[132]

Tule Lake had changed in the prior year and become a "high security" camp for Japanese war resistors and "No-No Boys." The latter had replied "no" to questions twenty-seven and twenty-eight on the 1943 "Application for Leave Clearance" form, referred to as the loyalty questionnaire, which everyone over the age of seventeen was required to complete. The questionnaire asked for agreement to serve in the US Armed Forces (number twenty-seven) and denunciation of loyalty to the Emperor of Japan (number twenty-eight). Those answering "no" to both questions had various reasons for doing so, for example, young men so instructed by their parents for fear that if they answered yes, indicating agreement to serve in the armed forces, the family would be separated. Also, an affirmation foreswearing loyalty to the emperor implied that one had, in the past, been loyal to him, which was not the case for Nisei young men.[133]

The resistors were also motivated by a complex of reasons and circumstance. In any event, their incarceration and that of their families was a betrayal of American constitutional values. Some reasoned they could not fight for a country that had imprisoned them and their families.[134]

Upon his return, the tanks Min saw at the entrance symbolized how the camp's character had changed into that of a segregation center for the so-called troublemakers. Min did not re-enter the athletic or choral scenes but retreated into himself. His withdrawal included immersing himself in reading, because books took him away imaginatively from his surroundings. Tomes like *War and Peace* expanded his vocabulary and completed some of the education he had missed with the disruption caused by the forced incarceration and the transition to his senior year in camp.

He "yielded" to his mother's insistence that he "become Japanese" and studied in an intense Japanese language program, but simultaneously resented her and wanted to distance himself from anything Japanese. When he looks back, he describes himself as being very angry: angry at being deceived that he was released from camp for "the duration" of the war to attend college, which proved not to materialize; angry at Gustavus Adolphus College's rejection; and angry at his mother. He "used to swear like mad. Almost every other word."

During this bleak time of feeling betrayed and rejected, Min met Reverend Thomas Grubbs, a Presbyterian graduate of the San Francisco Theological Seminary. Grubbs visited his barracks regularly for long conversations. The relationship seemed to keep Min grounded, and he says that of all the places he has worshipped, he remembers the barracks and that worshipping congregation as the most meaningful.

Until those conversations with Grubbs, Min had not given a thought to becoming a minister. Rather, he characterizes his Christianity as a kind of "YMCA variety." What he means by that term can be inferred from his description of one of his Sunday school teachers. The man was a "YMCA guy, a humanist, the sort who would have been embarrassed to admit he was a Sunday school teacher, and nobody else would have identified him as that, either." During this confused period, Min made two decisions: as a Nisei, to renounce his American citizenship and to become a Christian minister.

When Min tried to retract his decision to renounce his citizenship, it was too late. In July 1945, President Truman declared those who renounced would be removed to Japan. Min was one of 987 plaintiffs trying to reverse their case. His choice had been made in anger and despair during the worst of his confinement, and his case was not resolved until 1954.[135]

His family was cleared to leave Tule Lake in November 1945 and lived in the basement of the Japanese Church of Christ, Presbyterian, San Francisco (Christ United Presbyterian Church). This was a common predicament for those released from the camps. They could not find housing, nor could they find work.[136]

Min was not cleared to leave Tule Lake until March 1946. In January 1946, and with no family by his side, Min learned of Shig's death. A repatriated friend, Spencer Takeshita, sent him the news in a telegram. Min's brother had died in 1944 as a Japanese lieutenant junior grade on an escort for ships in the South China Sea, northwest of the Philippines.[137] Profound grief added to Min's distress.

Basic to his second decision, that of becoming a minister, were the perspectives expressed in 2 Cor 5:19 and Rom 8:38–39: God has reconciled us to the divine self by Jesus Christ and has given us the ministry of reconciliation; and nothing can separate us from that love of God in Jesus Christ our Lord.

Before incarceration, Min thought of God's love as somewhat conditional, which meant the priority of a faithful person was to be nice in order to deserve divine favor. His experiences during the war—his displacement, the betrayal in his release from Tule Lake turning out to be provisional, being behind barbed wire again after experiencing the freedom of traveling around the United States and to the other incarceration sites, his anger, confusion, and isolation—were ameliorated by the constancy of his visits with Thomas Grubbs.

He came to believe that nothing, not even a foul life, restricts God's love. Unlike the deception when he was told he was released from Tule Lake for the duration of the war to attend college, he came to believe that God's love is not provisional. Something is not right in the world, and God is working to reconcile it to the divine self. In this drama of life, God the reconciler engages in dialogue with individuals. Min's growing conviction that life is circumscribed by reconciliation and love led him to the College of Wooster and McCormick Theological Seminary.[138]

Min and June met at the Northern California Young People's Christian Conference, an ecumenical, ethnic church conference at Lake Tahoe, after his freshman year at Wooster and the summer before she began graduate work at Mills College in Oakland. June notes that whether Methodist, Presbyterian, or whatever, the JaJAs in California attended ethnic churches. They did not think of going to others because "the major denominations certainly didn't want us there at that time, right after the war, when we came back from being incarcerated. Nobody could figure out what we had done to deserve it, but we had to have done something to deserve something so bad as incarceration."

She characterizes Min as a bit brash, as you would expect a college freshman to be, but also idiosyncratic in a funny, charming way. "He would take off his glasses, dive into the water, come up, and put his glasses back on to see where he had to go to get back to shore."[139]

An unintended, but poignant, metaphor. For the majority of persons of Japanese ancestry in the United States, the war had been a disorienting sojourn in the depths of a murky underworld, and countless numbers struggled for years afterward to find safe harbor. Men, especially, speak of being "angry all the time," but many others suppressed it.[140]

A typical response of those who were incarcerated was simply not to talk about those years. Nothing could be done about it, so just get on with life. *Shikata ga nai* is an often-used expression of this philosophy. It cannot be helped; do not look back. Move forward. Persevere.

Numerous authors reflect about the prevalence of this attitude about perseverance, even if one might feel helpless. Dr. Michio Kaku, professor, futurist, and theoretical physicist, whose parents were incarcerated at the Tule Lake camp, says of them that, although they were left penniless, they seemed to be without self-pity or anger. Their attitude was that the past was past, they would forge on and make sure such disasters did not happen again. By doing so they would bring honor to their people.[141]

Perhaps this determination and silence, combined with the value placed on humility, colored the way the JaJA community came to be generally perceived. The term "model minority," attributed to a 1966 piece in *The New York Times*, came to refer to them.[142]

In the late 1970s, this silence was called into question by a movement to redress the injustices of the forced removal and incarceration. Initially, the movement was unpopular because it depended on "the Nisei to break the years of silence that protected their psyches," but the arduous campaign for redress continued, nevertheless.

In 1980, the year of Allen's speech, President Jimmy Carter signed the legislation that authorized the Commission on Wartime Relocation and Internment of Civilians. The resulting "hearings, exposure, publicity, the change in the public attitude" led to the enactment of the 1988 Civil Liberties Act, which resulted in a formal apology from President Ronald Reagan for the forced relocation and reparations for survivors of the incarceration.[143]

Some try to balance this perspective about perseverance and humility, which led to silence in the face of the injustice of incarceration, by emphasizing other JaJA values. Eric Langowski (Sansei, or third-generation) prefers to express *kansha* (gratitude) to his grandmother for showing him her rejection letter to attend what became his alma mater, which led to his research about the extent to which Nisei students were shut out of higher education during the war. He writes: "*Shikata ga nai* no more!"[144]

Allen's references in his candidating speech to the suspicion and mistrust directed toward him during the war years takes place eight years before Reagan's public apology and in the very early days of more open conversations about the WWII incarceration of persons of Japanese ancestry. At the time of his 1980 speech, the injustices experienced by West Coast persons who were forcibly relocated were still largely unspoken and therefore hidden from many Americans. His brief reference to the unique history of Japanese Americans and the suspicion and mistrust directed toward him during the war, while it conjured vivid memories on the part of his family, particularly Dorothy, as well as Min and June Mochizuki, might not have penetrated the awareness of the majority of those in his audience.

After the attack, the memories of those who were incarcerated and Allen's experiences contrasted in a number of ways. As a young Japanese American living in the interior of the country, Allen functioned in a perpetual state of shock during the war, exposed in a confusing white majority environment that was alternatively cruel and protective.

The Denver Post, a primary news source in Colorado, as were many newspapers of the time, filled its wartime pages with racial slurs directed toward anyone of Japanese ancestry: "enemy race," "yellow peril," "mad dogs," "yellow devil," "treacherous vermin," "slant-eyed back stabbers," and "not, nor ever will be, Americans." After Camp Amache opened, the *Post* was obsessed with reporting about alleged negative internee related events that contained "as many lies as facts."[145]

In contrast, Allen attended a generally accepting Presbyterian church whose leadership was dominated by persons of Scottish ancestry. His church friend, Jim Petersen, and his athletic status protected him somewhat at school. When he was jostled in the hallways, his team buddies tried to shield him. On the occasion of an away game in Lamar, the town east of Las Animas and between it and Camp Amache, the team went into a restaurant, and Allen and another Japanese-American boy named Fukimara were refused service. The whole team stood up and walked out.[146] However, the team couldn't protect their two Japanese-American members from hearing taunts from opposing fans during the games who screamed: "Send the J*ps back!" and "Kill those goddamn J*ps!"

Petersen has told his family about a tense moment that occurred after a Lamar-Las Animas football game, perhaps on the occasion just mentioned. Jim was the quarterback and Allen the other half of the unbeatable passing duo. Las Animas defeated Lamar, and Petersen remembers that the Las Animas team bus was flanked by angry Lamar fans on the bridge going out of town.

At first Petersen thought the anger was because Lamar's loss meant Las Animas would be going to the quarter-round playoffs. Then it dawned on him that they had two Japanese-American players. He asked Allen about it later, and Allen said yes, the Lamar fans on the bridge were jeering because of the Japanese players, an anger intensified by the fact that Camp Amache was only sixteen miles to the east. Many of the Lamar businesses placed hostile signs in their windows indicating they would not serve the Japanese when they came into town on leave from Amache, and many citizens resented that a new high school and hospital were built on the Amache grounds, better facilities than their counterparts in Lamar.

Even so, Bruce Newman, a Colorado native and Presbyterian ruling elder, indicates there were other reactions to the camp. He was nine years old and living in Granada, the small town a mile from Amache. His father owned the pharmacy. Many of the Granada residents welcomed Amache due to the revenue it generated and had "amicable" relationships with those who were incarcerated when they would come into town. One of the young Japanese women was a nanny for his younger brother.[147]

Although Petersen was aware of the depth of hatred directed toward Allen and the rest of the Maruyama family, he did not shy away from the friendship. Every time Allen stayed overnight at the Petersens', Pete and Pearl, the parents, complained about not getting sleep because the boys "giggled all night." However, Petersen's steady girlfriend was appalled that he had Japanese friends. One of his cousins was killed on Okinawa, and Petersen's aunt held Allen's family personally responsible.[148]

This seesaw between acceptance and rejection surely kept the adolescent Allen off-balance. During his freshman year, Allen played on a six-man football team. The last game of the season was in McClave, a small town between Las Animas and Lamar, and the ground was frozen hard as rock because it was November. He was carrying the ball, got tackled, hit his shoulder, and broke his collarbone. He walked the school hallways for the next month with his arm in a sling, an injury signifying his commitment to the team but coincident with the Pearl Harbor attack.[149]

After the attack, the assault on JaJAs was unending, from immediate incarceration of West Coast Japanese community leaders who were suspected of sabotage (none was ever found to have been a saboteur), to Executive Order 9066 on February 19, 1942, that initiated the forced relocations, and other orders, for example, the one by which the treasury froze the Maruyamas' assets. Also, movement for Japanese in the interior was restricted without official permission. There were curfews. They had to turn in contraband, such as knives over a certain length. As of December 31, 1941, the attorney general ordered that "Axis aliens" surrender radio transmitters, short-wave radio receivers, and cameras to police by 11:00 p.m. on January 5.[150]

When Allen's emotional pain during these difficult war years is described to them now, his European-American high school classmates register surprise. At a 2015 high school reunion, their comments ran along the lines of "We didn't think of Allen as being Japanese. He was just Allen. He was our friend." How could they not have been aware of his anguish? Yes, they were only kids, but for them not to know how he suffered may have meant he was disciplined about hiding it, he suppressed it, or perhaps that he worked diligently at assimilation.

Allen talks about "running with" two groups, the "rowdy bunch" and the "Sunday school group." Some of his old adversaries from junior high

were part of the rowdy bunch, but Allen had access to his dad's car, which
they loved because none of them had that resource. As he reflects about
those "bully heads," he thinks most of them were from single-parent homes
or their families were very poor, and the kids were basically on their own.
The rowdy bunch, including Allen, did indeed chalk up a number of esca-
pades, such as racing the car through the alleys of Las Animas in the middle
of the night and tipping over trash cans, as well as stealing gas from the
filling station.

The Sunday school group included the son of Arthur M. Wimmell,
newspaper editor and active Presbyterian church member; the bank president Rawlings' son Robert and daughter Dorothy; and Jim Petersen, of
course. Both Petersen's granddaughter and Allen tell how Pearl and Pete,
the parents, would say, "All you boys in this Sunday school class have got
to become Presbyterian ministers, because the church needs ministers so
badly. You all have to think about being ministers."[151]

Allen says Pearl was especially influential and that she and Pete were
always preaching to them that they needed to become ministers. Theirs
were voices of authority not only as youth leaders but also because Allen
related to them as if they were his second parents.

Of that group, Allen, Petersen, and Dorothy Rawlings did eventually
attend seminary and become ministers, but the Petersens' urging came before and in the midst of war. The path to ministry would not be straightforward, especially for Allen. He tells the story in several interviews about how
the pastor, Richard Sammon, discouraged him from ministry, a memorable
enough admonition that Allen will articulate Sammon's reservation shortly,
in his speech on the floor of the assembly. Allen characterizes him as "a
very nice person," but Sammon cautioned that, although it was laudable that
Allen wanted to go into ministry, he would only be called to serve in the
handful of Japanese churches on the West Coast. Perhaps a Japanese church
had started up in Chicago, but he knew of no others. He said, "You're not
going to be serving white people."

Allen says he "didn't know what it would feel like to live in a pure
Japanese community, a pure Japanese culture. I had no idea what a Japanese
Presbyterian church would be like." The only Japanese community Allen
knew was the cluster of families around Las Animas, and they were like an
extended family, accepted by the surrounding white culture until Pearl Harbor, and even then, they were not completely ostracized. His only exposure
to an ethnic church would have been to the Second (Spanish) Presbyterian
church south of the tracks that Allen's congregation supported. However, it
discontinued regular services by 1938, when Allen would have been twelve
years old. He does not have a clear memory of it.

When Allen speaks of Sammon's admonition, the context seems to have been around the time of Pearl Harbor. Allen thought Sammon was a "straight talker who didn't mince words about what life was all about. He knew the way the Japanese were treated, and I think he thought it was wrong, but he didn't question racism." From Sammon's perspective, Allen's membership in the community of faith had limits.

Allen was of two minds. At several of the youth conferences he attended, "it was brought out very clearly that the church needed missionaries. If I went to seminary and was ordained, I could always become a missionary." On the other hand, Sammon's admonition did not entirely make sense to him. Allen began thinking he "really ought to get into something else."

Before Allen graduated from high school, a new Presbyterian minister arrived in Las Animas—John Wintermute. With his encouragement, Allen started thinking again about the ministry. Wintermute drove out to the farm to tell Mr. Maruyama he was happy Allen was thinking of seminary, but Mr. Maruyama's reaction was not encouraging. "To him, Buddhist priests were poor, and many were beggars. My dad thought ministry was the worst kind of vocation, because he didn't understand what a minister was."[152]

Allen's brief mention of the war in his 1980 speech, paired as it was with the significance of friendships with church members, surely evoked a variety of personal recollections for many in Cobo Hall. They might not have been Japanese American, nor had they grown up in Southeastern Colorado or Central California, but they shared the experience of World War II turmoil and the church's support.

Rose grew up in the southern Illinois town of Grayville, which happened to be the home of one of Eleanor Roosevelt's personal secretaries. In 1936, the first lady herself had visited, and the whole town and people from the surrounding area had a parade and picnic for her.

As Rose remembered it, the entire school sat in the big study hall and listened to the broadcast when President Roosevelt declared war. The community felt a closeness to Roosevelt because of his wife's visit, so even as a young teenager, Rose felt a personal connection to the gravity of the moment.

Grayville had also been the location of a Depression-era Civilian Conservation Corps (CCC) camp, and some of the local women had married men from it. Many of the men were drafted, and because they were known in the town, Rose thinks people followed the news of the war especially closely.

Her participation in church as a pianist and choir member began at a young age, and that musical interest expanded in high school choir and band. She sang in an octet that qualified for the state contest. Rose graduated in 1944 and went immediately to Eastern Illinois State Teachers College (now Eastern Illinois University). There were only about seventy-five male students when she started, but over the four years she attended, the men started coming back from the war "in droves." When she graduated in 1948 with her teaching degree, there were over four hundred men. From before the war to the years following it, Rose saw that "the world changed," with more jobs available and more men going to school to qualify for them.

When Rose returned to take a teaching position in Grayville, she continued her participation in her Presbyterian church's music programs but became more active when George Clemmenson and his wife arrived. George had been a classmate at Eastern, and she was startled when he appeared in Grayville's pulpit. She had known him as a guy with a great sense of humor, not a characteristic she associated with ministers. He worked at the church while attending Louisville Presbyterian Theological Seminary, located over the state line in Kentucky. Rose, "Clemmie's" wife Erma, a war widow, and Clemmie became close friends.

In the meantime, Rose bought a car and learned to drive. She visited the Louisville campus several times, and, when the Clemmensons moved on, Rose decided she had to get out of Grayville and her teaching position. Her love was accounting and business, but she was teaching typing and shorthand, which she had never wanted to do. She decided to "do something in the church," a decision she associates with her friendship with the Clemmensons. She corresponded with McCormick, got in her car, drove the three hundred miles north to Chicago, and enrolled in 1953, the "biggest chance that I had ever taken." Rose, herself, was part of the post-war changing world, and for her, too, the church was an anchor.

She and two roommates took a required philosophy class and needed a tutor for a big test. Allen was the "young man" the school recommended. They met in October, and by May 10, 1954, they were married.[153]

Another of Allen's contemporaries at McCormick was Dorothy Rawlings Nelson. Although she wasn't explicitly included in the group of "all you boys" that the Petersens urged to become ministers, as a participant in the Las Animas Sunday school classes and youth groups, she, too, internalized the message. Dorothy, Allen, Rose Jarboe (Maruyama), Jim and Janet Petersen, and Min and June Mochizuki—all landed at McCormick in the early 1950s, some well acquainted with one another and some whose friendships would develop later.

All adolescents during the war years, they cultivated their friendships and musical and leadership skills in the context of the church. Pastors and friends in their youth groups shored them up, offered consolation at their low points, and pointed them toward their respective vocations. As young adults, they even met their spouses through seminary or church activities.

Chapter 10

Reflection and Renewal

ALLEN CONTINUES HIS SPEECH with another succinct biographical reference. "The time that I spent in the United States Army and at the University of Colorado was a time of reflection and renewal."[154]

He and Joe were two members of the "droves" of young men returning from the war, and both ended up at the University of Colorado. Allen briefly stayed at a sorority house dedicated to the influx of returning veterans, one of many adjustments universities made to accommodate their numbers. The unfortunate house mother! She abandoned her post in the lovely facility as it became obvious the "boys" were trashing it. Allen particularly remembers that when the drains clogged, water cascaded down the central double staircase.[155]

Whereas Joe's service had been in MIS in the Pacific and George's in the U.S. Army Coast Artillery Corps in the Caribbean, Allen's had been stateside. When he had first asked his parents to sign the form (falsely) verifying his age eligibility to serve in the military, he was barely sixteen. He was seventeen at the time of his second attempt, which resulted in the letter notifying him that no one of Japanese ancestry would be accepted in the armed services. Perhaps the timing of this exchange of letters occurred prior to March 1943, when the 442nd Regimental Combat Team was constituted.

After 1943, by November of his senior year in 1944, eighteen-year-old Allen could enlist. He and several other classmates took extra credits, graduated in January 1945, and joined the army. Allen was sent to Camp Hood, Texas, for basic training, and he was aware that other young Nisei men from around the country were scattered around the camp. When the men in his unit began talking about their choices for where they wanted to go after basic, someone commented to Allen that he would have no choice; he would be sent to the 442nd. He had been unaware that would happen, but his attitude was "Okay. It doesn't matter to me."

One of the last ordeals of basic was a thirty-mile hike carrying a heavy pack. He was within about five miles of reaching the goal when he felt he could go no further. A truck had been detailed to pick up stragglers, but Allen did not have to use it because a "huge Texan" (Allen says at least six feet seven inches) came along and offered to help him with the pack. Allen accepted and was able to complete the hike.[156]

When the Nisei men from Camp Hood were deployed, he was in the hospital, having had a hernia operation, and did not realize immediately that all the Nisei had been gathered and sent out together to the 442nd. He asked the sergeant major when he would be able to leave, and the sergeant said, "They're gone, and I need a clerk typist. If you're willing to stay, I'll make you a company clerk. You can't go out until the next group [of Nisei goes to the 442nd]." That would have entailed three months, the time required for infantry training for the new recruits. Allen accepted his offer.[157]

The year 1945 was the start of the war's end in Europe. Still, replacements for the 442nd were sent. Allen has some regret that he was not in that group because it would have been a different experience for him, even though he surmises they did "only" occupation work at that point. That prompts him to weigh how he would feel were he to have been one of the replacements and awarded the Congressional Gold Medal, as all who served in the 442nd eventually were. To emphasize, the 100th Infantry Battalion/442nd Regimental Combat Team is the most decorated unit in military history for its size and length of service. Allen thinks he would have been ashamed if he had been awarded the medal because he would not have seen action.[158]

Joe was part of a group receiving it in 2011 for his time in MIS, presented to him and others at the capitol by speaker of the House John Boehner. The wording of the legislation authorizing the medal Joe received acknowledges the wartime discrimination faced by men of Japanese ancestry. "The United States remains forever indebted to the bravery, valor and dedication to country these men faced while fighting a two-front battle of discrimination at home and fascism abroad."[159]

Allen got along well with the sergeant major, a career military man in his fifties who was generous with his stories. Allen learned "so much about the army" from him. The regard went both ways, because Allen was soon promoted to private first class, then corporal. Before he was nineteen and transferred to Fort Bliss, Texas, as part of an anti-aircraft artillery unit, he was a buck sergeant. There, he had a desk job in headquarters with regular hours, lived in better barracks, and did not have to be at work until eight. After five he would head into El Paso, where he bowled regularly with friends, and he took side trips into Juarez, Mexico.

While in the army, he had a "real change in terms of my whole attitude about being of Japanese origin. . . . It can be one of the best places for people to begin to understand what life is really about, what other people are like." The boys who seemed to be more discriminated against were several who Allen and the rest thought were gay. They were accepted, although they were made fun of. The scattered number of Asians blended in, and he recalls few African Americans.

He says the men were in training seven days a week, and he did not attend church/chapel services, nor did he have a relationship with any of the chaplains. However, the values from Sunday school, summer church conferences, and basic church teachings, which he accepted without question, transferred into his personal behavior and faith, particularly in terms of ethics. That was one reason he loved bowling and "got all into it. . . . It's nice to have something else to do besides going out and drinking."

All the guys talked about "getting girls," and Allen vaguely remembers having a girlfriend who worked at the bowling alley. She was older, and they had long telephone conversations. His only other dating experience had been as a high school senior and overseer at the Las Animas corporate cantaloupe shed where all the farmers brought their melons for sorting, crating, and shipping. He had his first real date with one of the women who worked there, also "older than a teenager," but it was casual, nothing serious.

High school girlfriends were never serious, either. "I didn't get invited to birthday parties and events that included boys and girls. . . . You had girlfriends in school that you liked, and they seemed to like you, but you really didn't do any dating." He never went out with Japanese girls because "they were like sisters."

And then the relaxed conversation took a turn into unexpected territory. "In the army, there was a waitress that I liked in the restaurant, and I asked if I could take her home. She said, 'Yeah, sure.'"

When he finished his story about what he characterizes as his first serious date, which could be scripted as a comedy routine with all its clumsy moments, Rose was laughing. "That's a wonderful story!" she assured him. As an aside, she whispered, "Well, I'm learning his stories, but he doesn't know mine!"

Allen did not seem insulted that Rose laughed about his awkward date, and he had not lost sight of the main topic, that of his translation of church teachings into his personal behavior in the army. He concluded, "So, I think what I learned from the church about morals was good."[160]

The way he told the story, his conclusion, and Rose's reaction reveal many admirable elements of his personality and their relationship, including a plainspoken and open manner. Rose's stories were similar in tone but uniquely colored by her dry wit. Sarah and John reflect these qualities, and they emerge time and again in Allen's personal and professional life.

He is practical, frank, realistic about human nature, and typically takes what life offers with a sense of humor. This open stance is somewhat unexpected, given his adolescent shame about his Japanese lineage and the self-hatred flowing from it. Even without such bruising at a young age, many never speak about humiliating experiences, thereby giving those incidents more clout than they merit. Openness is his basic inclination—an inviting attribute that surfaces in his relationships, his willingness to engage opinions that differ from his, and his motivation to explore new ideas.

John, in particular, has benefitted from this attitude. He had his own adolescent difficulties but he ascribes his as to being "an out-of-control preacher's kid." "Dad" would get angry but consistently stood by him and helped him out of difficult situations. Finally, as a college senior, John stepped too far over the line. "My dad was beyond himself. He came and got me and said, 'Son, you're moving home. I'm not going to let you mess up your whole life.'"

The only other times he remembers Allen furious like that was when they lived in Iowa and Allen would get upset with Vince Lombardi and the Packers. John knew he had "screwed up really bad" because Allen was madder at him than he ever got at Lombardi.

Allen drove him home from the University of Northern Colorado (the Colorado State College of Education in Greeley, renamed) and asked not if he wanted to finish college, but where. John did very well in school. He answered, "If I get a choice, I'd like to go to the best school in Denver, the University of Denver."[161]

John's choice was realistic. As Rose commented, "John was never afraid of hard work. If he wants to do it, he'll do it."[162]

As John recalls it, he met with John Wesley Rice Jr., an assistant dean at the university. He was registered on the spot and started his last quarter of college the next day. Rice was also a Presbyterian minister and associated part-time on the staff with Allen at the Montview Boulevard church. He was the father of Condoleezza Rice, secretary of state during the George W. Bush administration, and was the first African-American pastor at Montview (1971–74).[163]

John's point in relating the incident is to credit Allen with rescuing him time and again during his high school and college years and to observe that people in the Denver community helped because of their admiration for Allen, a regard that he says Allen downplayed. John emphasizes that his dad, "never, ever put himself above anybody else."[164]

Allen's rescue of his son is reminiscent of his own parents' firm treatment of him at that age. Not yet twenty-one, Allen was discharged from the army in Chicago in 1946. His memory of the occasion is dinner with Mari Sabusawa, a Japanese-American friend from Las Animas who was living in Chicago at the time. Her family had owned a store in Las Animas, and she was somewhat older than Allen. Sabusawa married James A. Michener, the novelist, in 1955, his third wife. Allen and Rose visited with her several times throughout the years.[165]

He had not signed up for a specific time period in the service, and "if you wanted to get discharged, they were very happy to get people out of the army." He informed his parents he did not want to work outside in the fields. "Well," they said, "You have to get a job somewhere, but you also have to go to college." He wanted to attend the University of Colorado in Boulder. Throughout the summer, his parents kept asking, "When are you going to Boulder?"

He delayed giving his answer because he enjoyed the job he found at Fort Lyon, the nearby veterans' hospital for psychiatric patients, and his new friends, a veteran on staff and his wife who "were great bowling partners." He started dating another co-worker. At the same time, he somewhat regularly attended the Las Animas Presbyterian church again and sang in the choir. As Allen described his social life and church commitments as a young man, Rose observed, "He had two lives. A lot of us did."

His father's reaction to Allen's contentment with these arrangements was "Okay, if you want to stay working at Fort Lyon, rent a house yourself because you're not living here anymore." Allen did not have money to buy a car and rent a house, so he "chose" to go to college. He boarded the bus and away he went.

As a student at the university in the fall of 1946, Allen says he was somewhat more settled in his Japanese identity and eventually joined Theta Xi, where his brother Joe was already a member. The one observation he makes about fraternity life is to note his awareness of and discomfort about who was included and who was not. "There were no other racial/ethnic people in it, but after I'd been in there a year, I found out there was one group prohibited from joining. It was in the constitution that no Jew could be a member. Something about fraternities that started someplace like New Jersey or New England."

His expanding world included meeting Bill Muldrow and the Presbyterian campus chaplain, G. G. Goldthwaite, through the Westminster Foundation. Bill and Allen became close friends. On Sunday mornings, he and Bill would sometimes go with Goldthwaite to rural areas where the chaplain would conduct services; otherwise, they would attend the First Presbyterian Church in Boulder. In any event, they never missed a Sunday.[166]

In hindsight, Allen characterizes Goldthwaite as "middle-of-the-road" theologically and reflective of the neo-orthodox movement. Neo-orthodoxy had become a widespread theological movement in America that originated in Europe after the savagery and destruction of World War I.[167]

Allen was not all that fond of the Boulder Presbyterian minister, who "preached long sermons." Muldrow often teased Allen about his preoccupation with timing the length of those sermons. Allen concluded the minister was "conservative," by which he means not interested or involved in social action or peace and justice issues, a contrast to neo-orthodox positions. Allen also differentiated the Boulder minister from "fundamentalists," even though the minister's emphasis was on individual morality and tended toward a literal interpretation of the Bible, another contrast with neo-orthodoxy. In contrast, Allen's definition of a fundamentalist is someone who exercises a rigid, literal biblical interpretation and makes the Bible "kind of a magic God" in itself.

He also worked as a counselor at Highlands Camp, a Presbyterian conference center northwest of Boulder, reminiscent of his own experiences starting during the summers in junior high at the Beulah, Colorado, camp and sponsored by the Pueblo Presbytery. He doubts that he would "ever have gotten into the ministry if it hadn't been for those awesome summer conferences" throughout his adolescence and young adult years. He characterizes them as places where young people find fellowship, study and play together, and learn to pray and communicate in their own way with God, and where the conference leadership brings together the relationships the kids develop with one another and the meaning of Jesus Christ. "They always had these campfires where you made your commitment, you dedicated yourself, you gave your life to Jesus—everybody did that."

He had regularly attended leadership training events and been a counselor at junior high conferences when he was in high school because the leaders at the camps he had attended in junior high inspired him by their "lifestyle, their love, their openness. I felt they were not only friends, but more like parents, really family."[168]

Although Allen did not characterize himself as one of those inspirational leaders in these interviews, the local Las Animas newspapers regularly list his name during his high school years as one of several recurring young people responsible for the program at the Sunday evening youth group meetings at the Presbyterian church. From the regularity with which his name appears, one can infer that he was recognized as one of the group's leaders.[169]

Allen and Muldrow double majored in business and engineering, a five-year course, but John Wintermute, the minister at the Las Animas Presbyterian church, and Standley Scott at the Rocky Ford Presbyterian church convinced Allen he did not need such an extensive background for seminary. Allen completed his business degree in three and a half years because he took classes every summer. By the middle of the school year in 1950–51, Allen was in Chicago, enrolled at McCormick Theological Seminary.

Muldrow finished the five-year course, traveled to Princeton Theological Seminary, and applied, but was refused admission due to his business and engineering background. When he was walking across campus, the Boulder minister of the Presbyterian church happened to be there and saw him. After he heard Muldrow's story, he marched Muldrow to the dean's office, a man whom he apparently knew well, and got Muldrow admitted on the spot. However, Muldrow had to take, as Allen describes it, a "dumbbell philosophy course" before he could begin classes, also required at McCormick of Allen, the business major, and Rose, the educator.[170]

As Allen describes it, his Japanese-American identity did not hinder his acceptance by peers or superiors during his army years, years that corresponded with his late adolescence. It seemed he was quite comfortable as a member of this new "team." The "huge Texan" carried the burden of his backpack, and that gesture enabled Allen to complete the long hike. The sergeant major found an assignment for him, mentored him, and schooled him in the ways of army life. His bowling team friends provided a social outlet, and he luxuriated in his better quarters and working hours. Indeed, army life stabilized the young Allen.

This relative stability continued during his college years. Through the Westminster Fellowship and Muldrow's friendship, he more firmly established his church connections. He resumed his role as counselor at summer youth camps, a role that put him in the position of "parenting" youth as he had been parented during his younger years.

His army and college years seem to have moved him toward reconnecting with his pre-Pearl Harbor self: no longer the enemy alien but a valued soldier in the U.S. Army, a university student capable of earning a degree in less than four years, and a leader in his church community.

Chapter 11

Expectations

IN HIS SPEECH BEFORE the General Assembly, Allen jumps from mention of his university days to his first pastorates and does not allude to his seminary years. "And from the very beginning of my experience with the church, I had confidence in the church because it lived up to my expectations."[171]

There was a possible strategic advantage to omitting those years in the speech. In the charged atmosphere of the assembly, a common exercise seems to have been pinning labels of "conservative" and "liberal" on potential leaders and their points of view. His omission of his seminary years might have sidestepped the tendency of some in attendance to equate his theological orientation with the seminary he attended and thereby oversimplify his positions. Allen, himself, characterizes McCormick as "always having been a moderate to liberal seminary." The more important factor was that he had been told McCormick was "one of the best seminaries in the country," as early as his conversations with Rev. Sammon in high school.[172]

Allen's seminary years certainly "lived up to" his expectations and provided the essential bridge from his university days to establishing his professional identity. As he characterizes it, "Seminary was a big, radical step . . . in my spirituality, in my whole theology." The foundation of his faith when he entered was built on the structure of the church's confessions. "It was pretty basic. I'm a person who goes according to the rules. In other words, if the Apostles' Creed is the basic belief of the church, I'm going to learn the Apostles' Creed—and the Lord's prayer and try to remember the Ten Commandments."[173]

What had persuaded him to think about a vocation in the church was not a set of beliefs or doctrines, though, but the quality of the relationships he had with church leaders and members. He was drawn to the openness of the pastors, teachers, and youth directors he worked with—their lifestyle and their caring. As he says time and again, they were not only friends; they were more like parents, really family. "And that was very impressive to me."[174]

One of his vivid memories of seminary was not an idea presented in a certain class but his interaction with one of the professors. He presumed to take issue with the lifestyle of Dr. Trinterud shortly after arriving, which had the potential of jeopardizing their relationship. Coming from what Allen describes as his simplistic, Sunday school outlook, "I had the audacity to go to this professor of philosophy, . . . who everybody knew was smoking and drinking. I was not against smoking because I was smoking, too, but very cautiously then, and I wasn't drinking. I had given that up in college. I believed it was wrong. So, I asked to see him because I knew his reputation. I said, 'I have great respect for you. You're one of the best teachers here at McCormick, they say, but it's immoral for Christians to smoke and drink publicly.'"

The professor's reaction was to chuckle and acknowledge that many of the students held that view. However, he said, nothing in the Bible prohibits alcohol; in fact, it figures positively in many of its stories. He believed the difficulty was drunkenness. Allen appreciated the professor's balanced answer and his kindness—"a good lesson," presumably in that the professor did not take offense and also modeled a less constrained way of living in a complex world. Allen felt comfortable at McCormick and in its "more liberal" atmosphere, in comparison with "being raised in the very dogmatic framework set by Jim Petersen's conservative parents" (in the Las Animas church).[175]

Arriving at McCormick expanded Allen's horizons in multiple ways: the big city and the "L" stop right by the seminary, not fifty yards from the new men's dormitory and Loyola University ("It was huge!") right across the street. The McCormick campus was surrounded by a wrought-iron fence and organized around its courtyard with married students' apartments, faculty houses, large gymnasium with basketball court and all kinds of exercise equipment, dining hall, chapel, library, and classrooms.

The required but basic German and Latin courses the first year were tough; less demanding were the subsequent biblical Greek and Hebrew classes (these layered over his Japanese language background). He enjoyed singing in the men's chorus all three years, and he liked theology. One of those professors was his favorite, Joseph Haroutunian (1904–1968), a well known spokesperson for the neo-orthodox position, which Allen characterizes as "all the rage." He says he entered seminary with a simplistic theology and came out as neo-orthodox.[176]

A review of some basics about neo-orthodox theology (see endnote 167) and a tribute for Haroutunian written by a fellow theologian and colleague at the University of Chicago, Joseph Sittler, shed light on why the subject and the professor were among Allen's favorites. Sittler describes Haroutunian's manner as "ebullient and vivacious," characteristic of "an Armenian *joie de vivre*," with a "hurry-up impatience," and his person as one who loved companionship. These phrases could describe Allen, save for the Armenian label.

Sittler writes that Haroutunian was a professor who "coupled sheer humanity with a terrifying velocity of mind." He abhorred pretension. If he were part of a discussion in which someone was holding forth in order to disguise a vacuous monologue, Haroutunian would "puff all the more intently at his pipe, until the heat of the pipe and the temperature of his impatience coincided in a brief comment—of about fifteen minutes."

From Sittler's description, Haroutunian's energy seems to have equaled Allen's. Also, not only would Haroutunian's frankness and lack of pretension appeal to Allen, but so would his theological orientation, the foundation of which was relationship. Sittler describes Haroutunian's fundamental proposition as that of knowing our "nature" only in our human transactions. Haroutunian used the word "communion" for these transactions. By "communion," he meant that our speaking and thinking, our purposing and acting, are done in mutual transactions, in social processes, and in the context of social institutions. Accordingly, what we primarily and ultimately have "to do" with God is known in the community of faith. Sittler states, in Haroutunian's words: "The miracle of the presence of our brother is one piece with the miracle of the presence of Christ with us, and the presence of Christ signifies, and is, the presence of God."

Sittler paraphrases and quotes Haroutunian: the love of Jesus "is the love of a creature for his fellowman; a love that every man owes to another and hopes for another, a love that posits humanity and sustains it. The miracle that has occurred among us who surround Jesus is that he has loved us and forgiven us and thus reestablished the bond of humanity among us." Again, "a man is himself only as he is neighbor to his fellowmen. . . . Faithfulness is . . . acting toward oneself and toward one's neighbor in the love and fear of God. Love . . . is the respect and justice of the creature toward the creature. This recognition and respect are of the essence of love and . . . the kingdom of God among us."[177]

Admittedly, the above is an all-too-compact summary of Haroutunian's theology. Allen's even shorter description is that Haroutunian was a
"happy Calvinist."[178]

Suffice it to say, the perspectives and commitment expressed in Haroutunian's orientation to life and faith as "communion" parallel Allen's work,
words, and experiences time and again. Recall that Allen's basis for entering seminary and the ministry was the quality of the relationships between
himself and mentors such as camp counselors, Sunday school teachers, and
pastors, people who were "like family," and "that was very impressive to me."

Also, recall Allen's characterization of his way of handling disagreement and disagreeable people, encapsulated by Haroutunian's "recognition
and respect." Allen says, "To think of opposing groups as enemies and [those
agreeing with us] as friends distorts the truth. . . . I try to become a friend
and see if they are willing to be friends. . . . In the end, your friendship and
trust has been strong enough that you can live together and work together."

During Allen's seminary years, echoed in the experience of some
of Allen's friends, Haroutunian lived his devotion to companionship in a
number of ways. For example, Haroutunian traveled from Chicago to Las
Animas by train and preached the sermon at Allen's ordination in 1953 at
the Las Animas church. When Allen is asked if he thought those in the
congregation had any idea about the stature of the person who stood before
them, he laughs. "They had no idea."

Haroutunian stayed the night and took the train to Fort Collins the
next day, where he preached William Gepford's ordination sermon. Allen
and Gepford, close seminary friends, had decided they could afford to ask
him to come—and he did.[179]

When Allen was serving in his first position, pastor of two national
mission churches in northern Wisconsin, Haroutunian regularly visited
there. One summer, he and his family lived in the Maruyamas' home for a
month, and he preached in Allen's absence. As Allen reminisced about those
years, Rose asked if the two Wisconsin congregations appreciated who was
filling the pulpit. Allen answered, "No, but Joe appreciated it. He and his
family had a wonderful time! He had visitors from all of that area come
to church, and our people couldn't understand why so many strangers attended while he was preaching."[180]

Allen is skeptical that Haroutunian's four children enjoyed the sojourn
in Wisconsin as much as their father did. When Allen asked him how the
summer had gone, Haroutunian claimed the children loved it, which might
have been true, in part, because Gleason was a quaint little town and a fishing stream ran behind the parsonage. However, Haroutunian also claimed

his children loved the four hours he spent each day with them on their Latin, Greek, and German.[181]

The GI bill covered tuition, housing, and food during Allen's first year of seminary, but for the second and third Allen was on his own. He worked part-time at a settlement house several miles further west from the city. He traveled those miles on the elevated train and felt he was finally getting acquainted with the city, in particular, with its "poor" people.

Immediately after mentioning the settlement house, he speaks of his regret that he did not have the resources to help Jim and Janet Petersen and their children, whom he saw frequently at McCormick. Poor people did not live only outside the seminary grounds. "The Petersens didn't have any money. They didn't have anything. The kids would have to eat out of cans. I felt so bad that there was no way for me to help them because I just didn't have the money. Even though I went to the neighborhood house every evening, as I remember it, for two to three hours, they didn't pay that well."[182]

Min and June Mochizuki and their children were in a similar financial position at McCormick during those years. With a family to support, Min pieced together numerous part-time jobs and had no time for anything but work and school. Min had made his way to McCormick knowing he "didn't want to be a Presbyterian minister on the West Coast because that meant we were relegated to some ethnic church." Unlike Allen, for whom ethnic churches were unknown but described as "just a few Asian congregations" by Sammon, his Las Animas pastor, Min and June grew up in them. As a Japanese American living on the West Coast, Min would undoubtedly be consigned to one, which he saw as a restraint he wanted to avoid. He was taken under care (approved to begin the process of becoming a minister) by the San Francisco Presbytery, but he transferred to Chicago when he began seminary at McCormick, where, as it did for Allen, "another whole world opened up" for him.[183]

The other young people who established themselves in the Chicago area during those years were Joe and Dorothy Maruyama, Allen's brother and sister-in-law. Joe made his way to Chicago in 1948 after graduation from the University of Colorado with a management degree. His interest was to become a labor relations expert, and Chicago was the place to interview, with big companies such as Montgomery Ward and Sears Roebuck. One of the companies with which he interviewed, International Harvester, was "famous for having battles with the UAW and FE union [Farm Equipment Workers union], which was communistic. I immediately interviewed and got hired." He worked for International Harvester until his retirement.[184]

Dorothy had arrived in Chicago several years prior, when she was sponsored by an organization that "was helping all these people to get out of the [incarceration] camps and get jobs in big cities." Dorothy initially became a "house girl," similar to the work June's sister did in Denver, in a home sympathetic to her circumstances.[185]

Joe and Dorothy met through mutual friends and became active in a large Presbyterian church on the North Shore—"big, a mega-church, beautiful pipe organs."[186] A man, vice president of Curtiss Candy Company "who was responsible for relocating Japanese Americans out of the camp, was also a lay person at that church." He was quite supportive of Dorothy, and, when International Harvester was on strike, he would offer Joe work until the company was back in operation.[187]

Joe and Allen, two brothers busy with career and education, met infrequently in Chicago. Contact between the two couples was more regular when Allen worked in northern Wisconsin and Joe, Dorothy, and their children vacationed there. Joe and Allen enjoyed hours on the golf course and fishing. When Allen moved to Dubuque, where their older brother George and his wife Helen had settled, Joe and his family vacationed there. As for Jim and Janet Petersen, they moved to Michigan after graduation, as did Min and June Mochizuki.

Although Allen's statement in his speech that the church "lived up to" his expectations does not allude specifically to his seminary years, those years certainly did not disappoint. He met the woman who was to become his wife, and his perspectives about his faith and vocation matured and underwent significant transformation.

Chapter 12

Challenges

ALLEN MOVES FROM THE allusion in his speech about his confidence in the church because it lived up to his expectations to describe his first position following seminary graduation. "The national missions churches in which I served in northern Wisconsin were challenging churches, not at all like my pastor, the late Richard Sammon, when I told him of my decision to enter the ministry, said to me, 'Allen, your opportunities will be limited to just a few Asian congregations.' It's not been like that at all."[188]

In the spring of 1953, when Allen was awarded his master's of divinity degree, he was aware there were "a lot of vacancies, a lot of open churches. All these committees came to interview possible pastors, but none of them would interview me." The interviews resulted in job offers for his classmates.

Allen began to think that perhaps the caution Sammon expressed to him as a teenager during the war, that as a Japanese American he would be called to serve only ethnic congregations, was still true. He had asked Sammon at the time why he said such a thing because Allen assumed the Las Animas church had accepted him as a member without qualification. He went to summer conferences and was also accepted there by youth leaders and peers. Sammon's answer unveiled another reality: "Because they expect you to be preaching and being a minister in a Japanese congregation."[189] Sammon did not specify whom he meant by "they," nor did Allen ask, but he says that was a moment of realization that there might never be a place for him in white society.[190]

Allen not only explicitly references this conversation in his 1980 speech, he still revisits it. Each telling highlights different dimensions. In some cases, the young Allen does not contradict his pastor but does ask, given the circumstances Sammon outlined, why he should go into the ministry. Sammon proposed he could be a missionary to Japan, or perhaps anywhere in the world. In that case, being of Japanese ancestry would not be a problem. In fact, it might be a real advantage to have somebody like Allen from the United States working in the mission field. Allen told him it was "something I'll think about" because he had heard at several youth conferences that the church needed missionaries.

Upon reflection, Allen says at the time of Sammon's comments he was "surprised" but not insulted. He simply relates what he remembers Sammon as saying but does not comment further on the irony that Sammon characterized the positive aspect of having a Japanese American represent the PC(USA) in a foreign field, but did not think the church would accept him as a pastor in majority white churches on home ground. In retrospect, Allen notes that he himself did not realize persons of Japanese ancestry were that badly discriminated against—not until the aftermath of the Pearl Harbor attack—and observes that Sammon was simply not aware of his racism.

In his final year in seminary in 1953, Allen adjusted to the lack of opportunity. "I decided to stay an extra year and get a master's in Christian education because I knew that churches would hire me as a Christian educator if I had the master's."[191]

Although Allen does not verbalize it, at the time this decision would place him outside the spotlight of professional ministry. He would not be as far away from majority white congregations in the United States as Sammon would have him, in the mission field, but he would not be in what was seen as the more prestigious position of pastor as head of staff, either. However, in front of the General Assembly in 1980, Allen simply offers the conversation with Sammon as evidence that his pastor was mistaken.

During 1954, he was working on that second degree, tutoring Rose and her classmates for their "dumbbell" philosophy class and courting her when two small mission churches in northern Wisconsin contacted, interviewed, and hired him. Only later in his tenure there was he told the story of how it came about. A man from its search committee had come to McCormick to speak with prospective candidates, either students or graduates. He was told he had appeared rather late in the process, and only one graduate was still available. "'But he's Japanese American and nobody wanted to talk to him. Do you want to?' The man said, 'No, we don't want a J*p up there in Wisconsin.'

"He returned to northern Wisconsin, and the other committee members asked, 'There are no students available?' He said a J*p was, but he figured the committee wasn't interested. Their response: 'Why didn't you interview him?'

"So they called me," Allen says, "and I went up there, visited with the committee, and they asked me to come. That was my first student parish." His first year as a student pastor he took the train to northern Wisconsin on Friday nights, an overnight trip of three hundred miles, and returned to Chicago on Sunday nights.

Allen eventually learned who the man was, and by then they had a close relationship. He and his brother owned a lumber company. When the man vacated his house right across from the church to build a new one, he sold it to the church. It became the parish house, and Allen and Rose lived there for two years.

Allen served Hogarty Presbyterian Church and Riverside Presbyterian Church in Gleason, yoked national mission congregations, from 1953–1957. By a superficial measure of success, numerical growth, the congregations attained that goal during his tenure. The Hogarty congregation grew from twenty or twenty-five to around fifty members; the Gleason church, from fifty or sixty to over one hundred. However, Allen does not attribute their expansion to his ministry. Rather, he says "the Presbyterian church was growing nationally during those post-World War II years. . . . Also, President and Mrs. Eisenhower were Presbyterian, and they would vacation and fish on a lake fifty to seventy-five miles away. Presbyterianism was very popular up there."[192]

Assigning credit to factors beyond his efforts is a typical Allen gesture, belied by what can be inferred from how he describes his experiences from those years, nor is a simple increase in membership the extent of his success. He was effective in dealing with one of his first challenges, a dynamic typically encountered by young, single pastors—a congregation's matchmaking impulse. Allen cautions, "A single pastor shouldn't really go to a little church because all the divorced women and the mothers of single women really make it their intention of getting a single pastor to marry their daughter or divorced daughter. They chase you; you better be careful. Everybody is aware. They all know. They're not dumb."

Within the first few months, before he and Rose married, he sought counsel from a pastor in a nearby city about handling "this woman with two little children" who would stay after church every Sunday and "pester" him. The pastor said, "Well, Allen, you're smart. You've just got to say 'I'm sorry. I'm not available.'"

The next week Allen explained he was committed to someone in seminary. She persisted. She came from a nice family in town, and he sensed the people themselves thought it might be a good thing for them to marry. The outcome: she was upset by the conversation but did not stop attending church. "She didn't stay after again because she realized I wasn't going to respond to her constant nagging. . . . Any lonely, single pastor would really be tempted to take advantage of someone like that because she made it very evident that she'd be glad to entertain you, you know? Even if it didn't mean marriage. But in a town like that people would figure it out very fast."

Hurdle number one overcome, without serious repercussions. Hurdle number two—the placement of the communion table. In Allen's case, the dispute was whether to set it up in the center of the stage-like chancel or down the step, in front of the pews. As any pastor knows, an issue of this sort will arise, perhaps disagreement about the process of preparing, serving, or taking communion; the order of worship; the placement (or not) of the American and state flags; the style of music; endless pitfalls await. Allen calls these sorts of ubiquitous disputes "ridiculous" in the grand scheme, but how congregations and pastors handle them is basic to whether or not they immobilize the community.[193]

Allen had apparently entered an ongoing controversy, but he also had a definite opinion: the "ideal" placement of the table was up in the chancel, in the blank space between the organist and pianist on one side and the pulpit on the other. The simmering disagreement erupted into a "big fight" between three or four elders and families who were divided about it. "It was finally settled to put it where I wanted, but the tension that built up during that time continued to fester throughout my ministry there. We never had a good relationship with the one family who adamantly wanted the communion table down below. It could have been solved so easily by having it part of the year down below and part of it above. I learned my first lesson about arbitrating in a church [between factions]."[194]

He clarified that the lesson learned was for pastors to state the reason behind a certain position but let the congregation decide. That way, peace in the "family" is maintained, but even prior to that, the pastor needs to uncover the origins of the disagreement at hand.

In the case of small churches in small towns, though, he concluded later in his ministry that Christian community is developed very clearly in small congregations. Rose concurred. In the album she assembled for the twenty-fifth anniversary of his ordination, she has this notation beside a picture of the Hogarty church: "The church with the truest Christian spirit of any church we have ever known."

Allen believes that the townspeople in Gleason and Hogarty recognized the churches as "very dependable in terms of charity, compassion, and love." The two congregations shared with all the people in their towns, and "everybody, the Lutherans, Catholics, some with no religion, knew what a Christian community that small group of Presbyterians was. These little churches were the kind of fellowship that you always hope churches could be. . . . When I got down to the middle part of Wisconsin, bigger churches with one hundred to two hundred members, I realized that the bigger the church gets, the less there seems to be a sense of true community within the congregation. The bigger the church, the more cliques. The entire congregation doesn't have that kind of closeness and community and concern for each other. Consequently, even their mission projects don't have the unified force that those tiny churches had."

Again, it seems not to occur to Allen to speculate about his role in helping these two congregations build on and express their strengths. Rather, he perceives their virtue as resting with their size and members, but it is conceivable that a less diligent pastor would not have enabled them to so fully maintain their caring fellowship.

His role in building on their strength as caring congregations is implied in how he describes his approach to his ministry with them. Because of their size, the small churches gave him the opportunity to visit every family on a regular basis. Just as in any church, some "really like you and some don't, particularly, but it's your responsibility to overcome the negativity that families may have and make a little extra effort in your pastoral ministry of being helpful to those families that you feel are not as responsive to your ministry. You may not have a chance to do this in a larger congregation where it's much easier to ignore people who don't like you. But in a small congregation you have a chance to befriend them in a way that you can overcome some of their dislike. A challenge for every minister is to be responsive to the needs of all the people, regardless of their attitude toward you. Maybe they've got a reason to feel that way. They have a reason for not liking your preaching, or their theology is different. You need to be sensitive to parishioners who have negative feelings."

He contrasts his diligence about visiting with church members to the attitude of a pastor colleague in the area "who carried his fishing pole and golf clubs around in his trunk. That's what he cared about, and his church knew it and suffered."

As he reflected on his experiences in these two national mission congregations, Allen's other advice was to continue learning. He gave several examples. Pastors can participate in classes offered by educational institutions in their communities after seminary. "I know that I needed help in my speaking, so I took a couple of courses in oratory and public speaking." Also, learn about your own personality. "Are you overly aggressive? To understand yourself is the beginning of being helpful and knowing how to respond to people whose personalities are quite different from yours."

He continued his reflections about his time in those small churches with a variation on his refrain of maintaining what could be called a generosity of spirit toward those who disagree with the pastor. "Something that they can't teach you in seminary is reconciling differences in people's view of the Bible and theology. Just like what happens in politics. It is always helpful to listen to what the other person is saying and try to reconcile your feelings about the negativity you've had about the other party. It's easier to ignore the other side than to understand where they're coming from. Then try to revise your own thinking. Your ideology is in competition with theirs. The older you get, you realize theirs is not absolutely wrong, and yours is not absolutely right."

When reflecting about the high point of his ministry in Hogarty and Gleason, Allen moves from general observations of lessons learned to a specific, personal one about reconciliation. When he began his ministry there, he carried the residue of the pain of "so much prejudice directed at me during the war, my anger about my racial origin, and my immaturity in the armed services." On the part of the congregations, he "discovered from the very beginning there were people who didn't like me because I was Japanese, especially with the recent war and if they had family that were killed over in Asia. They had bitter feelings about Japanese. However, after awhile, they were able to accept me as a human being, and race really didn't have much to do with it. When I discovered they could get over that, I was able to realize that my own feelings about religion and life, my whole philosophy of life, had begun to change. Those little churches helped me realize that."[195]

In addition to generosity of spirit and reconciliation, another word to characterize what happened in Hogarty and Gleason, and within Allen, is reciprocity. From the moment the search committee decided to interview and hire a "J*p," in spite of the first man's hesitancy, and Allen's decision to fully invest himself in these small communities, he and the majority of people seem to have committed themselves to meeting one another halfway and making the relationship a mutual and productive one.

The congregations and Allen appear to have worked at raising up this young pastor who was not only new to his profession, but shortly after his arrival, was adjusting to marriage, as was his bride, whose life had taken a course different from the one she had mapped out the prior year. In her matter-of-fact way, Rose said, "Although I was going to school to become a Christian educator, I did not finish the [two-year] course. I got married instead."

She met Allen in October 1953 and on May 10, 1954, "we were married." When asked if it was love at first sight, she said, "Sort of. Close."

In most conversations, Rose said she did not think of their marriage as being interracial, but as she sketched the story of their courtship and wedding, she told it like this. "In the meantime, this was '54. World War II had been over for nine years. But there were plenty of people who remembered it as something drastic in their lives. So my [two] sisters, bless their hearts, just took it on as something they had to accept and push and make people realize this was going to happen. That I had met this man, and I was going to marry him. I remember one of them saying to me that people used to come up to them and ask, 'Is your sister really going to marry that J*p?' So they [my sisters] had something to deal with, too. They had to learn to accept it and defend me, which they did. So, it was my two sisters who made all the arrangements and plans for the wedding."

Her sisters, Rebecca Louise (Becky) and Mary Jeannette (Maynette), confronted the issue of race head-on, and so did Rose's father. She took Allen home in those months before they married to meet her parents. They were sitting in the living room, and she says that her dad, "who was not an educated man, said outright, 'Well, I'm not a prejudiced man.'"

Rose reflected that, indeed, he was not. "He did not look on someone and say, 'Oh, that person is not like me. I'm not going to like them.' He was much more educated in the ways of the world than that."

Her parents, Guy and Katherine Jarboe, owned a restaurant in Grayville, a type of business in which they encountered many kinds of people. Rose and her sisters grew up in the rooms above it and worked in it alongside their parents. A Christmas Eve fire in 1939 forced the family to move from the rooms to a home.

They called the restaurant the Old House, and her mother's pies figured prominently on the menu. Rose laughed that a piece of pie is, without doubt, an acceptable breakfast food.

The restaurant was open for about three hours a day, at noon and in the evening. They were closed on Mondays. Rose notes that everybody else got married on a Saturday. "Not us. We got married on Monday. One person told me they let the teachers out early so they could come to the wedding. That's a small town for you."

Some inferences can be made from the facts Rose relates about their courtship and marriage. That she was marrying a Japanese-American man (on a Monday!) was remarkable to family and friends, but once her sisters and father made clear that Allen was acceptable to them, the community seems to have acquiesced to the inevitable. Rose herself knew that a mixed marriage would encounter questions, if not difficulties, but just as she left the security of her high school teaching position and her home in Grayville the year before to drive three hundred miles north to Chicago and enroll at McCormick, sight unseen, once she decided to marry Allen, her course was set.

With the same determination, she defined her role as Allen's bride. By her account, she fit comfortably into the rhythms of being the pastor's wife in the small towns. She and Allen both observe that she went above and beyond by playing the piano and sometimes the organ. Rose simply notes that "that was expected of [minister's] wives in those days."

Then life turned in yet other directions, which Rose described simply as "changes," with no regrets. She had "left teaching to go into Christian education, and ended up going back to teaching. We needed the money." She taught school in Merrill, about twelve miles from Gleason, "just one year. Because then I got pregnant. That changes things."[196]

Judith Fischer sheds more light on Allen's years in Chicago and the young couple in Gleason/Hogarty. A classmate of his at McCormick his senior year, she remembers him as being "very gregarious, with a positive personality. No complaining, nothing negative to say about others. He liked people and enjoyed being with them if they enjoyed being with him."

After Christmas break, a friend of Allen's, Cal Fischer, asked him for an introduction to Judy. She speculates that Cal could trust Allen with his feelings for her "because Allen wouldn't tease."

She had arrived at McCormick from Arizona and had grown up in Casa Grande, where her father owned a drug store. The town was, coincidently, near Sacaton, the capital of the Gila River Indian Community and the site of the Gila River War Relocation Center, another of the incarceration sites for persons of Japanese ancestry during the war. She remembers the women in their native dress sitting on a long bench at the grocery store, nursing their babies and waiting for friends and family to finish their shopping. Her family moved to Tucson when she was ten, though, so she has no personal memory of the Gila River incarcerations.[197]

By the time Rose and Allen were settled in Gleason, the Fischers lived in nearby Merrill. Sunday evenings the couples would socialize over dinner and board games, often Clue. They introduced the Maruyamas to their cottage on a nearby lake and spent time together there. Rose and Allen both comment about the pressure they felt when the Fischers urged them to buy a cottage that was for sale nearby, but they were not in a financial position to do so. In addition, Allen points out that "I was so busy up there at Gleason, we wouldn't have had the time [to enjoy the cottage]. Rose was teaching in Merrill, and I had two parishes thirty-five miles apart."[198]

The two couples kept in touch over the years with visits in Dubuque when the Maruyamas lived there and later in Denver, on the Fischers' way to conferences at Ghost Ranch Education and Retreat Center in New Mexico, and in Colorado's Rocky Mountains, at the Maruyamas' cabin. The Fischers moved to Santa Fe, where the Maruyamas visited them in 1999, and eventually back to Arizona because Cal was very involved in ministry with Native Americans. Although Judith Fischer says that Allen helped with the adoption of their two-year-old daughter from Hong Kong through Church World Service, Allen does not remember playing a role. However, that she specifically remembers their many visits over the years and that she thinks Allen must have had a role in the adoption speaks to the way Allen and Rose stayed involved in their relationship over the decades, as they did in many others.

Unprompted, Fischer found it significant that Allen "did not talk much about his early years or his family" during that first period of their friendship. Because she repeats often how happy Allen seemed to be with people, how outgoing he was, the impression is that Allen was adept at covering the residue of his pain from the discrimination of the war years and his anger about his Japanese heritage. Her observations recall the surprised reaction of his high school friends upon hearing how distressed he was during the war, contrasted with their feeling that he was "just Allen, our friend." When Fischer emphasizes his positive personality, she adds that "perhaps it was because he knew life could be full of a lot of problems, and he wanted no part in adding to them."[199]

Her characterization of Allen's personality raises the possibility that Allen might have met members of the Hogarty and Gleason congregations and communities more than halfway, an inviting posture on the part of this person who represented a racial minority from a nation so recently identified as the mortal enemy of the United States. His approachability would have contributed to those dairy farmers and small business owners overcoming enough of their discomfort that they would interact with and eventually accept him.

Allen would agree that his open personality makes him accessible as a minority person in the dominant white culture. In fact, he cultivates it. "It's true for any minority that . . . personality and character will help you get past racism. . . . As a minority person you have to be especially nice. . . . The minority person bears the burden of taking initiative to reach out in a friendly, welcoming way.[200]

In turn, Allen, himself, was a recipient of their "charity, compassion, [and] love," so much so that he realized race need not be an impediment to relationship. "Yeah, [their acceptance] really helped me." If they could get over the enmity toward Japanese Americans, maybe he could accept himself, too.[201] Sammon had set out only two professional possibilities—an ethnic congregation or a foreign mission field. According to Sammon, "white society, " as Allen often refers to it, was closed to him. The little congregations opened the possibility that there was a place for him to be Japanese American in the majority culture.

After almost five years, Allen circulated his dossier. He and Rose felt somewhat isolated. "There were maybe three hundred to five hundred people, counting dogs and cats, in Gleason. They still had party lines, and when you called, you had to go through that operator." Rose added that the switchboard sat right in the operator's living room, and Allen says, "We used to kid her that she knew everything going on in the community."[202]

He specifies that, "The frustration I always had was the lack of opportunity to bring more people into the church. Where do you find them? I felt like I was wasting a lot of my time. Maybe I should have been spending more of it in studying Greek and Hebrew or something! There were low points. I didn't particularly like taking care of the furnace and doing all the custodial work. I just didn't have enough help, sweeping the floor and doing that stuff.

"But in those little churches I did get my education in sociology and class systems. The business people and a few of the dairy people were rich, though they tolerated well the poor people. You become much more aware of class and are able to deal with it [more] than you can in a larger community."[203]

In particular, he was interested in moving to two congregations near Madison—Prairie du Sac and Mazomanie. Translated, Ma-zo-ma-nie is Native American for "Chief Iron Horse," and Prairie du Sac is located in the Wisconsin River Valley where the Sauk Native Americans had a large settlement. The Mazomanie congregation was United Church of Christ and the Prairie du Sac was Presbyterian, but the two churches were small enough (about seventy members in each congregation) that they had arranged to share pastoral leadership. Allen was contacted for interviews and candidating sermons at each church.

The Mazomanie congregation voted to hire him without any hesitation. However, Allen learned several years after his arrival that the vote at Prairie du Sac was not without controversy. The moderator of the Madison Presbytery chaired the meeting, and there were four votes against Allen out of about sixty. The moderator noted that with the large majority, the invitation could be extended to Allen, but what did the congregation think? There were murmurs, and someone said, "Why do so many of us want him to come, and yet there are four votes against him? We'd like to get some idea of what the opposition is."

Finally a man stood and spoke. "Well, my two daughters and my wife and I are the four votes against him." When asked why, the man said, "I don't mind the fact that he's Japanese American, but we're against the fact that he's married to a Caucasian. We don't want our daughters to be married to anyone but a white person." At the time, Rose was about eight months pregnant with Sarah, their first child.[204]

Several at the meeting said they could see why the man was against intermarriage but didn't think it reason enough not to let Allen come. The man responded, "Well, you know, we kind of talked it over here, and we decided that maybe you're right. It's okay to let him come."

When Allen heard the story several years later, he was "astonished." By then he knew the family well, as he did many of the other dairy farmers who were church members. "They accepted me. They were very friendly." His take is that the general objection to mixed marriages at the time was not so much against Asian/white families but against black and white ones. "John was born a year later, so we had these two interracial children" in Wisconsin.[205]

For Rose, Prairie du Sac was, on the one hand, a happy time of giving birth and raising young children in a community of "wonderful people, wonderful friends," particularly a good friend, Sybil Tarnutzer, "who took over being my second mom," and helped take care of the children. "It was a small town. You could go anywhere. You were safe. John was only about five when we moved [to Dubuque], but he wandered all over Prairie du Sac. He loved fire trucks. He followed them any time." She described the church as "beautiful, like a New England church. It was such a wonderful time."

She sang in the choir, taught an occasional class, and was active in the women's association, but saw herself in this setting not so much as going above and beyond as the pastor's wife but as doing "what every good Presbyterian woman did. Almost every woman in the church was active, or you weren't a member."[206]

Allen remembers that in Prairie du Sac, Rose "didn't have time to do anything but raise kids." For her, the downside was that "I didn't do my thing. I was just there for Allen to do his thing. When I started teaching again [in Dubuque], I became my own person again. I think that's necessary. I feel for pastors' wives who never become anything except the pastor's wife."[207]

During those years, Allen felt he had a split personality. The two churches were "very different with different problems" and had little to do with one another. "You had to be one kind of person here, another kind of person over there to fit in with the different styles of community." He spent a day or a day and a half in Mazomanie doing pastoral work and developed "a lot of good relationships," but Prairie du Sac was the "easy, normal community where we lived." A former pastor of the church who lived in Prairie du Sac persuaded him to join the Optimist Club, "a vocal group in the community" that helped Allen get acquainted with people in the town. "I never developed the kind of relationships in Mazomanie that I had in Prairie du Sac."

Allen found some humor in the fact that, although the former pastor was a "good preacher, a good man, a good leader, and Presbyterian," he had given up parish ministry to take the job as director of a Wisconsin temperance group, "in the biggest beer-drinking state in the country!" His wife taught in the church school, and he often worshipped in the congregation.

Many ministers would chaff at the continuing involvement of a former pastor and spouse in a congregation, and often just the presence of a former pastor provokes split loyalties that undermine the current one's ministry. Instead, the Baileys and Maruyamas became close friends. Rev. Bailey baptized both Sarah and John. In deference to Rev. Bailey's commitment to temperance, Rose and Allen decided that, although they liked to drink wine, they would not drink it in public. Furthermore, they hid the wine in the basement, as the two couples often exchanged dinner invitations.

The Mazomanie church had strong lay leadership, which Allen says benefitted the congregation because it did not have access to a full-time pastor. The members also "wanted good preaching." Allen had to be there by 9:00 a.m. on Sundays and back in Prairie du Sac at 11:00. The towns were separated by only thirteen miles, and both were about twenty miles from Madison. Allen speculates that the United Church of Christ conference and presbytery leadership had arranged the yolked relationship, not the churches.

Most of his time was devoted to preaching and pastoral work, as it had been in Hogarty and Gleason, with very little community outreach. "I didn't have time, for one thing, nor did I have incentive. I didn't see any problems in either community that a pastor should really get involved in." Neither church had particularly outstanding mission projects within their communities or outside the country.

As did the Hogarty and Gleason churches, Mazomanie and Prairie du Sac grew during Allen's ministry, each from about seventy members to around one hundred fifty or one hundred seventy-five. Again, he downplays having much to do with the growth, saying not with cynicism but with humor, "they just automatically grew with little effort. They were friendly congregations and knew that to support a full-time pastor, they needed a bigger budget. That's one way to get a congregation to be very evangelistic, when they know they need money!"

Those were quiet years in somewhat idyllic communities located close to popular recreation opportunities: Baraboo, the headquarters for the Barnum and Bailey Circus; Devil's Lake, a beautiful area and supposed to be "the deepest lake in the country"; and the Wisconsin River with its fishing opportunities.

A telling incident, however, occurred when Allen and a friend caught a "great big carp" on the river. Some of the church elders used to joke that "white people don't eat carp, but black people love it." When Allen caught the carp, his friend said, "If you feel so strongly about racial equality and discrimination, why don't you take this great big carp down the river to the black community [from Madison, who did a lot of summer fishing on the river and sometimes set up tents there]?"

If the friend meant it as a dare, he had not reckoned with Allen's willingness to tackle most any obstacle or rise to any challenge, particularly if it meant establishing a personal connection. Allen's response: "Okay." They took the fish over, and the people receiving it seemed quite pleased, but Allen's thought was, "That's the way they treat blacks here. They have very little respect."[208]

There was room for him in "white society" as a Japanese-American pastor, but not for African Americans. As pleasant as most of their memories of the two towns are, the Maruyamas were ready to move on.

Chapter 13

Opportunities

As ALLEN IS POINTING out to the 1980 General Assembly commissioners, opportunities for him abounded and not just in northern Wisconsin. The move to Dubuque, Iowa, reinforced his comment in his speech that the trajectory of his ministry was "not at all like my pastor, the late Richard Sammon . . . said to me." It was never limited to "just a few Asian congregations."[209]

The move happened a decade after Allen began regular visits to his older brother George while in seminary in Chicago. George had located in Dubuque early in his career, and during those vacations Allen had gotten acquainted with that pastor.[210]

Allen and Rose continued those visits when Allen was a pastor at the churches in Wisconsin. Dubuque is only about one hundred miles from Prairie du Sac, and Allen highlights a particularly enjoyable and regular stop on those drives—Spring Green, the site of Frank Lloyd Wright's Taliesin. His and Rose's interest was an outgrowth of periodic trips into Madison to see the First Unitarian Society, another noteworthy structure Wright designed. That Allen makes a point about how meaningful these two sites were for their family is a reminder of how thoroughly he and Rose immersed themselves in their surroundings wherever they lived—including sports activities and the natural and cultural environments.[211]

Because George was an active member and elder at Westminster Presbyterian Church, Allen and Rose would worship there when they visited. Allen does not remember details, but an associate pastor position opened, and the church invited him to candidate for it. He was hired.

The congregation had relocated from downtown Dubuque in the early 1950s and built their new church across the street from the University of Dubuque and Dubuque Theological Seminary. The church school and fellowship hall sufficed for space until the sanctuary was dedicated in 1964. According to Harriet Heitzman, whose husband was an architect for the new building, its design reflected Wright's influence.[212] The soaring, angular style suited Allen's tastes.

Joe, the brother closest in age to Allen, implied that Allen's reputation "of being able to make churches grow" led to the Dubuque invitation. Joe had observed Allen in the smaller Wisconsin churches when he and his family vacationed there. He had heard Allen preach, been at social lunches with his congregations, and thought Allen was "kept quite busy in Wisconsin as a beginning pastor."

However, Joe saw the Dubuque years as the formative ones for Allen, the time in which he came into his own professionally. As Rev. Foresberg had indicated in his nominating speech with his description of Allen's work with the Dubuque youth and his mention of their nickname for him, Pastor Marijuana, Joe also said Allen was "very well known in the city. He worked hard with the kids."[213]

Although Allen does not refer specifically to his work in Dubuque in his 1980 candidating speech, it is certainly part of the multiplication of "opportunities" he references. In conversation, he too calls those years a high point of his ministry and when he matured as a pastor.[214] He recites a list of accomplishments, including addressing "interracial conflict, so much social work, and involvement with the county commissioners about improving the jail [that dated from the Civil War] and the nursing home." Allen says it was so deteriorated that it could have dated from the same period.[215]

Rose agreed that the Dubuque years represented the time that Allen "came into his own." Of course, she said, in every place he worked, he was the pastor, and "that was special" in terms of access to a wide circle of relationships, but in Dubuque he developed ever more inclusive ties.

She also came into her own in Dubuque. "I had my school friends, and Allen was always too busy to do anything with me and my friends from school. I sort of had friends on the side of our marriage. It didn't seem strange. It's just the way it was."[216]

Rose enjoyed her job as a teacher of business classes at Hempstead High School because it catapulted her into another world from the church, "with different perspectives and kinds of students." She treasured her memory of one student, in particular, who wrote Rose "such an honest letter, in her own hand. I think I might still have it somewhere. In her words: 'I was not a good student, but you were a good person for me to know.' I took the letter to my principal; I was so proud of it, even though it wasn't well written. As he read it, he said, 'Well, she could have used some more learning.'

"Her parents owned a restaurant in downtown Dubuque, just a little place. She invited me and my family to come for dinner. I didn't think it appropriate for the whole family to go, but I did. She was my most successful student, not because she got so much out of the class but because she knew who she was and was grateful for what she did learn."[217]

Rose's definition of success: playing a role in the development of a student's emerging self-awareness and that student's unpretentious expression of gratitude. A beautiful, ordinary moment that the principal did not quite grasp. The qualities Rose valued in the student were those she was valued for herself. When she spoke out, which she did not hesitate to do about those things of importance to her, people could trust that she meant what she said. No pretension.

In yet other respects, Rose came into her own during this time. In the prior small churches, she was needed; "everyone was needed." In Dubuque, though, because she started teaching again and could "draw further away, that was a good thing. I was still very active, especially in the choir. Always the choir, as an alto, but the choir was my thing. That's me because I want to be there. That's the way I participated in church. I did not want to be Allen's assistant. I just wanted to be an ordinary person, to be a member of the church."

Just as she would not stand in Allen's shadow in the congregations he served, she did not give a pass to her implied dismissal in Dubuque's *Telegraph Herald* article that reported the success of her business students in a national competition. She wrote a forthright letter to the editor and protested that the article granted her status only as "Dr. Maruyama's wife," not by virtue of her own competency. She explained that while she was proud to be his wife, she was a professional in her own right. They published an apology.

Living in a larger community had yet another benefit for them as a couple. "We became friends with people outside the congregation, belonged to other groups," Rose said. She remembers those shared relationships were very important for them both. "I would always recommend that a pastor, if you can, find friends elsewhere. I remember those people. And the annual New Year's Eve event, and so much more." She characterized the friends and activities as important outlets "that he needed—and I did, too."[218]

Allen served in Dubuque 1962–72 and attributes many of the exciting times there to the larger social and political context. He participated in the Council of Churches that "riled things up" and frequently "made television news." It was the era of the civil rights movement and the assassinations of the Kennedys and Martin Luther King Jr. Concurrently, "Pope John XXIII opened the doors and windows of the Roman Catholic church," and literal horizons dramatically expanded with the 1969 moon landing.[219]

Rose said one of her most vivid memories of Dubuque, "almost as if you are there again," was the night John F. Kennedy was shot. "All the churches came together that night for a service at Westminster, because it was a big church right across from the seminary. The church was full. Everyone was in a state of shock."[220]

The archbishop also arrived in 1962. Allen says Dubuque was 80 percent Roman Catholic, and newspaper accounts give continuous coverage of the archbishop's first days, including a large photo of his arrival at the airport.[221] Allen's appearance did not garner the same level of coverage.

He characterizes the archbishop as a less than enthusiastic ecumenical figure, but during Allen's tenure, various denominations came together in a number of ways. Allen received his PhD in theology from the Aquinas School of Philosophy and Theology (now Aquinas Institute of Theology in St. Louis), subsequent to a master's of sacred theology from Dubuque Theological Seminary. The Dominicans had bought St. Rose Priory and invited the University of Iowa's religion department and the Lutheran and Presbyterian seminaries to share the facilities. They also had a dormitory there, and Allen rented a space to do his doctoral work. Rose editorialized that "he spent more time there than he did at home" while he worked on his dissertation.

Various Catholic priests and Baptist, Lutheran, Methodist, and Presbyterian pastors in Dubuque shared meals and study groups. The priests "unloaded" about their frustrations, but what struck Allen was the "freedom they had, not having to worry about where to live and having their meals prepared."

Allen and one of the priests, Dennis Kuennen, led a study group. Of particular significance for Rose was the 1969 moonwalk because the group had gathered for a potluck that night. After dinner and watching news of the moon landing, Kuennen and Allen shared leadership for the celebration of communion, a "very, very special memory" for Rose. Allen speculates that the conservative Dubuque archbishop "would have had a heart attack, if he'd heard we were doing that."

Unfortunately, Catholic participation did not extend to the Council of Churches. The group "wasn't that big," but it included the Lutherans, the United Church of Christ, the "liberal Baptist" group, a minister from another Presbyterian church, and lay people from the member churches. The council was very active in Dubuque community affairs.

Allen felt he had the time to devote to it because he was not the senior pastor at Westminster. He only had to preach once a month, and the

Christian education director had responsibility for all the church school. At one point, he was council president. He chaired the social action committee, as well as other committees.

A council priority, though, was to tackle the "horrible" conditions at the county jail and nursing home. The Civil War-era jail had not been modernized and was plagued with rats and mice. The county nursing home was in not much better condition. The council advocated so strongly for changes that they made the news. In a positive sense, the fallout for Allen was that "once you begin to stir things up, people begin to know who you are."

Allen's visibility in the hoopla surrounding the college students hanging out on the church lawn resulted in the mayor appointing him to chair the youth committee of city council, which meant he had to attend the "big acid concerts" and other citywide youth events. He was responsible for getting adult chaperones to circulate among the kids and keep order, if necessary. In the context of the city opening up a nearby park to relieve some of the crowds hanging out on the church lawn, Allen persuaded the church to open the Milk House, the coffeehouse in the little corner restaurant/dairy store that had closed.

The adults had their equivalent gathering place, Licciardi's. Allen notes that students went to the coffee house, but businessmen and professors (and pastors) all hung out at Licciardi's. It was an old, red stone house with a bar in the living room. Frank Licciardi was an artist, and Allen so liked his rendition of Christ that was hung in the window of the local department store every Easter that Licciardi gave it to him.

In his typical, deferential manner, Allen credits factors beyond his control to his community visibility. He emphasizes time and again that "when the newspaper gets behind you, it gets the population to do the same. I was at the right age, and things just happened to fall into my lap."

When pressed to speculate why the community response was positive, he describes his leadership as just "always being around," which resulted in those "things" coming his way. He does not remember speaking publicly to any large group or ever attending a city council meeting. Instead, he describes speaking with and working through individuals. In the case of the Council of Churches, it accomplished its goals through its committees, so he worked through them.

That Allen was so active in the Dubuque community was not only attributable to the era and the flexibility he had as an associate pastor, it also had to do with the character of the church and of its senior pastors. Gaylord Couchman left in the 1950s to become president of the University of Dubuque, located across the street, which speaks to his strong administrative and intellectual skills.

Richard B. Heydinger, senior pastor during Allen's early years, was "very vocal about civil rights, and he even got session to let him go to Hattiesburg [Mississippi]" to join in the marches for voting rights. Allen does not specify the date of Heydinger's trip. In any event, Heydinger "was almost shot at" there.[222]

Heydinger's activities complemented Allen's involvement in civil rights. Although Allen would have liked to, he did not participate in the Selma to Montgomery march in 1965 because Heydinger did. Session did not think both needed to be there. Allen was sent by his presbytery to Washington, D.C., though, and stood on the steps of the Supreme Court with many other pastors when "the judges made their decision about civil rights. They came out on the steps. That was exciting." He says that members of the Senate were also on the steps, and he met some of them.[223]

Church membership also drew from nearby Dubuque Theological Seminary, which "was a very big help in terms of getting support [for the church] in the Dubuque community." Allen characterizes Westminster as already being a "strong" church when he arrived, a strength that continued throughout his ministry there.[224]

Daughter Sarah was five when the family moved to Dubuque and fifteen when they left. When asked about her experience growing up as a biracial child in the Midwest, she says she did not think of herself as being different in Dubuque. However, the move to the larger Iowa city from Wisconsin and her age did bring her face-to-face with aspects of herself that she had not yet encountered.

"It was a time of the whole civil rights movement and my dad would say, 'Well, you know we can't become members of the country club here because we're Japanese.' That exclusionary kind of thing. I was like, 'Really? That's so weird.' I found things like that to be so peculiar."

She relates an incident when they visited "Uncle Joe" Maruyama in Chicago and went to the Museum of Science and Industry. "That's just a huge mix of races. You didn't interact with black people in Dubuque because there weren't very many. I was about ten or eleven. We were going from floor to floor, and I said, 'I'm thirsty. I want a drink. I saw a water fountain on the floor below.'

"So I walked back down and stood by the fountain because there was a group of four or five black girls getting a drink. I'm just waiting, and they turned and spit water on me. And I was like, 'What happened?' I got a drink and went upstairs and told my parents, and I was kind of crying. They were like, 'Oh, honey. I'm so sorry. Don't hate black kids. They did that because that's been done to them.'

"My parents were so concerned that that did not flavor my opinion of people of different races. I didn't feel in danger or at risk or completely ridiculed. I just didn't understand it. Why would they do that?

"My parents said they were sure that's why, that that's been done to them. 'You're white; they're black. There's this black/white civil unrest going on in this country right now.'"

Sarah's experiences in Dubuque with the children of a black family prompted more observations. The civil unrest in the country "was interesting to me, and the other interesting thing was that finally in Dubuque, they got a black family with little kids. They might have been the first; I don't know, but they became members at Westminster. I was twelve or fourteen, and someone told them, 'The pastor's daughter is the best person to have as a babysitter.' They lived only about four blocks from us. I would babysit the kids in the summer in the evening, and we'd walk around the neighborhood and people would stare at us. I never realized how it is to be totally ostracized and treated differently because of your race until I was with these black children. The thing I found very, very powerful was to care for children that were obviously another race, and people were afraid of or not sure how to deal with them. I just thought, 'They're regular people, a nice family. I don't get why this is such a problem.'"

On the one hand, Sarah was aware of being excluded from the all-white Dubuque Country Club due to being Japanese; on the other hand, as she recalls it, her parents framed the incident at the water fountain as a contrast between the black girls and her, a white girl, an identity that also shielded her from the uncertain, perhaps disapproving, glances of white Dubuque residents that were directed toward the black children.

However, "My dad would sometimes remind us that we're Japanese and people don't always accept that. I was like, 'Really?' I had no idea. As I got older, I was proud of my Japanese heritage. People are interested and ask, 'So you're half Japanese? I thought maybe you were Hispanic.' They want to know more, and I tell them my grandparents came from Japan and theirs was an arranged marriage. Then they're like, 'Wow!'"[225]

John's proud account of his (four feet eleven!) father's courage in confronting those who were hostile to the students gathered on the church lawn and Sarah's memory of her parents' concern that she understand the source of the girls' hostility at the drinking fountain speak to Allen's dedication to civil rights during the Dubuque years. As pre-teens, they learned the vocabulary of exclusion and racism, and their parents tried to give them tools to deal with it.

There was one Chinese restaurant in Dubuque, and, in addition to Allen and George, his brother, Allen remembers that the restaurant owners were the only other Asians in Dubuque. He knew of just the one African-American family. Someone once told him that the city had a history of not allowing any African Americans to stay overnight.[226]

Sarah's stories raise several dimensions of racial politics in quite personal ways: the weirdness of being excluded from the country club because of her race—Japanese; the mystery of being spit on because of her race—white; the popular daughter of the pastor noticing the neighbors' fear of children she babysat because of their race—black. She juggles various aspects of racial identity as a mixed-race woman who can be characterized as white, such as in the incident with the black girls at the water fountain, but she is sometimes mistaken as Hispanic even while also being appreciated as the interesting descendant of Japanese grandparents whose marriage was arranged. It seems easier for her to navigate this ambiguity than it has been for Allen to cope with his relatively straightforward racial identity as a Nisei growing up during World War II.[227]

Sarah's awareness of racism was just emerging in those years, but friends of the Maruyamas, the Calians, saw it clearly from their adult vantage point. Dr. Carnegie Samuel Calian and Doris arrived in Dubuque in 1963, shortly after Allen and Rose, Calian as a theology professor at the University of Dubuque Theological Seminary and Doris as a biochemist at the facility where George Maruyama worked. One of the first stories Calian tells to characterize Dubuque is this historical anecdote. Dubuque citizens would apparently meet the boatloads of enslaved people fleeing up the Mississippi River and encourage them to "stay in the boat," that is, to go further upstream to settle.

He speculates that he and Allen were close because they both were seen as minorities, he as the son of Armenian immigrants and Allen of Japanese immigrants. Armenians (those who survived genocide) were displaced from their homeland, as the Japanese Americans were displaced from their homes on the West Coast. He and Allen never dwelled on what Calian saw as a shared minority position in the community; they simply enjoyed being together. Allen gave him fishing and golfing lessons, although Calian does not remember ever catching a fish and spent most of his time on the golf course in the weeds looking for golf balls. Calian says the activities were just excuses to be in one another's company.

Unlike the surrounding city, the seminary encouraged diversity. It was known for enrolling and supporting international students. Calian remembers that Allen was pulled into those conversations and was of particular help to the Asian students.[228]

Allen became impatient with the Westminster church's commitment to civil rights because it went only so far.[229] Session did pass an open housing covenant, but he "was so disappointed with the lack of activity." Because the church did not follow the decision with concrete steps, Allen applied for a regional position as a community organizer. It would have allowed him to focus on "social activism, open housing covenants—the whole civil rights business." He was one of the finalists for the job, but a prominent church member active in Republican politics, Edward D. Failor Sr., was on the hiring committee. He pleaded they not hire Allen "because the church needs him so badly." When Allen heard about Failor's intervention, he was "mad as hops."[230]

Doris and Sam Calian would agree that the church needed Allen. Doris characterizes him as the one to visit the sick and as possessing a quiet personality, that is, he is not a "charismatic" leader. He was accepted and loved. Sam appreciates that "he always had time for coffee" and that Allen's was a cooperative style of leadership more concerned about outcomes and results than being the "top guy." The Calians admired Allen and Rose for their integrity. When the four were together, the Calians felt they were with "honest, real people," who, by the way, were also "good parents."

Youth ministry and community activism represent only part of Allen's pursuits during the Dubuque years. Calian emphasizes that Allen and Kenneth E. Hindman, who succeeded Heydinger as senior minister at Westminster, were pastors to the seminary faculty when it went through difficult times with new leadership. Allen was also supportive of the university undergraduate faculty's struggle to unionize. Finally, the seminary faculty joined in their effort, and it was successful. In short, Allen was "a pastor in times of conflict and celebration."[231]

In the midst of all this community and church activity, Allen had opportunity to expand intellectually. In 1966, he completed his work for his STM (master's of sacred theology) from the University of Dubuque Theological Seminary, cum laude. He began work on his PhD, but the demands on his time prompted him to request a leave of absence. It was not granted; however, the church revised his contract to half-time for a period. When he applied for governmental financial assistance, he was told that because he had just reached age forty he was not eligible. Still, he continued his studies. Not surprisingly, and in her wry manner, Rose's assessment of the busy Dubuque years was that Allen "had time for everybody except me!"[232]

In retrospect, Allen ranks the personal significance of his PhD as quite high. He says it was another big step in developing his self-confidence as a Japanese American, and it validated him professionally. As for the research and the ideas in the dissertation, they became integral to his theology.

The title describes his subject: "A Theological Critique of Marshall McLuhan's New Man of the Electric Age." Allen's purpose was to examine

McLuhan's anthropology and his vision of the future and to critique them in light of Christian anthropology and eschatology (humanity's destiny). His guiding questions led him to address the issue of human nature; what technology does to it; and whether humans can improve themselves through technological advancement. In the first part, Allen summarizes McLuhan's positions. In the second, he offers his theological critique as he has represented those positions.[233]

As anyone knows who has written, heard about, and/or read a dissertation, Allen's is a dense, complicated treatment of his subject and is replete with the jargon of various disciplines. A summary of his conclusions discloses his concerns, thought, and theological perspective in the late 1960s and early '70s, but Allen sees so many contemporary connections to and implications of McLuhan's work that he often expresses a desire to revive discussions of McLuhan's relevancy.[234]

From this historical distance, the questions that might arise are who was Marshall McLuhan and why would a pastor be interested in him? In the 1960s, McLuhan and his analyses of popular culture, the media, and technology's exploding impact were ascendant. As a measure of his importance, then and now, he described the dynamics of and coined the phrases "the medium is the message" and "the global village." In short, he discussed how modern communication methods have shrunk the globe, and he postulated that the method, or medium, of communicating content influences (determines?) it, how it is perceived, and its integration. He is also said to have been one of the first to anticipate the World Wide Web thirty years prior to its advent. He imagined electronic media as a global network of communication systems similar to the human nervous system, linking everyone.[235]

An astute pastor such as Allen, whose basic skills rest on adeptness with multiple forms of communication, would not only have been aware of McLuhan but would have attempted to understand what he was getting at. In addition, McLuhan presented himself as a religious person. He had converted to Roman Catholicism in adulthood and drew on Christian concepts and images in his writing and speaking.

McLuhan was Canadian and spent the bulk of his academic life in Toronto, where Allen was fortunate to personally interview him in December 1971. Allen gives the impression that he softened his critique of McLuhan somewhat as a result of that encounter, because it seemed to him that McLuhan might have been confused about some of his own arguments.[236]

When McLuhan visited Denver in 1973, they met again. (Allen and Rose had relocated there in 1972.) As a followup to that meeting, McLuhan sent a note indicating that he had "dipped" into Allen's dissertation, "finding it full of interest and relevance and also full of new bibliography for me."

Allen had suggested that he wanted to publish his dissertation, but McLuhan discouraged the effort. He wrote, "I think it a bit premature to put out anything serious concerning my work . . . while I am still trying to do the jobs [that remain to be done]!"[237]

Allen's primary critique in the second part of his dissertation is that McLuhan has not dealt seriously with the problem of sin and evil. Allen attributes this to McLuhan's confused application of his Roman Catholic heritage, which traditionally asserts that sinful man does not have the capability to exercise his creative freedom without the assistance of God's grace. Rather, McLuhan opts for his own definition of sin as simply willed ignorance. McLuhan seems to believe that man can overcome this resistance to learning and will become aware and knowledgeable. He will escape technology's power and will control it for his future benefit. McLuhan goes so far as to assert that the outcome, the emerging global village, is, if not connected to, metaphorically similar to, the mystical body of Christ.

At points in the dissertation, Allen compares and contrasts McLuhan with the Roman Catholic theologian Pierre Teilhard de Chardin. One comparison is the similarity of McLuhan's conception of the changes in man wrought by emerging communication technologies to Teilhard's "interiorization." Teilhard uses this term to describe the process by which he believes the cosmos is evolving, that is, through multiple interactions between man and matter. The body of knowledge expands through interiorization toward a collective identity, a sort of "thinking layer" around the earth, a membrane Teilhard calls the "noosphere," from the Greek word *nous*, or mind. Layer builds upon layer with increasing complexity until it reaches the Omega Point, a universal reunion with Christ.[238] Both McLuhan and Teilhard put forth similar, positive endpoints of evolution, McLuhan toward reintegration in the global village and Teihard toward the ultimate Omega Point. This forward, integrative movement of humanity would eventually emerge as a central aspect in Allen's maturing theology.

At the time of writing the dissertation, though, Allen observes that because McLuhan's "new man" of the post-Industrial Revolution is a cultural construct, not a theological one, his insights are difficult to translate into theological ones, although the effort is worthwhile. McLuhan himself also claims to speak from a cultural perspective and rejects a theological label. Accordingly, Allen represents McLuhan's positions as those of a literary artist who paints a "mural" of a world influenced by mass media. As such, his positions offer a "new vision whereby man and his society can comprehend the influence of electronic media upon environment."[239]

Allen emphasizes that McLuhan is not so much concerned with man's nature as with man's communications, especially the electronic media. To control that media, McLuhan moves from a moral category (all technology is bad) to "a new survival strategy" that is based on creativity, on artistry. McLuhan is optimistic that this strategy might lead to the "new man's" development of insight and awareness and, therefore, control of the electric environment in which he is now enmeshed.

Allen supports McLuhan's emphasis on creativity because, when Allen puts it into a theological framework, he thinks that man's creativity as a steward of God's creation is fundamental to a Christian anthropological understanding. However, he criticizes McLuhan for being too optimistic about man's capability for creativity and for romanticizing human history.

Allen summarizes McLuhan's scheme as follows. Pre-literate, primitive man lived a rich communal life, but it was fragmented into individualism by the literate print culture. McLuhan celebrates that the contemporary, electronic era has the potential, through the creative, artistic efforts of the "new man," to reinstate the integrated, whole, and unified life of primitive man.

From Allen's perspective, this is where McLuhan's analysis falters. Human nature has not changed from early man to the present. There is not an ideal state to which man can return.

With this criticism, Allen's neo-orthodox perspective from seminary days clearly emerges: the nature of humankind is inherently sinful, and that brokenness is manifest in individuals and in social structures. Only divine grace can heal this brokenness and bridge the gap between God and humankind. Humanity has the responsibility to creatively engage with the divine in this effort but is not capable, in and of itself, of accomplishing it. Accordingly, Allen is somewhat pessimistic that humanity can achieve control of its electric environment as McLuhan posits it will.

By immersing himself in McLuhan's thinking and that of any number of theologians during his research and writing, twenty years after his seminary graduation, Allen equipped himself intellectually to be a resource to the church at its many levels of government. These responsibilities had begun to emerge when he started his work at the Westminster church in Dubuque with a 1962 concurrent position as chair of a General Assembly standing committee. They continued with his service as a commissioner to the General Assembly in 1969.

Heydinger relocated to Waukesha, Wisconsin. A member of that congregation, Lois Stair, was elected as the first woman to serve as moderator of the General Assembly in 1971 and appointed Allen to the position of Chairman of the General Assembly's Standing Committee on Christian Education. He was also vice-moderator of the Iowa Synod. By the mid-1970s, he would be a member of the General Assembly Special Committee that produced the report about the church's response to liberation theology.

Of practical importance, as of 1972, he had a PhD in hand, validation of his intellectual capacity and of his perseverance. He had indicated to Rose that he was interested in exploring new possibilities, and she agreed. It was also the right timing for the family. "We needed to move on. Sarah was in high school and John right behind her," Rose said.

She and Allen represent Sarah as always putting herself "in charge of everything," so perhaps a different environment might provide enlarged opportunities for her. John was not only beginning high school but also struggling with asthma and allergies. He was "sick all the time." A location change might help.[240]

Two possibilities emerged when Allen started circulating his dossier. Someone at Montview Boulevard Presbyterian Church in Denver saw his name as a pastor seeking a position and recognized it from Allen's role as chair of the General Assembly committee. Montview contacted him. Down-to-earth Rose observed, "It's always who you know!" The other possibility was a chaplaincy position at Carroll College (now Carroll University) in Waukesha, a Presbyterian institution.

Allen was torn. He "had wanted to be a chaplain all my life, but I knew religious colleges were dropping the position because they were all cutting budgets. I got acquainted with the chaplain who was retiring there, though, and he said they had the financial resources."[241]

The Montview church and Carroll College interviewed him around the same time, and both extended offers. The arguments in favor of Montview were that "I wanted to come back to Colorado, and the Montview church had a [national] reputation." He accepted Montview's offer, to Rose's relief. She was skeptical about how their lives might change if he switched career paths to that of college chaplaincy, even though as a pastor he had been "so busy in Dubuque, a difficult time for our marriage."[242]

Allen's success in Dubuque was recorded in its *Telegraph Herald*. His arrival in 1962 had not elicited the public fanfare that the archbishop's had, but his 1972 exit drew extensive comment. Mike Tighe highlighted Allen's Dubuque accomplishments in an article that was used simultaneously to introduce Allen to Montview. The article remains in Montview's archives.

Tighe observes that Allen was "one of Dubuque's first ministers to thrust himself into involvement with the city's problems, and at a time when such activity had not become the vogue." He records that, in Allen's estimation, the 1960s began an era of such rapid change that the church's traditional structures proved outdated and were not meeting people's needs. The church was reacting to social problems instead of taking the initiative. Consequently, Allen asserted that people were seeing it as "an archaic museum piece or fossilized institution."

In his discussion of Allen's collaboration with Rev. Charles H. Bixby, pastor of First Baptist Church, and the Dubuque Council of Churches in "the gathering storm around conditions in the Dubuque County jail," Tighe notes a "lack of supervision at the jail, bad living conditions, fights, and homosexuality."[243] The injustices in the jail precipitated a feeling in the church in the early 1960s that, Allen is quoted as saying, "we were not where the action was. [That feeling] catapulted me into the midst of community concerns. . . . The church determines its witness and its mission by the agenda of the world rather than the church determining what that agenda should be."

In addition to tackling the problems at the jail, Tighe identifies other needs that Allen and the Council of Churches stepped forward to meet. They steered a municipal open housing ordinance through the City Advisory Commission, which led to a comprehensive human rights ordinance in 1969. He also mentions the 1969 community controversy over the Westminster church allowing "unkempt youths" to "loll" on the church lawn and Allen's support of the young people.

When Tighe asks Allen for some of his predictions for Dubuque, Allen cautions that the advent of interstate highways, pollution, and ecological challenges obligate the city to seriously engage in advance planning, difficult because of political and public apathy. His "most oft repeated desire" is to involve citizens in community problems. He advises structuring more educational opportunities and encouraging citizen advisory commissions. Perhaps as a reflection of his familiarity with McLuhan's thoughts about the electronic age, Allen does think that cable television holds promise for stimulating public involvement because it "is a great tool for bringing facts into the homes." All in all, Allen is optimistic about Dubuque's future and mentions the Five Flags Center, a major new development, as having the potential to bring together professionals, businesspeople, education institutions, and blue collar workers to engage the city's future.[244]

Tighe's article gives contemporaneous testimony to what Allen and his family remember from those Dubuque years in which he "came into his own." It not only portrays Allen as immersed in community affairs but also as frank and articulate about compelling personal and professional commitments. Allen identifies areas of neglect, calls attention to emerging challenges, and advocates drawing on community resources to address them.

The article conveys a sense of respect, affection, and regret about the loss of a valued leader. The tone is not accidental. Over his years in Dubuque, Allen and Tighe developed a friendship, and Allen officiated at Tighe's wedding.[245]

To say that Allen's opportunities would be limited to just a few Asian congregations had indeed turned out to be a misrepresentation of the trajectory his career was taking.

Chapter 14

The Church Has Been Good to Me

ALLEN ASSERTS IN THE next sentences of his speech that "I've served in congregations of all sizes. I've been a pastor for twenty-seven years. The Presbyterian church has been good to me."[246]

Although it is the case that his professional successes had multiplied over those twenty-seven years, progress was not always smooth. One obstacle was the less-than-auspicious sequence between Montview's offer of an associate pastor position and Allen's arrival in Denver. His Iowa presbytery released him before arrangements were final with Montview. However, he did not foresee any difficulty and anticipated that completing the hiring process would be just a "matter of going through the motions."[247]

To his surprise, that did not prove to be the case. When the Montview congregation held its vote, unlike with the Prairie du Sac congregation where only four were negative, the numbers at Montview were close.[248] Advisors from Denver Presbytery were called in, who pointed out that the majority had approved the call. Furthermore, in their opinion, the close result had little to do with Allen and more to do with controversy swirling around the senior pastor, Albert Fay Hill. Allen speculated that, given the growing hostility toward Hill, perhaps some thought that if they could keep Hill from having another associate on staff, maybe he would leave.[249]

In Montview's historical records, the reason behind the close vote is represented with a not-so-subtle nuance. "Some Montview members were concerned Allen might be 'too liberal,' resulting in a close vote to call him."[250]

As it will be explained, the controversy swirling around Hill centered on his involvement in social issues, so the concern that Allen was too liberal may indeed have factored in the vote if Allen too was represented as liberal. This might have predisposed members displeased with Hill to assume Allen would be his ally.

In any event, the presbytery representatives advised that the church carry out the call. Montview's session and Hill concurred, and Allen was finally hired as the associate pastor for parish care. He was to work with the board of deacons (members elected and ordained primarily to exercise the responsibility for the ministry of caring for other members) and the visitation program. His other responsibilities, as listed in the June 14, 1972, *Montview Messenger*, included evangelism and stewardship.

The article in the *Messenger* also gives a contemporaneous profile of Allen. It summarizes his Dubuque responsibilities as having been adult education, senior high ministry, and pastoral care, and emphasizes his roles as vice-moderator of the Synod of Iowa and chairman of the General Assembly's Standing Committee on Christian Education. It concludes with this personal touch: "Those who have had the opportunity to meet him are very impressed by his warmth and understanding."[251]

If there was widespread concern about Allen being too liberal, perhaps emphasizing his "warmth and understanding" was meant to allay it. Ed O'Keefe, an active member in the 1980s and 90s, comments that Montview was comprised of conservatives and liberals, with the liberals being the stronger faction but "not the noisiest."[252] When "liberal" is used as a descriptor in church publications of the time, local and national, the impression is that those who attach the label "liberal" intend it pejoratively, implying stridency about social issues at the expense of concern for individual, emotional needs and matters of belief.

The presbytery's opinion about the divided vote, that the controversy surrounding Hill was more of a factor than Allen personally, proved to be accurate. The controversy led to several years of uncertainty and conflict—challenges for Allen, the other staff members, and the congregation.

In 1969, Hill had followed the twenty-year tenure of Rev. Dr. Arthur L. Miller, Montview's fifth pastor since its founding in 1902. Stepping into the senior position filled by someone of Miller's stature would have been a challenge for anyone. During Miller's time, the congregation grew from 2,203 to 4,000. Other sources say membership might have reached 5,000. A graduate of McCormick Theological Seminary, Miller was revered as "gentle, caring, firm, and a man of conviction." He was moderator of the General Assembly in 1959 and tackled "problems of race relations, collective bargaining, capital punishment, alcoholism, planned parenthood, and international relations" during his term.

Miller's influence was considerable throughout the years of his ministry at Montview. For example, in the 1960s, he led Montview members to sign a nondiscriminatory pledge when buying or selling real estate, and Montview joined with Blessed Sacrament Catholic Church and Park Hill United Methodist Church to make the Park Hill neighborhood (in which the Montview church is located) Denver's first racially integrated community, "indeed, one of the first in the United States."[253]

When Allen describes the 1960s in Denver, he says "Park Hill was fighting a war trying to keep the blacks out." Redlining had meant the black population was concentrated some blocks further north of the church. Montview and the other Park Hill congregations—Episcopal, Methodist, United Church of Christ, Catholic—had "many meetings" trying to get members to sign open housing covenants, one indication that the churches were playing a positive role in attempts to integrate the community.

Miller's success in integrating the Park Hill neighborhood had its downside. Because the Park Hill community had opened to blacks, blacks bought homes. That precipitated "white flight," and new residents tended to join Park Hill Methodist and the United Church of Christ, both of which were closer to the concentration of the black population. Additionally, Peoples Presbyterian Church, a predominately black congregation, was located less than three miles from Montview and also closer to the heart of the black community.[254]

Concurrently, expanding suburbs and the construction of more Presbyterian churches to meet Denver's growing population needs meant that, by the time of Miller's retirement in 1967, membership had declined to around 3,800. Montview had willingly "seeded" some of its members to the new congregations. However, some unspecified "unrest and division" at Montview during these years resulted in even more members following an associate pastor when he left Montview to help form one of the new suburban churches.[255]

Yet one more demographic factor had contributed to Montview's membership decline. Rev. Kenneth L. Barley, hired several months after Allen began in 1972 and with responsibilities as the associate minister of local missions, notes that the church was located in a sector near United Airlines' headquarters and Denver's major airport at the time, Stapleton. When United relocated to Chicago, a glut of housing went on the market. Barley says that Hill was hired to turn things around.

Demographic and cultural factors made that a nearly impossible task, but the congregation had residual strength in not only its past reputation but within its membership and from Miller's tenure. Both of his sons entered the ministry, and his daughter married Roy Romer, who became Colorado's first three-term governor, elected in 1986, 1990, and 1994.

Romer was an active member at Montview. Barley remembers his participation in a dynamic Sunday evening group, of which he and Romer were both a part, that had supported and encouraged Romer to re-enter politics in the 1970s after a near-decade hiatus.[256]

Romer and Allen were also connected by their childhood memories of Southeastern Colorado. Romer, too, played on his high school's football team during World War II, and that activity connected him to Camp Amache. Romer's hometown, Holly, was located near the incarceration site, and his Wildcats played the Amache boys on November 11, 1943, on Amache's dirt field, in preparation for Holly's state championship game against Burlington.

The day of the game, two thousand five hundred fans surrounded the field, none of them from Holly. The lack of Holly spectators was attributed to a combination of gas rationing, the crushing amount of farm work during the war, and the "psychological barrier" to entering the camp.

Most of the Amache team lacked "football shoes" and were described as "muscular, physical, quiet, and smaller" than the Holly boys. The Amache players threw themselves into the game, resulting in a number of team injuries. The Holly players, admiring the spirit of the Amache boys, repeatedly helped their injured opponents off the field. After the game, the Holly players were remembered as expressing their respect for the Amache team's excellence, a memorable and noteworthy expression of maturity, given that Holly lost, 7–0.

After the game, Romer's reaction to Amache was similar to that of the teenage Allen's. Romer is remembered as questioning "why these people had to be in this camp." He said something to the effect that, "It was crazy. Absolutely crazy [that they were confined]."[257]

Hill had entered the life of a congregation with a proud history, notable members, and strong pastoral leadership, but it was undergoing a period of decline. Although his challenges were considerable, the high hopes the members had for him are reflected in its historical materials. He was hired because of his "vigor and vision, his challenging sermons, and a call for social action." He had acquired a national reputation from his work as the pastor of the North Avenue Presbyterian Church in New Rochelle, New York, and its exposé of Mafia operations in the region. Those efforts had resulted in Hill's book, *The North Avenue Irregulars*, which was later made into a movie of the same name.[258]

Allen emphasizes the national attention garnered by the story of the New York church's exposé about the Mafia. Hill's picture had even been on the cover of *Look* magazine. The accompanying article described how Hill and his family had twenty-four-hour police protection. Montview had hired a celebrity.

According to Barley, Hill convinced the session that if he had a staff the size of Miller's, he could bring the church back, or at least stop the decline. Richard C. Hutchison ("Hutch") was hired in 1969 with the portfolio for Christian education. Hutchison came at the recommendation of Hill, who had known him through General Assembly work.[259] In Hill and Hutchison, Allen says, Montview had two magnetic leaders,[260]

Rev. John W. Rice Jr. joined in 1971 in a part-time position, Montview's first African-American pastor, and was followed by Allen and Barley in 1972. Barley asserts that the decision to expand the staff was not taken without both immediate and long-term cost. "They made the mistake of selling property to pay our salaries, and that was one-time money."[261]

Probably Hill's argument to expand the staff, supported by his leadership qualities, was received positively at the outset. His argument and his personality fit a familiar pattern established by Miller. According to Dr. Robert S. Hanson, an associate from 1959 to 1966, in addition to Miller's community activities, his guidance and preferred style of leadership had been one in which the clergy shared "in the pastoral ministry, preaching, hospital calling, weddings, and funerals." In other words, Hill inherited a congregation accustomed to the church's significant community involvement, led by an energetic pastor with a leadership style that encouraged shared responsibility among multiple staff members.[262]

Hill continued his efforts to uncover organized crime in his new environment by organizing a group of young women at Montview who researched and reported on it. The outcome, *Colorado, Target of Organized Crime*, was published in 1972 and was read into the Congressional Record on August 7, 1972. In addition, Hill's interest in criminal and penal system reform led to a church group visiting the state penitentiary in Canon City, and the formation of a church Prison Projects Task Force followed.

Unfortunately, prisoners rioted at the state penitentiary shortly after the Montview group's visit, and there was a violent altercation between organized crime bosses in Lakewood, a Denver suburb, attributed by some to media coverage of the church's report. The church's exposure was seen as negative, even somewhat unnerving. In any case, what had been Hill's strengths now became unattractive: "bluntly outspoken, [too quick to propose] aggressive changes, not a consensus builder, and sermons [that] challenged political and cultural norms."[263]

The storm intensified due to unfortunate personal circumstances. Hill's wife died during his first year in Denver, and he remarried a divorced church member. He brought five children to the marriage, as did she. The blended family of twelve collapsed.

Allen says the three associates knew the situation was "not good."[264] The church continued to lose members—and money. Allen estimates that membership dropped by perhaps one thousand from 1968 to 1972.[265] The congregation divided about whether Hill should leave, as did the Denver Presbytery, but there was "no legitimate reason for getting rid of him. He hadn't done anything wrong. . . . The collapse of his marriage was not a legitimate excuse."[266]

Allen's account of these events provides underlying details. The women who did the research about the Mafia connections, "especially in Colorado Springs, Denver, even reaching to Pueblo, Grand Junction, and some of the smaller towns to the north of Denver," had done such a good job that Hill gave the study to the FBI and the local police. "When the Mafia found out, there was a big fight in Lakewood. Maybe one of them was killed and the other one imprisoned. . . . [Whatever happened] really made news, and the congregation was not happy about it. Many said, 'We called you to be a pastor, not a policeman or detective.' But that still wasn't a good enough reason [to fire him]," even though the "only people who liked what he was doing in Denver were the police!

"We associate pastors started circulating our dossiers. Then Fay came in one day and said, 'I hate to tell you this in a staff meeting, but I've made up my mind. I'm resigning. I'm just sick and tired of all this bickering. I've been offered to have my new book [*The Deadly Messiah*] made into another movie. I'm just going to be a writer. I'm handing in my resignation. You guys take over.' And he got up and walked out."[267]

The associates had no idea that Hill "was going to pull this stunt. We were in a state of shock." As far as they knew, he had adamantly refused to resign to that point. Later Allen heard that some members had even offered him money to leave, perhaps as much as $25,000, which he had refused.[268]

Barley thinks "what finally ended Fay's time [in 1974] at Montview was that he took responsibility for a bad decision" (funding the salaries of the additional staff by the sale of church property). Barley remembers that "Fay announced he was finished on a Friday and the joke was, 'How did the three of you decide who would preach on Sunday?' We always said, 'Well, we flipped a coin,' and it went from there."[269]

Allen has a personal memory that he cherishes from early in this difficult period. Apparently the three associates, Hill, and members of session were discussing all the unrest and unhappiness. Allen was still somewhat

awed by Montview's membership profile that consisted of not only personalities such as Romer but also of a number of "big wheels—around 275 doctors, lawyers, dentists. Several of the older, respected members who didn't
even know me, whose say meant a lot, remarked, 'Dr. Maruyama ought to
take over leadership.' Fay and the other associates seemed to agree. I was
embarrassed. But it shows the influence of a PhD."[270]

Perhaps—or this could be yet another instance of Allen deferring to
external factors, as when he attributed the popularity of his public leadership in Dubuque to the cultural unrest of the 1960s and newspaper coverage
of his work. In this case, he credits his PhD as the basis for confidence in his
leadership. Certainly the graduate degree marked a significant moment for
him personally. "I know the day that I passed my doctoral examination and
the day I finally graduated, I felt I had arrived at a place of recognizing my
own self, that I didn't have to prove to anyone that I was just as good as anybody else—a sense of having arrived at a point of not having to apologize for
my existence [as a Japanese American], of having reached a certain maturity
where I could stand up to people."[271]

Surely he communicated this maturity, but his energy, likability, and
genuineness must also have prompted respect. Additionally, at a difficult
time for the congregation, his abilities and quiet commitment to reconcile
difference might have been more apparent than he realized.

When he looks back at his ministry from the present, in his 90s, he
describes his approach to congregational conflict in these terms: the importance of uncovering the origins of disagreement, of clearly stating the reasons for particular positions in a dispute, of letting the congregation decide
the outcome in order to maintain "peace in the family," and of making an
extra effort to be responsive to those who might not agree with his positions. These were lessons learned from his first years in ministry in Hogarty
and Gleason, perhaps somewhat refined and apparent to others by the time
he reached Montview more than a decade later.

At the time of Hill's resignation, Allen and Barley had been on staff
for several years, Hutchison for nearly five. They went to session for advice.
Session proposed that the three associates act as co-pastors in the interim
because there was no money to hire a senior pastor to come in temporarily.
In the meantime, the session authorized a committee of thirty-five to study
the possibilities over the next several months and come up with a plan.

Attendance began to pick up; money started to come back. Session
proposed they make the arrangement permanent, if the three were to agree.
Barley and Allen did so without condition, but Hutchison stipulated that
his own participation be reviewed after three years. The three became co-
pastors with that qualification.[272]

Barley notes that "we were very different. Hutch was an educator. Allen was a pastor. I was more of an administrator/social action kind of guy. It really worked well, because we each had our compartments. Hutch left first, [in 1980], I left later [in 1988], but Allen was the long-term person who was there from the beginning until his retirement" [in 1992].[273]

Initially, Miller, who had returned to Denver after completing a year-long interim position in the Northwest, was skeptical about the arrangement. "He said, 'Different members like different people. When Allen preaches, Allen's friends will come; when Hutch preaches, his people will come, and so forth.'

"It never developed that way," Allen observes. "They didn't care who was in the pulpit. After a couple of years we said, 'You know, either we're awfully bad preachers or awfully good!'"[274]

O'Keefe observes that when he knew the "triumvirate," which was composed by the mid-1980s of Allen, Barley, and Rev. Dr. Glendora ("Dusty") Taylor, none of them were "stem-winding, spell-binding speakers."[275]

Allen attributes their effective teamwork to several factors in addition to those identified by Barley. First, they had been functioning in such a hostile situation before Hill left that they had established working relationships in which they held onto and supported one another, as well as Hill. Second, throughout the conflict, the three associates "did our work. Whatever assignment we had, we held our regular meetings. We tried to keep everything as normal as possible. . . . There was no problem picking up the pieces [after Hill resigned] because we realized, by that point, all Fay was really doing was preaching."[276]

Longtime Montview member Shirley Burkhart frames all the furor as "a big hullabaloo." Her memories give substance to how painful that period was for the congregation. She liked Hill and his preaching. She thought he was a "good person, but a lot of people were unfair to him and those of us who liked him had no chance. The worst Sunday I'll ever experience happened at a church meeting after one service. The things that were said [about Hill] were unbelievable. Horrible things. And one [man] who spoke, whom I knew, had no business making the accusations that he did. I was tempted to turn around and say that to him, but I thought, 'Keep your mouth shut.'" The challenges for the three associates to heal the congregation were considerable.[277]

When the decision was made to initiate the co-pastorate, the three men put a great deal of effort into designing the plan because it was new to Montview and there was less than a handful of models for it in the denomination. The arrangement was organic to the three of them, not imported.

As Allen describes it, the plan consisted of choosing a co-pastors' committee consisting of three members, each of the pastors choosing one member. The co-pastors would consult with the committee regularly, in addition to staff meetings with everyone else. They decided to share responsibilities based on what each liked to do. The practical effect was that, initially, little changed, except the order of who was preaching.[278] They alternated each Sunday, as well as Christmas and Easter. About baptism, weddings, and funerals, they left it to the people to decide. After two to three years, they saw that they all had about the same number, so preferential selections had not resulted in inequalities.

These numbers "amazed" Allen because he had figured that congregants would choose one of the two European-American pastors to do a funeral or wedding, rather than an Asian. "It never happened that way. How the numbers broke even I will never know."[279]

That he will never know is probably accurate because again he is prone to discount the strength of his pastoral appeal. Congregation members apparently responded to the person, of which the race was only a part.

The "troika's" (to which it is sometimes humorously referred, with an acknowledgment that terms such as "troika" and "triumvirate" were discouraged in favor of "collegium" and "co-pastorate") success from its inception and throughout the years had at its base pastors who committed themselves to it and worked hard at it. Barley says they generally agreed that if difficulties emerged among the pastors, the discontented one would have to leave. The co-pastorate would not be sacrificed. They would not allow a situation to develop in which the congregation would have to choose between disputing pastors. "We rotated the preaching, rotated moderating session. We really tried to keep, symbolically, the sense of one person. We also said to the congregation, 'Let's try it for a year and you vote again.' That happened several times, before the intervals got longer between the congregation having an opportunity to say whether they wanted to continue."[280]

Montview's historical record characterizes the 1974–75 period as one of "Crisis, Change, Challenge." It represents the church's response to the congregational division and Hill's resignation as "immediate and unique." Session took only one month to come up with a plan, which it adopted on a trial basis. The "new formula for leadership" directed that: 1) the three associate ministers "adopt and implement" a collegial model of administrative staff responsibility; 2) the three associates work together as colleagues on an equal basis and share authority and responsibility; and 3) the three associates be considered the Head of Staff Team. The plan was seen as an opportunity for healing and renewal of a "divided and hurting" congregation.[281]

Rev. Dr. Cynthia Ann Cearley more fully describes the collegium model in her 1995 dissertation for advanced pastoral studies at San Francisco Theological Seminary. Cearley was initially hired at Montview as an assistant pastor with responsibilities for Christian education for children and youth. She became part of the co-pastor "team" in 1988, elevated from the assistant position upon Barley's departure.

In her dissertation, she notes that Barley, Hutchison, and Allen expressed their ideas about how the model would work in a 1975 *Montview Messenger* article. They emphasized that the "collegium" model rested on their shared bond of common interest, their commitment to work within this style, and, in particular, their agreement that it would require a sense of humor.

She expands her summary of the co-pastors' thoughts as follows: 1) the staff and session would agree upon areas of responsibility; 2) preaching and presiding at meetings was to be rotated; 3) they committed to a consensus model of decision making; 4) conflict that might emerge would be directed toward renewal, restoration, and growth; and 5) each pastor was responsible for the collegium's decisions. The model was to be instituted only if the congregation committed to entering the shared ministry.

Cearley elaborates by describing Montview's model as requiring diffused leadership. Importantly, where one of the three pastors acted, all had acted. Authority rested in the team, not the individual pastor. The concept of diffused leadership extended to the congregation. Power was to be shared not only within the clergy team but also with the congregation, who were to function individually as team members. After a trial period, 77 percent of the congregation voted on October 25, 1975, to accept the new pattern.[282]

As a measure of its uniqueness and the hope it symbolized for the congregation, Rev. William Keesecker, moderator of the General Assembly that year, was invited to preach at the co-pastors' installation service on December 28. Keesecker's presence as moderator symbolically gave the unusual staff arrangement the recognition and blessing of the entire denomination. A full evaluation of the collegial style of ministry was conducted again in 1978, and the congregation concurred with session to continue it by a vote of 219 to 72, again, three quarters of the voting membership.[283]

Foresberg, in front of the entire General Assembly in his nominating speech just two years after this confirmation, highlights Allen's role in this unique model of staffing, describing it as "inconceivable." Certainly Foresberg's five-minute time limit in 1980 did not allow him to fill out the details of the model, but the adjective is not much of an exaggeration. Considering that less than a handful of congregations had instituted models of shared ministry, the ideas were not widely articulated or circulated. Additionally, because consensus determined a course of action and each of the three co-pastors was equally responsible for any decision that the team made, commissioners would have had a difficult time conceptualizing how consensus worked, functioning as they did by majority rule.

The idea of decision-making by consensus would have been especially foreign for many in Foresberg's 1980 audience who were members of congregations whose pastoral leadership was authoritarian, a common pattern at the time. What the senior pastor wanted, the senior pastor got. He (overwhelmingly a "he") was in charge. Majority rule itself was a stretch in congregations that functioned hierarchically, in which concurrence by session served, in effect, as a rubber stamp of the senior pastor's will. Even if Foresberg had given a more extended explanation of the co-pastorate, his description of the "inconceivable" leadership team of which Allen was a part might not have registered with all that many General Assembly commissioners.

Barley and Allen never felt the Denver Presbytery itself fully understood or affirmed the co-pastorate. Barley says presbytery "always resisted" it, because "they just couldn't understand how it could possibly work."[284] Allen notes that although Montview was one of the larger churches in the presbytery, a "big steeple church," the co-pastors were never fully accepted as "big steeple" pastors with the authority and power that often accrues to clergy in those positions. He says presbytery, including other clergy colleagues, just "didn't know what to do with us. We were seen strangely by other pastors, not as real pastors of a church."[285]

Cearley is also aware that people in other churches "made fun" of Montview for decades. She knows of correspondence between senior pastors and presbytery executives about "how silly Montview was, really hurtful things. Here's the cathedral church of the presbytery, and they've got these three yo-yos running it. They should have a big senior pastor in there."[286]

The daily milieu in which Allen worked at Montview, at times even puzzling to others in the Denver Presbytery, could not have been further from the tone of the 1980 confrontation that morning with the conservative pastors before the assembly began, nor from the push and pull between liberal and conservative forces at the assembly in which it seemed winner must take all. With his mention of the "inconceivable" co-pastorate, Foresberg did not communicate—perhaps could not—that what Allen brought to his candidacy were many of the elements that the assembly needed to overcome its own "division and hurt."

How close the Montview pastoral team came to the ideals of consensus and shared responsibilities outlined in the written record would depend on the personalities involved. Those who worked with Allen relate anecdotes that disclose the humanity of the co-pastorate, a quality that supported its success, and they tend to be humorous.

Barley says, "We accepted each other for what we were. Allen would fall asleep in worship when he wasn't preaching. He'd ordinarily sit behind the communion table in the center (on those Sundays), and everybody could see. He'd just nod off. Maybe he's narcoleptic. Then, again, maybe he was being inscrutable, in an Asian way. So I accepted it. 'That's just Allen being inscrutable. He's not really sleeping.' I never said, 'Allen, you have to stay awake!'"[287]

Cearley also refers to this behavior, but when she became a member of the co-pastor team, she approached it from a different perspective. Rather than describing it in a humorous tone, she noticed that Allen's bout with throat cancer in 1985 and the subsequent radiation treatments had depleted his energy. She concluded that the sleeping was symptomatic, and when she was sitting at the front with him and he would nod off, she would subtly shift position or move objects around to wake him.[288]

Rev. Harriet Isbell's memories of her time at Montview also convey these gracious aspects of the co-pastorate. Isbell was Cearley's predecessor as the staff member responsible for the education of children and youth, and her tenure overlapped that of both Hutchison and his successor, "Dusty" Taylor. Isbell was not an ordained minister at the time and was not routinely included in staff meetings. However, she felt that she too was included in the circle of the Head of Staff Team's enthusiastic support. She gives the youth mission trip each summer "to Mexico, North Carolina, all over" as an example. In particular, she remembers Allen instigating a massive annual garage sale to raise money for them. People would start bringing items six months before the sale, and "we'd make thousands of dollars to take with us on the trip."

As if to emphasize the incongruity between the "formal church, so Gothic," as Isbell describes it, and the staff congeniality, she tells the story of one summer Sunday when Allen was preaching and the two other co-pastors were away. The lay member who was to be the liturgist did not show. "Allen said, 'Harriet, you've got to be the liturgist.' And I answered, 'Well, it's summer, and I have on sandals and am not really dressed appropriately.'"

He told her to go find a robe. She located one and also went into the kindergarten room to grab the black heels the children used for playing dress-up. She and Allen were processing down the aisle, got to the steps going up to the chancel, and she lost one of the shoes. She "turned around, picked it up, and put it back on. He laughed about that. The relationships at Montview were very congenial."

Isbell, apparently not wanting to set Allen on an unrealistic pedestal, added that maybe there were some who did not appreciate him. She infrequently heard murmurs among members active in the children's education programs that perhaps he had been "in charge of something that had happened and they weren't pleased with how he handled it."[289] Not unexpected, given how active Allen was in promoting new ideas and how spontaneous he can be. Barley's take is that "Allen is a people person. There were very few people who disliked Allen that I knew."[290]

Two stories that church member Burkhart tells could also potentially imply that the members at Montview, many of whom think of themselves as fairly sophisticated, had varied reactions to someone as spontaneous as Allen. She introduces the first story after describing Allen as "very active" and "a caring person, always a dear, kind man." Those descriptors are followed immediately by her account of her daughter's wedding. Her daughter is "very tall" (six feet one), and her daughter's husband is six feet four. Allen stood on a milk crate "to be tall enough to look them in the eye, because he's so short."

Burkhart's story is reminiscent of Allen's humorous account of his experience as the shortest, by far, as a groomsman at the banker's daughter's wedding; however, the dynamics were different because he was officiating at the Burkhart wedding. The ceremony, moved from an outside garden due to rain, took place inside the tennis club, so the informality of the crate was not the negative it might have been in the formal sanctuary. Of more importance is the inference, first, that Allen thought to compensate for his height so the discrepancy would not distract from the ceremony and, second, that, his eye-to-eye interaction with the bride and groom took priority over the mechanism (the crate) he used to achieve it.

Moreover, Montview's tradition of outreach also values looking at situations and people "in the eye" and stepping forward when needed, a characteristic that emerges in Burkhart's second story. She was part of the Catering Crew. It had its beginning at one of the Palm Sunday breakfasts when the paid chef had a heart attack during the preparation. The ambulance crew carried him out of the church kitchen on a gurney, and Burkhart stepped in. Her first task: make muffins, six hundred of them!

She and two other cooks eventually expanded their catering to the point of preparing meals for such occasions as presbytery meetings when they were held in churches without adequate kitchens, for Senior Support Services in downtown Denver, and for Central Presbyterian Church's men's shelter. "A big cook" meant five thousand meals on a single Saturday.

Reflecting on Allen's spontaneity, Burkhart remembers that when the Catering Crew had ideas for projects, Allen was the one to say, "'Do it.' He never hesitated." Perhaps some members and staff would have preferred hesitation, when considering not only the Catering Crew's projects but also the many activities Montview supported. From Burkhart's perspective, though, "you could always count on him to find a way to help."[291]

To give perspective on the extent of Burkhart's own energetic activities at Montview, Allen notes that she was the one to "organize all the dinners, and she had, like, fifteen people working in the kitchen with others helping serve." Over the years, the Catering Crew's operations were considerable.[292]

Isbell emphasizes another dimension of Allen's ministry at Montview. She saw him as "the one people called on when there was illness or things that needed pastoral care. Allen was part of making that formal church real because he did so much of the pastoral care for the congregation."

She offers herself as an example of Allen's insights and responsiveness. She turned to him when staying in her marriage became unbearable. "My husband would come home drunk and say, 'You know, I couldn't ever kill my children, but I wouldn't have any trouble killing you!'"

Allen's response: "'You get out of that house right now! You and the children can come and stay with us.'

"And I said, 'You're right. I need to leave. But I'm going [home] to North Carolina.'" She did return to North Carolina, attended Duke Divinity School, and was ordained as a Presbyterian minister. She served a congregation in the Chapel Hill area for years.[293]

Isbell characterizes Allen's personality as one of "go, go, go," and that would not appeal to every congregant's temperament. However, in times of personal distress and emergency, complete pastoral engagement and a quick response such as Allen's can be life-giving and life-saving.

Upon Hutchison's departure in 1980, session again solicited congregational feedback about the "collegiate" model. A number of members wrote letters, and one refers to the 1978 congregational vote to continue it. The writer reminds session that approval was based on the feeling that "all three pastors were liked, and there was no desire to designate any one over the other two." Furthermore, the co-pastorate is the "best situation for church members because each member can take from each minister what they want. The sermons every Sunday are something to look forward to. . . . The different personalities and interests of the co-pastors have created an environment in which most of the members are able to find one to whom they relate comfortably."

A staff member notes that the co-pastors are "so kind and helpful" and are equally accessible, which creates a feeling of equality among the entire staff, a sentiment that echoes Isbell's experience. Yet another writer reminds session that the church committed originally to a model that has worked well, not to three individuals. They learned to work together. By implication, a new, third personality can also learn, and the model itself should not be abandoned.

The theme of how the model highlights Montview's unique strengths emerges in several letters. It is "wonderful that Montview has been innovative and explored new patterns." This theme is expanded by the person who writes: "The co-pastor model enhances a great strength of Montview—its well-informed, articulate, and highly motivated laity. It enables involvement and responsibility, and allows a better opportunity for hiring a woman minister."

One letter specifically addresses the contemporaneous circumstances of Allen's 1980 run for moderator. It is a "huge advantage for all ministers on staff to have approximately equal knowledge of all activities. It allows for better support when one is involved elsewhere, as with Allen's preparation for General Assembly."

Concerns about the co-pastorate's future do emerge in these letters to session. One is that a third pastor "might not be as well qualified as these two fine men" (Barley and Allen). Also, another notes that the original team was comprised of "three unselfish ministers not seeking power, unusually open-minded, cooperative, and free of jealousies" and hopes that a new, "third person with these qualities can be found."

Others were not as hopeful about a newcomer being "as well qualified as these two fine men" who "both give excellent sermons." Accordingly, "Barley and Maruyama are up to the task [subsequent to Hutchison's resignation], as though they, combined, are the 'head man.'" The writer proposes that an assistant be hired for them and a modified version of the model be continued with just the two, Barley and Maruyama, acting as "senior."

Another proposed option was to revisit the senior pastor model and elevate one of the two. However, this writer admits the proposal might not be viable because "neither Barley nor Maruyama wants a 'promotion' to a senior position that would result in more administrative duties." In addition, if the church were "to revisit the scheme of a senior minister model, no one should be brought in to supersede Rev. Barley or Dr. Maruyama. Then, again, how would we choose between these two good men?"[294]

The outcome of all the back and forth was congregational affirmation of the co-pastor model. Session hired Taylor, the second woman to be ordained as a teaching elder in Denver Presbytery. Her ordination had taken place in 1975, shortly after that of the first woman, Rev. Betsy Muldrow, spouse of Bill Muldrow, Allen's close friend from university days. Initially, Taylor was the interim third member of the collegium, and the congregation subsequently hired her to fill the position permanently. The prescient letter writer who wished for such an outcome, the "opportunity of hiring a woman minister," was surely pleased.

Allen, Barley, and Hutchison had stabilized the pastorate at Montview, but parallel to the ebb and flow of activity at the church was Allen's involvement in a dynamically changing Denver Presbytery. As Barley mentioned, each of the three had their own areas of interest: Hutchison, the educator; Allen, the pastor; and Ken, the administrator and "social action guy." Similarly, the three had different levels of involvement in the presbytery, Hutchison and Allen being more involved than Barley.[295]

Rev. Larry Angus, Allen's close friend and campaign manager for his 1980 candidacy for moderator of General Assembly, summarizes Allen's increasingly active role. Angus was called by the Wheat Ridge Presbyterian Church in 1973, one year after Allen's arrival in Denver. He had served as an associate pastor in Greeley, Colorado, and prior to that, as an associate in a large church in Oklahoma, his home state. The Oklahoma congregation had integrated its summer Bible school and also started an integrated coffee house. Angus says, "We'd have anywhere from a hundred to two hundred kids every week [in Bible school]. The First Baptist Church started their own coffeehouse and said there were not to be any blacks. Can you believe that?"

When Angus moved to Greeley, he expected to continue this kind of inclusive outreach. The opposite happened, and he became increasingly disappointed with ministry, to the point of wanting to leave the profession. The immediate cause was that the minister's wife "turned charismatic," and "before long, so did my boss." They pressured him to do the same, that is, to adopt such demonstrations of the presence of God's spirit by "speaking in tongues" and "faith healing." The church "turned very conservative. I wasn't sure I ever wanted to be a minister again. . . . It was awful, . . . a very judgmental, hateful kind of thing."

When the Wheat Ridge church in suburban Denver approached him, though, he agreed to an interview. The church was "dying on the vine," but based on the strengths he saw in its members, he decided to give ministry another try and "was there for thirty years."

When he moved to the Denver Presbytery, what Angus saw happening "was a relief," even though conservatives had come to dominate the presbytery in the five or so years before his arrival. By using the word "conservative," Angus simply means "biblical fundamentalists, not the charismatics" that he faced in Greeley. Reassuringly, Allen and several other ministers had started meeting monthly, usually at Montview, to strategize about ways to rebalance the presbytery's orientation and guarantee that progressives had a voice.

Angus saw Allen as "being highly respected" by the group. Angus notes that Allen transferred his skill as a member of Montview's co-pastor staff that "keeps everybody communicating" to his participation in the presbytery. "He's subtle. His leadership style is not direct. He moves where he needs to move and presents his ideas."

By "progressive/liberal," Angus means both a liberal theological and social stance, but the "real issue with our group was more, 'Who is going to run the presbytery?'" The gathering grew to at least twenty or thirty ministers, and they were dubbed the "Raucous Caucus." Their members became increasingly involved in presbytery activities. Angus attributes Allen's election as moderator of the presbytery in 1979 to the advocacy of the caucus.

According to Angus, the activities of the Raucous Caucus continued for about twenty to twenty-five years before a new presbytery executive came in and told them they were being divisive and not helping the presbytery. Caucus members "voluntarily stepped back and let it be." This happened several years after Allen's 1992 retirement.[296]

Allen provides yet more background on the origins of the caucus, which he attributes to Hill. When Hill arrived in Denver from New York in 1969, "presbytery was overjoyed to have a man of such stature become a member. He surrounded himself with the liberal pastors [of the presbytery] and shortly brought with him Richard Hutchison, who was also a very charismatic kind of person. Between the two of them, they developed a following of at least a half dozen pastors from good churches around Denver. That's when the Raucous Caucus developed and why presbytery consistently voted to back Fay [Hill]."[297]

Angus emphasizes that the three churches that left the denomination during Allen's tenure as presbytery moderator in 1979 were "ultra conservative. They didn't like anything about the Presbyterian church because of all the issues, particularly abortion. The Presbyterian church was basically for choice at that time. Since then it has gone back and forth, but all those issues of abortion, civil rights, evolution . . . were tossing around. A lot of churches were withdrawing. And Allen had been in the thick of it [the controversies in Denver] before he ran for Moderator of the General Assembly [in 1980]."

From Angus' perspective, the conservative/liberal tension was an undercurrent in Allen's candidacy, "but whether you won or lost depended on your candidating speech. It wasn't like you could campaign much before you got there." He says the extent of Allen's pre-assembly campaigning consisted of a committee in Denver Presbytery who worked to get him nominated by the presbytery and to commit all six of its delegates elected to General Assembly to cast their votes for him. Most of the campaigning outside the presbytery was limited to members of the campaign committee calling ministers with whom they were acquainted "all over the world" and saying, "'Hey, who is your delegate? I want to send some information about Allen, a really dynamic person.' A kind of underground politicking. Then when you get there you have a booth and campaign buttons to pass out."[298]

As mentioned, Allen visited Dubuque Theological Seminary, where the reaction to him was "hostile." He also visited his other alma mater, Mc-Cormick Theological Seminary, as part of his campaign strategy. Friends of his associated with San Francisco Theological Seminary advocated for him there. "Hutch [Hutchinson], a graduate of Princeton Seminary, and Ken [Barley], a graduate of Pittsburgh Seminary, solicited support for me from those institutions."[299] In addition to the Denver Presbytery's endorsement, John Knox Presbytery also supported him.[300]

Angus emphasizes, "It was an honor that the presbytery twice [again in 1990] would choose him to run for moderator [of the General Assembly], because it's not Allen's decision. It has to be the decision of the presbytery whether you run or not."[301]

Despite the challenges at Montview, perhaps as an outgrowth of them, the Presbyterian church had indeed been good to Allen. He was in place when Montview chose the innovative co-pastor model, one which suited Allen's temperament well. While the Denver presbytery was not always consistent in its support of the model, neither did it uniformly view the co-pastors as "three yo-yos," because it put forth Allen twice as its nominee for moderator of the General Assembly. The hope in 1980 was that he would follow in the footsteps of Miller, another of its favorite sons and moderator of the 1959 assembly.

Chapter 15

Chosen

TRANSITIONING TO THE SECOND half of his candidating speech, Allen builds on biographical information that emphasizes his dedication to the Presbyterian church. He says, "I was born a Buddhist, I chose Jesus Christ as my Lord and Savior, and I have committed myself to his service in his church."

In the next sentence, he pivots from his focus on himself to highlight the characteristics he so values about the church: "And I believe in the United Presbyterian Church because it is a church of justice and righteousness. It's a church that's been faithful to its witness, its mission, and message."

Having established that the church has been constant in its commitments, Allen pledges his loyalty, in turn. He proclaims that, "I shall seek to help to serve to lead it always in paths of faithful service."

Allen has disclosed before the assembly who he is in the first half of his speech. Now he reminds the gathered representatives of the United Presbyterian Church (UPC) who they are and what he and they can become and accomplish together in "paths of faithful service."

He intensifies his pledge by switching to an exhortatory mode in the sentences that follow. In them, he introduces a passage of Scripture, a reference to church history, and draws out their implications for what the church must be and do.

"Peter says, 'You're a chosen race, a royal priesthood, a holy nation, God's own people' [1 Pet 2:9–10]. Yes, we Presbyterians know in good Scottish Calvinistic tradition that we are God's own people and we can battle against principalities and powers. We believe we are God's own people, and we stand for human rights and peace and justice for all."[302]

At first glance, Allen's segue from a biographical mode to an exhortatory one is somewhat jarring. Perhaps he thought the parallels between the church's stand for human rights and the story he has told about the church's acceptance of him as a Japanese-American teenager, as well as of him as a successful pastor, did not need elaboration. Also seemingly self-evident were the connections between his life and these familiar Scripture passages and images.

The tone in this section of his speech also changes. It moves away from a personal, almost conversational one, to a quality of lament. In biblical literature, lament is often a plea to God that the divine self remember its identity and act accordingly to relieve pain and suffering. In effect, Allen laments before the General Assembly that, just as he has proclaimed who he is, the church must declare who it is by standing for "human rights and peace and justice."

In these paragraphs, he recaps his progress from his childhood Buddhist background to his acceptance of Jesus Christ as Lord and Savior. Such acceptance necessarily means commitment to Christ's service and his church, in Allen's case, in its particular manifestation as the UPC. For him, commitment embodies service to Christ within the structure of the UPC because it is a church whose message is Christ's message—one of justice and righteousness. Moreover, it is faithful to its witness to Christ in that it fulfills its mission; its actions and message cohere. It lives what it proclaims. Allen asserts that his leadership will move the church along those familiar paths of faithful service.

He has traced how his Christian identity superseded his Buddhist one, and he has reminded those gathered before him of their shared Scottish Presbyterian heritage. In this section, he starts with the theological basics—the image of the church in 1 Peter as a chosen race, a royal priesthood, a holy nation, God's own people—and includes a reference to Calvin, the Presbyterians' spiritual ancestor of the sixteenth century. He emphasizes that any distinctions derived from human designations of race are erased by the new heritage all Christians share as God's chosen race. No countervailing forces are stronger than the sweeping movement of God's chosen people, as long as it stays faithful to its mission of human rights, peace, and justice, which is based on its correlated message of justice and righteousness.

If the audience remembered their Bible lessons, they would be hearing that Allen was emphasizing the message of 1 Peter that being "chosen" means to understand and live the "direct connection" between "faith and conduct," between "doctrine and ethics." Although attributed to the apostle

Peter, they would remember that this letter was likely not written until the end of the first century of the Common Era and was addressed to persecuted Christians in Asia Minor to assure them of their future as a "spiritual house."

As those early Christians were identified to be a holy priesthood, nation, or people, terms used in the Hebrew Bible to refer to Israel, Allen is reminding the General Assembly of its identity and purpose. As were those in Asia Minor, Christians in Detroit are the "spiritual society of Jesus," and their calling is to live blameless lives, submissive to Christ and following his example of patience, love, and even suffering in his service. They have been chosen not be be an exclusive people, but to be a people who serve with an attitude of humility.

In these paragraphs, Allen seems to be recomposing his biography in theological terms in parallel to the church's biography. Having been born into a Buddhist family, he has been reborn into a Christian one with distinctive values and a purpose derived from them. This transformation to "God's chosen race" is vivid and significant for Allen, but it contrasts somewhat with the transformation of those early Christians in Asia Minor to whom 1 Peter is addressed. Their new status as Christians made them aliens in a surrounding culture that was familiar to them, a culture of which they had been a part. The words of 1 Peter direct them, as a consequence of this new and threatening exposure, to live exemplary and humble lives. Being chosen is not "grounds for complacency" but a "challenge to live a holy and obedient life."[303]

The Maruyama family's conversion had inadvertently meant a movement in the opposite direction. They were no longer members of a minority, Japanese-Buddhist aliens in the surrounding white society, but Buddhists-become-Christian, received into the religious majority. Because Allen communicates his spiritual journey in traditional biblical images and does not make the point more explicit, the audience might have heard these all-too-familiar biblical words as part of a straightforward sermon about the connection between "divine revelation and human action" rather than the spiritual biography that it was.

The underlying details are these. Allen has distinct memories as a very young child of the little statue of the Buddha that his mother kept in the cupboard. In those days, Mrs. Maruyama "made regular offerings to the Buddha," and "she had regular meditation with the Buddha." She was demonstrably religious, but his father was not.[304]

Mr. Maruyama might not have expressed his beliefs overtly, but it was this same "liberal Buddhist father," as Allen describes him, who gave permission to the Purvis family to take the Maruyama children to the Presbyterian church's Sunday school in Las Animas. The outcome was, as Allen has just told the audience seated before him, that the whole family eventually became Christian. In this section of his speech, Allen seemingly implies this transition came with a shift in "race." The Asian "race" (as well as the white), is a limiting category that at times in his life has led to emotional injury and exclusion. This "race" is superseded by the more expansive "chosen race" and its accompanying responsibilities that he shares with those in Cobo Hall and in the churches they represent.

In the present, in his 90s, when he retraces his spiritual journey, he returns time and again to the Las Animas church and the conferences of his youth. "My idea of God did not come into existence until I went to the Presbyterian church, when all the Maruyama and Purvis children went to Sunday school and church on a regular basis."

His marks the beginning of his spiritual life as a member of this "chosen race" with the "awesome influence of those summer church conferences" in junior high. He characterizes them as "mainline, not conservative" and as following a common pattern, apparently based on structures developed by the national church. The routines included fellowship with "a lot of playing," teaching the young people to pray, by which he means, "to learn to communicate in their own way with God," and integrating the relationships the young people developed with one another with "the meaning of Jesus Christ." Relationship lay at the core. Most "impressive" were the lifestyles, love, and openness of the pastors, teachers, and leaders in the youth fellowship, church school, and at the conferences. "They were not only friends, but more like parents, really family."[305]

The summer conferences drove his spiritual development, and Allen never tires of repeating these experiences. He passed on their traditions as a counselor himself at the junior high camps when he was in high school and, after the war, when he was a university student and leader at senior high conferences in the mountains west of Boulder. Even as a young pastor in Wisconsin, he "put together" and led youth camps at Onaway every summer. He says the setting was ideal "because once the youth got on the boat and landed on the island, there was no way they could get off!" On a more serious note, "it got to be a very special place for everybody."[306]

Relationship remains central in his spiritual development even when he specifically discusses theology. While he characterizes his pre-seminary beliefs as "pretty basic," when Rose asked if he ever questioned his beliefs, his answer emphasized how intertwined belief was with his relationship to those admired figures of church leaders who were "more like family. . . . I wouldn't question any of those beliefs because that's what I was taught. To question them would have been kind of heretical in the context of a summer conference environment. There you're inspired to deepen your prayer life, your communication with God in worship. That was more important than questioning the confessions of the church. I had no problem with the whole business of Calvin's idea about original sin. Even when I got to McCormick Seminary, the basic structure of the confessions of the church was the foundation of my faith."[307]

However, McCormick was a "very big change, a big step in my spirituality. When I went to seminary, I was very conservative." In addition to not questioning the confessions of the church, recall that "conservative," in his terms, meant an emphasis on individual morality and literal biblical interpretation.

This "big step" was prompted by his exposure to neo-orthodoxy. He characterizes many seminaries affiliated with mainline churches in those years as facing its "onslaught." He embraced it wholeheartedly. When Allen distills neo-orthodoxy's influence on him, he focuses on "the whole difference in the interpretation of the Bible, a more liberal interpretation of the Bible with an understanding of its cultural context." For him, that interpretive method spilled over to a deeper understanding of the church's confessions, that is, "as representing ancient, historic positions of the church reflective of the backgrounds out of which they came." He associates this method with the "whole transition of how literature was being interpreted, an emancipation of literature itself."[308]

Neo-orthodoxy's influence emerges in his 1980 candidating speech in that it posits humanity as basically sinful, both individually and in its organizational structures, which leads to an awareness of institutional and structural injustices and to a motivation to ameliorate such injustices as economic exploitation and racism. From this perspective, of course Allen would proclaim in his speech that God's own people "stand for human rights and peace and justice for all." Theologically literate members of Allen's Cobo Hall audience and the majority of those listening who attended seminary during the years that neo-orthodoxy exerted its influence would be familiar with and sympathetic to these values and recognize them in his assertions.

Allen mentions specific theologians who influenced him throughout his ministry, particularly neo-orthodox ones such as Joseph Haroutunian and Reinhold and Richard Niebuhr. Another influence Allen mentions is Paul Tillich, a contemporary of the Neibuhrs whose name is not associated with the neo-orthodox movement; rather, Tillich's work was focused on correlating philosophy and theology.[309]

When Allen delivers his 1980 speech, seminary and his work on his master's and doctoral degrees are not that far in his past. His speech reflects these theologians' continuing influence from McCormick in the early 1950s, Dubuque Theological Seminary in the mid-1960s, and his extensive use of their work in his dissertation in the early 1970s. The candidating speech is a dense compression of these influences.

In conversation, Allen is quick to add that, as emancipating as seminary was for him personally, he was very cautious about not upsetting members he served in the little churches in northern Wisconsin in the 1950s upon his graduation. He had come to know that entertaining different viewpoints and questioning his prior beliefs did not mean he was "going to hell," but "those people had such a simple ABC understanding about Christianity, I didn't want to upset them. . . . I used to think when people said, 'Oh, Christianity is just about doing to others as you would have them do unto you,' that is such a simplistic view of faith and Christian ethics. But I didn't want to break that up. It's better than nothing." Again, his concern to nurture relationships dominates, in this case, his with church members and theirs with their faith community.

By 1980, though, Allen's experiences, reputation, the office he sought, and the issues the church had been dealing with throughout the 1960s and 1970s meant he did not hesitate to articulate a more complex theology with its implications. On the one hand, in wording his choice of "Jesus Christ as my Lord and Savior" and his commitment to "his service and his church," he is speaking the language of, and directly to, the concerns of the conservative pastors' caucus and devout readers of *The Presbyterian Layman*.

On the other hand, when Allen asserts that the stance of the church is one for "human rights and peace and justice for all," he shifts to another perspective. "Human rights" could have been heard as code for a number of decisions taken by prior General Assemblies to support causes of "oppressed peoples" worldwide.

When Chapman, in his article in *The Presbyterian Layman* the prior year, had excoriated the General Assembly for its grants to the World Council of Churches Programme to Combat Racism, he was not alone in this perspective. He used the money the Council gave to the Patriotic Front in Zimbabwe as an example of the pitfalls of "theologies of liberation which inventively portray Jesus of Nazareth as hardly more than an early-day Che Guevara," that is, the equivalent of political revolutionaries. He had castigated the Presbyterian Church as one of those "fashionably liberal denominations" that give their money with no strings attached to "aggressively radical third-world Protestants, mostly from Africa and Asia," the "poor non-whites" who end up controlling the spending. Allen's emphasis on human rights, peace, and justice for all could be heard by those with Chapman's biases as simply justifying support for these movements.[310]

Also, Allen's name was tied to liberation theology due to his membership on the General Assembly's Special Committee on the Theology of

Liberation and Renewal (1975–77) and its 1977 report. In the event any-one had forgotten his involvement, the denominational publication *The Presbyterian Outlook,* which had published a profile of the five candidates and their views on May 26, 1980, had referred to his membership on that committee.[311]

Allen still marks that service and its report as a major influence on his theology. An expanded discussion about what he saw as liberation theology's implications was reported in a 1977 interview with Virginia Culver, the religion editor of *The Denver Post.* First, he offers the report's definition of liberation theology as seeing "the suffering of oppressed people as a real and central concern for believers in Jesus Christ. It sees this concern theo-logically, that is, as God's own concern . . . that emerges out of oppressed people's need to be free."[312]

Second, he is specific in the *Post* interview that economic, political, and social suffering experienced by people in less affluent countries has its source in the oppressive practices of affluent countries that depend on cheap labor from the less affluent. In addition, theological oppression is intertwined with economic, political, and social suffering because the Christianity that was imposed on other cultures during European expan-sion (colonization) had "transposed Christianity's Jewish roots to fit an ex-clusively white, European context." In contrast, liberation theologians strive to fit Christianity into whatever culture it finds itself, rather than imposing this "European look." Their method of accomplishing this is "action and reflection," which they call "practice" (praxis).[313]

This viewpoint sounds similar to the one Allen expressed in 1972 in his interview with Tighe in Dubuque's *Telegraph Herald* in that Allen already understood a basic orientation of liberation theology prior to im-mersing himself in his work on the committee in the mid-1970s. In the 1972 interview, he had said, "The church determines its witness and its mission by the agenda of the world [including the cultural context in which it finds itself] rather than the church determining what that agenda should be."[314]

By the time he became thoroughly familiar with liberation theology through his work on the committee and was giving his Cobo Hall candidat-ing speech, he would have had no trouble embracing this perspective that valued evangelism and mission as growing out of community need rather than as being imposed. In contrast to Chapman's orientation, from Allen's perspective, third-world Protestants should most definitely control the decision-making and spending in their own communities.

In her 1977 article, Culver reports that Allen is excited by liberation theology's implications as a tool for evangelism and by its potential to "cre-ate tremendous pluralism" in the church of the twenty-first century. Just as "Martin Luther emancipated people from religious bondage," liberation theology will "emancipate people from social, political, and economic bondage." He does note that freeing people who are suffering economic oppression poses a real threat to "European whites" because they will lose access to all that cheap labor.[315]

Allen's profile in *The Presbyterian Outlook* in May also included a summary of his "General Statement on Issues before the Church." As with the candidates' speeches, the summaries of their positions in the *Outlook* are compressed versions without much of the context of commitments and thought processes they had developed over time. For his summary, Allen had written that he "would like to see the 192nd General Assembly continue to further the goals of eliminating racial and sexist discrimination in its personal and corporate life." Furthermore, it should "move ahead on issues of justice and peace. . . . Peacemaking, reconciliation, and living with pluralism" are "necessary steps toward progress in the 1980s," again, terminology embracing the majority of the General Assembly's commitments but also clear indicators of what might be inferred as a liberal stance.

Allen's appropriation of the 1 Peter image of the church as "God's chosen race," with its implications that ethics and doctrine are inseparable, might have washed over the ears of many of the people in Cobo Hall as a familiar Bible quotation. His application of the image to the church's mission as being one of human rights, peace, and justice, not for just some but for everyone, might have caught their attention, though. The speech reinforced the emphasis he had placed on "peacemaking, reconciliation, and living with pluralism," all relational terms, from the *Outlook* summary.

Also of note in this section of his speech is the string of verbs Allen uses to offer his candidacy and express his intent. He does not say, "I shall lead the denomination always in paths of faithful service." Rather, he says "I shall seek to help to serve to lead the denomination always in paths of faithful service." In his estimation, leadership is not an assertion of one's will; it is entirely relational. It rests on seeking, which implies collaboration and building consensus. Leadership rests on helping, which implies empowerment of others. It is service, which means obligation and responsibility, not an expectation that one will be served.

Compressing one's biography, spiritual journey, and vision for an entire denomination for the coming year into a five-minute speech is daunting. The temptation might be to rely on these well-known phrases and Bible verses as the only sufficient way to express one's faith and to exhort the audience to remember who they are, to what they owe allegiance, and to act accordingly.

The danger lies in the familiarity of the words. As a crowd the size of the one in Cobo Hall rustles and strains to hear, the well-worn phrases might simply drift past. Allen is using them in all earnestness, though, because they best express what he believes to be true. The faithful service in which he seeks to lead them as a "chosen race" is to maintain coherence between their message of justice and righteousness and their mission of peace and human rights.

Chapter 16

The Inclusive Church I Love

ALLEN'S INTENTION IN FRONT of those gathered before him in 1980 is not to protect them from the complexities of faith and practice as he felt he should do for members in the small Wisconsin churches in the 1950s. The people attending the assembly are leaders in their presbyteries and synods and are presumably in Detroit expecting to be challenged. Accordingly, he extends and intensifies his exhortatory tone in the next section of his speech to impress upon them what it means to be chosen for service. Not only must the church's spoken message and mission cohere, so must its witness, its behavior. To make this point, he offers another familiar image of the church—the body of Christ.

He proclaims that "The Presbyterian church is a church I love because it is part of the body of Christ, and as his body we witness to unity and love. Paul said, 'The hand cannot say to the foot I have no need of you or the ear to the eye I have no need of you' [paraphrase of verses in 1 Cor 12].

"Quite the contrary. God has so adjusted the body that there is no discord. If one member suffers, we all suffer. If one is honored, we all rejoice. We are the body of Christ, individually members of it. And it's an inclusive body. As Paul said, 'There is neither Jew nor Greek, neither male nor female, neither slave nor free, for we are one in Christ'" (Gal 3:28).

Whereas the "chosen race" image might imply a singular identity that subordinates difference and diversity to accomplish a task, the body metaphor highlights the interaction and mutual dependency of its distinct parts. To be members of the same body does not mean suffocating variety of thought and function, nor does diversity of parts undermine the possibility of unity. By enlisting this image and pairing it with the one of "chosen race," Allen completes his plea for an identity that includes both unity and diversity.

Allen engages the two representations to address his concern about the various divisions within the church that have grown into such hostile camps. His approach, dependent as it is on familiar biblical references, will surely remind the delegates who they are and whom they serve.

He continues, "The body recognizes that there is no difference between the physical and spiritual. The body knows in its rich heritage to learn to live together as conservative and moderate and liberal because we are one Lord, one faith, one baptism, one God and Father of us all. We're the people of God and part of the body of Christ, and I believe it. We must live in unity and peace."

Again, his words border on lament, that is, a plea that the UPC wholeheartedly claim its identity and act accordingly. In case anyone is taking the body analogy only literally, he emphasizes that there is no difference between the physical and spiritual. The various ideological factions of the body of Christ—charismatic, conservative, moderate, liberal—must function together just as the various parts of a physical body do, in order to be a viable whole. He does not chide the audience for their divisions. He accepts them, but these divisions need not result in fracture. Rather, he pleads that the various factions remember that they must live together peacefully and constructively.

Angus thought the divisions between the conservative and liberal camps might have been simply an undercurrent of the assembly, but liberal and conservative positions and pleas for unity are identified so many times in the speeches and written materials that the enmity has to be taken seriously. That Allen is calling for "unity and peace" as the past moderator of the Denver Presbytery when churches withdrew, and as the first Japanese American, so disparaged during World War II, to stand for moderator of the General Assembly, Allen has lived the negative outcomes of division and difference. Difference need not lead to alienation, though. Just as the images of the church as a "chosen race" and as the "body of Christ" seem to pull in opposite directions, toward uniformity on the one hand and variability on the other, in his person, he bridges the seeming contradiction. The church can simultaneously embraces unity and difference without descending into conflict and rejection.

He asserts that the church is not just any physical body, though. It is the body of Christ, and in it he has found "family" and a home. The "chosen race" and "body of Christ" images together underscore the implications of being closely knit, akin to the family affiliation he felt when growing up in the Las Animas church. In offering these differing biblical images of the church, Allen suggests a way to embrace and respect division and difference, just as he was embraced, without discarding the value of unity. He implies that a conservative member suffers if a liberal does, and vice versa. When one is honored, all rejoice. Members do not have to abandon their positions or beliefs, but they must remember they are part of the one body and honor those who hold differing positions.

He has already described how crucial it was that the church befriended him in his adolescent distress when the surrounding culture identified him as "alien" during the war. Moreover, he has noted that the pastor of his youth was wrong when he doubted that Allen would serve only ethnic churches. On the contrary, the UPC has offered multiple opportunities for service, thereby reflecting the church as one body that embraces difference. "It has been good to me." If they have not yet grasped the meaning of his remarks, he is now reminding them that the apostle Paul spoke and wrote the same encouraging words and offered the image of one inclusive body to the early church in the face of its divisions, an image of itself that Allen urges the General Assembly to recapture.

Allen embodies the link between "God's chosen people" and the "body of Christ"—unity in service strengthened by diversity in function. By implication, he invites those listening to make a similar move. Being part of "God's chosen people" is not a privilege but a call to service. He has made that commitment to "his service in his church," not because the Presbyterian church is an inert organization but because it is a live entity. "It is a part of the body of Christ." He is motivated to love it for any number of reasons, among them its faithfulness "to its witness, its mission, and message." Again, he does not criticize but offers a vision of reciprocity in which a church faithful to its message and mission encourages and equips its variety of members, in turn, to be faithful to one another in their unified commitment to serve.

Just as the prior section of his speech focused on the image of the church as a "chosen people" but did not convey underlying personal detail, in these paragraphs he relies on familiar biblical phrases and the image of the "body of Christ" at the expense of incorporating personal information. His speech might have carried more weight had he explicitly disclosed some of the biographical details that lay behind his choice of these images.

He could have spoken about how he lived into the reciprocity of unity and difference most overtly in Dubuque in the 1960s where he and his family say he "came into his own" as a pastor. Allen consistently attributes this "high point in my ministry" to any number of historical and cultural factors: an era of rapid change, the expansion of human understanding of its place in the universe with the moon landing, the opening up of the Roman Catholic church, the civil rights movement in which the nation at least gestured toward realizing its declaration of the value of human equality under God, the positive publicity growing out of his association with the Council of Churches that pressed for improving the deplorable conditions at the jail and the county home, his advocacy for disaffected youth, and the strength and community reputation of the Westminster Presbyterian Church itself.

The Sixties was a decade of awakening—scientifically, culturally, socially, and spiritually. Segments of the church were grappling with all of it, as was he. Those segments matched the energy and commitments of his "go, go, go" personality. He engaged the church wholly, even if that meant sometimes challenging the laggards, for instance, by telling the Dubuque *Tribune Herald* editor that the church's traditional structures proved outdated in the face of those rapid changes. He cautioned that the church must take the initiative to meet people's needs, physical and spiritual, or risk being seen as a "fossilized institution."

By the time of the 1980 speech, he approaches the need for the church to take the initiative by highlighting what it is called to be, not by chiding the General Assembly for its division and failures or threatening what it risks if it is not faithful to its mission. By using the image of the church as the embodiment of Christ, he proclaims that the essence of the church is not "fossilized" but dynamic and reciprocal among its various parts.

Having made his case, he approaches a conclusion by explicitly naming "conservative," "moderate," and "liberal" factions and proclaiming them all to be people of God, called to service, and unified as part of the body of Christ. Living together in unity and peace is not a matter of choice; it is basic to maintaining the UPC's identity. These words cap his logic and plea that the church reclaim who it is. They sound like his conclusion.

However, he does not stop. "Like a few other presbyteries, the presbytery of Denver has paid the price to be Presbyterian, to be faithful to our tradition, to have integrity in our mission, and yet we must seek the peace and unity of the church. I'm confident that's why I'm here, my friends. I'm a product of mission, and I symbolize mission in the whole United Presbyterian Church. Thank you."[316]

At first glance, the initial sentence of this final paragraph takes an abrupt turn. The mention of the troubles in the Denver Presbytery seems to negate the conclusion to which he was headed, one of unity and peace. He circles around after mentioning Denver, though, and ties together how he represents the church's mission in his person as a Japanese American Buddhist child who was accepted into membership in God's "chosen race";

in his dedication to its mission and message of human rights, peace and justice; and the promise of God's people moving into the future, unified in its diversity, as the body of Christ.

Rhetorically, there might have been advantages to bringing up the difficult subject of Denver's loss of several churches. If the conservative pastors who threatened Allen immediately before the General Assembly convened were representative of a widespread sentiment, that a massive walkout would result if he were elected, better that he acknowledge the difficulties in the Denver Presbytery with the hope of diffusing that sentiment.

These difficulties were at the forefront of conversations leading up to the General Assembly. In the May 26 issue of *The Presbyterian Outlook*, an article had focused on Denver. It spoke of Faith Presbyterian Church, the largest in the presbytery and second largest in the state, as being "the third church removed since September last." The article specifies that the presbytery would not co-sign a loan for a building expansion because Faith was not giving at least 51 percent of its missions budget to presbytery-approved causes. Specifically in reference to Faith, it "consistently rebuffed presbytery efforts to work out differences and seek reconciliation." The article represented the presbytery's difficulties as ongoing. It stated that a fourth church had also voted to secede, but presbytery had not taken action.[317]

If Allen had ignored the widely known problems faced by the Denver Presbytery, he might have been seen as hypocritical in light of his exhortations for peace and unity. To acknowledge the problems was also to establish rapport with any number of those in his audience. The issues confronting Denver were so widespread throughout the denomination that Allen's reference to them could have elicited understanding and a spirit of camaraderie.

Allen's conclusion goes a step further than simple acknowledgment of the pain the Denver Presbytery has sustained. As a leader who does not shy away from confronting difficult subjects, akin to that five-feet-two-inch high schooler tackling a six-feet-three-inch end, he reminds his audience there is a price for maintaining integrity as the body of Christ. The churches that willfully refuse to abide by General Assembly decisions (ordination of women, equitable financial support of mission projects, and so forth) and walk away do shatter the body's unity. If the General Assembly abides by its actions, there might be a price, and the Denver Presbytery is a cautionary tale about the consequences of that choice. Will the General Assembly put in the effort that dealing with these difficult issues requires, recognizing the potential cost? If the answer is yes, he is equipped by virtue of his experience to lead it through the morass.

On the other hand, choosing to mention Denver's woes and confronting those assembled with the reality of the hard work of reconciliation might have deflated his audience. Ending on the high note about "unity and peace" might have been a better strategy. Actually, on the notecards that Rose preserved from the speech and included in the album she put together of materials from the 1980 candidacy, the final paragraph referencing the price Denver has paid to maintain integrity does not appear. The last paragraph on the original notecards concludes with "We must live together in unity and peace." Allen does not remember the details of the speech, but he seems to have extemporized what became the final paragraph, perhaps in response to the earlier confrontation with the conservative pastors.

It is not realistic to think that the inspiring images of the church he has offered, images that have sustained it for millennia, and that sustained him thus far in his own ministry, do not carry challenges within them. Allen is a realist. As optimistic as he is with his assertion of the "good Scottish Calvinistic tradition's" confidence in battling "principalities and powers," claiming to be God's chosen race with the task of carrying a message of unity and peace is to be under constant siege in a world fractured by vying religious perspectives and traditions, ethnicities, races, gender representations, and national identities. When it comes to logistics, the body of Christ that is on a march for human rights, peace, and justice will continually encounter resistance and divisions along political, social, cultural, and economic lines.

After recognizing these realities, Allen asserts that he is the very person to lead the church through these complex and challenging times because he has survived them personally as a Japanese American and professionally as moderator of the Denver Presbytery. Not only has he survived, but, as the Montview church had observed, his leadership, based on consensus and service, brings healing. He does symbolize hope for unity in the church's mission.

These conclusions can be drawn in retrospect and after an analysis of his speech. However, it is doubtful that anyone other than Allen's family and Angus was paying close enough attention at the moment of its delivery to grasp why these familiar Scripture passages revealed so much about his passions and his spiritual journey. His remarks were probably simply accepted as a "nice" speech that passed the litmus tests of propriety and piety.

Chapter 17

The Candidates

ALLEN MAKES HIS REMARKS fourth in the order of the five candidates. To a person, they all sound similar themes of maintaining unity in diversity and offer various ways to achieve this goal.

The first candidate to be nominated and to speak is another clergyman, Charles Hammond, who has been active at presbytery and synod levels of the church. He is from Indiana and was introduced in the May *Outlook* article as being "all about the church preserving a variety of expressions without losing its unity."[318]

In his speech, he too calls the church his family, but the biblical images he develops come from the story of Jesus bringing Lazarus back to life. He says he chooses that story because his primary concern for the church is its declining membership. Only Jesus Christ can bring life back to the church. Following the example of Jesus, the church must first "roll away the stones" of class, privilege, race, and pride in the past that has resulted in the church facing its future unadvisedly, with fear. The church must also clear away "the rubble" lying between the "graceful word of God" and those needing to hear that word. Secondly, the church must unbind the grave clothes that prevent it from welcoming "those into our midst who are different." He pledges to be a moderator who will be a careful listener.

Second in the order is August John (Jack) Kling, a clergyman who was presented in the *Outlook* article as chairman of the Joint Hispanic Ministries of the South Florida Presbytery (1972–1976), editorial advisor for *The Presbyterian Layman* since 1969, and member of the Board of Directors of Presbyterians United for Biblical Concerns. He resides in Alabama and begins by greeting the commissioners with a few words in Spanish, which reinforces the information given about him in his nominating speech. In it he was introduced as one who can "unite the conservatives and the liberals" and as one who reaches out to "the stranger" in his ministry. As a pastor in Miami, he extended hospitality to Cuban refugees, spoke fluent Spanish, and paved the way for a Spanish-speaking pastor as his successor. He was also instrumental in seeing that a Spanish-speaking chaplain was hired at the area hospital, established a multiracial day care center, and was active in ecumenical leadership in Miami.

Following his greeting in Spanish, he quotes those who say he is a "model and warm pastor." This turns out to be a self-deprecating joke. He says he is only a model, not the real thing, and because he is just warm, he's "not so hot."

He moves into identifying five issues facing the 192nd General Assembly: 1) the disputes over the disposition of property when churches withdraw; 2) the commitment to education; 3) peacemaking, reinforced by the fact of the thirty overtures on that topic brought to the assembly for consideration; 4) the question of whether the church can grow again; and 5) spiritual renewal.

Rather than using a biblical image, he offers the analogy of bicycle repair to guide the church in how it should deal with these issues while maintaining its identity. The church is at the hub of the bicycle wheel, and balancing competing interests is like adjusting the spokes. As it makes these adjustments, the church needs to approach the task in the spirit of 1 Cor 13:13: "So faith, hope, love abide, these three; but the greatest of these is love."

The third candidate to speak is a ruling elder from Iowa, Louise Lyon, a registered nurse and teacher of thirty years. The *Outlook* had introduced her as a past president of the Iowa Parent Teachers Association and the League of Women Voters. In a strong, deliberate voice, she says she looks into the "vast space" of Cobo Hall before her and sees people who represent the "extravagance of God's love." Central to her speech is her story about the prior year. Her presbytery had asked if she would run for moderator, and her husband supported her. However, he died. She is humbled that, in spite of that loss, she stands before them, believing that "all things work together for good." As Allen does, she evokes the image of the church as the body of Christ and says "we have to be sensitive to the Spirit's leading." She cares more for the people behind the issues than the issues themselves.

Allen as the fourth speaker is followed by the fifth, a businessman and ruling elder named Earl L. Peterson. According to the *Outlook*, he has served

as executive director of United Way in Springfield, Missouri; in a number
of presbytery and synod positions; as past president of United Presbyterian
Men; and as member of the General Assembly Program Agency Board. He
cites the concern of the current moderator for the peace and unity of the
church and promises to deal with issues creatively, not destructively. He
urges those gathered to listen to each other carefully and to receive other
viewpoints with patience.

Allen, Kling, and Lyons are somewhat self-disclosing in a personable
manner. Peterson's speech, his written materials, and his answers to the
questions that are about to be put to the candidates are all marked by their
brevity, and Hammond typically expresses himself in generalities. Common
to each is an awareness that the issues the General Assembly is about to deal
with over the next several days are weighty and potentially divisive, and
they each, in their own way, are committed to leading in a manner that will
respect difference for the sake of unity.

An hour has been set aside for questions from the floor, again with
a time limit on the candidates' responses. They will continue in the same
order—Hammond, Kling, Lyon, Maruyama, and Peterson—but the starting
point for each successive question will rotate through the order.

The questions can be understood to reflect some of the primary
concerns of the 1980 General Assembly: peacemaking and nuclear disarmament; evangelism (what is it, of what value is it, and how do you do it, alluding to the widely shared concern about decline in church membership);
the candidates' positions on an overture that would dilute the requirement
to involve more women in positions of leadership by changing the wording in the *Book of Order* from the requirement that church bodies "elect"
women to serve to "nominate" them (none of the candidates support it);
and how often to hold the General Assembly in the interest of conserving
human and natural resources. Several of the questions repeat those asked
and answered in the May issue of the *Outlook*.

Curiously, one question flies in the face of the candidates' somber emphasis on unity in diversity. It lifts a statement from an unnamed candidate's
campaign publicity that a "rejection of this imminently qualified servant of
the church could be a signal to many that conservative evangelicals are unwelcome in our church." The commissioner asking the question says, "I would
like each of the candidates to comment on whether their election or failure to
be elected will be a signal to the church and, if so, what is the signal?"

It seems that, from this questioner's perspective, all the candidates'
emphasis on careful listening might only be window dressing. He (the person asking the question is a "he") might intend to expose all of them for
an empty piety or to challenge them to "get real" in the face of intractable

difference. He seems to imply that the "conservative evangelicals" are hanging on for dear life.

Hammond is the first to answer with a position that he summarizes as "My election or failure to be elected would not be a rejection of any particular group in the church."

Kling follows: "I'm not sure the failure to elect me would be a rejection of me. . . . It's been a wonderful experience [running for moderator], regardless of the decisions you make. Our presbytery would probably agree."

Lyon: "Only if those who choose to view it in that light do so." Several sentences later, almost as an aside, she inserts, "I hope you will view me as one of the minorities in the church. Woman, single, senior citizen." Is she implying that only a person who represents a minority position can identify with "conservative evangelicals," also apparently assumed to be a minority?

In his answer, Allen follows the pattern he has established during the questioning period by referring back to the commissioner who asks the questions, sometimes by thanking them, usually by repeating the question. In this case, he acknowledges that the person asking poses a difficult theological issue about the nature of the church and the ways churches and individuals raise questions about contentious issues. His "simple answer" is the one he has given to commissioners who ask him what he stands for. "I stand for mission, evangelism, and reconciliation. I can't imagine how that would be any basis on which anyone would want to withdraw [if I were elected]." He continues by proposing that synods establish task forces to seek to reconcile alienated churches so they might overcome their estrangement and that the prayer retreats begun by Howard Rice (the current moderator) be continued so "we as a denomination grow closer together in more unity and peace." His answer attempts to reframe the question by establishing general principles about which all can agree. Further, he offers several solutions to overcoming enmity.

Peterson's answer is characteristically brief and to the point: "I have no groups who give a hoot if I'm elected or not, but I would be proud to represent this church in any capacity on a moderatorial level."

Four of the candidates (wisely) deflect the question from what could be implied as its intent: to construct an either/or issue for the General Assembly in which if some are "in," others will be "out." They use the question as an occasion to rise above the seeming attempt at reducing the election results to a hostile takeover.

Of particular note, however, is Lyon's answer. She uses the questioner's inquiry about what has come to be called identity politics to stake a particular claim. Possibly, she assumes that membership in a minority group grants certain electability advantages. Perhaps Kling's bilingual ministry gives him some "minority" credentials she lacks, and Allen has overtly used his minority racial status as a positive for his candidacy, that as a product of mission he symbolizes it for the whole church. Her claim: "I hope you will view me as one of the minorities in the church. Woman, single, senior citizen."[319]

Lyon trumps her Japanese-American and Spanish-speaking rivals with a minority trifecta: gender, marital status, and age. Her claim builds on the sympathy undoubtedly generated by her reference to her husband's recent death in her candidating speech. She forcefully reminds the audience of her laudatory determination to stand for the position of moderator in spite of the obstacles she has faced the prior year.

Allen does not remember her trifecta claim, only that she was well-spoken, "with a kind of warmth," and that she had made it well known that she was recently widowed in her printed materials. He thought she was well qualified for the office.[320]

Whether or not her three-minority claim struck him in the moment, his answer, which immediately follows hers, sidesteps the identity politics she has asserted. Perhaps this is due to the earlier confrontation in which the conservative pastors threatened to walk out if he were to be elected. The confrontation might have been foremost in his mind because the question now posed for all the candidates is a thinly veiled version of that threat, and it is possible the man who asked the question was part of that group.

Even if the intent of the questioner is the opposite, that is, to disarm the "conservative evangelicals" by explicitly naming them as a contentious issue, Allen's answer is the one that most directly redefines the question. He addresses it in broad theological terms. His response is an implied challenge of its own, for the questioner and the "conservative evangelicals" to join him so they might stand together in mission, evangelism, and reconciliation, potentially all unifying principles. He goes one step further by suggesting practical steps for conversation and bridging difference: synod task forces and prayer retreats.

The similarities of the candidates' positions as articulated in their speeches do not reveal great differences between them. It seems they are careful to follow unspoken standards of presentation and content. The question-and-answer period, though, allows the commissioners to witness the abilities of the candidates to speak spontaneously, possibly revealing more telling strengths and weaknesses than the five-minute prepared speeches did, but even the questions seem to follow polite norms. The only uncomfortable question is the one that raises an implied litmus test for belief, of whether "conservative evangelicals" will feel welcome under the leadership of the new moderator. The candidates do not lose their composure, though, leaving the commissioners with no obvious choice.

Chapter 18

The Election and Its Aftermath

WHEN THE ALLOTTED HOUR for questions expires, the clerk explains the voting process to the assembly. Commissioners will vote by secret ballot. The ballots will be collected and counted in the sections where the commissioners are assigned to sit, approximately thirty commissioners in each section. The twenty-two section leaders will then report the totals from the microphones available at their sections. The Youth Advisory Delegates (YADs) and the Seminary Advisory Delegates (SADs) are allowed to vote, but their votes, while reported, will not be included in the final tallies. The new moderator must win by a majority vote. There are 617 voting commissioners, so the winner needs 309 votes. The five candidates are taken to another location.

The voting is complex and tedious, which has the unexpected effect of creating suspense. It takes about fifteen minutes for the secret balloting before the section leaders are ready to report. The clerk records the totals as they are reported for each section, and the candidate totals are then tabulated: Hammond—176; Lyon—169; Maruyama—134; Kling—130; Peterson—8. Hammond leads, followed by Lyon and Maruyama. Only seven votes separate first and second place. The youth and seminary student votes follow a different pattern: Lyon—57; Maruyama—38; Hammond—30; Kling—16; Peterson—0. Lyon leads, followed by Maruyama.

No winner on the first ballot.

The second ballot. Same process, only this time someone makes an adding mistake, which takes an interminable time to identify and correct. It is finally sorted out: Hammond—228; Lyon—197; Kling—95; Maruyama—95; Peterson—2. The youth and seminary votes still do not follow the trend: Lyon—69; Hammond—41; Maruyama—29; Kling—12; Peterson—0. Lyon is still first in the youth vote; Hammond has moved to second place. There not being a majority, a third ballot is necessary.

Howard L. Rice, the moderator of the 191st General Assembly who is conducting the meeting, asks for a cup of coffee. "I'm fading quick!"

Rice was confined to a wheelchair due to multiple sclerosis. From the laughter on the tape, his plea seems to have been variously heard with amusement and sympathy.

A discussion ensues about modifying the process to narrow the possibilities so someone will be more likely to reach the required number of votes on the next ballot, but it is determined there is no precedent for dropping any of the candidates. A few of the commissioners also seem to need coffee because the total number of voters has dropped to 609. The winner now needs a majority of 305.

The third ballot results: Hammond—318; Lyon—246; Kling—28; Maruyama—17; Peterson—0. The youth and seminary delegates maintain their preference for Lyon: Lyon—78; Hammond—47; Maruyama—17; Kling—11; Peterson—0.

The moderator: "I think this is it. I think we just got it. Hammond has been elected." Hammond is brought into the assembly to applause.[321]

It could be, as Angus and Calian said, that it all depends on the speeches. For whatever reasons, Allen may not have delivered his as forcefully or clearly as the others. When Min Mochizuki recalls Allen's candidacy, he says he does not remember the speech. "Perhaps I wasn't all that impressed."[322]

Then again, it would seem each candidate took care to speak about the "unity and peace" of the church. That they almost pointedly eschewed identification with "liberal," "moderate," or "conservative" positions in their answers to the questions, both from the floor and in written materials, is perhaps an indicator that the tension between the positions was a significant undercurrent, certainly more than Angus thought it was. Allen was clearly identified with the troubles in the Denver Presbytery and the "conservative" churches withdrawing, an issue he himself brings up in his speech. Hammond might have had the advantage of being neither too "hot" (liberal, as Allen was tagged) nor too "cold" (conservative, as Kling's credentials would have identified him), but as "just right," expressing himself in generalities as he did.

It is also difficult to determine the extent to which the constituents of each candidate effectively "politicked" for their respective nominee. It could have turned out differently, perhaps, if Allen had deeper roots in the Asian caucus. Min does not remember that Allen specifically reached out to it during the campaign.

Then again, Allen did not grow up in an ethnic community as Min and June did. Although Allen presents himself as Japanese American in his speech, he also explicitly says things never turned out the way the pastor of his youth predicted, that he would serve only ethnic congregations. He could have been perceived as simultaneously presenting himself as "assimilated" and as Asian American, which might have obfuscated his unique racial heritage.

Allen says one of the first things he did when he got involved in General Assembly work was to join the Asian caucus because "I'm an Asian." However, immediately following this assertion, he says, "I wanted to find out what these people are thinking about. In Wisconsin there were no minority pastors, and still none in Iowa. In Denver, minority pastors, especially Asians, were almost nonexistent. But I guess I'm a typical Asian, as typical as any minority person who lives and associates and socializes mostly with Europeans. I've rarely experienced being in a minority group."[323]

His words express a conundrum. Being Asian in America for Allen is to be seen as a minority but to live as a member of the majority culture, an experience that he thinks many members of minority groups share. To be Asian but with a more direct connection to one's Asian heritage than his is also to be a minority person but set further apart, in a group whom he refers to as "these people." Identity is fluid as it moves between cultural, social, class, and racial categories.

From his perspective, Min says he thinks it was difficult for Allen to reach out to the Asian caucus. "He was a Japanese American but did not share the Japanese-American experience [of being incarcerated during the war]. I think he found it difficult to reach out. Then again, although there was the Asian caucus, I don't think there were Asian commissioners, as I recall."

June quickly added, "Remember, he tried to be non-Asian. He wanted to be an American as he grew up."[324]

Min and June easily identify what being Japanese American means. It means sharing a particular and traumatic experience, that of incarceration, and they are definitively part of that group. Allen is not.

From the perspective of white commissioners to the 1980 General Assembly, all three are Japanese American without distinction because JaJA forced removal and incarceration during World War II was not (and is not even now) well known.[325] If the majority of the commissioners thought about Japanese Americans at all, it might have been in the context of that Japanese-American "model minority" stereotype. The tag implies

compliant, quiet accommodation, which is not a promising leadership quality in American culture.[326]

After two decades of work in General Assembly affairs, as he stood
before the commissioners in Cobo Hall, Allen's identity may have been ambiguous. He was an assimilated male pastor of a prestigious urban church
and a past presbytery moderator, but he also presented himself as a member
of a minority group with a "unique" history on which he did not elaborate.
Kling's solid identification with Cuban immigrants in Florida and Lyon's trifecta minority claim might have superseded Allen's Japanese-American one.

In particular, Lyon's three-fold minority position as woman, widowed,
and senior citizen could have tapped into constituencies representing a
number of members in the audience who were not in positions of power
due to various combinations of those very characteristics. It is somewhat
puzzling, though, that a woman presenting herself as a widow and senior
citizen definitively captured the youth vote, particularly when Foresberg
represented Allen as a champion of youth in his nominating speech.

There could have been other random influences on the vote tally, difficult to identify from this historical remove: 1) The order as determined by
lot. The first to be nominated, the first to speak, the first to be introduced in
The Presbyterian Outlook May 26 issue, and the first candidate on the ballot
was also the winner. 2) The tedious voting that caused even the moderator
to "fade." The audience would have seen the way the voting was trending,
so by the third ballot, they knew which way to cast their ballots to move
things along.

In any event, Hammond is the new moderator. Among other appointments, he designates Lyon as the vice-moderator and Allen as chairperson
of the General Assembly Committee on Congregational Mission.[327]

The assembly moves on to its business and will have to deal specifically
with issues that promise to threaten the "unity and peace" of the church that
all the candidates had hoped to maintain. Even a report that, on the surface,
seems relatively innocuous garners controversy. It is presented by Allen several days into the assembly when he speaks as chair of the Committee on
Congregational Mission.

One of its recommendations is that "a mass media ministry 'extend the
claims of the Gospel to all persons' and strengthen the self-esteem of United
Presbyterians." The media task force itself was comprised of twelve special-
ists from across the church who had researched the issues throughout the
prior two years and come up with strategies for addressing them. Certainly
Allen's research on McLuhan and the exploding influence of mass communication had qualified him for a role in the group.

The assembly receives the report and approves the funding for "a denominational witness via radio and television," which includes the half-hour television project already underway, *Video One*, via RCA's Satcom I satellite that links 430 cable systems. Allen was surely pleased by the approval as he had recognized the potential of cable television almost a decade earlier, an enthusiasm reported in Dubuque's 1972 *Telegraph Herald* interview upon his departure from that city.[328] The assembly also approves the Support Agency to seek additional funding for more media projects from individuals and foundations.[329]

The discussions surrounding the report, though, give an intriguing snapshot of the church's approach to the increasing dominance of the media environment and of the critical tone taken by those in opposition to the report. Perhaps the tone reflects that taken by those opposed to any number of positions approved by the assembly and gives insight into the level of acrimony that seems to underlie many of the debates.

A May 26 *Outlook* op-ed piece by J. W. Gregg Meister, even before the committee's work was presented to the assembly, had criticized the committee for not going far enough. In the first paragraphs of his piece, Gregg Meister approves that the report encourages using technologies of broadcast television and radio, but he charges that it ignores other "information technologies." Examples he offers include transmitting ideas and information via teleconferences, the way medical centers do by beaming grand rounds to regional hospitals and professors by offering continuing education with videocassettes. The editorial notes that Roman Catholic dioceses are even leasing cable channels to broadcast worship services and educational materials, which Presbyterians should emulate. Thus far, the editorial seems to offer constructive criticism.

However, the editorial takes issue with the fact that the report does not address the "theology of the television camera's inevitable distortion of reality," a criticism it connects to Malcolm Muggeridge's position that the media (press, television, and radio) exists to exploit sex and violence. From Gregg Meister's perspective, the media task force should not discount Muggeridge's particular claim that television is incapable of portraying anything but fantasy.[330]

Such a critical analysis is important, but by quoting Muggeridge, a British gadfly whose ideas were evidently a bit out of the mainstream, the editorial draws on a rather unconventional argument to make the point that using these technologies brings with it potential distortion and misrepresentation. Certainly the UPC needed to thoroughly inform itself about pitfalls of information technologies, but the tone of the editorial suggests a certain level of partisan bickering rather than an invitation for informed discussion.

Other subjects discussed and reports adopted by the General Assembly with more potential for dispute are represented by the resolution on "violence and racial strife" presented by the Committee on Social Justice and the Rights of Persons. The issues the report raises have only multiplied and intensified in subsequent decades, two in particular: the devaluing of black life and immigration. In particular, the resolution calls attention to "the unpunished police violence against blacks, . . . the social and economic impact of the heavy Cuban and Haitian migration, and the systemic violence committed against racial minority people, as in the shooting of Vernon Jordan."[331]

The resolutions presented to the assembly had been widely discussed for months in the presbyteries that had put them forth, in publications leading up to the assembly, and in the questions addressed to the candidates in those pre-assembly materials. The issues were also debated in any number of other forums prior to and during the assembly.

For example, former U.N. Ambassador and United Church of Christ clergyperson Andrew Young addressed the assembly at a breakfast that was attended by "1,500 United Presbyterians." He asserted that progress in domestic race relations "is directly proportional to the degree of involvement by the churches in that struggle. . . . 'When America begins to see a moral dimension to political questions, American politicians do respond.'" Of additional interest, his observation that "'security and national defense is not going to be increased by proliferation of nuclear arms'" was met with applause.[332]

Of the issues and efforts that came to the fore in 1980, most had evolved over prior decades and have subsequently become more complex and urgent in the twenty-first century. The majority of resolutions before the assembly concerned peacemaking. At the forefront was apprehension about nuclear proliferation and the then-ongoing hostage crisis in Iran.[333]

Even on that first morning of the assembly, one question posed to the candidates concerned those thirty or more resolutions about peacemaking. Although not as pointed as the question that brought up the potential rejection of conservative evangelicals if certain candidates were to lose the election for moderator, it also had divisive potential. The person asking it said that Carter had sought peace in Afghanistan and Iran without any real success and may have contributed to renewing Cold War fears through his position on SALT II and other recent policy decisions. The person had asked that, if elected as moderator and spokesperson for the denomination, how would the candidates speak to the ever-increasing tensions in our world, especially if political parties and candidates do not address them in the manner the denomination deems necessary? (The candidates in the 1980 presidential election were Ronald Reagan, Republican, and Jimmy Carter, Democrat.)[334]

Allen was second to answer and began with an accurate rephrasing of the question. He indicated one reason he repeated it was that the people up on the platform were having a hard time hearing those speaking from the microphones on the floor of Cobo Hall. After being assured he heard the question correctly, he indicated that it is up to the General Assembly whether or not the moderator speaks to these issues. He reminded the audience that all the candidates had endorsed the peacemaking report that would be coming before the assembly for approval and that he had no question in his mind that "peacemaking is a priority for the church of Jesus Christ in our decade." He had concluded by noting that "the persuasion we bring to political candidates and political parties must be exercised by each of us wherever we live."

The other candidates' answers to the question were similar to Allen's in that they were careful not to introduce their personal political opinions. Instead, they consistently signaled that, if elected, they would reflect the positions taken by the General Assembly on any issue in question. They avoided any indication that they might advocate for positions taken by dissenting factions. In any event, Iran, Afghanistan, nuclear armament, and the church's place in the political process remain salient topics for dispute.[335]

The commissioners, including Allen as one of six representing Denver Presbytery, continued to listen to speakers and preachers and to receive and read and discuss and act on reports throughout the subsequent days of the 1980 assembly. In any assembly, some reports are of book length, commissioned by the assembly and presented by the committees and task forces that have worked on them, perhaps for years. The deliberations are daunting, and when the time comes to present the report in question, the assembly might not accept the opinion agreed to and recommended by the majority of the committee members.

In Allen's experience, often "the committee report loses. That happens many times. . . . A good example is our Christian Education committee report [at another General Assembly] on the language requirement for pastors to pass basic Greek and Hebrew seminary courses. We recommended the requirement be dropped, and here it is, decades later, our constitution still has the language requirement for ordination unless the presbytery makes an exception." In democratic processes, debate continues and issues linger and evolve.[336]

This ongoing dynamic emerges in any number of ways, but its prevalence is indicated by the space given in the May 5 *Outlook* to reflections by the outgoing moderators of both the northern UPC and the southern

Presbyterian Church in the United States (PCUS). Among Albert Winn's concerns (PCUS) is hospitality for the Hispanic churches. "They are Presbyterian. . . . They don't have to become Anglo to be Presbyterian." He thought that they could take joy in their language, food, dance, and ways of worship.

His statement embodies the dilemma faced by both Allen and Min. While former moderator Winn undoubtedly intended to be respectful and inclusive, he speaks of the Hispanic churches as "they," not "we." Winn's position reflects a desire that churches whose membership base originates in other cultures and countries be validated and accepted, but it can just as easily consign pastors and members to ethnic churches who might not want to be there. As Nisei (second-generation), neither Allen nor Min wanted to serve ethnic congregations. The two pastors are Presbyterian. End of conversation.

Outgoing moderator Rice's (UPCUSA) observations are part of another stream of argument, this one about the General Assembly's monetary support of various causes. Specifically he points out that the World Council grant to Zimbabwe was an issue at the beginning of his term, but that it has "calmed down." He asserts that peace in Zimbabwe has shown that perhaps the grant was wise and did not fuel war. Screeds like Chapman's condemnation of the grant to "aggressively radical third-world Protestants" in his 1979 *Presbyterian Layman* article had evidently been more widespread than one might have expected.

On the topic of liberal/conservative tensions, Rice is optimistic. He thinks the church is healthy and that the rise of "evangelical social activism" has, in turn, increased the interest of the "so-called liberal wing" in devotional life. His point seems to be that each faction is learning from the other. Evangelicals are recognizing the need for social engagement, and liberals can be both activist and evangelical.[337]

Perhaps Rice's optimism was premature. What irritated Allen most about the 192nd General Assembly was not his loss of the election. He was upset by the new moderator's performance throughout the ensuing year. Angus was equally disappointed by the winner. Allen and Angus thought "he was one of the worst moderators the church ever had. He just did not do a good job representing the church." When pressed for detail, Allen says, "He pushed himself [forward] and not the church, and he played politics with his friends, appointing them to positions. He had kowtowed to the conservative pastors, had the conservatives backing him, and had pushed that I was just so liberal. I thought he would change his position if he got elected, but he wasn't the leader type of person. He was wishy-washy on so many things. He appointed the woman [Lyon] as vice-moderator, but she would have been so much better as moderator than he turned out to be.

I doubt he ever let her do much." In Allen's estimation, Lyon would have engaged, but Hammond played it safe, and, even more disappointing, he used his position for personal ends.[338]

In his 2002 reflections for the one hundredth anniversary of Mont-view, Allen describes the 1980 loss and the congregation's response to it. He remembers "coming back from Detroit at Stapleton Airport when a delegation of Montview members met the plane with a huge sign saying, 'We love you, Allen, welcome home' (in all caps!). I thought the group had gotten the wrong message so I reminded them that I lost."[339]

When he approached their home in Aurora, a suburb east of Denver, he caught sight of more Montview church members and banners and balloons. He thought they had not heard the results of the election, either, and were welcoming him as moderator. When he tried to correct the misunderstanding, they responded, "We know you lost, Allen, but it doesn't matter!" An evening of celebration and dancing to a live band followed in the backyard on the large cement basketball court they had built for John. Allen's run for moderator was in the past; Allen and Montview were ready to move forward.[340]

At the 1980 General Assembly, Allen's ministry, commitments, and personal history were clearly visible in his speech and as they played out in the issues, personalities, and debates swirling around in Detroit's Cobo Hall. Just as he struggled in his adolescence during the years of World War II, exposed in a marjority white community, and lived the early years of his ministry in the milieu of the civil rights movement, he did not shy away from political, cultural, and ecclesiastical disputes in 1980. Losing the election would not change this level of engagement, which means his biography is not his alone. He would continue to live in tandem with, vulnerable to, reflective of, and proactive in addressing ongoing cultural tension and conflict.

The Maruyama Family
1916–2017

Masakuni and Umeyo Maruyama wedding photo

Masakuni and Umeyo Maruyama with their five children:
Allen on his father's lap; Virginia; George and Joe, standing; Ted, seated.

Becky, Rose, and Maynette Jarboe

Allen's high school photo

Allen's U.S. Army photo

Allen and his mentor, Rev. John Wintermute, 1953

Rose and Allen Maruyama wedding photo, 1954

Rose and Allen's children, Sarah and John, 1960s

The Dubuque years: Rev. Richard Heydinger, Judy and Bob Roussell, Allen

Rose and Allen with their two children, John and Sarah, 1975

Brothers George and Allen

Rose and Allen: A pensive moment at the 1980 General Assembly, Detroit, Michigan

Allen and John relax, Japan, 1986

Rose, the consummate hostess, at Sarah's wedding reception, 1988

Allen, 1993

Allen and Rose, 1994

Allen and granddaughter Amanda, 1996

Allen, Sarah, Rose, Mike, and Amanda, 2017

Mike, Sarah, John, and Jonathan, 2017. A favorite Maruyama pastime,
second only to Denver Bronco games!

Amanda at the Maruyama Park, Kyoto, 2019. Sarah and John visited it
with their parents in 1986 during Allen's sabbatical.

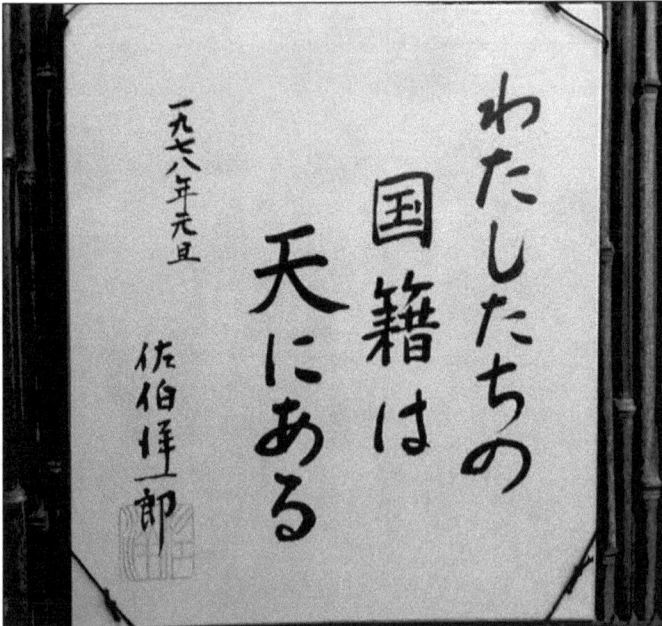

一九七八年元旦

佐伯理一郎

わたしたちの
国籍は
天にある

Shodō (Japanese calligraphy): "Our citizenship is in heaven."
Phil 3:20, Rev. Yoicho (Yoichiro) Saeki

PART II

Without a Dream, the People Perish

Chapter 19

The Promise and the Dream

On the occasion of Montview's year-long hundredth anniversary celebration in 2002, the congregation invited Allen and other former Montview pastors to preach. His Sunday occurred on April 14, ten years after his 1992 retirement. He says the sermon for the occasion is a particular favorite of his, and it is one of a few for which copies still exist.

In it, he replays earlier convictions but in the context of an evolving theology. His focus in 2002 is still mission, evangelism, and reconciliation, with changed definitions. The sermon's text is Prov 29:18, which asserts that where there is no vision, the people perish. The passage characterizes Allen's commitments well, given his forward-looking posture and his pursuit of concrete goals. Even if attaining the dreams is not accomplished in a single lifetime, the impetus to achieve them gives direction and purpose.

The sermon copy begins with the notation that the congregation will be asked to chant this phrase for several minutes: "People without a vision shall perish." Given that Allen had retired only a decade prior, perhaps many in the congregation would not have been surprised with this introduction that invites their active participation. They would have remembered such rhetorical moves, which possibly reached as far back as the energetic style of his time as a youth leader at conferences in Colorado and Wisconsin.

Those who arrived at Montview after his retirement might have wondered about this dynamic opening that invited vocal participation from the listeners, not the usual practice of Presbyterian preachers. Inviting congregational engagement would be congruent, though, with his "go, go, go" personality. A Japanese expression captures this energy level: *issho kenmei* or "all in, full throttle and nonstop." With this rousing lead-in, Allen amps up the congregation from the outset.[341]

When he launches into the sermon proper, he reminds the congregation that the Hebrew prophets gave Israel a promise and a dream. The promise was that they were God's people, and God was their God. The dream was that, as God's people, they would bring a blessing of peace, joy, and prosperity to the whole world. The promise and their participation in achieving the dream are inseparable.

Even in these opening paragraphs, Allen is echoing his 1980 candidating speech. He voiced the belief then, held throughout the Judeo-Christian tradition, that the assembly he was addressing was part of a certain spiritual lineage, that of God's chosen people. With the Montview congregation, he also establishes that this promise carries within it an inherited commission—to bring a blessing of peace, joy, and prosperity to all creation. In the 1980 speech, he had cast the commission in slightly different language but with similar intent—to stand for human rights, peace, and justice. In the speech, the commission was a call to action that summarized his vision and leadership goals for his anticipated moderatorship.

In the sermon, the commission serves as a shared vision meant to encourage the congregation to recommit to its meaning and purpose. Allen asserts, "Whether it is a nation, a church, or an individual, unless we have a vision, a dream, unless we see our goals clearly, we will indeed perish. We will lose heart, enthusiasm, zest for life, desire, and motivation—we will lose the essence of life."

He notes that the vision for Christians is referred to scripturally as the "kingdom of God." Specifically, Jesus Christ commissioned his disciples to "Go into all the world, preaching the gospel [of the kingdom], teaching and baptizing and healing."[342] Allen says, "This is our mission: to bring the kingdom of God, to preach that the kingdom of God is coming," an objective characterized by peace, joy, prosperity, healing, and justice.[343]

Appropriate to an anniversary sermon, Allen rehearses some of the historical ways Montview has fulfilled this shared vision of biblical Israel and the Christian church through its mission and evangelism, the same foci of his 1980 speech. Montview did not join "white flight" to the suburbs in the 1960s but engaged its Park Hill neighborhood to become interracial. Although Allen does not mention it, longtime members might also have remembered that Montview hosted an audience of about three thousand upon the occasion of Rev. Martin Luther King Jr.'s speech in Denver as a visiting dignitary.[344]

Allen adds to his list that Montview opened its doors to a preschool, a new venture in education; it provided space for the League of Women Voters and the Gay Men's Chorus, groups that represented engagement with political and social issues and with change; it gave a "constant stream" of clothes and food and shelter to the homeless; and it expanded its supportive and healing mission to Alaska, Switzerland, and Nepal, to mention several more distant commitments.[345]

This retelling of Montview's history of mission and evangelism, particularly with its final listing of the food, clothing, and health care ministries, might have been heard by newcomers as a relatively benign tribute to Montview's faithfulness. Longtime members could have read between the lines, though, each with memories about the genesis of particular ministries. This breadth of outreach, spanning the years of social change that it did, was not always without controversy.

Shirley Burkhart, decades-long member, remembers two "bad" Sundays. The congregational meeting in the early 1970s, at which Rev. Fay Hill's person and ministry were excoriated, was the "worst," but the second was a meeting after the Sunday service that focused on disagreements about hosting the Gay Men's Chorus.

"We were home [to them], and they rehearsed and gave wonderful concerts here. . . . They would make some wonderful scenery and put it in the sanctuary. One was kind of a Madam's house. . . . Some of our members had a fit about that, but it really was a fun concert. The [chorus members] were good people.

"Well, this [one member] was just bound and determined that when his daughter walked through the fellowship hall [where they practiced], she was being tainted and, well, he was crazy, to be honest with you. We had a meeting on Sunday and they carried him out. He was just so wild about this. [His feeling was] we just couldn't be around gay people because they were awful. . . . He sat on the front row and injected stuff [while people were speaking]. Five or six men went up and picked him up and carried him out . . .

"We had some pretty active loudmouths, . . . but the co-pastors were peacemakers [when these difficult situations arose]. Standing tall, offering support, being strong and not offering their opinions but wanting to console/consult/encourage the church members."[346]

In his anniversary sermon, Allen quickly moves beyond Montview's past and its memories to imagining a vision for its work in the third millennium on a radically transforming planet earth. The first task is to recognize how fundamentally the world is changing—people, nations, the earth, and all its creatures. So fundamental are these changes that the earth is, in essence, becoming a new creation.

In light of this transformation, Montview's mission becomes one of teaching and preaching a God of creative change. Change is not to be feared, whether it be space travel, genetic engineering, the maturation of world religions, cloning—whatever—because God is divine process and exists in the midst of change.

The second task is to pursue Montview's prophetic vision in light of change, building on the promise to the Hebrews that they are the people of God and upon Jesus Christ's directive to preach the kingdom of God. It can do this by reconceiving its traditional emphasis on mission and evangelism in order to meet the challenges of the present context—that the earth exists as a global village in an age of instant information. Although he does not name him, Allen draws here on McLuhan's image of the global village formulated three decades prior, as well as McLuhan's assertion that humanity is bound ever closer via networks of mass communication.

Allen notes that in this era of the early twenty-first century, evangelism is not a "fanatical drive" to convert non-Christians. Rather, its goal is to keep Jesus Christ and what he taught and lived in the gospels at the center of faith. This evangelism will be influential in a number of ways, first, by enabling humanity to "preserve the beauty of the good earth's creation." Second, it will replace dehumanizing cultural elements such as discrimination and intolerance with freedom as articulated and enacted by Jesus Christ. A marker of this freedom is human dignity, which Allen refers to as "humanism in the best sense of the word." Other markers of keeping Christ's life and teachings at the center of evangelism are love, forgiveness, and peace.

He praises Montview's adult education programs and lecture series because they help in this effort. They provide information and inspiration that members need to keep pace in a constantly changing world. They indicate that Montview is attempting to stay "on the cutting edge of new theology and science." He specifically notes that Barley introduced him to the World Future Society, and he mentions the Institute of Noetic Sciences. These are among several groups in which members can participate that "open up a new frontier of God's wonders."[347]

Allen's final reference is to the Jesuit philosopher and scientist Pierre Teilhard de Chardin, a figure who had appeared in his 1972 dissertation as possibly one of any number of influences on McLuhan's thought. Allen reviews Teilhard's concept of the Omega Point for the 2002 congregation. Teilhard believed that everything in creation is physically and spiritually evolving toward "christianization," the Omega Point. Allen emphasizes that when everything—including humans, but also birds and bugs, flowers and weeds, rocks and rivers—reaches this point, all will live in love.

For those in the congregation conversant with the Judeo-Christian tradition, Allen's description of Teilhard's Omega Point may have sounded strikingly similar to Scripture passages that convey comparable yearnings for what is sometimes referred to as the "peaceable kingdom." A familiar passage that sounds this theme is often part of the Advent liturgy during the four weeks prior to Christmas and the celebration of Jesus's birth. Isaiah 11 speaks of lambs, leopards, calves, and lions eating and resting together, and of children playing over the hole of the asp and putting their hands on the adder's den. The passage includes this verse: "They will not hurt or destroy on my holy mountain, for the earth will be full of the knowledge of the Lord as the waters cover the sea."

Allen says of Teilhard's Omega Point, "What a vision! And Montview church will be in the forefront of the evangelism and mission" that proclaims and participates in striving for this re-articulated hope for realizing the realm of God that includes the animate and inanimate. He leaves his message about attaining this vision there.

His conclusion is one of gratitude to Montview, where he acknowledges he spent half his ministry. "You saw me through humble efforts to be a leader in the national church and through sickness and joys. You were parent and family. . . . I could never give you what you gave me."

To examine the sermon in greater detail, Allen builds on themes that he articulated as far back as the 1970s. For instance, Allen's reformulation of mission and evangelism for the twenty-first century integrates the methodology of liberation theology that looks to local need for guidance.

Just as he has not named McLuhan, he does not refer to liberation theology specifically, but its worldview lies behind his assertion that Montview does not approach evangelism as a "fanatical drive" to convert the "heathen" but knows that other religions are "meaningful and redemptive" in their context. This viewpoint echos the striving of liberation theologians to base Christianity in local culture through "action and reflection" about local values and needs rather than imposing an external evangelism burdened with its own cultural accretions.

The sermon elaborates his commitment to mission and evangelism, which found expression in his 1980 candidating speech and his answers to the questions put to the candidates. In the 1980 speech, he described the Presbyterian church as standing for "human rights, peace, and justice for all," and as witnessing to "unity and love as part of the body of Christ," which is "an inclusive body." In his answer to the question from the floor of the assembly about whose election as moderator would mean sending a message that conservative evangelicals would feel unwelcome, he had emphasized that he stood for "mission, evangelism, and reconciliation." He did not see "how that would be any basis on which anyone would want to withdraw."

While his focus in 2002 is still mission and evangelism, his definition of them has evolved. In 2002, he describes their overarching goal as engaging with the "Creator God . . . by embracing change and eliminating dehumanizing elements such as discrimination and intolerance from all cultures—including our own." This humanizing of the world is the evangelism, the church's message, of the twenty-first century, along with having a "driving evangelical fervor to convert the masses of people to preserve the good earth." His emerging definition of evangelism emphatically embraces the spiritual and material health of all creation.

This evolution represents a separation between the 1980 speech and the 2002 sermon. In the speech, he saw mission and evangelism as unifying the ideological positions of conservative, moderate, and liberal. His overarching theme then was that "The body [of Christ] knows in its rich heritage to learn to live together as conservative and moderate and liberal because we are one Lord, one faith, one baptism, one God and Father of us all." He implies that effective cooperation is possible.

In the sermon, not only has he given up on the possibility of working productively with those who embrace a certain type of conservative perspective, but he makes a point of praising Montview for its prophetic vision that has withstood "the cyclone, the tornado, of conservatism that has engulfed our nation and our culture." He is optimistic that Montview's resistance will continue because the congregation engages with the "majority of theologians and biblical scholars who are beginning to enter the twenty-first century."

In contrast, those who resist change "still live in the nineteenth century" and take their cues from theologians and biblical scholars who lived and wrote over a century ago. Inferred in this characterization is a conservatism that takes entrenched, absolutist positions. In 2002, Allen's emphasis is not that the various factions of conservative, moderate, and liberal live and work together productively, but that forward-looking Christians press toward the vision of peace, joy, prosperity, healing, and justice.[348]

His emphasis would be no surprise to Montview members who were thoroughly familiar with his forward-looking orientation tempered by realism, a perspective that finds expression in the song "The Impossible Dream" from the musical *Man of La Mancha*. He never kept it a secret that it is his favorite. Some of its realism, bordering on despair, is echoed in the 2002 sermon. The song was sung in his honor ten years prior at his 1992 retirement dinner. He also wants it in his funeral liturgy. On the occasion of the 1992 dinner, one member teased in her tribute that "I have been known to express some dismay to Allen about the number of times we have heard 'The Impossible Dream' from the pulpit!"[349]

The song's performance history from its Broadway appearance in 1965 parallels much of Allen's adult life. In particular, he says he admires the main character because his was a lonely voice, just as Jesus Christ's was. Jesus Christ and the character embody the message that what is true and right will not be popular.[350]

He would not go so far as to equate himself with this character, but he not only admires him; he is somewhat reflective of him. He, too, wants to run "where the brave dare not go, . . . to fight for the right." He, too, sometimes feels "scorned and covered with scars." In spite of the hurdles, he hopes it will be said of him that he "still strove with his last ounce of courage . . . to reach the unreachable star," that vision toward which he believes all creation is straining.[351]

While people who lack vision might indeed perish, the person who strives toward a vision perceived to be critical of or outside culture's norms does risk ridicule, if not outright persecution and isolation. If that person is not a member of the majority, which is Allen's situation, he or she is even more suspect and vulnerable.

To the Montview congregation, Allen's sermon would have sounded themes longtime members had heard from him before. Those who had worked with him in the years between his 1980 run for moderator and his retirement would have easily read between the lines. They were familiar with the formative events of those years. They would have lived through the progression of his thinking, punctuated by health crises, a lengthy sabbatical in Japan, and his commitment to a new, post-retirement vocation.

Chapter 20

The Physical and the Spiritual

ALLEN'S BELIEF IN THE unifying potential of mission and evangelism in 2002 is distinctly different from that of 1980. He retreats from his 1980 call for conservatives, moderates, and liberals to respect one another and live together as the body of Christ. Rather, he implies in 2002 that conservatives have become more strident to the point of generating a "cyclone" that threatens not only the church as the body of Christ but also its movement toward the realm of God. In this climate, the church can affirm physical difference, such as race and gender, and survive spiritual and ideological controversy only if it resists this "tornado."

His 1980 commitment to the inseparability of physical and spiritual health remains, but it has expanded. In 1980 he said, "The body [in the context of the church as the body of Christ] recognizes that there is no difference between the physical and spiritual." By 2002, he conceives of spiritual and physical health as including the animate and inanimate elements of creation. This shift is accompanied by a change in focus from the image of the body of Christ to the biblical imperative to strive for the kingdom (realm) of God, which places even more emphasis on the unity of the physical and spiritual aspects of life. He uses Teilhard's formulation of the universal impulse toward the Omega Point in the sermon, which he presumably equates to the realm of God, to emphasize that everything is swept into the movement toward this vision, including humans, birds and bugs, flowers and weeds, rocks and rivers.

One way to track this expansion in Allen's theology over the intervening decades is to compare his reserve about Teilhard in his 1972 dissertation, chronologically closer to his 1980 speech, with his embrace of Teilhard
in the anniversary sermon. In the dissertation, Allen observed that Teilhard
conceived of the evolution of matter and spirit as a trajectory that generally
shows progress, and Allen's concern was that this view is not compatible
with the biblical doctrine of "man" as sinner, a prominent aspect of Allen's
neo-orthodox anthropology at the time. Accordingly, the problem Christian anthropology has with evolution as a generally "upward" movement
is that the essential nature of humanity has not changed appreciably since
the beginnings of its recorded history. Humans are incapable of progression
through their efforts alone.[352]

However, a good deal changed for Allen between his neo-orthodox
anthropology as expressed in his 1972 dissertation, which prompted him
to question Teilhard and McLuhan's optimistic assessments of human potential. By 2002, he enthusiastically embraces Teilhard's vision, that "rocks
and rivers, everything in creation, including humans, will be christianized.
And we will all live in love." Revisiting the intervening years and unearthing
some details of a complex of events in Allen's life sheds light on this shift.

The specifics of his 1980 vision of unity and peace, inclusive of physical and spiritual difference, correlated closely with challenges the church
was facing then. However, the vision of unity, peace, and love that he proclaims in his 2002 sermon is sweeping and timeless. This dream is not an
abstraction for Allen. An endpoint of unity and love implies that creation
currently suffers from disunity and discord. Evidently, in his mind, the "cyclone, the tornado of conservatism" is a significant contributor to disunity.
In order to arrive at unity and love, creation is in need of healing, spiritually
and physically. And to this Allen even more purposefully devoted his life
between 1980 and 2002.

In the decades leading up to the 1980 speech, pastoral care was a
prominent characteristic of Allen's work: ministering to those confronting
personal crises, illness, and death. His caring also focused on healing ecclesiastical and social fractures: making room for the expression of differing
theological orientations, in particular, third-world orientations that led the
church universal to seriously address "the suffering of oppressed people as
a real and central concern for believers in Jesus Christ," God's own concern
"that emerges out of oppressed people's need to be free."[353]

Whether it was in Dubuque on behalf of inmates at the decrepit county
jail; poor and elderly residents at the crumbling county home; disaffected
youth on the church lawn; or, more widely, women at the margins of church
leadership; redlining and other civil rights inequities; or simply listening

to individuals in a search for common ground and establishing relationships with those who disagreed with him, he was striving to heal fractious
division and subsequent social and personal injury. Some who knew him
during the Dubuque years characterize him as "very kind, with a big smile,
always."[354]

Surely his commitment to those suffering from exclusion and oppression can be traced to the spiritual pain he experienced as a teenage Japanese
American during World War II. Pain of such magnitude that he would lie
about his age in order to enlist and kill the enemy that was the cause of so
much loss before being killed by them, an enemy he saw in his own reflection in the mirror. Pain upon being told that, as an Asian, he would
not be hired to pastor majority white churches. Lingering pain, inflicted by
what can be called microaggressions, such as his daughter's memory that
evidently they could not join the Dubuque country club because they were
Japanese, as much as Allen loved golf.[355]

However, 1985 was a turning point. His earlier candidating speech assertion that "there is no difference between the physical and the spiritual"
took on personal urgency as he faced a life-or-death physical threat.

Prior physical crises had not affected him in quite the same manner. In
fact, he only recognizes the first one in retrospect. As a slight eleven-year-
old on the farm in the 1930s, he could grab onto the family's large German
shepherd-collie mix and ride it. The dog and he were "real good friends."
But this particular time it growled. Perhaps his brothers, who were playing
basketball in the yard, yelled for him to get off because the dog seemed to
be injured. If they did, Allen ignored them. He was having too much fun.
Suddenly, the dog twisted and bit him on the throat. His parents wrapped
his neck with cotton and rushed him into the town doctor. After the doctor
stitched up the wound, he told Allen's parents that he had a clear view of the
throbbing jugular. He said that if the penetration of the dog's teeth had been
off by even one-sixteenth of an inch, . . . The doctor marveled that the vein
was intact and that Allen lived.

The wound healed but did not disappear. Allen can still feel the scar
from the thirteen or fourteen stitches and remembers his concern for the
dog, who was checked for rabies. The dog was clear, but they tied him up in
the yard for the remainder of his life, "at least another ten years." The kids
rarely played with him. Allen "felt so sorry for that dog. I think he suffered.
It's too bad they just didn't put him down." Both Allen and the dog carried
residual damage from the encounter.[356]

Another brush with physical crisis occurred in 1974 when he was
plagued with abdominal problems. Eventually he sought treatment, and
the diverticulitis required surgery. The surgeon reported that he "just kept

pulling out damaged intestine, but it's okay. You don't need all that intestine anyway."[357]

Allen was hospitalized for thirty days, and he says that, verified by those who know him, he was "not a good patient." He remembers the period as one of several during which "Montview people supported me when I needed it so desperately." He heard that "those who visited me made bets on who would be able to stay the longest before I rudely dismissed them." Church members and staff apparently handled it effectively by tuning into his cantankerous spirit and giving back as good as they got. A member who sent a card every day wrote on one: "Don't worry about your job while you're in the hospital. The custodian is doing your work during his lunch hour."[358]

Rose remembered the reaction of Allen's pastor colleagues. "They knew when to leave his hospital room because Allen was blunt about it. He'd say, 'Don't you have other work to do or somewhere else to be?'"[359]

Allen has been told that waist-down surgery, in particular, affects mood. His grumpy attitude could also be that he, the exemplary host, was not in a position to play his usual role of offering beverages, snacks, and engaging conversation to his visitors. Unable to properly host them, better to dismiss them.

The prelude to what became the most significant health crisis, the one that confronted him in 1985, was the growth of a tumor on his cheek, below his eye. The surgeon described the radical surgery he would perform as involving a skin graft from Allen's leg to rebuild his face. Allen insisted the surgeon take only the tumor, not as much as the surgeon intended. The surgeon argued. Allen pressed him. Why such a total reconstruction? The answer: "That's just how we do it." Allen's response: "It's my body and I decide. Take only the tumor." The doctor wanted Rose to come back to the examining room, presumably to persuade Allen otherwise. Allen stood firm. He signed a release form. Following the surgery, samples of the tumor were sent to several labs. One reported that the tumor was not the serious cancer the surgeon had assumed. Allen never had any more trouble with it.[360]

Each time, both after the abdominal surgery and the tumor removal, Allen recovered and moved ahead, active as ever, until he was increasingly bothered by what became a chronic "popping" in his ears, similar to that experienced with an altitude gain. A fingertip-sized growth was detected at the back of his throat. The examining physician called Rose with the report that Allen had a "violent cancer." She hung up the phone and cried. He told Allen he had "maybe a year or two to live."[361]

The third doctor Allen consulted was retired army and had experience with Asian patients. Evidently he had seen similar growths in that population and said he knew immediately what it was. He scheduled surgery the next day. A regimen of radiation treatments for thirty days followed. Allen speculates that the side effects of the radiation did more damage than benefit to his body, but the doctors insisted the treatments were essential. This time he acquiesced to medical authority.

Until that diagnosis, surgery, and treatment, Allen described his life as typical of that of many ministers—crammed with visitation; planning and leading worship services; writing sermons; teaching; attending meetings, conferences, and retreats; and, in his case, extensively traveling to fulfill his responsibilities as a member of national church boards and committees. Approaching the age of sixty, he was confronted by a diagnosis that drove home the lesson about the "brevity of life," and, if he were to survive, he began to question what he should do after he retired.[362]

During his whole ministry to that point, he says meditation and prayer were simply not significant personal practices. He began to pay attention to them. He was always physically active so perhaps had thought that sports, golfing, and fishing sufficed for self-care. Now it seemed self-care involved more than physical fitness and the busy social life he and Rose enjoyed. The physical crisis prompted a spiritual one, suggesting that he should no longer neglect such practices as prayer and meditation. He marks his confrontation with this "violent" throat cancer as one of the turning points in his faith, one he ranks alongside the broadening effect of seminary education in the 1950s and his affirming experiences as a pastor in Dubuque throughout the 1960s. The immediate physical and spiritual challenges in his own life opened him to a more expansive sensibility.

Chapter 21

Pilgrimages

THE CELEBRATION OF THE twenty-fifth anniversary of his ordination back in 1978 had signaled another significant turning point: an overt acknowledgement that Allen's emotional distance from his Japanese ancestry was healing. He had already discovered as a young soldier that being Japanese American in the army was not the disadvantage he thought it would be in white society, nor was it during his student years at the University of Colorado. Acceptance as a pastor by the majority white Hogarty, Gleason, Prairie du Sac, Mazomanie, and Dubuque congregations in the 1950s and 1960s had moved the process along. Being awarded the PhD with its attendant affirmation and being hired by the also majority white Montview church in 1972 significantly breached the emotional distance, and by the the twenty-fifth anniversary of his ordination, he was more than open to embracing his Japanese heritage and to visiting Japan.

Montview presented Allen and Rose with a $3,015 check in recognition of the occasion. The April 1978 solicitation letter for the monetary gift read, in part: "The Session authorized the creation of a special fund to be presented Sunday, May 14. [Its] purpose is to make it possible for Allen and Rose to visit Japan. As many of you know, Allen is among the first Japanese Americans to serve a non-Asian congregation in the Presbyterian Church. His parents came to America from Japan at the turn of the century and settled as sharecroppers in Southeastern Colorado where Allen grew up. It has been Allen's dream to visit Japan someday, returning to the villages where his father and mother were born and raised."[363]

On their visit to Japan that summer, Allen and Rose renewed ties between the Colorado family and Allen's Japanese kin, ties that had never been severed. When Allen was a pre-teen, cousin Paul Maruyama not only visited the Maruyamas in the United States in the early 1930s but lived with them for a time. Paul had graduated from high school in Japan, and his father, Mr. Maruyama's older brother Yoshihiro, wanted him to have some US education. After taking classes and graduating from high school in Las Animas, Paul went to Colorado Western State in Gunnison, where Allen's oldest brother George would also attend.

Paul played golf in Japan and brought some of his clubs to the United States. Allen describes a "nine-hole sand course out on the prairie just north of the Maruyama's Colorado farm. Paul would ask, 'Allen, want to go with me and carry my clubs?' So I'd carry those heavy clubs and follow him around. That was my introduction to golf!"

At the time of the Pearl Harbor attack, Paul was teaching Japanese in the Sacramento Japanese-American community. That circumstance subjected him to the forced mass removal of persons of Japanese lineage from the military zones of the West Coast. Paul was incarcerated, but his Maruyama cousins lived free, in Colorado. He was sent to Tule Lake, the location where Minoru Mochizuki's family was also held and where Paul continued to teach Japanese. After the war, Paul settled in St. Louis, started his own business, and became a community leader and liaison between the Japanese government and Missouri business interests.

The two branches of the Maruyama family in the United States maintained contact over the years, and Allen conducted Paul's memorial service in St. Louis in 1995. Although Paul was Buddhist, his wife was Christian, so he had requested a Christian funeral out of respect for her. The service was held in a community hall, and over five hundred people attended. Allen regrets that he did not make it a Buddhist/Christian service because "that would have been so easy" and would have honored Paul's spiritual heritage, also.[364]

Allen and Rose renewed connections with the Japanese Maruyama family during their 1978 trip, and they were also hosted by Mrs. Maruyama's relatives, the "really rich" Aminos, as Allen refers to them. In her album of the trip, one of the photos Rose included, a bit blurred, is of the narrow road leading to the Amino home place where Mrs. Maruyama was raised.

The story of Allen's desire to re-establish contact with his Japanese heritage as an assimilated Nisei tells of a gradual reconciliation, uniquely his and facilitated by the church. It takes on added dimension if told in contrast to the reconciliation with heritage undertaken by his contemporary, Minoru Mochizuki. Many of their experiences are similar—having support of Presbyterian churches and colleagues, attending McCormick, both active in the national church and averse to serving ethnic congregations. As noted, Min attended the 1980 General Assembly and was another Japanese-American Presbyterian pastor who was "among the first to serve a non-Asian congregation in the Presbyterian Church."

Min's journey to reconcile with his heritage differed from Allen's in several ways, most significantly in that Min was one of the incarcerated West Coast Japanese Americans. To recap Min's wartime experiences, he endured, as he describes it, "the wrenching upheaval of the evacuation and incarceration" at Tule Lake. His older brother, Shigeaki, was the only family member not incarcerated, as he had gone to Japan for university studies in 1938. It was while Min waited for his release from Tule Lake in 1946 that he learned of "Shig's" death, which had occurred back in 1944 in his service as a member of the Japanese navy.[365]

Grief, betrayal, and anger marked Min's incarceration. He went so far as to renounce his American citizenship, a hasty decision that he was not able to reverse until his court case was resolved in 1954.

Min had begun what he characterizes as his "very dramatic journey" to reconcile with his Japanese heritage somewhat before Allen did, but it started only after he had surmounted several barriers. First, he had to overcome his resentment at being confronted from an early age with his mother's determination to return and live permanently in Japan. Accordingly, his family had spoken only Japanese at home, and she had been very pleased that he was appointed the spokesperson at both his elementary and junior high Japanese language school graduations in San Francisco.

She was particularly insistent during their confinement at Tule Lake that he enroll in intensive Japanese language study. He finally "gave in" and enrolled. He so resented his mother's continuous talk about Japan and their Japanese relatives that he shut out everything she said. Not until his late thirties was he finally ready to explore his heritage.

Second, factors such as the incarceration, his brother's death, and renouncing his citizenship raised any number of barriers for him in the process of "becoming an American."[366]

Although he conceives of his brother as having lived in two worlds, of Japan and America, he himself was caught between those two worlds. Min resented his mother's overbearing insistence that he was Japanese, not American, and would likely live as an adult in Japan. The incarceration gave him the clear message that the US government did not accept him as American, either. Min's brother, a sailor in the Japanese navy, was killed by Allied forces.

In Allen's case, two of his older brothers and he were all in the US military during the war, and he was never forced from his home, nor did he have to leave his high school and friends and graduate from behind a camp's barbed wire. He always had a home in the United States, even though sometimes during the war it was nearly unbearable; Min did not.

What they shared was their resentment about their Japanese ancestry, a loss of heritage that took them years to recover. Min was ready to immerse himself in it in the 1960s. By the mid-1970s, Allen was more than ready to reclaim it, but his fluency in Japanese was never that of Min's, much less that of his older brother Joe. Allen's older brothers had benefitted from several more years than he as students in the Japanese school in their Colorado farming community, because the school closed in the mid-1930s.

Now Min speaks with gratitude about his fluency in the Japanese language and his connections to Japan. He contrasts them with those of many Nisei, "almost none of whom can carry on a conversation in the language as I do." He expresses regret that the majority of them who visit the country and seek out relatives cannot say much beyond "hello" and that they are virtually spectators, tourists, in the country of their ancestors. He is also pleased that he was always able to talk with his mother-in-law in Japanese, something his wife June admitted she could never do well with her mother.[367]

Min, June, and their five children lived in Japan for one year, 1964–5, during his sabbatical from Western State in Michigan. He worked in Tokyo at a student center with Methodist roots. Min observed that the country was still recovering from the war, as was the Japanese-Protestant church, which, in his opinion, relied too much on mission support from churches in the United States. While the center still had some Methodist ties, Min describes it as part of the *Kyōdan* system, the United Church of Christ in Japan.[368]

During the sabbatical, the Mochizukis renewed Min's connection with Rev. Thomas Grubbs, the Presbyterian pastor who had visited Min so faithfully during his incarceration at Tule Lake. Grubbs had become a missionary in Japan.

Min also attended a pan-Asian Christian youth conference sponsored by the World Council of Churches and held that year in the Philippines, the first year it had taken place in Asia. All the other pan-Asian conferences had been in either Europe or North America, purposefully staged on neutral territory. The suspicion and hostility between students from various countries that had been or were at war were almost impossible to navigate. The Philippines had been occupied by Japan during the war, Korea had long endured Japanese occupation, India and Pakistan were embroiled in conflict, as were Malaysia and Indonesia—the antagonisms were deep-seated. "Of course, for any Christian gathering, reconciliation is an integral part of the undertaking. I think it was a ten-day conference, and close to the end was the period required for the Koreans and the Japanese to meet. An ambitious gathering.

"I'm embarrassed, though, that I left June in Japan with our five kids."

June forcefully dismissed Min's discomfort about leaving them for the conference. Her dismissal reveals volumes about the expectations put on ministers' wives in the 1960s. As she put it, "I was the minister's wife, and a minister's wife can do anything! It never occurred to me to say, 'Hey, wait.' I wanted him to have all those experiences of being a minister. It amazes me that I encouraged him to go!"[369]

June and Rose both came to terms with their husbands' professional and academic involvements in ways that affirmed both the marriages and the wives as individuals in their own right. Rose openly acknowledged that, especially in the 1960s in Dubuque, Allen "had time for everyone but me." Rose's response was not to stand in Allen's way, though. She was of a mindset similar to June's. She carved out places for herself with her own friends and professional commitments, as a choir member expressing her musical talent, and as a high school teacher. Both women took on their own roles in the church and outside of it, June with her position as a national leader for Presbyterian women's groups and as an employee in Western's counseling office.

Min, along with June and various children and grandchildren, visited Japan a total of eight times over the subsequent decades. Allen and Rose traveled there twice, first for several weeks in 1978 and again in 1986 for Allen's sabbatical. Joe, Allen's brother, also visited Japan on a number of occasions.[370]

On a 1984 trip, Min was able to connect with Keio Gijuku University friends of his deceased brother. Keio University is equivalent to American Ivy League institutions.[371] For Shig to have gained admittance as a graduate from an American high school and to have completed his studies from the university in 1943 speaks to his considerable abilities. Min also grants that Shig was the obedient, good-natured oldest son.

Min and the Keio alumni enjoyed a memorable retreat together in the mountains. Of special meaning for Min was their presentation of the text of Shig's 1941 diary and his biography. The biography was written by Admiral Kichisaburo Nomura, one of two negotiators in Washington at the time of Pearl Harbor.[372] After thirty-eight years, from the time of getting the report about Shig's death when he was alone at Tule Lake in 1946, Min felt he came to know his brother through the tributes paid him at that retreat by those who knew Shig as a young man. By reclaiming his heritage, Min integrated both his worlds and came to know a brother lost to him during the war.[373]

However, well before these numerous visits, their early professional experience underscores both Min's and Allen's determination to establish themselves as professionals beyond the confines of their racial heritage. Their contemporaneous calls to serve non-Asian congregations as seminary graduates in the early 1950s indicates how effective their efforts were.

John Vander Meulen, pastor at First Presbyterian Church, Dearborn, Michigan, recruited Min out of McCormick to work with him as assistant pastor. To put the Mochizukis' move in the context of race relations in Dearborn at the time, Min eventually learned that, before he and his family moved in, members of the congregation polled the West Dearborn neighborhood where their home was to be. The purpose was both to gauge the reaction of the homeowners and to prepare them that a Japanese-American family would be joining them.

This cautious approach was well advised. Orville Hubbard was mayor of Dearborn during those years and well known for his racist views. In fact, after Min arrived, approximately fifteen clergy association representatives met with Hubbard to confront him about his policies. For example, even as late as 1954, it was rumored there was an ordinance against "non-whites" staying overnight in Dearborn, ironic because a sizable Middle Eastern population lived (and still does) in East Dearborn. "Non-white" was vaguely defined; Min never saw such an ordinance, nor does he know if it was ever enforced.

Hubbard's response to the clergy delegation reveals his prejudices: "How long do any of you intend to stay here? Six or seven years, maybe? I intend to stay a long time." Min remembers that Hubbard's comment put a stop to the conversation about inclusion that the delegation had hoped to begin with him.[374]

Min's installation as a Japanese-American pastor in a majority white congregation was so "auspicious," according to Vander Meulen, that Vander Meulen invited Eugene Carson Blake to participate. Blake served as stated clerk of the denomination from 1951 to 1966, a position of considerable authority in the national church, and was widely known for his forceful personality and public positions on any number of issues. He was one of the group of civil rights leaders who called for the 1963 March on Washington for Jobs and Freedom, and he spoke from the steps of the Lincoln Memorial on that occasion, immediately prior to John Lewis.[375] Blake himself lent star power enough to the occasion, but Vander Meulen also invited Kenneth Nye to participate. Nye was the synod executive at the time and also eventually worked at the national level.

Indicative of Blake's personality, when he noticed that Min's only dress shoes were an oxblood pair, which he was wearing with his new black robe that the church had given him, Blake pulled June aside. He gave her money and said, "Buy him a pair of black shoes."[376]

Blake was a ubiquitous presence. For example, he is recorded as the guest speaker in the 1956 minutes of the Synod of Wisconsin's annual meeting held at Carroll College. He was introduced as stated clerk of the Presbyterian Church in the U.S.A. and president of the National Council of Churches of Christ in the U.S.A. Allen is recorded as being present at this meeting. Few Presbyterians would not have been familiar with Blake's name.

A revealing cultural sign of the times is this notation: Blake's speech was followed by a reception prepared by "the ladies of the church." In the 1950s, "ladies" tended to be in the church kitchen; men stood at the podium.[377]

In spite of the differences between their childhoods as Japanese Americans, one spent on the West Coast and one in the interior of the United States, Allen and Min followed strikingly similar professional paths in the PC(USA): graduating from McCormick Seminary, church dignitaries speaking at their ordinations (Haroutunian and Blake), early ministries in the Midwest, decades of significant involvement at the national level of the church. Their impulse to reclaim their Japanese heritage also followed similar paths.

In the early decades of their ministries, both Min and Allen were accepted and encouraged by a denomination that traces its roots to Western Europe and identifies strongly with that cultural context, but one that also embraces a larger vision of itself. On their part, both Japanese-American men worked diligently to define their roles in this predominately white American church while re-establishing their Asian ancestral ties, often with the church's encouragement and support.

Chapter 22

The Sabbatical

IN 1986, ALLEN TRAVELED to Japan a second time, and this trip immersed him in the culture in a way that more closely resembled the depth of Min's experiences. Allen benefited from Montview's new policy that, following ten years of service, pastors became eligible for six-month sabbaticals. Not only would Allen have a more comprehensive exposure to his ancestry, but the trip would give him opportunity to explore Japan's religious milieu. Allen's sabbatical focus was "The Christian Mission in Japan" with this guiding question: Why, if Christianity has been in Asia for centuries following the birth of Jesus Christ, does it have so few adherents, with the exception of South Korea and the Philippines? If he were to study its development in Japan, he might discover some answers.[378]

The sabbatical was not simply Allen's opportunity. Rose, Sarah, and John each have distinct memories of their travels in Japan. Their reflections add a personal dimension to Allen's more academic report.

Rose was also granted leave from her teaching position in the business program at Gateway High School in Aurora for her own research. She visited a number of Japanese schools, primarily in the Kyoto region, to observe their methods of instruction. She was particularly impressed with the discipline of the children and the orderliness of the classrooms. Not only were the children respectful, but they helped clean the rooms at day's end. Even the youngest ones were expected to contribute to the effort.

When she and Allen spent a month in Tokyo, they regularly attended not only Japanese churches but also an English-speaking service at an

Episcopal church. One Sunday, they ran into a group of teachers on an exchange between departments of education in the United States and Japan. The teachers complained that they had had to go through quite a bit of red tape to get into the various schools they wanted to observe. Rose had encountered no difficulties because a friend who also taught in Aurora had put her in touch with a friend in Japan. Through the Japanese teacher and other contacts, Rose had access. No red tape. She described her sabbatical experience as rewarding and productive.[379]

Perhaps Allen's more limited ability with the Japanese language did not give him the level of cultural penetration that Min's fluency did, but his sabbatical was no less satisfying. It came on the heels of his encounter with the "violent" throat cancer that reoriented his perspective about the "brevity of life," opened him to practices of prayer and meditation, and motivated him to think about what he should do after retirement. This context set the sabbatical in motion, along with two months of studying Buddhism at the Naropa Institute in Boulder, Colorado, now Naropa University.[380]

The agenda for the trip included four months in Japan, three weeks in China, and four days in Seoul, South Korea. While in Japan, they took several weeks off and traveled by rail as far south as Nagasaki, where they visited a friend and the various memorial sites to the bombing victims, and north to Hokkaido, off the coast of Russia. Rose especially enjoyed the side trips when they would randomly stop, walk around a city, and get back on the train. Sometimes they would spontaneously decide to stay overnight.

During their time in China, they visited a number of cities, including Beijing and Nanjing, and they saw the Terracotta Army excavation in Xi'an. A lot of their travel in China was also by train, but a vivid memory was of flying on a plane with folding wooden seats. Rose said the acronym for the Chinese airline was CAC. "We joked that it stood for 'China Always Crashes.'"[381]

The recent cancer surgery and radiation treatments meant that Allen's ear still seeped blood and required attention, so he sought follow-up care at the Baptist Medical Center in Kyoto, the city where he and Rose did much of their research. The center's rate structure was similar to that of medical facilities in the United States, and Allen thinks some of the cost might have been covered by his health insurance, but it was expensive. After several visits, the physician did not know what other steps to take to promote his healing. She recommended he see a colleague at the Kyoto Medical Center, which was part of the Japanese health system. When Allen registered and they saw his last name was Maruyama, they billed him for his many subsequent visits as they would a Japanese citizen. The cost was significantly less, and under the physician's care, his ear began to heal.[382]

Allen not only had the advantage of being a Maruyama in Japan, he had personal connections. He knew he would be preaching one Sunday at a relative's small church. Before he left the United States, he had asked a friend fluent in Japanese to phonetically translate the sermon he had been invited to deliver. Following the service, he had the impression that the congregation did not understand much of what he said, but they appreciated the effort. He also visited Yoicho Saeki, a classmate from McCormick days and a pastor in Tokyo. When Rev. Saeki and his staff held a retreat for several days in the mountains, Allen and Rose were included, to their delight. The food was outstanding, as was the time spent in the *onsen* (hot spring baths).[383]

The sabbatical was more than a research project not only for Allen and Rose, but also for Sarah and John. "It was the first time John and I had ever been anywhere," Sarah says. "We were only in our late twenties."

Sarah, the daughter her parents describe as "always being in charge," former high school cheerleader who also embodies *issho kenmei* (go, go, go), as her father does, recalls the day they visited the Amino and Maruyama family members. Some still lived in Yamanashi Prefecture. She says, "It will forever be my best story." Her telling and John's memories of the trip reveal a good deal about the ways not only Allen as Nisei but his children as Sansei (third-generation), mixed-race children encountered their heritage.

A relative in Tokyo picked them up early and took them to the area by car. "I sat in the back seat with my cousin who didn't speak English, and I didn't speak Japanese. I thought, 'This is going to be a long ride.' We got to the first family house, and John and I are whispering to each other, 'We're kind of hungry.' They brought us fresh fruit and some cake and we wondered, 'This is it? We better eat a lot.' We're just wolfing it down because we're starving.

"Then they drove us to the Buddhist temple where all the Amino family is buried, and they have us sit down. They say, 'We're going to eat here.' And we're like, 'Oh, we have to eat again!' So they bring out bento boxes, and John and I are going, 'I don't recognize anything.' It's like a flower tempura and a leaf tempura. John and I are picking through it and trying to decide what we're going to do, saying 'Well, I guess it's a good thing we ate all the fruit and cake.'

"Then we drove to the Maruyama family farm. A nice home. They welcome us and give us cloths [to wash up] and then ask if we want beer. John is like, 'I know beer. Yep, I'm in,' because he's twenty-something. They open the doors to this room and there's this table that's twelve feet long, just filled with food. We both went, 'Oh, my gosh. We have to eat again.'

"The food is amazing, but I'm blown away because there are no women. They are all in the kitchen preparing the food. But we had a nice time. We ate all that and got in the car to head back to Tokyo. The cousin that drove us says, 'Oh, my mother has dinner prepared for us when we get back.' John and I are like, 'We have to eat again?' We walk in, and it's another twelve-foot table. There isn't even one inch of space that doesn't have food on it. They've made American dishes and Japanese dishes. They want to make sure their American family friends find something they like. It was just mind-blowing, really nice."[384]

John's story of the events of that day give yet more details about families negotiating cultural difference and the unexpected, extravagant hospitality. The ride to the mountains outside of Tokyo took "a couple of hours. Kind of reminded me of our place up in the mountains here [west of Denver]. We had an interpreter, and he was our driver. I couldn't speak any Japanese; my dad could understand it but couldn't speak it very well.

"A funny thing I remember is that when we were ready to leave one of the homes, my dad and I said, 'Grab the beer and chug it down. We have to go.' We'd set the glass down, and they'd turn around and fill it up. They did this like three times, and finally we drank all the beer at the table. They ran in the back and got some more. We're going, 'We're trying to leave!' We didn't understand the culture. You're supposed to leave your glass full, not empty. The same in all the beer gardens. Everybody would leave their pitchers full. It drove me nuts. Everybody wastes their beer. Hilarious, until we understood."[385]

When Allen remembers the experience, he explains, "They always put out more than they can eat. If it goes empty, that means they didn't have enough. The job of a host or hostess is to completely satisfy your guests in any way possible."

Allen lives this expectation, one he learned from his parents and their Issei contemporaries in Southeastern Colorado. He welcomes guests, even for brief visits, with offers of soda, tea, coffee, ice cream, cookies, crackers, perhaps the gift of a book or some other object. More often the invitation is for lunch or dinner, preferably at one of the Denver area's Japanese restaurants. Of course he was impatient when visitors came to his hospital room in 1974 as he recovered from abdominal surgery and he could offer them nothing, not even a pleasant disposition.

When he describes the duties of a host, Allen emphasizes that the guest also has obligations. "In the same way, when you go visit anybody, you don't go empty-handed. You have to take a gift. It's an insult if you don't. My mother, with her closest friends, she had to take some fruit or candy or something or she couldn't go visit them. *Omiyage*—present."

At the mention of *omiyage*, Rose reacted negatively to a custom with Japanese origins, the only time she did. "That gift business really instigated a problem. I got irritated by it many times because it was the first thing his mother would think of. The minute we'd talk about seeing someone. 'Oh, we have to have a gift.' That's more important than seeing the person. Irritating, but that's the way she was, so I had to accept it."[386]

John had another surprising encounter with Japanese customs during those visits with the family in Japan. "The Amino side did a lot of business with people in the United States and was very successful. A big operation. They did the automatic docks in most of the ocean bays. I was an accountant working for Union Carbide back then, so they offered me a job and a wife and a house if I would come work for them. But I was young, a single guy in my twenties, and they were serious. My offhand response was, 'Can my wife be blonde and blue-eyed?' They all laughed. 'No,' they said. 'It doesn't work that way.'"[387]

Sarah described the multigenerational Amino home: the younger son and his wife and two children lived on the main level; the senior Kunio Amino and his wife lived upstairs; and the base level was a garage that held perhaps up to twelve cars. They rented parking spaces to neighbors. A lush garden with trees, bushes, and grass was planted outside, around the living space, on a layer of soil several feet deep on top of the cement. On the roof of his business Mr. Amino practiced his golf swing.

The Amino-Maruyama visits continued in both directions across the Pacific. On one occasion, when one of the grandchildren got older, he came to Denver for school and stayed with, as Sarah says, "Uncle Joe," Allen's older brother. She remembers a delightful Christmas Day skiing with Joe, his daughter, and their Japanese cousin.

As a young professional, Sarah had opportunity to travel to Japan again in her role as a training manager for General Electric in 1995. Her prior exposure in 1986 had been as a visiting family member and with the guidance of her parents. Now she was a working woman traveling with colleagues.

Her boss asked her to go to Tokyo where they were opening an office. The company was doing short-term international rotation assignments for a month, but Sarah's daughter, Amanda, was not yet a year old. She told him, "If it were for two weeks, perhaps." The next day he called and said, 'Sometimes a half loaf is better than none. Go for two weeks. I'm sending several people who speak English and Japanese to be your translators.'

"I was still hesitant to leave my baby, but my parents were moving to be near us in Kansas City. They said they would be available to help Russ [Sarah's husband] take care of Amanda.

"I just loved immersing myself in the culture. It was so interesting to be a businesswoman working in Japan. The president of the company there was Ivy League-educated and spoke English very well. The women were very young professionals. They would say, 'Sarah-san, you have baby?' I said, 'Yes,' and they asked, 'Ah, you go to work; who take care of baby?' I said, 'I take her to a daycare center.' 'Oh, what is daycare center?' Because they didn't have any daycare centers then. I asked what they would do. They said, 'Quit work. You have to.' They knew if they got married and had a baby, their career was over until their children grew up. Maybe never."

From this new perspective on Japan as a mixed-race Sansei, she was struck by the influence of Japanese habits and cultural values on her father's behavior. "My dad taught me that you should be gracious and host people. That's what I experienced in Japan because they were constantly taking care of us. They were absolutely wonderful hosts and took us out to lunch and dinner. They gave up their personal lives to entertain us. In America, people will say, 'I can't entertain [visiting colleagues] tonight.' That's rude. These people come from England, from all over, and they're excited about going out with their new American friends, and everybody is like, 'Can't go. Can't go.' What is that?"

She had many memories of her Japanese colleagues' hospitality. "One guy commuted to work from Kamakura, on the coastline about an hour-and-a-half ride on the train from Tokyo. On one weekend, he said to us, 'You come to Kamakura, and I show you the town.' Here he is, early in the morning on the one or two days he has off, and he meets us at the train station, shows us these beautiful temples, and takes us to this amazing res-taurant. Kamakura has a two-story Buddha from perhaps the 1600s. Just massive. A tsunami washed away the supporting structure, but the Bud-dha is still there. The colleague took us to a little place where they do the traditional Japanese tea ceremony. We walked through the bamboo forest nearby. What a fantastic experience we all had because this man unselfishly gave his time, who really had no time with his family anyhow because of his work circumstance. It just blew my mind, and I thought, 'It's such a differ-ence in culture.'

"On another occasion, a colleague asks, 'Sarah-san, you like sashimi?' I answer, 'Sure,' but I'm lying through my teeth. She says, 'I take you to my husband's restaurant.' I say, 'That would be wonderful,' but to my American colleagues I say, 'Phil and Betsy, if I have to eat raw fish all night, I'm in trouble.' At that time I hadn't quite acquired a taste for it. I said to Phil, 'If it's something I just can't eat, I'll hand it to you under the table.' He goes, 'Okay, I'll do it.'

"You have to be gracious. You're the main guest, the special honored guest from the United States. Turned out they brought cooked things that were really, really good, but eventually they brought us a shrimp that was completely raw with the head still on, just out of Tokyo Bay that morning, very fresh. Phil is giving me the look like, 'Is this the thing you want me to eat for you?'

I thought, 'I've had enough beer. I can do this.' I ripped off the head and ate. It really didn't taste fishy or bad. It was just kind of slimy. But it's one of those things where you have to have a plan. The meal was outstanding and so thoughtful because she wanted us to have that experience."

Sarah reflected, "It was an interesting time because I felt my culture. I felt who I was, and yet I wasn't the Japanese person. I was the American, but they all thought I was cool because of my Japanese heritage. That heritage has always been pretty much a positive thing."[388]

Her reflection displays an ambiguity similar to Allen's about their Japanese-American identity. It is not an either/or proposition. Sarah expresses it by saying, "I was, but yet I wasn't." However, her positive evaluation contrasts with what her father's heritage has meant for him as Nisei, sometimes negative in the extreme. His heritage also influenced his experience of his visits to Japan differently than Sarah's in that he was more intimately connected via his parents' viewpoints and values, lifestyle, diet, and language. Not only had he studied Japanese language and culture as a child in the Japanese school, taught by a Buddhist priest, but among some of the trappings of Japanese culture in his immediate surroundings were a bathhouse in the back yard, the Japanese periodicals his parents subscribed to, and the holidays they celebrated with nearby Japanese farm families. Rice was a staple, and they even had access to (raw) fresh fish when a Mr. Taguchi came by the farmhouse with it packed on ice in the back of his pickup, fresh from the West Coast via Denver.

Even so, Allen was born and raised in the United States. The Presbyterian church was influential from middle school; as he says, the church was like another family. His perspective as he approached his sabbatical research was that of a Western-educated Christian pastor going through a profound spiritual re-evaluation subsequent to his bout with throat cancer. Still, although he encounters a foreign culture, frequently he discovers the familiar.

Chapter 23

The Christian Mission in Japan

As Allen immerses himself in his 1986 sabbatical study of the reasons why there are relatively few Christian adherents in Asia, Japan in particular, he comes across a familiar poem that he quotes.

THE FLEETING DREAM

Flowers blossom beautifully,
But they are destined to fall.
Nothing in this world lives forever.
By crossing the deep mountain of transiency,
And awakening from the fleeting dream,
I shall not be deluded again.

He comments that "When I learned it as a child, I had no idea that it was communicating ideas about Buddhism, Japanese culture, and Japanese life. Life is transient. One of the earliest expressions I remember was when some tragic event happened, my parents would say, 'It can't be helped' [*shikata ga nai*]. This was resignation that in this transient world there would be tragedy, sorrow, sickness, and death, and we would simply have to accept it and bravely face the future. This is a Buddhist idea and teaching."[389]

He explains in the report that he learned the poem as a child in Japanese school in Colorado because it was the mnemonic device used to teach the kanas, or Japanese characters, of the language. He was surprised to

185

encounter it again in Japan and to discover it is used for the same purpose for Japanese children.

Learning the kanas is no easy task and demands explanation. Even a brief description reveals the complexity of learning the Japanese characters. The written language consists of two parallel systems, the hiragana and katakana, each comprised of forty-six characters. The hiragana, or "plain" kana, are simplified cursive outlines of the original Chinese characters. The katakana, or "partial" kana, are even more simplified versions and with fewer strokes, many with just one part of the Chinese symbol.

The poem Allen learned as a child employs all the letters/symbols one time each and was in use as early as the tenth century as a teaching method. The order, or the arrangement, of the current Japanese alphabet started developing around the eleventh century, but was initially used only by scholars. By the late nineteenth century, the poem was so widespread it was used in classroom instruction books. Not until 1952 did the current alphabet become the official one for all public documents.

Japanese-speaking children learn hiragana first, but the sounds/order of hiragana/katakana are the same. Hiragana are used to phonically render the Japanese reading of the Chinese characters, as well as for Japanese words that do not have Chinese characters. Katakana are mainly used for foreign words.

Kanji is the Japanese word for the underlying Chinese writing system. "Kan" refers to the Chinese Han dynasty (206 BCE–220 CE) and "ji" means letter. Some three thousand to five thousand kanji or more are in general use in Chinese, and Allen notes that through the ninth grade, Japanese students learn about eighteen hundred kanji. Using kanji means reading and writing with the Chinese characters. A typical written passage in Japanese might contain all three: hiragana, katakana, and kanji symbols.[390]

In this section of his sabbatical report, Allen is not making a point about the complexity of the Japanese writing system. He simply accepts it as something he had to learn. Rather, he is emphasizing how Buddhism is so completely intertwined in Japanese culture that it is even foundational in its language. He writes that "in Japan you are born into Buddhism," and one might assume that, given his childhood, raised by Buddhist parents who later converted to Christianity, Buddhism was also interwoven with his early home life.[391]

In his report, Allen also explores the influence of Confucianism, Shintoism, Taoism, and, to some extent, Christianity, on Japanese cultural values, but he focuses on Buddhism.[392] Its influence includes obedience within hierarchy, humility, avoiding confrontation, the significance of silence and of empty spaces (especially prominent in paintings and calligraphy), repaying debt because owing someone results in loss of face, and industriousness.

He quotes from Takashi Ishikawa in *Kokoro: The Soul of Japan* to point to yet other areas. "Many aspects of Japanese culture, such as the tea ceremony, ikebana (flower arranging), Noh drama, landscape gardening, swordsmanship, and archery" are all influenced by Zen Buddhism.

Buddhism had spread into Japan in the eighth century, but Zen Buddhism's influence, introduced in the twelfth century, is particularly noteworthy as one of the more popular schools. Given its seven-hundred-year history, its aesthetic influence also permeates "the preparation of food and the works of art. . . . Sculpture and architecture come from the Buddhist teachings concerning nature and the need to develop sensitivity and awareness of all that is beautiful and simple."[393]

Allen's written reflections on his encounter with Japan as a Christian pastor reflected his academic study decades after World War II and the subsequent American occupation. The young Shig Mochizuki, Min's brother, also traveled to Japan for academic study, but in a different historical context—back in 1938, over forty years prior to Allen's sabbatical.

Shig also encountered Japan and Buddhism from a Nisei Christian perspective, and he too was struck by Zen Buddhism's pervasive influence. He had been active in the Christ United Presbyterian Church in San Francisco, the Japanese YMCA, and the Northern California Young Peoples Christian Conference. Allen and Shig differ in that Allen's report is based on his research, but many of Shig's recorded reflections are based on his lived experience.

Shig's observations are included in his biography, written by Admiral Kichisaburo Nomura (given to Min by Shig's Keio Gijuku University classmates at the 1984 retreat). They appear in Shig's essay titled "Random Thoughts of Experiences at Zen Cloister, March 1940." The general theme of the essay is that to fully understand and participate in Japanese culture, one must experience Buddhism.

Shig stayed at the cloister for several weeks and, among his summary thoughts, he writes that the aim of Zen is to open one's mind's eye in order to see the nature of existence. In essence, what is seemingly most mysterious is actually most practical and vice versa. His experience at the cloister that approximated this Zen aim was when he participated in the upkeep of the grounds: "By sweeping the sacred grounds spotlessly clean, the mind of the sweeper is also cleansed and purified."

In his diary, Shig also writes that, "Zen teachings are the fundamental source of the Bushido spirit," which, he asserts, is "the basic principle of the

Japanese race." The impression is that Shig is doing a sort of field study to understand more fully the culture of his parents' homeland in which he now finds himself during a time of war.[394]

The Bushido spirit that Shig identifies is the Samurai code, a value system that appeared in the eighth century. It was influenced by any number of historical events and ideals, including those of Buddhism and Confucianism, and eventually emerged as a code of conduct for everyone. Shig seems to be witnessing how important these unifying values are in a time of national stress, perhaps in the hope of incorporating them into his own emerging Japanese identity—values such as honor, integrity, loyalty, courage, and self-control.[395]

In comparison, Allen reports in his research decades later that "I was very influenced by Professor Idemi of Buddhist University who studies Buddhism and Japanese culture." He quotes Idemi that "every aspect of Japanese culture has been influenced by Buddhism." As one example of many, Allen writes that "the loyalty of company employees and the length of service in the same company come from the Buddhist belief that loyalty and faithfulness in one's vocation are the expectations of a good religious practice." In this sentence, without naming it, Allen reflects the Zen/Bushido spirit.[396]

As was the case with Allen's dissertation about McLuhan, his sabbatical report is thorough, detailed, and dense. It includes historical, religious, cultural, and psychological sections, to name several. However, he does not lose sight of its originating question: Why, if Christianity has been in Asia for centuries following the birth of Jesus Christ, does it have so few adherents, with the exception of South Korea and the Philippines? He proposes that perhaps a study of the Christian mission in Japan will provide some answers.

He reports that only 1 percent of Japan was Christian at the time of his visit; in the Philippines and South Korea, 10 to 20 percent were. Partial answers he gives are that in the Philippines, Christianity has been present for hundreds of years in that Roman Catholic Spain occupied the Philippines from the sixteenth through the nineteenth centuries.

This is not so in Japan, even though the sixteenth century Roman Catholic mission from Spain, Holland, and England was initially successful. The Tokugawa shogunate began to see Christianity as a threat, however, and evicted missionaries and forbade Japanese people from becoming Christian. Those who did were severely persecuted. The Shogunate ruled for over two hundred sixty years, and those centuries of enforced isolation were marked by stability and accompanied by a "surge of intellectual and scholarly activity." Japanese national identity became firmly established, and universal education was made the norm. Christianity was simply not part of the culture during those formative centuries.[397]

The emphasis on education initiated during shogunate rule carried into the twentieth century. Allen notes that it remains a "very significant industry" with a five-and-one-half-day school week. The literacy rate in Japan is 99 percent.[398]

He reports that the more recent Christian presence is paired with Commodore Matthew Perry's 1853 arrival in Edo (Tokyo) Bay and the first commercial treaty between the United States and Japan, the (Townsend) Harris Treaty of 1858. These developments renewed Roman Catholic missions and initiated Protestant ones.

Whereas Christianity's contemporary influence in Japan began with the country's opening to the west, Allen attributes Christianity's prominence in Korea to the crisis of the civil war between North and South Korea (1950–53). The popularity of Christianity in South Korea is sometimes attributed not only to its reaction against communism, but also to the end of the Japanese occupation after World War II. In addition to filling a religious void during those critical periods, Allen notes that the church in Korea is "indigenized," unlike in Japan. Just as Min had noted twenty years prior, during his 1960s sabbatical, Allen too sees the Japanese Protestant church's dependency on American churches as inhibiting the process of indigenization, on which he thinks a more widespread acceptance of Christianity in Japan would depend.

Allen writes that the Christian influence in Japan is positively associated with several developments, though. First, it contributed in the area of education. He notes that many institutions of higher learning still reflect their missionary beginnings in their names. He gives the example of Doshisha University, one of the oldest continuing universities and still church-related.[399] Consequently, a number of government officials and professionals have been educated in Christian institutions at some time in their lives.

He observes, in addition, that most churches have nurseries and preschools. Sarah's conversation with her young female colleagues who were not familiar with many childcare options during her 1995 visit nine years after Allen's sabbatical indicates this remained an unfulfilled need. Perhaps because the number of Christians in Japan was so few, access to these church-supported options was quite limited.

A "social consciousness" was the second Christian influence identified by those whom Allen interviewed. While it would seem that the emphasis in Japanese culture on the group would give rise to concerns for the social good, he notes that "this is not true." Those who were not part of groups that would be viewed positively tended to be shunned or worse. Namely, the church advocated for the handicapped, that is, "misfits" cared for privately, including the elderly without families and lepers, and for minorities, such as Koreans and "burakumin, the outcasts of Japan who butchered meat in the vegetarian days and buried the dead." He names Toyohiko Kagawa, a Japanese Christian pacifist, as "an inspiration to Japanese society in this regard because Kagawa believed the poor, the sick, and the indigent needed care."[400]

Although Allen does not make note of it, Kagawa (1888–1960), in addition to his pacifist beliefs, was a reformer and labor activist and was twice nominated for the Nobel Prize in Literature and twice for the Nobel Peace Prize. Initially though, Kagawa's activism for the disadvantaged was controversial and landed him in jail more than once in his home country of Japan.[401]

Allen writes that the government's "quasi-socialized medical program" and its "expanded welfare program to assist the needy" have moved to address social needs, but "the church can claim much of the credit for bringing this concern to the forefront. . . . Urban development, neighborhood concerns, etc., have often fallen to the church to promote because of its vision of the social needs of the larger community."[402]

Min's sabbatical year (1964–65) in Japan occurred midway between Allen's visit and Shig's World War II sojourn. The experiences of Min's family that year provide additional insight into the seeming contradictions between the emphases on group loyalties and a certain carelessness regarding the social good. They ran into it in terms of hospitality, rather, the lack of it. Their home was at the top of a hill, and their children's school bus would drop them off at the bottom. The children were constantly bullied as "outsiders" on their walk up the hill. No one ever intervened, and the neighbors were never friendly. One of June's Japanese aunts sympathized, describing her experience as an "outsider" when she moved from one town to another. After twenty years, she was just getting acquainted with her "new" neighbors.

Min had a similar experience of isolation while working at the Tokyo student center with its Methodist roots. "Here I was, part of the student center, but no minister approached me to welcome me. No one. We were on our own. We were outsiders."[403]

Societies embrace any number of contradictions. Extravagant hospitality shown to honored guests, as experienced by Sarah and John on their visit to Japan as extended family members and Sarah as a work colleague, exists side by side with strong group cohesion that draws firm lines between "outsider" and "insider." As family, John was offered a home, a wife, and a job, but when he jokingly suggested the wife might be blonde and blue-eyed, the response, although good-natured, was immediate. "It doesn't work that way."

In his report, Allen mentions another feature of Japanese society, its hi-
erarchical structure, in the context of his discussion of the tension between
the emphasis on the group versus the individual. The "relations between
the various classes and their sub-groups," while not as rigid as they were
historically, were still apparent at the time of his sabbatical. "The Japanese
are nevertheless very conscious of social status, educational achievements,
position in business and industry, etc. . . . [One] knows one's own position
and place." Social position determines the depth and duration of bowing,
for example, and who is obligated to give what gifts to whom.[404]

Allen is especially sensitive to the, from his perspective, unfavorable
place and status of women in this hierarchy. He introduces his discussion
with this Confucian saying: "A woman should in youth obey her father, in
maturity her husband, and in old age her son." He notes that, although the
severity of this feudal subservience had given way in the twentieth century
to grant women equal rights constitutionally and supposed equality of job
opportunities, "they are still subjected to considerable discrimination. . . .
They do not usually go with their husbands to social occasions and their
place is in the home," more particularly, as Sarah noted, in the kitchen. He
concludes this discussion by saying "the modern Japanese woman is becoming emancipated but she is fighting her cultural mores all the way."[405]

Allen's observations are based on his research and visit in the mid-
1980s; Sarah's came from her experience as a professional woman on temporary assignment in Tokyo a decade later. Entrenched cultural norms are
difficult to displace, even if they are perceived as no longer workable. Even
in 2019, a front-page article in the New York Times indicates that, while
there is movement to make way for Japanese women in the larger society
as independent actors, the majority are tangled in a web of contradictory
expectations.

According to the article, husbands also bear burdensome expectations. They often stay at work late or go out drinking with clients, a commitment to work, hospitality, and group cohesion that Sarah observed in her
Kamakura colleague and for which she, as a visiting colleague, was grateful,
but husbands have little choice if they are to meet rigorous targets for raises
and promotions. Some households meet these demands by accepting that
the woman will work part-time, but the husbands continue to work "brutal
hours." Yet other factors impinge on working men and women. The aging
population cannot continue to meet labor needs, and longstanding opposition to immigrant workers keeps that door shut as a source of relief.[406]

In 1986, Allen had observed that such high expectations for academic
and professional performance have their source in Buddhist beliefs that
"loyalty and faithfulness in one's vocation are the expectations of a good

religious practice." These expectations contribute to "the drive for education, pride, the need to succeed and a disciplined determination that nothing is impossible."

This line of thinking leads Allen to note another seeming contradiction, one between the Japanese attitude of humility and a certain stubbornness. "Underneath the ideal of humility is a strong stubbornness and belief that they are right." Any person, by his own power and determination, can become a "super" person. He correlates this attitude with the Zen principle that, through spiritual discipline, anyone can attain Nirvana, the height of human achievement. As a humorous aside, he quotes a saying that "'Americans think they are right; Japanese know they are right.' This is a Buddhist teaching!"[407]

Allen's offers a possible workaround to this sense of cultural superiority and the tendency to value "insiders" over "outsiders." He asserts that another of Christianity's contributions to Japanese society is "the idea of the importance of the individual soul." This emphasis has introduced the potential that an individual acting with "integrity against the group or crowd" will not be dismissed out of hand.

That he counts the "importance of the individual soul" and social consciousness as important contributions of Christianity is better understood in light of his observations earlier in his report about the significance of group identity in Japanese culture. He writes that the Japanese place the group above the individual. That is, "beginning with the family, the group's will should prevail when in conflict with the individual's will."

Complementary to this orientation is a belief in the "harmony of relationships," which puts a premium on avoiding conflict. "Every attempt is made to make all decisions by consensus. . . . Avoiding confrontation and maintaining group solidarity are the goals of decision-making." Accordingly, Japanese society emphasizes "maintaining good rapport and relationships."[408]

Whereas Allen recognized the Buddhist influence on his early years in the poetry mnemonic used to teach the written language, he does not identify aspects of his own behavior in his discussion of the significance of group identity and its complementary values. His point is to contrast the Western emphasis on the value of the individual soul with the Japanese emphasis on the group's will, consensus decision-making, and harmonious relationships.

However, he was one of the three originators of the Montview co-pastorate, which successfully adopted a style of decision-making by consensus. Additionally, the three pastors agreed that if any one of them was in conflict with the others to the extent that it would compromise the team, that person would leave. The team (group) would not be sacrificed. Also, Allen's colleagues and some Montview members describe his style of leadership as focused on building relationships, as Allen himself does, a style they credit as a key factor in the collegium's success.

As represented in the 1980 evaluative letters from members of the congregation, many recognized that the original members of the collegium were "three unselfish ministers not seeking power, unusually open-minded, cooperative, and free of jealousies." That is, the interactions of the co-pastors themselves were powerful examples of how the collegiate staff model could work in terms of team building and decision-making.

This emphasis on relationship and consensus, as well as the priority on the integrity of the team over individual egos, were characteristics of the co-pastorate that neither the Denver Presbytery nor the national church ever fully understood or believed could work. The model flew in the face of a Western cultural emphasis on individualistic "strong man" models of leadership.

Certainly the Montview congregation recognized their staff configuration as innovative and took pride in developing such a unique model. And it did work. After four decades, it still works at Montview, surely in no small part because a Japanese American helped create and sustain it, unaware that he was perhaps enlisting and comfortably embodying values from more than a Western cultural perspective.

Allen's bibliography for his sabbatical report is extensive, and he spoke with many pastors, professors, and others during his time in Japan about how the US church could be of most help. He discusses their responses at length, but Masao Takenaka, professor of Christian ethics and sociology of religion at Doshisha University, offered a particularly succinct list: 1) Asian churches must establish their own identity; 2) The United States and Europe can provide resources, one of them being how the church adapted Christianity to their cultures. In turn, Asian churches need to learn how to be multi-racial; 3) Because Asian churches look to the West for leadership, it is important that American churches take responsibility for their country's government. Namely, they should not crusade for "ultra-right" (totalitarian) or "ultra-left" (communist) political leaders. Those positions are "very distasteful to Japanese and other Asian churches"; 4) Churches in America need to take a hands-off approach in regard to the Japanese churches and respond with resources and moral support only when asked.[409]

Allen's summary indicates that he respects this opinion that churches in America need to take a hands-off approach. He writes that one task of the American church is to encourage the church's indigenization in Japan and elsewhere in Asia. He believes that the "exciting dialogue" taking place between Buddhism and Christianity in Japan is encouraging in this regard.

Both are studying how to make faith relevant in a secular age, and Christians should also engage Confucian, Shinto, and Taoist scholars. Their common bond of enhancing human life can "enable all the religions of the world to work together harmoniously."[410]

The importance of this "hands-off stance" was reinforced by his visit to Nanjing Theological Seminary in China. He was told that help from the church in the United States would actually be harmful in that it would jeopardize religious freedom and reduce government aid. Rather, the Western church must recognize that "three self-movements are dominant in China: self-support, self-direction, and self-propagation." He unequivocally asserts that "this attitude seems to be quite prevalent in Asia because of the desire to separate Christianity from Western civilization."[411]

As for Japan, Allen emphasizes that religion and culture intertwined over centuries of shared history. So, too, Western Christians must recognize "that Christianity has been so deeply encrusted with Western cultural traditions that we cannot separate one from the other." This requires "doing some missionary work on ourselves," to sort through what is Christian practice and belief and what are Western cultural practices and values. The two have bled into one another.[412] That Allen correlates Christianity's most recent arrival in Japan with the incursion of Western culture (Commodore Perry's appearance in Tokyo Bay) hints that a possible reason for the scant Christian presence in Japan is its close identification with an "outside" culture.

These reflections led him to ask in 1986, fourteen years before the new millennium, "What is the mission of the [US] church in the twenty-first century? This should be the title of the next sabbatical paper." In this section of the sabbatical report, themes about the future and change emerge that will be echoed in his 2002 favorite sermon: "Without a Vision, the People Perish."

The church should take its cue for mission from the problems humanity will face. These include nuclear war, overpopulation, disappearing natural resources, global economic breakdown or an international depression, starvation, and the plight of refugees—"all mind-boggling and overpowering."

Further, now that the Christian gospel has been taken to every continent, should the church's mission be extended to include space and other planets potentially with living beings? And how is theology relevant in the computer age? He enlists robots as an example. If they become independent beings, do they have civil rights? Because of all these challenges, he asserts that the church needs a new vision because the twenty-first century is a new frontier.

He concludes the report by admitting that when he began the sabbatical, he had no idea it would lead him "to search for a clearer understanding of Christianity and a better definition of mission in the twenty-first century." Those insights provided him, first, with a more defined direction in which he wanted to head in the next decade of his own ministry.

Second, he observes that the US church needs to become more conscious of its total environment. It exists and does mission locally, regionally, and internationally. Accordingly, it lives throughout the global village. This awareness should lead it, for instance, to influence US political leadership to avoid unilateral movements toward violence by helping it realize that the United States is only one nation among many. Re-conceived, then, mission is not "the Christian mission in Japan." Rather, mission would be first to the US church, then to the nation, and then to the world. He quotes Luke 24:47: "Repentance and forgiveness of sins should be preached in his name to all nations, beginning from Jerusalem," taking that to mean, beginning with ourselves.[413]

It is not surprising that a study of other cultures redirects a researcher's focus to his or her own environment, assumptions, and practices. Perhaps by seeing the intricate ties between Japanese culture and its religious traditions firsthand, from Allen's sympathetic perspective as a person of Japanese heritage, he emerged from the sabbatical even more sensitive to the web of Christianity and Western cultural traditions. As a Japanese-American Christian in Japan, his lens was bifocal, as it is for him as an assimilated Nisei in America. From one perspective, he is an outsider in relationship to both cultures; from another, he can claim a certain insider status in each.

The sabbatical certainly reoriented his definitions of mission and evangelism. Mission does not begin elsewhere; it begins at home. As for evangelism, his definition of its task will emerge explicitly in his 2002 sermon, shaped, in part, by his experiences during his sabbatical.

In 2002, he will assert that evangelism is not a "fanatical drive" to convert the "heathen" because other religions are "meaningful and redemptive" in their context. The point is not to obsess over the percentage of Christians in Asia. Rather, evangelism's goal is to keep Jesus Christ, what he taught, and the example of his life at the center of faith. The consequences of this evangelism will be to "preserve the beauty of the good earth's creation" and to replace dehumanizing cultural elements with freedom as articulated and enacted by Jesus Christ, "humanism in the best sense of the word." His vision in 2002 will be based on the dream that this replacement will result in communities of love, forgiveness, and peace.

Chapter 24

Advocacy

ALLEN'S SABBATICAL SUMMARY INDICATES he will be re-evaluating the direction of his own ministry, but such an assessment will be taking place in the context of his many ongoing commitments. Of particular immediacy is his responsibility on a General Assembly Task Force on Pornography, which is congruent with his goals to begin mission at home and to replace dehumanizing cultural elements with freedom as articulated and enacted by Jesus Christ.

Tracing the evolution of the denomination's concern about pornography and how the task force came about gives a sense of the continuing nature of the church's focus on social justice issues and the thoroughness of the work the task forces do to address them. Allen was no stranger to these demands. He had already served on many of these projects, such as examining, making recommendations, and developing study materials on liberation theology, on the church's effective use of mass communication, and on the efficacy of the required Greek and Hebrew language examinations for ordination.

For more than a decade before the study on pornography was authorized by the 198th General Assembly in 1986, various councils and boards of the two precursor bodies that formed the PC(USA) in 1983, the "southern church" and the "northern church," were engaged in combatting the abusive treatment of women. Both had authorized studies and reports, developed educational materials, and recommended action to that end. Of particular concern of these various groups were "obscenity, pornography, sexual harassment, and other forms of sexual exploitation."[414]

The Task Force on Pornography was part of the work of the Council on Women and the Church and the Committee on Women's Concerns. It consisted of sixteen members and advisors from throughout the United States and the Dominican Republic. Allen is quick to point out that all the members were very impressive female theologians, pastors, and academics—all but two, he and James Spalding, a professor of theology at the University of Iowa Department of Religious Studies.[415]

Allen laughs about being one of only two men, as though the small number could be read as filling token slots. However, Allen came to the work he was assigned with firm convictions and public credentials regarding his advocacy on women's behalf. His commitment is particularly clear in the steps he took for the full participation of women in church employment. This commitment is noteworthy because it is not something he articulates. He might have taken his advocacy for granted, but the women with whom he worked did not.

Glendora ("Dusty") Taylor was working as an assistant pastor at Littleton First Presbyterian Church when, in 1980, Hutchison was leaving Montview. It began the search for an interim co-pastor. The Taylors had some familiarity with Montview because Hutchison's wife Pat had been the music director at the Littleton church, and Taylor's son Greg took organ lessons from her. Pat gave the lessons at Montview, and Greg would practice on the organ there.

However, Taylor did not apply for the position; she was recruited. She says, "I think Allen had a lot to do with [bringing me on board]. He was a big reason I was invited to Montview. Allen was always very active in presbytery," as was Taylor. She remembers having lunch with Barley and Allen, when she thinks they possibly explored the prospect of working together.[416]

On his part, Allen mentions he knew Taylor through their work together in presbytery, but he does not remember playing a role in her selection to be the interim co-pastor, a position for which the session does the hiring. "She was an exceptional woman. Even in presbytery, she was a leader, and she's a good preacher."

Evidently the congregation was also impressed with Taylor because, after one year, they wanted to hire her to fill the position permanently. For Allen, this is the more memorable part of the sequence of events leading to Montview hiring Taylor on a permanent basis. He says, "I think when the congregation did their interviews for a third co-pastor, they had a whole bunch of people to choose from. Ken [Barley] and I stayed completely out of their choice. You would think that in a co-pastorate, the two other co-pastors should have a voice in the choice, but we had no voice about the selection or the vote of the congregation. It was totally up to them."[417]

Hiring Taylor as interim co-pastor and then to permanently fill the position created no small difficulty for Montview. Denominational practice precludes a congregation from voting to install the person who has served as interim. Taylor thinks her installation was the result of a persistent lobbying effort, and she credits at least one influential member at Montview for persuading presbytery to make the exception.

For a woman to be hired as a Presbyterian pastor by a "big steeple" urban church in 1980 was remarkable. Also remarkable, from Taylor's perspective, was the way in which the issue of salary equity was handled. She recalls that the new team member, regardless of who that person might be, did not begin at the salary level of the other two. Montview's policy was to pay the new co-pastor 80 percent of the others' salaries the first year, 90 percent the second, and "then it was to be equal."

From Taylor's daughter's viewpoint, this was significant—that in the early 1980s "a woman was going to work somewhere with equal pay as men." Also memorable from those years was the fact that her mother was to give the sunrise service sermon at Red Rocks Amphitheatre in 1991 (or perhaps 1992). To speak at the Red Rocks interdenominational service is quite prestigious, because the occasion draws people from the entire metropolitan Denver area. Thousands of people. A magnificent venue: towering red rock formations framed against the Rocky Mountains' Front Range.

Kathy felt pride but also fear for her mother. In a recent conversation, Kathy told her, "I was scared because you were so exposed. There were still a lot of men who weren't happy about having women pastors. And your sermon [that morning] was about who saw Jesus first after he arose. The women! What if some crackpot got mad? I'd never had that feeling before because it's one thing preaching in the church, but somebody is so exposed on a stage."[418]

Cynthia Cearley also remembers that Allen was particularly supportive when she joined the staff as the assistant pastor for youth and children in 1980. Her friends told her she "was crazy to go work for three people. They said, 'That can't work.' But it was absolutely fine. I found these three very different but very collegial people: Dusty Taylor, Ken Barley, and Allen. I remember thinking that all of them, specifically Allen, had made very intentional decisions to share ministry and be collegial. That wasn't being done much in the church. For Dusty and Allen, because they weren't white males, a co-pastorate was a way to move into leadership of a church in a significant way, given their race and gender. Any of us who are not white male in the church know it's not the same road if you're not a white guy."[419]

Allen would be the first to agree. When he reflects on his call to Montview in 1972 to be an associate pastor, he says, "If I was running for the senior pastor position, it [race] would have been a major issue. . . . But having one of the three associates be non-white was a blessing to the congregation. In Park Hill, it would be a significant symbol that this congregation is not racist."[420]

In 1988, when Barley moved on to become pastor at First Presbyterian Church in Kalamazoo, Michigan, Cearley became the new member of the co-pastor team. She emphasizes a number of times how "when you're a brand new pastor, your bosses cover for you all the time because you don't know what you're doing. . . . Each of the co-pastors were wonderful mentors. Allen mentored me by being very enthusiastic about me and my ministry. He clearly wanted me to get involved in presbytery and broaden my experience so I would have recognition beyond Montview. . . . [After I had children], I would have had to go on long work trips [with the youth] and leave my kids. I didn't want to, so Allen actually took on the youth and some of my job for a short time in order to allow me to be moved into the role of co-pastor. To the end [before his retirement], he was enabling my ministry and helping. . . . He was a good friend in ministry, always. After he retired, we would go have lunch and hang out and talk."[421]

When asked how Allen handled working with two female colleagues as co-pastors or if he ever commented on it, Taylor laughs. "Two women! He did very well with that. . . . I don't remember him saying anything about it. That's just the way it worked out."[422]

The only time Allen highlights that his two of his colleagues from 1980 to his retirement in 1992 were women is in the context of a non-church member coming into the office to arrange a funeral for her husband. He somewhat gleefully tells the story. "They brought her into my office and I greeted her. She was obviously shocked that I was not white. She asked, 'Isn't there another minister available?' And I said, 'Yes. There are two other ministers. I'm sure we can make arrangements.' She says, 'I'd appreciate that.' And I said, 'Okay.' I ushered her out [and directed her down the hall]. She didn't realize the other two were not white men. They were two women! I think either Cindy or Dusty did the funeral. But it was obvious she could not fathom there wasn't a white man who was a minister at that church."

When Allen refers to Taylor and Cearley as colleagues, it is in the context of the interests and competencies of the three co-pastors, not to them as clergywomen. "After Hutch and Ken left and I was there with Dusty and Cindy, Cindy had more funerals than Dusty or I did simply because she was really good at doing funerals. By then, I was so busy with General Assembly, I wasn't much interested in doing pastoral work. I think Dusty did more weddings than I did then, but I had done enough to have my fill of funerals and weddings."[423]

All of which to say, Allen was no token male member of the task force on pornography. He advocated for and actively supported women in ministry without fanfare. Presumably he was seen as someone who would invest himself similarly in investigating the issues of sexual violence and economic disadvantage that forced women into the sex work that the task force was commissioned to investigate.

Starting in December 1986, only months after his return from his sabbatical, and continuing throughout 1987, the committee as a whole met four times: in New York, Minnesota, New Mexico, and Georgia. In addition, individual members attended any number of related events and workshops and conducted interviews. They read books, articles, and legislation, and they wrote reviews, which they shared with each other. In December 1987, the report was complete and approved for recommendation to the upcoming 200th General Assembly (1988). It was received by the Advisory Council on Church and Society, and the council took action to support it. The study paper was adopted by the assembly, an achievement because, as Allen notes time and again, acceptance of reports by the General Assembly is never a foregone conclusion.

Taken together with the decades-long history of the various task force reports, recommendations, and study guides produced by any number of committees on these related topics, a number of church professionals, staff, and members had been involved in the constellation of issues surrounding sexual exploitation over the years. Allen's task force was a piece of an evolving effort on the part of the church to inform itself, ameliorate conditions, and minister to those affected by it.

Allen particularly remembers the occasion that task force members visited a sex shop in New York City to listen to some of the women who were part of its operation. Some of the sex workers made it clear that that was the only way they thought they could generate sufficient income.

As he recalled the women's words, Rose interrupted. "The task force visited a sex shop? You never told me about that! How could any woman be happy with that choice?"[424]

Allen answered that he did not remember they were particularly happy. What struck him was that they had few options, and sex work provided them the best income, given their circumstances. The question for him was what conditions needed to be addressed so they had better opportunities.

The report itself briefly discusses this experience. "When the task force visited a Times Square sex shop, its members were struck with how ordinary and unexotic the women seemed. The same women might well be seen behind the counters in the fast food restaurants, and that sort of low-wage work may be their other best option." The report also notes that work in a sex shop "is surely safer than street prostitution, which poses constant dangers to health and safety." It concludes this section with the observation that "the pornography industry draws from a populous labor market of unskilled and economically needy women whose other options are not especially promising," and rumors of big money may be an (illusory) "enticement for women to take part in the production of sexually-explicit films and videos."[425]

The report is not just an abstraction of definition, history, and theology, although it also considers those aspects. Many of the convictions it expresses are congruent with Allen's personal commitments. At the outset, it states a theological vision of community as a covenant people striving for "shalom," people who are committed to living together in health, wholeness, unity, and peace.[426]

This vision of community is basic to Presbyterian theology, as it will be basic to Allen's favorite 2002 sermon in which he reminds the congregation that the church shares in the promise God made to Israel and to the church: as God's people, they were given a dream as well as a blessing to share with the world. He did not use the words "covenant" or "shalom" in the sermon, but they are congruent with the "promise" and "blessing" of Allen's sermon.

The pornography report also notes at the outset that in the story of the creation and the fall, the sexual relationship between male and female has been viewed as expressive of the covenant relationship between God and humanity. God is said "to know" the male and female, a Hebrew word that refers to the sexual encounter between a man and woman. The word "connotes mutuality and intimacy."

As "closely tied to the eros quality of love in human relations" as it is, the Hebrew verb that expresses the divine relationship with humanity "is also connected with agape love as a concern and care for the other." The interrelationship between divine love for humanity and the erotic love between humans is extended in the passages in the biblical Song of Songs, "where man and woman take pleasure in and celebrate one another's bodies, passages [that have] been seen through the centuries as symbolic of the relationship of God and the people of Israel, of Christ and the church." In short, as Allen says throughout his ministry, there is no separation of body and spirit in which one is valued less than the other. Body and spirit are complementary. Violation of one is violation of the other.

Pornography: Far from the Song of Songs rehearses any number of definitions of pornography, various attitudes toward it, and legislative approaches to dealing with it, in particular the 1986 *Final Report of the Attorney General's Commission on Pornography*. The *Pornography* report analyzes the strengths and weakness of these attitudes and approaches. It confesses the "role of the Christian church in the relationships between pornography, sexist attitudes, and sexually aggressive behavior" in that throughout history and into the present, the church contributes to sexual exploitation by promoting the unequal status of women.[427]

In its summary, it says pornography demeans human dignity and mutuality in relationships, and it is symptomatic of "deeply embedded cultural problems." Among these are the extent of social isolation in US society; assumptions that women (and children) exist to serve men's needs; a viewpoint that sex is an adversarial relationship in which one person exercises power over another; that violence is natural, acceptable, and sexually stimulating; that commitment to human relationships threatens individual freedom; and that self-gratification is the highest good.[428]

Pornography: Far from the Song of Songs offers a number of both targeted and general recommendations. The recommendations urge developing and using educational materials in local churches, including sex education for junior high and high school members; "reaffirming the policy of previous General Assemblies regarding the use of inclusive language in the entire life of the church"; urging individuals to take action, including writing letters to "television networks and cable service opposing programming considered to be pornographic," while keeping in mind and balancing First Amendment rights of expression; and reaffirming the General Assembly's historical support of the passage of the Equal Rights Amendment.

The list of proposed actions is lengthy and continues with a recommendation to monitor the church's investment in companies that might be benefiting financially from activities that promote sexual exploitation and to contribute $10,000 to the World Council of Churches in its effort through the Ecumenical Decade of Churches in Solidarity with Women to "address the issues of violence against women." The report urges reaffirming support for the United Nations Convention on the Elimination of All Forms of Discrimination against Women.

The progression of the recommendations follows the template Allen used to conclude his sabbatical report. They begin with self-examination and renewal before extending reform measures outside the church, nationally and then globally. Also, as with his membership on the task force to study liberation theology in the 1970s, Allen was in the midst of cutting-edge and controversial issues for the church in the 1980s: sexual exploitation, inclusive language and sex education in the church, the Equal Rights Amendment, World Council of Churches and United Nations' programs advocating for women's rights.

As a measure of Allen's clear-sightedness and that of the other task force members, their report and most of its recommendations address seemingly intractable issues of injustice and sexual cruelty against women and children that remain at the forefront of the news three decades later. One sample among many is a headline on a 2019 front page of *The New York Times* that reads: "Behind Illicit Massage Parlors Lie a Vast Crime Network and Modern Indentured Servitude." The words below the headline give this detail: "Foreign Women Caught in Cruel Indentured Servitude."[429]

Without breaking stride, Allen had not just the intent but the opportunity to follow through on his sabbatical resolve of beginning mission "in Jerusalem" through his General Assembly work. In 1988, not only was the *Pornography* report adopted, but the entire nation was in the process of revisiting the injustice of its forced removal and mass incarceration of JaJAs during World War II. The movement had started in the 1970s as JaJAs began to talk more openly about their dislocation and loss and determined that the injustice they suffered should not happen ever again to any targeted groups. The effort took form in such organizations as the National Coalition for Redress/Reparations.

In response, in 1980, Congress had formed the Commission on Wartime Relocation and Internment of Civilians to investigate the effects of incarceration and possibilities for redress. The Commission held hearings around the country and concluded that the "imprisonment of a whole population of people . . . was because of racial prejudice, war hysteria and a failure of political leadership—and not because of 'military necessity.'"

Redress legislation was making its way through the process when the 1988 General Assembly met. The General Assembly passed a resolution urging President Ronald Reagan to sign what the assembly refers to as the Japanese-American and Aleut redress/reparation bill. Some political leaders were advising Reagan not to sign, but, according to others, he seemed open to the possibility.

In August, Reagan did affix his signature to what became known as the 1988 Civil Liberties Act. At the signing, he recalled his participation in 1945, as a young actor and army captain, along with General Joseph Stilwell and other celebrities, in the recognition of Kazuo Masuda, a Japanese-American member of the 442nd Regimental Combat Team who was killed in action in Italy. Stilwell presented the Distinguished Service Cross, awarded posthumously, to Masuda's family.

Reagan was present when Stilwell made the award, and Reagan made the following remarks at a rally marking the occasion at the nearby Santa Ana Municipal Bowl: "America stands unique in the world, the only country not founded on race but on a way—an ideal. Not in spite of, but because of our polyglot background, we have all the strength in the world." He apparently referred to his 1945 remarks at the 1988 signing ceremony as a way to convey the constancy of his values.[430]

The 1988 act called for an apology and payments of $20,000 to survivors of the incarceration and their heirs. In a public ceremony in 1990, President George H.W. Bush apologized to the first Issei to receive the checks, and payments to the rest of those eligible were made into 1993. Educational provisions of the act were eventually fulfilled under the Clinton administration.[431]

Allen does not mention the 1988 General Assembly resolution urging Reagan to sign the 1988 Civil Liberties Act. Perhaps the presentation of the pornography task force's report was uppermost on his mind, but the apology and reparations certainly met his criteria for church mission beginning at home to right a terrible injustice. In this case, "at home" could even be read in a literal sense as his sister-in-law Dorothy and her family were among those eligible to receive the payments. Perhaps by 1988 Allen was secure enough in his sense of himself as an assimilated Japanese American that the apology from the US government, while it would have made a great deal of difference to the teenage version of himself, was simply accepted as a long-overdue recognition of arbitrary exclusion and hardship.

In what was to be more formative personally for Allen, Mother Teresa was invited to the 1988 assembly and spoke at a worship service he attended. A hopeful inference from her appearance is that the PC(USA) was following the injunction of liberation theologians. Rather than imposing its priorities on her work in Kolkata, it listened and responded to her expression of need and hope.

As Allen describes it, he "met Mother Teresa," albeit along with "hundreds of other fans." Her presence at the assembly, its affirmation of her work, and Allen's encounter with her sparked his concern for homeless ministries in Colorado. He continues to be an advocate for the homeless, yet another instance of promoting mission that begins "in Jerusalem," a recognition of the biblical imperative to meet immediate need.[432]

Chapter 25

Tenacity and Partnership

ALSO DURING 1988, ALLEN met Lesley Shearer, an acupuncturist and one of the leaders in Colorado who lobbied for and was successful in gaining certification for acupuncturists. Neither of them remember whether they first met at a "Science and Consciousness" workshop in Albuquerque, New Mexico, which Allen attended with several Montview members, or at a craniosacral workshop in Denver conducted by Hugh Milne, a Scottish osteopath, around the same time. From their meeting to the present, Shearer remains one of Allen's biggest supporters and a friend.[433]

A characteristic she finds remarkable about Allen is his tenacity, and she gives an example from a trip she, her husband, Allen and Rose, and some Montview members took to Kathmandu in 1993. As part of that trip, some of the group visited Kolkata, India. Not one to shrink from inconvenience or human pain, even Shearer found herself "overwhelmed" by the crushing poverty, the numbers of people, the smells, and what seemed to be chaos on the streets. "Kolkata is culture shock, absolute culture shock," she says.

She questioned the wisdom of the visit Allen wanted to make to Mother Teresa's internationally known hospital in Kolkata. Rose would accompany him. Two strangers to the city heading out on their own? Shearer says she would not have considered attempting it. Allen hailed a taxi, reassured by the driver that he knew the way. But Shearer was correct about the hazards. The taxi drove into the middle of a demonstration, a picture of which Rose took from inside the cab and included in her photo album of the trip. The people in the demonstration got angry at the driver because he was forcing his way through. They started shaking the taxi and almost overturned it. Rose was scared. Allen assured the driver, "We're not in a hurry. Take your time." They waited until the demonstration passed by.

They arrived at the hospital door, only to be told that Mother Teresa was out of the country. They were not allowed entry. Rose took a picture of the door, and Allen says that, while they were disappointed not to meet her or tour the facility, finally seeing the hospital in its surroundings was satisfaction enough.[434]

Another risky adventure on the same trip involved a flight in a small plane to view the summit of Mount Everest. Rose and Allen weighed the opportunity. Chances were they would not see the summit, since, more often than not, it is covered in clouds. The ride would be bumpy, to say the least, and the cost was nearly prohibitive. But, Mount Everest! Surely it was worth the gamble. Rose writes these words on the page of photos that show the summit through the plane's window, clearly visible and seemingly within reach—"$200 pictures"!

Rose thought of that particular trip with the Shearers as extraordinary, even though she had already been to Japan (twice) and China and Korea. She said, "Who would have thought that a little girl from Grayville, Illinois, would be in Nepal—or Kolkata?"

Allen's calm reaction to being surrounded by the demonstrators, his trust in the taxi driver, and a similar reliance on the pilot of the small plane, along with his determination to see Mount Everest in spite of the unlikelihood, are reminiscent of the way he handled a more threatening incident as a college student. In his second year at the University of Colorado (1949), he got a call one afternoon that his father was desperately ill. He immediately enlisted a fraternity brother to drive him the forty miles from Boulder to Denver, where he intended to "thumb" rides on south to Pueblo, a distance of over one hundred miles. There he would catch a bus going east for the remaining eighty miles to Las Animas.

"I was somewhere south of Denver. Cars and trucks would just zoom by, and I was getting discouraged, but suddenly one car stopped. I didn't ask any questions. I just threw my suitcase in and my jacket and jumped in the front seat.

"The guy started laughing. He said, 'I'm headed for Mexico. Where are you going?'

"I said, 'I'm only going to Pueblo, to the bus station.'

"And he said, 'You may not go to Pueblo. I want you to go with me. You're riding with a criminal.'

"He said something about robbing someplace, and he was pretty inebriated. I talked to him, and by the time we got to Colorado Springs, I persuaded him to stop and have a cup of coffee.

"But he was saying, 'I really need company to go to Mexico.'

"And I said, 'My father is dying in Las Animas, and I need for you to take me to the bus station in Pueblo.'

"I finally persuaded him to drop me off there. . . . There was no reason to be scared, except he was so drunk we could have been in an accident. It was good for me to talk to him that much because he was willing to have a cup of coffee. I suppose I could have grabbed my suitcase out of his car. I didn't see any gun or anything. . . . I know I got him sobered up."

Allen's father had suffered a cerebral hemorrhage. He died shortly before Allen arrived that evening.

With unexpected partners—taxi driver, small plane pilot, inebriated thief on the run—Allen reached his destinations, more often than not with Rose's companionship. One of the more surprising goals Allen determined to achieve, after his 1986 sabbatical and as part of the process of redirecting his ministry, was to begin the certification process for becoming a massage therapist. Although he believed that there is no separation between the physical and the spiritual in terms of healing and faith, the church at large did not share that belief when it came to massage therapy. In the late 1980s, "massage" equaled massage parlors, which equaled prostitution. End of story, but not for Allen, who persevered through one thousand hours of training to obtain his state license.

His friend Larry Angus had other plans. Larry approached him with the idea that Allen should again stand for moderator of the General Assembly in 1990. Rose was doubtful. "He'd be disappointed again if he didn't make it." Rose believed he did very well the first time and said, "I thought, that was enough." That he ran again in 1990, she believes was "Larry's fault. He insisted."

From Allen's perspective, the lesson from 1980's loss was that "you learn humility and to understand yourself much better when you lose than when you win." For Larry and Allen, surely the time had finally come for the first Asian-American leader in the national church. Allen determined he would make another run.[435]

In the decade since the Detroit General Assembly, any number of changes within the church, the nation, and the world pressed upon the PC(USA). In 1983, the "southern" (PCUS) and "northern" (UPCUSA) branches of the Presbyterian church reunited, an accomplishment many years in the making. Even into the present, real and imagined differences in style and values remain sources of friction.

During the three years following reunification, world affairs intruded somewhat dramatically on the Presbyterian church. Rev. Benjamin Weir had survived for sixteen months as one of the hostages held in Lebanon by the Islamic Jihad, fourteen of them in solitary confinement. Upon his release, he was a national hero, and the reunited PC(USA) denomination fully embraced him as its voice of moral leadership by electing him moderator of the 1986 General Assembly.

Weir, having lived and worked in the Middle East for nearly three decades, consistently expressed the view that a "one-sided American policy . . . that ignores the dispossessed Palestinians is a factor in the troubles now faced by Americans in that part of the world." Throughout his career, and during his year as moderator, Weir communicated his commitment to "international forgiveness and reconciliation."[436]

In that Weir urged the United States to examine its own policies and their impact on global issues, his views paralleled Allen's belief as he was to express them in his sabbatical report: mission, in the sense of self-examination, redemption, and recommitment, must begin at home. Allen had contextualized the belief scripturally, as originating "in Jerusalem."

The expanding diversity in moderator profiles throughout the intervening decade supported Angus's optimism about the viability of Allen's candidacy. The prior year, 1989, Joan Salmon Campbell was elected moderator, a black woman and Presbyterian pastor. Outspoken and a talented contralto with a degree from the Eastman School of Music, she was known to burst into song from podium and pulpit. During her tenure, she addressed the ongoing fracas between liberals and conservatives over any number of issues with her characteristic proclamation, "There's room for all of us!" Her statement underscored the need to reconcile differences within the church, again congruent with Allen's conclusion after his sabbatical that the mission of the church begins with itself. Such attempts at unity were seen as crucial to maintaining the denomination's vitality as it had lost one million members in the prior two decades.[437]

The same refrain for unity while affirming diversity had emerged explicitly in 1979, even before the 1980 assembly convened, when Allen first ran for moderator. As has been noted, that assembly was dominated by the concern about churches withdrawing over such issues as ordaining women and accepting presbytery jurisdiction concerning matters like a local church's appropriate amount of giving to the mission of the wider church.

The outgoing moderator of the southern church had noted back then that it is "difficult for a pluralistic church to grow. Homogeneous churches grow easily." He contrasted the value of pluralism with what he saw as the profile of another denomination, the Presbyterian Church in America

(PCA), which many of the departing ministers and churches from both the northern and southern churches were joining. He said that the PCA "has chosen to be homogeneous with similar beliefs, similar socio-economic status, and probably the same race. The challenge for pluralistic churches is to keep the tensions of pluralism in a healthy balance."[438]

One example of the church's continuing efforts to meet challenges of pluralism is reported in the 1987 General Assembly publication of its daily activities. In noting the assembly's vote to reaffirm its commitment to racial justice, the report lambasts the "heretical nature" of the "Christian Identity" movement and its racial interpretation of Christianity. The report character-izes the movement as a "pretext for hatred, racism, including anti-Semitism, and sexism." Evidently not only the Presbyterian Church but other main-stream Protestant denominations, Catholics, and even "fundamentalist" churches had withstood "vicious attacks" by white supremacist groups and gangs loosely affiliated with this movement.[439]

As indicated in its choices for moderator and its public stances, sub-sequent to Allen's 1980 candidacy, the now-united PC(USA) had continued to value diversity, which would surely bode well for his 1990 candidacy. In addition to Angus's determination that Allen could be the first Asian-American moderator, Allen himself thought he had the necessary personal support. His endorsements came from such luminaries as Dr. Daniel A. Ruge, President Ronald Reagan's physician at the time of the assassination attempt in 1981 and now a member at Montview; Colorado's Governor Roy Romer (who would be re-elected that fall), also a Montview member; and a number of other well-known figures.

Allen was even more visible throughout the denomination in the decade since his last attempt to win the position by virtue of all his leader-ship positions in the national church. Perhaps most significantly, the link conservatives had made between his term as 1979 moderator of the Den-ver Presbytery and churches departing over the ordination of women and other issues would not impact his candidacy as it had in 1980. He decided to run, although Rose was still hesitant. A busload of Montview members accompanied them to Salt Lake City, the site for the 1990 assembly. Those attending included Dr. and Mrs. Ruge.

Chapter 26

Vision and the 1990 Salt Lake City General Assembly

No recordings exist of the 1990 Salt Lake General Assembly (May 29 to June 6). The lack of audio robs any summary of the proceedings of its vitality and also means a loss of both Harriet Isbell's speech nominating Allen, which he recalls as "beautiful, outstanding," and his candidating speech. Nor does either of them have written copies.

One can only imagine the wit and perhaps drama of Isbell's remarks, given her energy and sense of humor. Perhaps she even had proper shoes for the occasion and did not have to rob a nearby children's nursery for a dress-up pair. After the election, Allen told her that, on the basis of her speech, "if you had been running for moderator, I think you had a chance to win!"[440]

Written materials have to suffice for context and to present the candidates. As was the case in the 1980 election, the 1990 gathering consists of lively contests of personalities, ideas, and goals. It too engages salient political and social issues, ones that remain at the forefront of challenges in the twenty-first century. In 1990, though, these discussions take place in the context of sorting through the implications of the 1983 reunion of the northern and southern branches of the denomination and the continuing squabbles between liberals and conservatives. Whether it be debates about organizational restructuring, allocation of resources, theological emphases, or liturgical practices, the reunited denomination is engaged in articulating its vision.

June Suzuki Mochizuki said she remembered the 1990 assembly well. She was a member of the nominating committee, and for the prior decade, her husband Min had served on General Assembly Council. As had Allen, Min and June had remained quite active in the denomination at the national level following their attendance at the 1980 assembly.

When the church reunited in 1983, Min was chair of a committee of five that had chosen Salt Lake City as the 1990 meeting site, an "unusual recommendation. No General Assembly went to Salt Lake City as there were very few Presbyterians there." He says it competed with San Fransisco and Seattle for the bid, but the folks in Salt Lake City were remarkably receptive to hosting Presbyterians. The committee anticipated that the experience would be unique and informative.[441]

That "there were very few Presbyterians" in Salt Lake City was an understatement. E. Kenneth Tracy, executive presbyter, Presbytery of Utah, notes in his welcome to the General Assembly that there were "only twenty-four churches and 4,976 Presbyterians" in the entire presbytery.

However, Min and Tracy both recognized the value of having the assembly in a location where mainline Protestantism was not comfortably represented. Not only might the experience bring fresh perspectives to matters under discussion, but, as Tracy points out, the PC(USA) would witness "the very special and unique ministry that is carried out in your name, in a land called Zion [by Latter-Day Saints], by Presbyterians as a religious minority and, in many cases, in very isolated rural communities within the states of Utah and Idaho." By choosing this location, the PC(USA) affirmed the value of ministry in rural and agricultural areas, as well as in coastal and larger metropolitan settings.[442]

Min and June traveled to Utah from Denver, having retired to Colorado in 1988 to be near family. They now attended Montview regularly and had finally established a friendship with Allen and Rose after decades of briefly crossing paths.

Also during the 1980s, Min's emotional attachments to Presbyterianism were strengthened by an experience that somewhat parallels Allen's sense of having been adopted into the Scottish Presbyterian "family." Neither Allen nor Min use the term "assimilation" for their sense of inclusion. For Allen, it is "adoption"; Min calls it "convergence" and "identification." The phrasing implies that participating in this particular religious community does not require erasure of their Japanese-American identity. Rather, they have become part of it on their own terms.

Min describes his "identification" experience as originating in 1983 with his task of negotiating the severance pay with William Thompson, the stated clerk of the church's northern branch. Thompson had lost re-election for the position in the reunited denomination to James E. Andrews, the stated clerk of the southern branch.

"I went to New York [the location of the national offices of the northern branch] for the conversation. . . . Well, he knew better than I what the terms were because he was stated clerk. I'm sitting outside his office, and I look around and see pictures on the wall of these old guys with beards—historical church figures. I suddenly felt such a kinship with these Scotsmen. The feeling was incredible. I consider Presbyterian history my history, too, but this was the strangest moment of identification. That we are Presbyterians, and somehow we are physically linked."[443]

The link Min recognized as he gazed at those portraits spanned two centuries, during which Presbyterians in the United States survived any number of changes. However, the changes in the decade between Allen's 1980 candidacy and 1990 were particularly significant for both Min and Allen and for the denomination—the Mochizukis' retirement to Denver, the start of Allen's massage therapy training, the church's embrace of such diverse leaders as Benjamin Weir and Joan Salmon Campbell, and the 1983 reunion, which in itself prompted a whole cascade of adjustments.

Even the geographical center of the reunified church bodies shifted. Initially, the headquarters for both the United Presbyterian Church in the United States of America (UPCUSA—northern) and the Presbyterian Church in the United States (PCUS—southern) were to shift to Kansas City. At the last minute, Louisville made a more enticing offer, including property along a waterfront. Unexpectedly, Louisville won the bid.

Throughout the prior decade, any number of committees had worked on other basic tasks having to do with reunification. A hymnal using inclusive language in the lyrics was proposed for the new entity, the PC(USA). A new confession of faith took shape, and redesigns of organizational structures meant to tie up fundamental changes subsequent to reunion were negotiated. Many of these adjustments would be presented to the 1990 assembly for approval.

Illustrative of how foundational these changes were, a new confession meant amending the church's constitution. If approved at the Salt Lake General Assembly, it would be sent to the one hundred seventy-one presbyteries for their agreement, similar to the process of amending the U.S. Constitution.

The committee working on it was comprised of representatives from the two branches and had started on the task back in 1979, in anticipation of the 1983 reunion. If approved, this "Brief Statement of Faith" would be the first new confession since 1967 and the eleventh in the church's two-hundred-two-year history in the United States.[444]

The significance of this "Brief Statement" lay in the fact that it would become the agreed-upon vision for the new denomination. Also significant was its poetic form. It was hoped that this format would lend itself to liturgical use in worship services throughout the member churches, thus engaging local congregants in widespread and repeated articulation of its perspectives.

The thoughts of Susanne Langer, a twentieth-century philosopher writing for an academic audience decades prior, shed light on the dynamics that underlie such endeavors. Her framework makes less puzzling why so much time was devoted to writing a new confession and why it loomed so large on the 1990 assembly's agenda. Her work also offers a foundation for thinking about the importance placed on its anticipated liturgical use.

Langer's definition of religion, one that pertains to any faith tradition, establishes the framework. She defines religion as "a gradual envisagement of the essential pattern of human life"—gradual in that religious traditions develop over spans of time, historically and as they are embraced in the lives of their adherents. Another way to conceive of Langer's "pattern" is to think of it as a "vision."

Such a pattern or vision shapes questions like why we exist and how we should act in the world, as well as answers to those questions. It considers the origin of individual souls and their course prior to birth, during life, and after death, or if such souls exist. It sets forth the nature of the divine and that divinity or divinities' relationship to the universe, its theology. The pattern suggests a religion's cosmology: creation's origin and where it is headed.

However, an abstract pattern does not in itself sustain a religious tradition. Langer says it is sustained in objects and concepts that become "charged with meaning" or sacred for the practitioners of that particular tradition. In addition, that which is sacred would be nearly useless were those meaningful "objects and concepts" and that "essential pattern" to stay remote from faith practices. They are made accessible through ritual, that is, "a disciplined rehearsal of right attitudes,"[445] such as Friday prayer, Shabbat, Sunday Mass, chanted mantras, pilgrimages, and so forth.

In the Reformed (including Presbyterian) tradition, confessions are statements of the "essential pattern" envisaged by the faithful that reach through history to the present. Although Presbyterians would not go so far as to call confessions sacred, they do function as "charged" historical repositories.

Finally, that the authors of the new "Brief Statement" consciously shaped it poetically for liturgical use meant they hoped it would not languish within the pages of books studied only by clergy, seminary students, and professors. Rather, it would be regularly and ritually used as "a disciplined rehearsal of right attitudes" throughout local congregations as a repository for faith and action and as a vision for the future. To state its significance in the terms of Allen's 2002 sermon, it would express the vision without which the people (and the reunited denomination) would perish.

The text of the "Brief Statement" is not altogether that brief. Even a cursory reading reveals how closely Allen follows its major tenets in his 2002 anniversary sermon at Montview, "Without a Vision, the People Perish": the divine promise to Israel and the church and the call to be a blessing to the families of the earth by embodying justice, freedom, and peace; and the redemption of all creation (although couched in Allen's sermon in terms of Teilhard's Omega Point), with no distinction between the physical and spiritual (the new heaven and earth). The "Brief Statement" also uses the term "body of Christ," with implications similar to those used by Allen in his 1980 candidating speech: male and female, every people and race living as one community. In general, Allen's vision and the statement explicitly embrace inclusivity and a dynamic, divine presence.

Allen lives the "essential pattern" expressed in the statement, a happy coincidence that its approval might take place at the assembly where he would stand for the second time for the position of moderator. In all probability, the majority of those attending the 1990 assembly would also recognize the statement's tenets as reformulations of those with which they grew up and which they embraced in their confirmation classes. Min would have particularly recognized himself and his call to ministry during his incarceration at Tule Lake in a concluding phrase: "With believers in every time and place, we rejoice that nothing in life or in death can separate us from the love of God in Christ Jesus our Lord."

The topic of approving the "Brief Statement" appears so frequently throughout the 1990 General Assembly that most commissioners probably would have been familiar with its form, content, and purpose. Its spirit might have influenced the tone of this assembly, in particular. A summary follows.

The first stanza sets out its trinitarian structure and concludes with the core of Reformed faith—the sovereignty of God. "We trust in the triune God, the Holy One of Israel, whom alone we worship and serve."

The second stanza focuses on the second person of the trinity, Jesus Christ. Its emphasis is his proclamation of good news to the poor, release to the captives, blessing the children, healing, inclusiveness, repentance, and forgiveness. The stanza concludes with statements about his unjust crucifixion and his resurrection.

Themes common to Allen and Min's beliefs about God emerge with particular clarity in the third stanza. God, "whom Jesus called Abba Father," created the world good, and all are equally made in God's image. Humans rebel against and hide from God and ignore God's commandments. The consequences of that behavior are violation of God's image in self and others and exploitation of neighbor and nature. Even though humanity deserves divine condemnation, God is everlastingly faithful and redeems creation. God chooses a covenant people to "bless all the families of the earth." Christians are heirs of the covenant through Christ.

The fourth stanza emphasizes the work of God the Holy Spirit, who justifies by grace through faith, inspires, and calls women and men to ministry. The Spirit binds believers together "in the one body of Christ, the church." It gives courage to the faithful to "unmask idolatries in church and culture to hear the voices of people long silenced and to work with others for justice, freedom, and peace."

The concluding phrases were quoted above. They function as a doxology, together with the final words: "Glory be to the Father, and to the Son, and to the Holy Spirit. Amen."[446]

A prose summary hardly does justice to the cadence and imagery of the statement or to its emotional impact. The 1990 General Assembly adopted the statement, and it was sent to the presbyteries for their approval. It has been included in the constitution throughout the subsequent decades. Because of its length, churches rarely use it in its entirety in any single worship service. Depending on the liturgical focus of the service, when it is used, one of the three stanzas about Son, Father, or Spirit is typically combined with the first and/or last stanza for congregational recitation.

The task for the hymnbook committee also touched congregation members at the emotional level of "ritual" and with the functional purpose of reinforcing the denominational vision. The new *Presbyterian Hymnal*, emblazoned with the reunited church's logo, had already been approved and was published in 1990.

The committee members reminded Presbyterians in a June 1990 *Outlook* article, at the time of the Salt Lake assembly, of what had been its task and methods. The direction of several prior general assemblies was that the committee use "inclusive language [while being] sensitive to the diverse nature" of the church. The committee recognized that the more difficult task was dealing with the emotional impact of changing, possibly eliminating, hymns near and dear to congregants' hearts. Hymns that, in some cases, had been sung for generations of Presbyterians underwent significant transformation as they were adjusted to meet contemporary demands for envisioning the "essential pattern of human [and divine] life."

Even though the new hymnal was an accomplished fact by the time of the 1990 assembly, the committee admits that congregational adjustment to differences in dearly loved and familiar hymns (as Langer's objects "imbued with meaning") will be a drawn-out process. Altering or replacing familiar elements of ritual is emotionally disruptive at best. The committee can only acknowledge the importance of being "increasingly attuned to the depth of feeling for and attachment to hymns by church members."[447]

While the committee's *Outlook* article explains the general principles it followed in its determinations, the hymnbook committee does not address specific concerns raised in what were undoubtedly any number of prior discussions and *Outlook* articles, such as one by Richard C. and Florence M. Cole. The Coles begin by addressing congregations "throughout the land" who will "decide whether to replace the 1955 *Hymnbook* with the 1990 *Presbyterian Hymnal*." The *Hymnbook* had occupied Presbyterian pew racks for nearly a half century, a measure of how charged and momentous adopting the new hymnal would be for congregations.[448]

As one indication of how thoughtfully and thoroughly the committee worked to review and revise the hymnal, it was explained that "texts which promote self-righteous militarism, self-righteous nationalism, self-righteous triumphalism or self-righteous mission activity" were not included. Terms used pejoratively were altered, such as "'darkness' or 'black' to denote evil and sin."[449]

Although the Coles do not explicitly dismiss the new hymnal, they imply the effort is misguided in that it compromises the "essential pattern" of Reformed theology in any number of ways. It remained an open question whether congregations would replace their 1955 hymnals with the new one, which partnered with the new confession, the "Brief Statement," to re-articulate the denomination's vision of greater inclusivity and divine engagement with human suffering and injustice.

Rarely is it easy to maneuver change of such magnitude. Most of it required a good deal of give and take. Any number of articles in the *Outlook* set the stage for the 1990 assembly with added details of ongoing debates, but the parameters it set out in the first issue of the new decade are not surprising in light of all the change. Its list of "Hopes for the Nineties" focuses on regrouping, individually and institutionally.

Most of the items on the list call its readers back to the basics of what would be recognized as the Reformed religious pattern. The list is long and includes a revival of faith and faithfulness, an increasing focus on Jesus Christ and less on the particular "issues" that currently divide the church, a widespread increase in biblical literacy and devotion to Scripture study, a recovery of theological vision rooted in Scripture . . . that manifests itself in public faith and practice, and a continued commitment to work for justice in the church and the world.[450]

This list that, in effect, calls for re-examining and recommitting to the "essential pattern" of Presbyterian belief and practice is congruent with Allen's 1986 sabbatical conclusion that mission, particularly following change and its disruptions, should begin first in Jerusalem, that is, with self and one's purpose. As sabbaticals are meant to do, his gave him distance from and insight into his regular work routine and familiar surroundings in 1986. Reunion in 1983 had given Presbyterians a similar sabbatical, a time for an interior re-examination throughout the 1980s before presenting an "essential pattern" of Reformed faith in 1990, as expressed in the "Brief Statement of Faith" for themselves and to contemporary society. Also, in spite of the nearly 24/7 schedule of the General Assembly, an assembly itself provides a sabbatical opportunity of sorts for teaching and ruling elders—time apart for reflection, renewal, and recommitment.

An earnest and thoughtful editorial in the February 12 issue follows the January list of hopes. It is entitled "Cultural Pluralism in the Church." A comparison of this editorial with the "Hopes for the Nineties" list suggests the denomination is see-sawing between the stability offered by the regrouping focus of the January list and an invitation to imaginatively meet the challenges of the future prompted by all the change.

The pluralism article rehearses the steps that have been taken to deal with the disruption prompted by reunification. It notes that the 1980 assembly of the UPCUSA (northern branch) had mandated a series of colloquia on the topic of pluralism, culminating in an event held in San Francisco titled "Authenticity before the Altar" at which participants from different cultures had "celebrated diversity in oneness."

At the heart of this series, and in a guide adopted by the southern branch of the church (PCUS), also on the theme of pluralism and during the same period of time, were efforts to address tensions highlighted by reunion. Can there be a culturally plural inclusive church? Is it possible to appreciate diversity while valuing the contribution each makes to the whole? The writer cautions against "ethnocentrism," that is, "applying our own cultural concepts and values to a culture other than our own."[451]

Not only was the reunited denomination integrating southern and northern cultural distinctions, structurally and otherwise, but there was growing awareness that Western cultural values, even more specifically, white values, were ubiquitous throughout the denomination's theology and practices—which is to say, this awareness was not unique to Allen. Written materials throughout the 1980s frequently urge members to study and critically examine these values and to appreciate other cultural perspectives.

The following week, in February, Gene Williams' interview with S. David Stoner, the General Assembly Council executive director, appears in the

Outlook. The interview also addresses the broad concerns about pluralism by juxtaposing "doing justice" with "spiritual growth" and the latter's emphasis on evangelism. The focus is the tension between the "whole church" and local congregations. The interview emphasizes that two of the eighteen priority areas established by the 1989 assembly addressed maintaining balance between doing justice and doing evangelism.

The section of the interview that addresses doing justice specifies what this entails. Williams quotes Stoner as reminding Presbyterians "the basic call for Christianity is to feed the hungry and clothe the naked and house the unhoused and to work with the poor.' . . . In addition, 'We try to work on biases and prejudices as well as real economic problems. . . . And there are issues [about] how we live our lives and use nature's resources. . . . We're called to solve the structural problems inherent in our society that cause these things to continue."

In the discussion about doing evangelism, Stoner notes that most major Protestant denominations have lost members, not to other churches as much as "to the secular world." Given that dynamic, the task is to support local churches as they define their ministries in ways that are perceived to be significant in their communities. Additionally, the church at all levels needs to focus on spiritual development so people are clear about their faith and purpose.[452]

Combined, the two articles, "Hopes" and "Cultural Pluralism," as well as the Stoner interview, serve a similar purpose: to define a contemporary vision of a relevant church in an increasingly secular world, that is, a viable and inspiring "essential pattern" for the reunited denomination. These multiple conversations also foreshadow Allen's favorite 2002 sermon's themes of vision and change: God is divine process and exists in the midst of change; and, without a vision [of living into change, while not losing sight of the goals of peace and justice], the people perish.

The last week in February, Williams published his interview with James E. Andrews, the stated clerk of the PC(USA), in the *Outlook*. Again, the underlying theme is that of articulating a vision. How will the church respond to change in the coming decade of the 90s?

The very layout of the page hints at playfulness. The intriguing sidebar reads, "Andrews Speaks Out on Breakfasts." In support of his less than positive view of the first meal of the day, Andrews notes two biblical morning occasions: Luke 22:54–62, which describes Peter's denial of the Christ to the people who gathered around the fire to warm themselves in the courtyard at the high priest's, punctuated three times by the rooster's pre-dawn crows; and John 21:4–14, the seaside breakfast that Jesus shares with his followers after the crucifixion. Andrews concludes that breakfast begins in tragedy;

that at least 50 percent of breakfasts should be eaten out of doors, preferably by the sea; the menu is fish half the time; and breakfast should be limited to the cataclysmic times of life.

Andrews's freewheeling exegesis of these biblical passages might have been seen as sacrilegious or as an effective engagement strategy. Not unexpectedly, given his droll wit, Andrews frames the 1990s as a decade of change that will present not-to-be-dreaded challenges prompted by the "wave of freedom that has swept Eastern Europe in the past several months" and the "shifts in demographics . . . of people in different kinds of religious organizations growing out of a very different kind of spiritual understanding."

One demographic shift that Andrews notes is the increase in the number of Muslims in the United States, soon to outnumber Jews. He considers Christian spirituality to be closely aligned with Jewish spirituality, so recognizing Muslim spirituality, as well as "practitioners of Eastern religions—Buddhism, Hinduism," will "open us up to new things."

This thought leads him to speculate about what those "new things" could be. He acknowledges his own shortcomings with contemplation and that he is trying to maintain an "attitude of prayer" for stretches of time lasting at least ten minutes. With characteristic dry humor, he observes he is "paid to know how [to pray]. The average person in the church is lucky if he [or she] can do it for sixty seconds! We're going to have to learn that" (spiritual disciplines of meditation and prayer).

Allen had come to a similar conclusion about the efficacy of prayer and meditation after his brush with mortality five years prior. Also, Allen had expressed a comparable desire to learn from dialogue with other religious traditions, a desire clearly expressed in his sabbatical report in 1986. That he was fully engaged with developments and ongoing discussions within the reunited denomination throughout the 1980s is reflected in these *Outlook* interviews and articles.

In Williams's interview with him, Andrews returns to a discussion of the "sweep to freedom" in Eastern Europe to make the point that "the Presbyterian tradition has always been identified with revolutionary movements—every place. The Reformed church in France was always in opposition to the monarchy. The Dutch Reformed Church came into being in the midst of a civil war with Spanish Catholicism, and they really weren't sure whether they were fighting Catholics or Spaniards or both or neither or what. The English Puritans and the Scots the same way. We [Presbyterians] were identified with the American Revolution."

He names several contemporary Presbyterian/Reformed political leaders. "I look at Czechoslovakia and suddenly realize that one of their deputy prime ministers, Josef Hromadka, is a Presbyterian minister I have known for years."

Andrews's fearless engagement with change and his attribution of a revolutionary spirit to the Reformed tradition echo Allen's *issho kenmei* (go, go, go) personality. As Allen does in his 2002 sermon, in 1990, Andrews assumes that coping with, even fomenting, radical change is not only very Presbyterian; transformation is integral to the divine nature.

Andrews adds this caveat: change should be intelligently managed. He describes what he thinks is the successful move of the national offices of the UPCUSA from New York and the PCUS offices from Atlanta to Louisville after reunion. He assures readers that when local churches and presbyteries need to call on the national offices, they will be in place.

He offers his own vision that undergirding the capacity to meet the challenges of change will be education, as Presbyterians have traditionally emphasized not only public education but also church school for all ages and strengthened ties with denominationally affiliated colleges. Also, the church can focus on overcoming the fragmentation he sees in its own membership and in the various communities it serves. Signs of ever-present brokenness are isolation and people lacking common goals and understanding. If the church demonstrates its primary calling, that is, its devotion to Jesus Christ that is expressed in obvious concern for one another, it can be a model to a broken world and "reach out to points of need in the community."[453]

As a public voice, given his position as the stated clerk of the reunited denomination, Andrew's sense of humor, his optimism, his openness to other religious traditions, his confidence in the face of change, his energy, and his awareness of the need for a unifying vision come through clearly. These characteristics and commitments are congruent with those Allen embodies and with the vision for the denomination that Allen consistently articulates. Perhaps Larry Angus correctly assessed that 1990 is Allen's moment to step into the position of moderator of the General Assembly.

Chapter 27

Identity and the 1990 Salt Lake City General Assembly

IF ONE ELEMENT OF the context for the 1990 General Assembly is the need to articulate a vision for the reconstituted PC(USA) in light of reunion, another is the ongoing tension between liberal and conservative perspectives. This tension is variously expressed, for example, when it emerges as a binary choice of whether to emphasize justice/mission or evangelism. It also emerges in the question of whether the PC(USA) can be culturally pluralistic and still maintain its membership numbers.

However, save for the Andrews interview, the articles also betray an underlying sense of vulnerability and tentativeness that contrasts with the confidence conveyed by many of the pronouncements at the 1980 assembly. For example, when Rev. Andrew Young spoke at one of the breakfasts in 1980, he assumed churches should, can, and do play an influential role socially and politically when they communicate and act on the basis on their faith commitments: "'When America begins to see a moral dimension to political questions, American politicians do respond.'"[454]

The *Outlook* articles in 1990 suggest that the PC(USA), as representative of many mainline Protestant denominations, is cautious and searching for ways to engage its evolving relationship with a dynamic social and political context as it approaches the last decade of the twentieth century. Even as it seeks to establish stability following reunification, it is facing external attacks from an increasingly aggressive right-wing fringe, is dealing internally with tensions between its own conservative and liberal factions, and is losing members in a society characterized by its growing secularism.

Some church leaders, such as Allen and Andrews, optimistically engage the tasks of establishing new patterns, to use Langer's term. Others are either hesitant to adapt, fearful, or outright insistent on staying within what they think of as tried and true parameters.

A thread of argument in the *Outlook* publications leading to the 1990 assembly opens a dialogue that addresses this uncertainty. The dialogue is carried on in a series of articles prompted by a March piece entitled "The Two-Church Hypothesis." The piece tackles the central questions of identity: who are we and what are we about? Louis Weeks and William Fogleman had proposed that the "struggle going on in our denomination" has its source in two "deeply related but distinguishable denominations." They were referring not to tensions between the southern and northern branches but to differences in perspective that are dependent on where a person locates him- or herself in the church's organization. Their "two-church hypothesis" argument has the additional benefit of shifting discussion away from the conservative-liberal binary.

Their argument is summarized in an article by Richard G. Hutcheson Jr., which includes his reaction to their hypothesis. He notes that Weeks and Fogleman call the one "denomination" the "Local Church" and the other, the "Governing Body Church." The life of the first "denomination" is "centered in the congregation," and the other is "made up of the majority of the ministers (all of whom belong to presbyteries) and those lay people who participate in and identify with activities at the presbytery, synod and General Assembly levels." The Local Church pattern dominated in the first centuries of the church in the United States, only to give way to the Governing Body Church in the twentieth century. The two churches are marked by differences in attitudes toward homogeneity, inclusiveness, forms of ministry, and views about the role of conflict. The two models compete between top-down initiative and control versus independent decision-making at the local level.

Hutcheson thinks the Weeks and Fogleman hypothesis rings true in terms of structure and process. The "Governing Body Church" bemoans "creeping congregationalism" (the local church acting as the seat of authority and decision-making, replacing the model of shared decision-making by mutually connected governing bodies), "declining contributions to governing bodies, and complaints in local church circles about 'General Assembly pronouncements' and 'Washington lobbies'" with which local churches disagree.[455]

The 1979 departures of the Denver Presbytery churches over such issues as the ordination of women and equitable financial contributions to
the mission of the larger church illustrate these disagreements. In his 1980
run for moderator, Allen had tried to explain the departures of the disaffected churches in these very terms. Their departure did not have to do with
him personally as moderator of Denver Presbytery but with the tension
between those who approved of decisions taken by the General Assembly
and those who did not. The conservative pastors at the breakfast caucus who
confronted him back then did not buy his explanation and personalized the
conflicts by blaming Allen.

Hutcheson's critique of the "two-church hypothesis" is lengthy and
serves as prelude to any number of *Outlook* articles about the subject that
continue to appear in the months prior to the assembly. One of his observations, in particular, previews an issue that will spark a good deal of disagreement at the assembly, that of monitoring "special interests organizations"
within the denomination.

He bases his discussion on the chapter from Robert Wuthnow's *The
Struggle for America's Soul: Evangelicals, Liberals, and Secularism* that
uses the PC(USA) as a case study of liberal-conservative polarization.[456]
Hutcheson centers his reflections on the "Chapter 9" organizations that
have been sprouting at the national level of the denomination. He notes that
these "'struggle groups'" advance special interests "'specifically to engage in
combat'" around polarizing issues.

"Chapter 9" organizations derive their name from the Chapter Nine
constitutional provision in the *Book of Order* that allows for and regulates
them. In addition to their inflammatory affect are questions about the veracity and appropriateness of their publications.[457]

As a reminder of the sometimes incendiary rhetoric used by "Chapter
9" groups, a decade prior, as prelude to the 1980 assembly, this language
was easily identified. For example, the Presbyterian Lay Committee, one of
the "Chapter 9" organizations, had carried the "Killing for Christ" article
in its publication, *The Presbyterian Layman*. To recap, the article critiqued
liberation theology as an inventive portrayal of "Jesus of Nazareth as hardly
more than an early-day Che Guevara." Stephen Chapman, the author, had
concluded his screed by accusing "fashionably liberal denominations" (such
as the Presbyterian church) of naively handing their money over to "aggressively radical third-world Protestants, mostly from Africa and Asia."[458]

By 1990, some in the denomination were of the opinion that there
was "no place for one-issue people," such as members of the Presbyterian
Lay Committee. Chapter Nine should be eliminated from the constitution,
thereby obliterating such "struggle groups." Another objection to the groups

was "that lay people confuse the public positions of Chapter 9s as actions of the national church; they consider, for instance, *The Presbyterian Layman*, the paper of the Presbyterian Lay Committee, . . . as an official document."

Leading up to the 1990 assembly, it seems that two "Chapter 9s" had engaged in hot debate—the Presbyterian Lay Committee and Presbyterians for Lesbian and Gay Concerns. The debate centered around "brochures that Presbyterians for Lesbian and Gay Concerns (PLGC) displayed at their booth at the 1989 national Youth Triennium, which included 'safe sex' material." While the PLGC group was the target for widespread outrage about the display, it was the Lay Committee that the General Assembly censored. Its "privileges were suspended for two years by last year's Assembly, pending study by a special committee" that was prompted by its "sensationalist" representation of the brochures at PLGC's Triennium booth.[459]

In addition to Hutcheson's illustration of the charged issue of "struggle groups," Jack Rogers also responds to Weeks and Fogleman and their two-church hypothesis. Rogers, a theology professor, is of the opinion that the problem is much more complex than they represent. The division is not so much along local church and governing body lines as it is a division that aligns local and governing body officials elected by their judicatories against "General Assembly Entities." Members of the "Entities" group are people who "were not elected to those positions by any local congregation or governing body." They represent caucuses; ecumenical entities; agency, seminary, and governing body staff; and members of committees and task forces.

Rogers engages in a lengthy analysis and concludes that the church is called to do both justice and evangelism, echoing Stoner's position. Setting up a polarity with evangelism/message on one side and justice/mission on the other offers a false choice. Rogers is optimistic. He thinks Presbyterians are not as divided as the "two-church hypothesis" makes it appear, and he welcomes the conversation it has prompted.[460]

The "two-church" discussion stays lively in the *Outlook* throughout the months leading to the assembly. Rev. Dr. Eunice Blanchard Poethig, at the time the executive presbyter in western New York, weighs in with an opinion piece published in the early days of the 1990 assembly that promises to erase the dividing lines. She offers a perspective as someone who served as an educator for nearly two decades early in her ministry in the mission field in the Philippines. She says the church has historically been both particular, (roughly equated with local congregations) and catholic (equated with the governing body). "Our denomination is intricately designed so that both characteristics are to be experienced in all arenas of its life. . . . Setting up polarities invites hostility, competition, and boundary setting. Instead, we should affirm the strengths of the various arenas of life and witness and respect each other wherever we are currently serving."[461]

Based on his position as pastor of a local congregation and his involvement in General Assembly task forces and on committees, Allen would comfortably agree with Poethig's call for mutual respect. He is simultaneously an active participant in the church as the "local body" and the "governing" church, as well as a member of any number of Rogers's groups that fall within the "entities" category. Also, in Rogers's formulation of two camps, Allen has consistently expressed himself as being squarely in both— evangelism *and* the church as God's agent of social change. Additionally, Allen certainly had experienced the personal pain of the conflict between Hutcheson's "hostile camps" of liberals and conservatives. On one hand, the difficulty of categorizing him could play to his advantage as a candidate; on the other, perhaps someone more easily classified would appeal in such an unsettled time of transition.

The "two-church" discussion signals how engaged Presbyterians are about the reunited denomination's basic identity, about causes for turmoil, and, if causes could be isolated, perhaps the discussions would give rise to solutions. However, other contributors to the 1990 *Outlook* articles are looking outward at a different set of challenges, those exacerbated by rapid political and social change. They wonder if the church in the twentieth century's last decade will be up to the tests facing it and the world. If one set of debates focuses on "Who are we?," another set is addressing the issue of "In light of who we are, what shall we do?" to fulfill the church's mission.

A particularly articulate example of the "What action shall we take?" concern is written by the Rev. Dr. Aurelia T. Fule. In her *Outlook* article, she gives insight into the denomination's participation in any number of social and political issues. As associate for Faith and Order in the Theology and Worship Ministry Unit of the PC(USA), she is part of that unelected "Entities" staff as identified by Rogers.

However, to so classify her and leave her biography at that is to dismiss her extraordinary history. During World War II, she was a teenager in Hungary. Concerned that her opportunities for higher education were compromised by the war's devastation and aftermath, her parents shipped her off to England, where she began university studies at Oxford. Desperately homesick, worried about her parents, and new to academic study in English, she endured. Years would pass before she would see her parents again. She received undergraduate and master's degrees in theology from Oxford, immigrated to the United States, and completed her ThD in 1960 under Reinhold Niebuhr's tutelage at Union Theological Seminary in New York. She was ordained as a teaching elder in 1963.[462]

Fule's report on the World Council of Church's World Convocation on Justice, Peace and the Integrity of Creation, which met in Seoul, South Korea, in March, is included in the April 30, 1990, *Outlook*. She highlights one of the four "covenants" that was agreed to by the four hundred voting participants from more than one hundred countries. The covenant in question is the concern about "preserving the Earth's atmosphere and for building a culture that can live in harmony with creation's integrity." She thinks the covenant gives the PC(USA) churches and their larger communities the opportunity for a "second round of learning."

She reminds readers that the "first round" of acquiring knowledge stays in our head only as floating facts, but on the "second or third learning," those facts are incorporated into our understanding in a way that "makes a difference in our thinking." Members of the PC(USA) had their "first round" on April 22, 1970, the first Earth Day. It had an impact—the Clean Air Act, the Environmental Protection Agency. However, the Clean Air Act had been compromised, and air and water were still polluted. "We have been warned about global warming trends that could alter the climate and raise sea levels radically in the next five decades."

She thinks that the Korea World Convocation gives the PC(USA) its opportunity for a "second learning"—to incorporate the information and take steps to develop "new theological perspectives concerning creation and the place of humanity within it, and to be open to learning from the insights of indigenous peoples and people of other faiths and ideologies as well as from the traditional wisdom of women."

About the other three covenants agreed to by the World Convocation conferees, she reports that one advocated for a just economic order, another for the security of all nations and peoples and a culture of nonviolence, and the last for the "eradication of racism and discrimination on national and international levels." Fule concludes with a question: "Shall we commit ourselves to work and to engage our church to work for the sake of creation?"[463] In 1990, Fule's clearly articulated vision for the church's mission took its place among the discussion of issues the assembly would address.

As he expresses it throughout his ministry, visible in his 1980 candidating speech, in his 2002 sermon, and again in 1990, Allen's vision of the church's task is reflected in these various *Outlook* articles. He also consistently embraces the task as both mission and evangelism. Allen is clear. The answer to the question of "What shall we do?" rests in the answer to the question of "Who are we?" The church is the body of God's people chosen to bring God's kingdom of human rights, peace, and justice to all creation and to preach the vision of that coming kingdom. Presumably he has been a participant in many discussions such as the ones reflected in the church's publications leading up to the Salt Lake General Assembly, and he seems to be comfortably positioned to be a participant in debates about both the church's task and its identity.

Importantly, in his position as a pastor in a local church, in his roles in presbytery and synod, and in his many involvements at the General Assembly level, he exemplifies that the divisions outlined in the "two-church" discussions do not really exist in the lives of many church members and staff. Their work and relationships move between and among all levels of the denomination's life over time. Allen's pilot educational curriculum at Montview, for instance, was included in the 1970's Liberation Theology Task Force's report to General Assembly.

Also, the comment of one of the letter writers during Montview's 1980 evaluation of the co-pastorate claimed as one of its strengths that the model allowed for Allen's considerable time commitments to the General Assembly with no sacrifice in the church's ministries. Implied is the local church's approval of his peripatetic life throughout church structures and that each cross pollinates the other.

Those traveling to Salt Lake City represented all these concerns and perspectives and many more. Some approached the 1990 General Assembly with the view that the church was overwhelmed by all the changes of the late twentieth century; others thought change offered opportunity for creativity and spiritual growth. Some approached the assembly with dread about the "radical polarization rending the church"; others saw possibilities for affirmation and mutual respect. The task would be to elect a moderator capable of managing the turmoil, of generating a common vision for the future, and of uniting church members in pursuit of strategies to achieve that vision consistent with their perceptions of denominational identity. Could anyone meet such ambitious expectations?

Chapter 28

The Candidates

Six candidates have been nominated by their presbyteries for moderator of the 202nd General Assembly. The contenders are all men, two ruling elders who are businessmen and four teaching elders: three of them veterans of World War II; two of them members of minority groups, Allen as Japanese American and one "Latin gentleman," as he refers to himself; and four have roots in the former PCUS (southern branch). Allen is one of only two candidates with histories in the northern branch. In various ways and with different emphases, their profiles indicate they all have made significant contributions at each of the structural levels of the denomination.

In addition to the complexities of the ongoing tension between liberals and conservatives and the reuniting northern and southern churches are numerous political and social issues not unique to religious bodies: What about the Troubles in Northern Ireland and elsewhere? What about equitably sharing the rising costs of health care? What about climate change? Racial profiling? Monumental disruptions in Eastern Europe and the Soviet Union?

Also not unique to religious bodies are the questions of whether an organization can value diversity and simultaneously maintain its membership and financial assets, establish common goals, and represent diversity in its leadership. Some of the questions have evolved during the decade between Allen's first candidacy and his second; some have emerged in 1990 with more immediacy.

To give the commissioners and the larger church a sense of the candidates and their positions on any number of these challenges, *The Presbyterian Outlook* May 4 issue publishes the candidates' profiles and asks a series of questions similar to those posed in 1980: 1) What is the most significant matter to come before this General Assembly? 2) What are your goals for your moderatorial year? What particular strengths do you bring to the task? 3) What is the most urgent need in the PC(USA) in the 1990s? The candidates' responses appear in alphabetical order.

Most of the men are already familiar to General Assembly attendees. Josiah Beeman, first on the list, is a ruling elder and director of a government relations firm in Washington, D.C. He is "active in the church at all levels" and is the youngest candidate at age fifty-four. Many commissioners to the General Assembly were probably introduced to him through several prior *Outlook* articles, some of which reported his work as chairman of the General Assembly Council (GAC) Structural Design Review Task Force.[464]

The task force's title implies a relatively benign set of administrative responsibilities. Not so. Apparently he, a Washington lobbyist, and James E. Andrews, stated clerk, are primary participants in ongoing debates about basic structural issues of accountability and decision-making in the reunited church.

For instance, Beeman suggested Andrews "relinquish his authority for choosing legal counsel for the Office of the General Assembly's legal matters." Instead, the authority should "go through the GAC structure." Andrews disagrees. This and other issues, such as altering certain relationships involving the Board of Pensions (with responsibility for the life insurance, retirement, and health insurance programs for church employees at all levels) are so contentious that all parties eventually agree to postpone many of the decisions that were to come before the assembly until further study and discussion by either a review committee or the Advisory Committee on the Constitution. In other words, structural changes are so complex and contested that their resolution is determined to be premature even before the assembly begins.[465]

During the assembly, the *Outlook* runs an article that quotes Andrews's observations, which implies the ongoing discussions have been more than animated, and the article perhaps gives insight into Beeman's reputation. Andrews says, "We'll probably fight hammer and tongs in the review committee and we'll see who should prevail. We're real good at that; it's sort of our chief means of recreation. Joe [Beeman] and I reserve for each other the privilege of making very strong verbal statements about these things. It's very possible that the people around us get more uncomfortable with that than we do. But the man is a first-class antagonist. You don't come up against him half-cocked."[466]

Beeman is also a member of a joint working group on Northern Ireland, drawn from both the Global Mission and Social Justice and Peacemaking units. The group will be presenting a resolution to the assembly calling "for nonviolent resolution of the conflict, an end to religious discrimination, more integrated educational exchange programs, . . . and increased foreign investment to alleviate high unemployment."[467]

Not surprisingly, at the time of the May article that presents the candidates' views, for Beeman, the most significant matter before the assembly is a structural one that expresses the church's values: the Pension Study Task Force report that deals with the impact of rising health care costs that fall disproportionally on lower paid clergy and church staff and on smaller churches. He also alludes to the "Brief Statement of Faith," but he thinks it was debated throughly at the 1989 assembly and only needs approval.

His goal is to bring the diverse elements of the church into conversations in which they listen to one another and build consensus in an open process. He puts forth his strength as giving a variety of views the opportunity for expression. He says the most urgent need is to "equip the laity so that they can reach out into the world as Christ's instruments for reconciliation, peace and justice" and to better train them for leadership in the church.[468]

Price H. Gwynn, III, one of the two oldest candidates at the age of sixty-seven, has just retired as vice president, director, and member of the executive board of Lance, Inc. He confirms its identity as "the peanut butter cracker people." Honorably discharged as an army captain in 1946, his biographical information emphasizes his golfing, running, and mountain climbing interests. His father and grandfather were Presbyterian ministers, and Gwynn has been active in his (originally PCUS) local church and in presbytery in many capacities throughout his life.[469]

He answers the question about the most significant matter before the assembly in three parts: theologically, consideration of the "Brief Statement of Faith"; politically, the Chapter 9 organization question; and administratively, the report of the Pension Study Task Force, specifically, the problem of rising health care costs. He, too, recognizes the significance of the issues swirling around structural change as it is focused on the pension problems.

His goals center around "kinship." If the church recovers a sense of community, linking around common bonds and open discussion, it can reaffirm its connectedness. His list of strengths complement this goal: leadership; communication and listening; interpersonal, managerial, and analytical skills; a lay perspective; and "a family tradition of concern for the life and witness of the Presbyterian Church."

The urgent need for the 90s "is dual." Externally, it is speaking an authentic and understandable word to an increasingly secular public. Internally, it is living with difference and keeping the church obedient to the gospel. The good news is that the "framework and structure for an inclusive church are in place." The challenge is to live into that inclusivity as individuals and as an institution.[470]

The third candidate listed, M. Douglas Harper Jr., age sixty-two, has served as pastor for thirty-two years in the same Texas presbytery, on most presbytery committees, on synod committees, and as a member of the Joint Committee on Union, which prepared the Plan for Reunion of the southern and northern denominations in 1983. That role, and as a current member of the Special Committee to Prepare the "Brief Statement of the Reformed Faith," gave him a good deal of visibility prior to the assembly. His PhD is from Duke University.

Not surprisingly, the most significant matter before the assembly for Harper is the "Brief Statement of Faith." He gives three reasons. First, in the Reformed tradition, everything—structure, program, and witness—grows out of faith. Translated into Langer's words, if faith is synonymous with embracing the "essential pattern for human life" envisaged by a particular religion's tradition, of course the statement is the basis for structure, program, and witness.

Second, Harper believes that as the first constitutional theological statement of the reunited Presbyterian Church, it "will declare our present theological identity to the world."

Third, because voting on it will be a year-long process on the part of the presbyteries, debate about it will stimulate significant theological discussion. Harper has a clear sense of the new confession's significance as a late twentieth-century "envisagement" of faith and identity that has potential to stimulate conversation at all levels of the church's life and that promises an informed and recommitted laity.

The process of working on the statement has convinced him that the "heart of the church is sound; theologically, the center holds." His goals, therefore, are to recall the church to "these central realities and to the true center, Jesus Christ" and to "promote healing and reconciliation." Not only does he believe it was God's will that the northern and southern branches of the church heal their 122-year split, but that God intends that the church "help restless congregations remain." He is speaking of former PCUS congregations. They have another year to decide if they want to leave the reunited denomination "with their property under the provisions of Article 13."

To explain, because individual churches do not own their property and forfeit it to their presbyteries if they withdraw, this provision is uniquely designed to give the southern churches freedom to opt out of the reunited structure and maintain their property, but for a limited time. That such a provision was necessary implies that a number of congregations in the southern branch were doubtful about rejoining their counterparts in the north.

He says his greatest strength is his "commitment to Jesus Christ and to the PC(USA)." Also, he claims broad and deep knowledge of the church by virtue of working at all its levels for many years.

Harper sees the most urgent need of the church as a desperate one for a unifying vision. The only adequate vision is "of Jesus Christ as the Reconciler and of ourselves as Christ's servants sent out to reconcile the world to him and through him."[471]

Allen's brief biography and answers to the questions appear fourth in the May article. He had already been introduced as a candidate in the February issue of the *Outlook*, along with Beeman. The first sentence of Allen's February announcement had read that he professes "straight-forwardly that he seeks the position of moderator of the PC(USA) solely because he believes sincerely that someone of either Asian or Native American or Hispanic background ought to be moderator once in the denomination's history."

The February article rehearses biographical details and emphasizes that his father sharecropped for a series of Scottish Presbyterian families. Allen represents this history in 1990 with more detail than his mention of it in his 1980 candidating speech. He describes one of those farmer's wives. She was "very evangelical and wanted to take the Maruyama children to Sunday school. My father and mother were both Buddhists, and they thought that sounded wonderful—somebody to take the children off their hands on Sunday. . . . We all went, from the time of kindergarten and first grade," and the family all became Presbyterians.

In that introductory article, Allen also emphasizes that the church must adapt to massive changes taking place at home and abroad while reclaiming the Presbyterian heritage and identity. He hopes for "stabilization in Louisville and the church at large."[472]

The shorter biographical sketch introducing Allen in the May *Outlook* article that presents the views of the candidates draws together a rather comprehensive list of his service to the church. It implies a fluid ability and long-term commitment to work across all levels of the denomination's structure.

He has been moderator of presbytery, vice-moderator of synod, and on many presbytery and synod committees. "At the national level he has served on the Vocation Agency, Council on Women and the Church, and is currently serving on the Nominating Committee [as was June Mochizuki] and a member of the Consulting Committee on Professional Development of the Church Vocations Unit. Other Assembly service has involved work on special committees on liberation theology, languages for ordination, judicatory relations, and pornography. He chaired standing General Assembly committees in 1962 and 1980 and was nominated for moderator of the 1980 Assembly."[473]

Whether intentionally or not, this list also demonstrates that even though his Japanese ancestors were not Presbyterian, a heritage claimed by other nominees, Allen's experience and dedication to church service is lengthy and substantive. Gwynn's father and grandfather might have been Presbyterian ministers, apparently giving him an exceptional claim to a Presbyterian heritage, but Allen—and Min—feel the connection no less. Both of them claim full membership in the Presbyterian family and a visceral connection with its history.

Allen's explicit reference to being adopted into the Presbyterian family does not appear in this printed material as it did in his 1980 candidating speech; however, he mentions the evangelical efforts of the Presbyterian farmer's wife in relationship to his Buddhist parents. Both the 1980 reference to adoption and his 1990 emphasis on the conversion of his entire Buddhist family highlight why he places such importance on electing an Asian candidate, or a Native American or Hispanic one, as it would so broaden the racial and ethnic markers used to legitimate church leaders as to eliminate them. His commitment to this goal highlights the familiar biblical image of the church as one family, united by its shared faith. The church is "God's household," comprised not of "strangers and aliens" but of "fellow citizens" (Eph 2:19).

Allen is quoted in the *Outlook* article as thinking the most significant programmatic issue before the assembly is the report from the Pension Board Task Force appointed by the General Assembly Council. As noted, the pension proposals were so complex and controversial that they were eventually delayed for further study and recommendations. His particular concern is that the outcome not burden small churches and their pastors.[474]

His background in the small-town Las Animas church and the mission churches he served in Wisconsin make him particularly sensitive to the needs of small churches, a loyalty he and colleagues indicate that he never abandoned. Cearley, his colleague at Montview, observes that "he had a very big place in his heart for small churches in the presbytery, I think because he came from a small church and loved being at a big church, able to empower and help and make a place for small churches. Inner-city parishes and places like that benefitted a lot from Allen's being at Montview because he was always moving in the direction of, 'How can we connect [resources] to what's happening over there?'"[475] Small churches and inner-city parishes stood to benefit even more were he to be elected moderator of General Assembly.

Of greater significance for the 1990 assembly in his estimation, though, is the potential acceptance or rejection of the new "Brief Statement of Faith." He succinctly states its significance. "It symbolizes our identity in a pluralistic society." The importance he places on the statement is not surprising, given that by articulating the church's identity, it also sets out its purpose—its vision.

This becomes explicit in his statement of his goals as moderator. They are to spread a positive image of the PC(USA) by emphasizing the mission of the church, its growth, and evangelism. He wishes "to provide a vision and a dream for the whole church . . . that will enable us to be leaders in an increasingly complex world."

In that such limited written materials from Allen's ministry remain, it is difficult to know how frequently he uses this formulation of "a vision and a dream" or when he started using it. The phrase is explicitly part of his public presentation of his goals in 1990, and it functions similarly in his favorite sermon in 2002. This repetition underscores that he is not one to dwell on the past. The "essential pattern" of faith for Allen is insistently oriented toward the future.

His answer to the question about the strengths he brings to accomplishing his goals is that "as an Asian American I feel very sensitive to the global needs that challenge our church. I would be an effective witness to our Presbyterian inclusiveness, diversity, and mission."

Allen's next statement about his strengths, although brief, is not said lightly. "I have had the experience of being a good moderator, complimented for strong qualities of leadership and reconciliation. I would seek to be fair, honest and straight-forward."[476]

His memories of how he moderated church sessions support this claim. When he describes the contentious meetings while the Dubuque session was coping with all those "hippies" loitering on church property, he says, "the session wanted me to be acting pastor during the period when Dick Heydinger left to take a new church, and that was when the kids were hanging out on the lawn. . . . We used to have some real knock-down, drag-out debates about, 'What do you do with these kids?' . . . One of the things I had studied in college was *Robert's Rules*. That was very helpful. Our denomination has a nice, orderly, democratic way to keep debates from becoming closer to violence."[477]

"I've never had a session where you finally call an end to the meeting because of too much disagreement that can't be solved. But it's obvious when two groups are not going to get together that you ask for a motion to create a committee to try and solve it. At the next meeting they can come in with some kind of compromise. I used it as the final possibility when we couldn't resolve something, but I didn't have to do that very often.

"I could be very stern in a meeting and would explain that's what a moderator is supposed to do. Our responsibility is to keep order. Session members were reasonable people. There aren't many who are so unwilling to understand that there are certain discussions and issues that cannot be resolved, and you just have to accept the [majority] position. You don't have to give up your own, but you need to accept it. . . . I've had some elders very unhappy with me, who would tell me after the meeting how unhappy they were. I'd try to calm them down and explain to them that I certainly wasn't unhappy with them. I've never had anyone quit the session."[478]

Although it is a standing Presbyterian joke that too often the resolution to conflict is to "form a committee and study the issue to death," this standby tactic does allow for tempers to cool and compromise positions to emerge. When it became apparent that the contention swirling around certain task force proposals for the Salt Lake assembly were nowhere near resolution, they were referred for further study even before the assembly began.

Allen assumes a sermonic pose when he considers the *Outlook* question about the most urgent need in the church in the 1990s, similar to the tone of the second half of his candidating speech in 1980. As much as he is future oriented, on both occasions he purposefully draws on the Judeo-Christian tradition as a whole to contextualize his thinking. This rhetorical move reminds the faithful in the twentieth century that their beliefs have taken shape, and continue to evolve, over spans of millennia, as Langer would say, as a "gradual envisagement of the essential pattern of human life."

He believes the most urgent need "is to be faithful to our biblical and prophetic witness in the world." This belief is consistent with the way Foresberg represented Allen's approach to making decisions about the life of the church in his 1980 nominating speech. He said that Allen always asks whether the decision is biblically grounded and what its theological purpose is.

In Allen's 1990 answer to the question about the church's most urgent need, he compares the time of Jeremiah and Israel during the Babylonian captivity to the "siege from the forces of change and revolution in our culture and society," a siege the church has withstood in the past. "We have lived in captivity to a complex series of religious, political, social, and cultural . . . reaction to rapid change. The tendency for a people in captivity is to adopt the culture and religion of the captors, but Jeremiah prophesied that the people of God must be faithful to God. The urgent need of our church in the 1990s is to listen to God's Word and discover God's agenda for our church. . . . We have spent enough time and energy restructuring and relocating the church. Let us now move forward into being the body of Christ in the world. . . . Like the Judges of the Old Testament, we tend to be a church divided into regional enclaves, and what we need in the 1990s is to unify our church to be God's instrument on earth. . . . We are Christ's presence to the world; therefore let us be reconciled to each other so that we can reconcile the world to God."[479]

The theme of reconciling comes up again and again in denominational publications and candidates' statements prior to the 1990 assembly, so it is difficult to determine if Allen's formulation of it, in the context of the prophets and judges of old, stood out. Certainly, his embrace of the "Brief Statement" and the pension plan issues as the most urgent matters before the assembly do not distinguish him from the other candidates. They are the most urgent matters for all six.

Herbert Meza, whose views are presented fifth, is sixty-seven years old. A pastor from Florida, he is the third veteran, serving "in the U.S. Marine Corps in the South Pacific during World War II." His name might have been the one of the six most immediately recognized by assembly attendees as he was vice-moderator the prior year, when Joan Salmon Campbell was moderator. Like Allen, Meza had once before been a nominee for the position, but in the PCUS in 1976. He, along with Allen, claims an international perspective, as he was the first PCUS missionary to Portugal. He served three terms on the PCUS Board of World Missions and on any number of other committees and institutional boards.

His answer to the first question is that, "In terms of lasting effects, the most significant issue before this Assembly will be the Brief Statement of Faith. . . . The most intense issue revolves around the medical benefits [the Board of Pensions issues], which will generate the most discussion." In that assessment, he too proves to be correct. Meza is concerned about how decisions to be reached in regard to the medical benefits will "have implications as to how we define ourselves in terms of community." That is, "it will make us struggle with our self-understanding in terms of covenant support for those who are on the bottom scale of income. . . . The struggle . . . should sensitize us to the fact that there are thirty-five million of our citizens [in the United States] without health insurance."

Meza introduces his answer to the question about goals and strengths with this approach: "I am the 'product' of a home mission project that our General Assembly began many years ago among Cubans in Ybor City,

Florida. Through that mission I came to know the love of Christ, and even now, when I go back home, I visit my old hangouts to remind myself how far the love of Christ can reach. But if you had told me about the love of Christ and denied me the strength of your witness for justice and fairness, you might have turned me into a cynic. However, you kept telling me that in Christ I could move beyond stereotypes . . . and I believed!"[480]

Allen Maruyama, Herbert Meza, and Minoru Mochizuki—each makes clear that through faith, they are integral parts of the PC(USA), with distinctive contributions to make. Allen has been "adopted"; Min feels somehow physically linked to those bearded Scotsmen through their shared history; and Meza embraces the Presbyterian witness that the love of Christ erases stereotypes.

Allen and Meza are calling on the body as a whole to act on the belief it has sung in a favorite hymn for the past century, "In Christ There Is No East or West." Rather, in his name there exists "one great fellowship of love throughout the whole wide earth."[481]

Although Meza thinks the role of moderator is largely symbolic, that symbolism is powerful. He himself is symbolic "of the fact that the gospel is first personal and always social. . . . I symbolize the wide dimension of the gospel. I believe in and have labored for the inclusiveness of the church. I speak Spanish and Portuguese fluently. No Latin has ever been moderator. It is time to make that affirmation. I symbolize the church's pilgrimage with peace as an ex-Marine, twice wounded and once cited for valor. . . . The great issues that are tearing our world apart are hunger and prejudice. The crisis of our church is one of divisiveness and depletion." His leadership will enable the church to see "there is a faith on this Earth . . . that can call men and women to that undefeated love of Calvary. . . . I know that experience."

Meza has already identified one of the church's crises as "divisiveness and depletion," so it follows that the "urgent need" he identifies is first to determine the causes for this state of affairs, as reflected in "our statistics." He reviews the prior three decades and identifies the '60s as the decade when the church focused on issues of race, the '70s on hunger, and the '80s on peace. "In the '90s we shall have to focus on the renewal of the church."

Although Meza articulates the crucial role of the church's "witness for justice and fairness" (mission), he asks a series of questions that highlight his priority on the need for church renewal. Is the crisis of "divisiveness and depletion" a crisis of confidence? Is too much expected of the churches? Is its institutional style too cumbersome and "perhaps bi-cephalic" (his way of referring to the the "two-church" debate)? Are we "squandering our energy and resources in our squabbles with each other, stalemated behind a variety of barricades?" Are "housekeeping details" distracting the church from its mission? He understands that institutions in crisis want simple answers, but such answers will not do. In any event, "the one luxury we cannot afford is to lose heart. The one tragedy we cannot abide is to lose touch with each other."

The views of Fred A. Ryle Jr. are the sixth and final ones to be reported. Age fifty-five, he is also from Texas. Most of his activity as a teaching elder has been in his pastorates, his communities, and his presbytery and synod. He has been a commissioner to several General Assemblies, and he currently serves on the General Assembly Task Force on Christian Obedience in a Nuclear Age.

As did each of the candidates, Ryle does not answer the question about the most significant matter coming before the assembly by naming a single issue. He begins with the approval of the "Brief Statement of Faith" (the all-important "envisagement" document that each of the other candidates mentions), adds the Pension Board Task Force report, as do the majority of the others, lists several other matters, and concludes by discussing the importance of the "cluster of concerns related to the Chapter 9 organizations." He points out that the assembly will be debating how much authority it has over what these organizations do, what material they publish or distribute, even if their existence will be tolerated at all. The only other candidate to spotlight the Chapter 9 matter is Gwynn.

Ryle thinks it is crucial to listen to the "deep feelings and beliefs of all of our sisters and brothers" in these Chapter 9 groups that represent "minority positions." They are, after all, "formed to promote particular concerns." However, "we cannot allow polarity to paralyze the church."

His goal is to communicate a vision of the church as knowing it is called to obey Jesus Christ as sovereign, as being committed to the transforming power of biblical and Reformed faith, and as celebrating difference in unity around common faith in Christ. His strengths grow out of his experiences as a listener who has a pastor's concern to find a common base for ministry.

The urgent need he sees is to address the pain in the church and the world. Specifically, the church must define itself by trusting in Jesus Christ and by advocating and working for justice as commanded in the prophets, by seeking an end to dehumanizing poverty, by showing compassion on all in pain, and by healing broken lives and society "by evidencing the reconciling love of God."[482]

All six candidates show remarkable similarities in their diagnoses of significant matters facing the church, their strategies for dealing with them, and their assessments of their strengths to meet the challenges they identify. As was the list of hopes for the 1990s that the *Outlook* identified back in January, the matters before the assembly of note for the candidates are inward-looking—namely, the "Brief Statement of Faith" that will express the reunited church's identity and mission and the Pension Board Task Force report dealing with such issues as equitable distribution of insurance and retirement benefit costs. Their comments tend to begin, as had the January *Outlook* list, with a "revival of faith and faithfulness" and recovery of a "vision" rooted in the sovereignty of Jesus Christ and Scripture that will result, as the *Outlook* list concluded, in a "continuing commitment to work for justice in the church and the world."[483]

The ongoing discussion about the "two-church" hypothesis reflects overriding concerns about "polarity," internecine "squabbles," and a general sense of imbalance in the face of complex change. Certainly all the internal tussles prompted by the 1983 reunion demanded time and energy, but reunion did not account for membership loss and all the disputes around any number of issues. In light of these crises, "renewal," "transformation," "vision," and "reconciliation" become watchwords the candidates use to signal hope and confidence as the church anticipates the 1990s.

As in 1980, by virtue of Allen's last name beginning with the letter "M," he appears midway in the order of the candidates in publications and possibly in the same position of the order of speakers when it came to the nominating process. Given that he was introduced in the 1990 February publication as the "60-year-old soft-spoken co-pastor of Montview Boulevard church in Denver," it seems not much about his "soft-spoken" personality nor his positions on the issues dramatically differentiate him from the other five men. Because recordings of the 1990 assembly do not exist and therefore the segment of questions from the floor and answers is not available, it is difficult to determine what, other than Allen's concern that an Asian, Native American, or Hispanic be elected, sets him apart from the others. Even in that, he shares Meza's perspective.

Chapter 29

The Vote and Assembly Business

THE ELECTION WAS HELD on May 30 at the Salt Palace Convention Center in Salt Lake City. Suspense built due to a glitch in the electronic voting system, which lasted for thirty minutes. "Outgoing Moderator Joan Salmon-Campbell summoned her many talents to get the Assembly through the interlude," presumably by leading a rousing hymn sing.[484]

The history of the site itself presented its own irony, given that Allen Maruyama, a Japanese American, was a candidate for moderator. In 1967, Salt Lake City "officials used eminent domain laws to force the Japanese community to leave the area deemed 'Japantown' to make way for the proposed Salt Palace, the main event center for the city." Their action was a blow to the self-sufficiency of the Japanese-American community, many of whom had settled in Salt Lake City to re-establish themselves after the war.[485]

At first glance, Salt Lake City, a relatively homogeneous community of Latter-Day Saints and far from the West Coast, was an unlikely home for Japanese Americans, many of them Buddhist—until one recalls that they were among the almost nine thousand incarcerated at the War Relocation Authority's Utah site, Camp Topaz. Having nothing to return to on the West Coast upon their release in the mid-1940s, many headed toward the nearest metropolis.

However, Presbyterians were generally aware of and had been supportive of the nationwide movement to address the injustice of incarceration. For example, the 1980 General Assembly adopted the resolution of "violence and racial strife" presented by the Committee on Social Justice and the Rights of Persons that included support of "the call of the Japanese American Citizens League for a congressional inquiry into the incarceration of 110,000 Japanese Americans during World War II."[486]

It would seem that the 1988 Civil Liberties Act, which was the outcome of that inquiry, resulting in reparations being paid to the surviving prisoners of the camps and eliciting President Ronald Reagan's apology for the injustice suffered by persons of Japanese ancestry during World War II, would have been part of recent memory for many Presbyterians descending on Salt Lake City. Perhaps some were even aware of the history of the Salt Palace and of Japantown's displacement.

However, Min does not allude to it as part of the unique Utah history that factored into choosing Salt Lake City as the 1990 assembly site. Apparently Allen did not make anything of it either. On one hand, that might have been a missed opportunity. Calling attention to the irony of the venue in light of his candidacy for moderator of the General Assembly of the PC(USA) could have positively differentiated him from his competitors.

Alternatively, even from a 1990 perspective, at a forty-five-year remove from the closure of the camps, many Japanese Americans still experienced the incarceration as a source of shame and did not discuss it.[487] As June Mochizuki observed, after the war "nobody could figure out what we had done to deserve it, but we had to have done something to deserve something so bad as incarceration." When Allen visited Camp Amache as a teenager and saw his California friends who were imprisoned, his reaction was similar: they must have done something wrong to deserve imprisonment. If the displacement of Salt Lake City's Japantown was generally known, perhaps prudence kept Allen silent about it.

Even so, given the similarity of the positions of the six men as reflected in the printed materials distributed before the assembly, distinguishing oneself would seem to have been a primary task in the speeches and answers to questions from the floor. Another tactic might have been to capitalize on the occasion by presenting oneself as uniquely charismatic and compelling.

The course of the voting suggests one candidate did successfully set himself apart. Even though a majority of 303 votes was needed to win, Gwynn did lead comfortably on the first ballot with 248, "followed by Harper, Meza and Maruyama, each with 101, and Beeman, thirty-two, and Ryle, twenty-two." The separate (non-binding) votes of the Youth Advisory Delegates (YADs) and the Theological Student Advisory Delegates (TSADs), as harbingers of the leanings of a younger generation, reflected a similar pattern. The totals for the YAD vote were Gwynn, seventy; Meza, thirty-five; Maruyama, thirty-three; Harper, seventeen; Beeman, three; and Ryle, two.

The TSAD vote totals were Gwynn and Maruyama, ten each; Meza, four; Harper, two; and Beeman and Ryle, one each.

The second ballot totals put Gwynn over the top with 322 votes. Meza received ninety-two; Maruyama, ninety-one; Harper, ninety; Beeman, seven; and Ryle, six.[488]

Allen says the results were unexpected. He thought he was in a strong position to win and had anticipated that Meza would be his most serious competitor.[489]

The *Outlook* also represents the results as a surprise. Gwynn is described as "less well-known than some of the other nominees and was considered something of a dark horse by veteran Assembly watchers." The article observes that "the election of an articulate elder with impeccable business credentials may have in part represented a collective wisdom seeking to reach out to disaffected elements in the Presbyterian Church who may be thinking of leaving."

Perhaps preference for a lay moderator reflected the timeliness of the many discussions that focused on the "two-church hypothesis." Members might have been ready for what they perceived as "bottom-up" leadership. Also, Gwynn's heritage was thoroughly grounded in the southern branch of the reunited denomination. As emerges several times in pre-assembly materials, one concern was that former southern churches would exercise their option, in this, the final year during which it was available, to leave the reunited church with their property intact. Gwynn's southern background could have been a mollifying factor.

Contrasted with Gwynn, Allen was one of only two nominees with a northern church background (Beeman as the second), the branch that was apparently looked upon with some suspicion by the other. Also, it seems to have been a negative to be both a teaching elder and closely identified with the national church. If so, that Allen received the number of votes he did speaks to the respect he garnered.

As a way to introduce the new moderator to *Outlook* readers, the article reporting the results summarizes Gwynn's nominating speech given by Rev. Ann Clay Adams of North Central Iowa Presbytery. It speaks to the appeal of his personality. She says that Gwynn is "'a gentle spirit with a probing mind,' with a winsome way about him, altogether a stimulating person." She also says he does not hold rigid positions, and is "one who could bring the church together."[490]

Allen would not only agree with the article's representation of Gwynn as "stimulating," but goes so far as to describe him as "brilliant." Allen says it is certainly true that the response of commissioners to anyone's candidacy hinges on the candidates' speeches, and he thinks Gwynn's was remarkable.

He does not begrudge Gwynn's win in the least, and his enthusiasm about Gwynn's leadership capabilities did not diminish throughout the following year during which Gwynn was moderator.

"I was so happy he won. Price Gwynn was a very impressive man, . . . one of the best moderators we've ever had, . . . a born leader." In fact, Allen emphasizes that Gwynn continued to be a major positive influence in church matters for a number of years, and Allen enjoyed working with him.[491]

Gwynn's challenges were considerable. Many of the *Outlook* articles leading to the 1990 General Assembly portray an inward-looking denomination struggling to balance itself after reunion and in the face of declining membership. Each of the six nominees are of one mind, in that they name the same issues internal to the life of the PC(USA) as the most urgent, namely, the approval of the "Brief Statement of Faith" and the Pension Board Task Force controversy.

However, even a short overview of actions taken by the assembly indicates the denomination was fully informed about and grappling with the "increasingly complex world" to which Allen alludes in his *Outlook* profile. The number of actions reported on just one page of the *General Assembly Daily News* gives a sample of the issues receiving attention. Given that the assembly ran for nine days, the actions, meetings, and discussions reported on the page represent only a fraction of the church's recognition of its responsibility to reach out to a world "in pain," as candidate Ryle expressed it.

Although the General Assembly as a whole does not yet express itself in these terms, it is attempting to address white privilege and systemic injustice. "By an overwhelming vote, the assembly acted to make the problem of the African-American male a priority and to designate one million new dollars over a five-year period to address the problem." This problem was defined as African-American males being "a population segment at extreme risk." The assembly called for "regional hearings among African-Americans in the helping professions" in order to formulate and implement programs "of outreach, self-help, self-development, and reconciliation."

A cluster of issues raised in the Peacemaking Committee's report included calling for "normalization of relations between the United States and Cuba and encouraging Presbyterians to continue to build bridges of understanding between the two churches and peoples." The Northern Ireland conflagration was addressed with a twelve-point program for supporting "non-violent solutions to political, economic and religious strife." The assembly voted to support "removal of American military bases in the Philippines." It approved the committee's recommendations to develop "creative ministries to respond to the needs of immigrants" and to reaffirm "previous stands about the Middle East while condemning continuing violence and calling for specific efforts by all parties for peaceful settlement."

In the category of human rights, a resolution urged the US government to "work for the full restoration of the dignity and human rights of all Koreans in Japan." Another "stated unequivocally that 'authentic Christianity can have no complicity in anti-Semitic attitudes or action.'"

A whole raft of overtures and resolutions dealt with reproductive rights and human sexuality, discussion of which was delayed until the 1991 assembly. In the meantime, the Special Committee to Study Human Sexuality, made up of six pastors, three physicians, five academics, two presbytery executives, one nurse, and one professional educator, made available a booklet of its working papers, *Body and Soul: A New Look at Human Sexuality and the Church*. Topics included sex and singleness, women's issues, men's issues, sex and the elderly, gay and lesbian concerns, reproductive technology, violence and coercive sex, sexuality issues related to the ordained ministry, and teen sexuality.

The General Assembly also voted to send a communication to Presidents Bush and Gorbachev, meeting during the same week in Washington, D.C. The concluding sentence read, "We join together in prayer with peoples around the world for the establishment of just societies, for peace among all nations, and for preserving the environmental integrity of our earth."[492]

Most of these issues and topics were complex and certainly did not resolve in 1990 in Salt Lake City. In fact, many of those studied at the assembly only gained in intensity and still seem intractable: reverberations from the dissolution of the Soviet Union, the "extreme risk" confronted daily by African-American men, gay and lesbian (and transgender) rights, sexuality and ministry, violence in the Middle East, dispossessed Palestinians, anti-Semitism and white supremacy, reproductive rights, threats to "environmental integrity," unequal access to health care and its rising costs, creative ministries to deal with the needs of immigrants, Cuba-US relations, resolving questions about the border between the Republic of Ireland and Northern Ireland (which emerged again in Brexit discussions), and numerous others.

When Ed O'Keefe, an active Montview member who participated in the proceedings, reflects on the 1990 assembly, he focuses on Allen and Rose's reactions to the loss. He does not represent Allen's emotions in quite the same way as Allen does. Allen communicates a gracious attitude and wholehearted endorsement of Gwynn's victory and his capabilities, but O'Keefe says, "The loss was very tough on Al. When everyone gathered after the defeat, it was a sad get together. However, Al and Rose's attitude was,

'But we move on.'[493] As Allen's parents would have said, *"Shikata ga nai."* It cannot be helped. Do not look back. Move forward. Persevere.

O'Keefe might not accurately reflect the complexity of Rose's reaction, either, in that he underplays her regret. At the time she might have put on a brave show as being ready to "move on," but she was so skeptical about the 1990 candidacy that, decades later, she emphasized that she had not encouraged Allen because she had not wanted him to be disappointed again. He had done well enough the first time. No need to try a second, even though he assured her that, in retrospect, he realized he learned humility and self-understanding from loss and did not regret it. Still, for her, one run and loss were more than sufficient.[494]

Because Allen was already preparing for significant transitions in his personal life, he seems to have quickly moved past the defeat. He and Rose would be retiring together, the date yet to be determined. Save for his responsibilities on the General Assembly Nominating Committee, he was satisfied with his work at the national level of the church and was ready for it to "draw to a close."[495] Closure was not immediate, however. Perhaps he began redirecting his emotional energy, but even in 1993, Allen was continuing his General Assembly activities by serving as Chair of the Consulting Committee on Professional Development.

Chapter 30

Swimming Upstream

ALMOST THREE DECADES AFTER his retirement, Allen reflects on his time at Montview by contrasting it with his years at Westminster in Dubuque. Rather than being immersed in the local church and community as he was in Iowa, "the national church had more influence on me when I was in Denver, and in terms of my accomplishments. Maybe that was due to being a co-pastor, and every year we would change our responsibility. One year it would be Christian education, one year congregational care, another year stewardship and administration, and then we would switch around again."

The fluidity of responsibilities meant any one pastor's efforts could not be easily pinpointed, either by the pastors themselves or the congregation. None of them settled into specific roles, but they did have flexibility, as Barley noted, to pursue their preferred areas of interest, such as Allen's focus on pastoral care, Barley's preference for mission and administration, Hutchison and Allen's interest in presbytery, and Allen's in the national church.

Unlike at Westminster, where Allen's position as associate in relationship to the head of staff was clear, Allen is sensitive to the fact that the Montview co-pastors "were seen strangely by the other churches. They didn't see any one of us as *the* pastor of the church. Sometimes we would be chosen [to participate in community activities] for one particular reason. Within the Denver community, I was the only Japanese-American pastor, so they would sometimes ask me to be on a city committee, like when they established an interfaith group. The archbishop was the chairman, Rabbi Foster was vice-chairman, and I was secretary-treasurer."

Perhaps the clearest contrast with Dubuque and his community connections there is Allen's more remote professional relationship with Denver. "I never really felt I was involved in the community itself. I didn't even get much involved in Park Hill [Montview's location], even though we got to know and work with the neighboring churches. We were too busy trying to keep Montview's head above water, not just because of the controversy over Fay Hill, but because all the churches were under a lot of stress."[496]

Cearley, who was a member of the collegium when Allen retired and worked at Montview as part of the team for three decades, affirms his perceptions. First, she says no one saw any one of the three as *the* pastor. Cearley observes that the co pastorate is a "different animal. . . . I even have a hard time identifying what I did particularly, what I brought. . . . It's a bit like an amoeba moving around. If this person has [really strong opinions], the whole thing moves that way. If there's conflict, they pull back and say, 'Oh, I'm not good with what's happening here.' It sometimes frustrated people watching from the outside because they'd say, 'They don't know what they're doing.' The answer was, 'They know perfectly well what they're doing. You're just not used to seeing leadership function in this way.'

"The point was to be part of the team. We'd sit together and all throw out ideas, then everybody would go do their jobs. It's very difficult to single out one person in this model and say, 'Montview's success is due to this or this.' That was the point. We were trying to model in our staff what we wanted the congregation to be, which was 'This is not about individual attainment. The success is really the priesthood of all believers. . . . It is all about what we do together.' That came from somebody like Allen for whom that is success. . . . It doesn't have to be about *me* succeeding."

Allen reflects this frame of mind in his reaction to Gwynn's 1990 unexpected win of the moderator position. Yes, Allen was disappointed to have lost, but once he saw that Gwynn was an inspiring, effective leader, he did not hesitate to give him his full support. The team's success was the point.

For many, it is *all* and *only* about *me* succeeding. Allen's genuine pleasure in the success of the group is a less common attitude. Cearley notes, "I think it's probably safe to say Allen swam upstream his entire ministry, first because he was Japanese American and second because he was part of a church [Montview] that swam against the current. That takes a toll."

Her second agreement with Allen's observations about his focus during his Montview years is that most churches were "under a lot of stress." Montview members, Allen, the other co-pastors, and their colleagues in other faith traditions were fighting against a culturally strong current: the increasing secularization of the United States. She describes how Montview's experience of it was colored by the events that initiated the collegium.

"The co-pastorate wasn't the end-all, and some people still don't like it, but it was born out of crisis, and we were able to heal the really deep rift at Montview that came from the whole Fay Hill experience. But it took about twenty years. Churches don't heal quickly. It was a real struggle for them in those first ten years, especially. I give Allen, Ken [Barley], and Hutch [Hutchison], then Dusty [Taylor], a huge amount of credit for holding together and working together. We had a facility built for 4500 people that now a congregation of 1400 was supporting. It was constantly about money and resources, as it is with all churches."

Third, Cearley affirms Allen's assessment about the extent of his involvement in the larger church during his Montview years. She thinks of him as "Mr. Presbyterian." He rarely missed General Assembly or presbytery meetings. "A lot of his time went to presbytery." Even as he approached retirement, "He never lost energy for connecting people to the larger church and for mission, and he always looked forward to going to General Assembly and renewing acquaintances."

The image of Allen that emerges in Denver is of a professional constrained on all sides: the countervailing expectations derived from his race; the professional ambiguity of his position as a co-pastor; the Denver Presbytery's lukewarm relationship with Montview; fallout from his stances on controversial theological, social, and political issues; his position in an institution, the PC(USA), buffeted by its own conservative/liberal tensions; and an increasingly secular society.

Cearley is correct to note that in many ways Allen is someone who swims upstream, but she also points out that he was twice nominated for moderator of General Assembly. Even as she credits the honor, yet another obstacle that he faced can be inferred from her observations. She says, "That's a huge win. . . . That he took his place in the grand scheme of bringing the denomination to a place to even consider his nomination—a little guy from Las Animas."[497]

When Cearley, a "big-city" colleague, refers to Allen's achievement, not in spite of race but as "a little guy from Las Animas," she introduces class as yet another constraining aspect of Allen's identity. Taylor, also a Montview co-pastor, is somewhat class-conscious, too. She gave the nominating speech at the presbytery meeting where Allen was endorsed to run for moderator of General Assembly in 1990. When she reflects on that speech, she points out that "to go from his [origins] to where he was eventually was amazing. He had very humble beginnings."[498]

Even though Allen frames his childhood as the son of a sharecropper, he is more inclined to highlight the fact that his family was relatively well-off in small-town Las Animas, were it not for the racial prejudice ignited by the war. The Maruyamas had adequate horses and equipment to work the fields. Mexican migrants labored for them. In high school he had access to the family car, the envy of his rowdy circle of friends. He benefitted from the GI Bill through university and his first year in seminary. He only mentions the lack of financial resources in seminary when he did not have disposable income to help his friends, the Petersens, with their expenses, but the Mochizukis, Rose, and any number of other McCormick students were also stretched financially. Penury was a painful but not unusual state for someone preparing for that particular profession in those years.

Allen does not characterize his class origins as a disadvantage. He hints at his small-town football team's limitations in the playoff against the husky Pueblo players, but discovered that "when you tackle someone that tall, they fall HARD. It was fun!" Perhaps the fun was to take down the cocky, big-city guys.[499]

His respect for the "big wheels—around 275 doctors, lawyers, dentists" at Montview might have reflected some class intimidation, but he in turn inferred from their support that they respected his pastoral leadership. His conclusion about their regard: "It showed the influence of a PhD." His professional and academic achievements seem to have overcome the inferiority he might have felt as a farm boy from the High Plains.[500]

Unlike Cearley and Taylor who mention class disadvantage, Allen typically expresses his sense of being on the fringe in terms of race. Particularly in the case of race, education was the tool that ameliorated disadvantage. It "was something that belonged equally to you [as Japanese American], and you could succeed in it."[501]

In terms of class, he shared army service and access to the resource of the GI Bill with many millions of other small-town young men of his era, so he does not talk about "very humble beginnings" holding him back. Perhaps, though, Cearley and Taylor's perception was shared by others.

Rose was certainly conscious of her small-town origins and marveled that Eleanor Roosevelt's personal secretary also came from Grayville, a connection that brought about the never-to-be-forgotten visit from the first lady. Rose surprised herself by her own courage when she made the three-hundred-mile drive north to Chicago to attend seminary, a drive and educational opportunity that eventually took her, a daughter of restaurateurs in southern Illinois, as far as Nepal.[502]

This is not to discount Taylor and Cearley's awareness of Allen's humble origins and race in his swim upstream, only that Allen prevailed in spite of a complex of factors. The achievement was not without personal cost, though. On his part, Allen also identifies with the "Man of La Mancha" character and the quixotic pursuit of an impossible dream, an identification based on taking principled stances. The one who pursues such goals will be scarred because, as Allen says, what is true and right will not be popular.[503]

Cearley, a pastor who engaged her own battles in a denomination marked by its win/lose historical conflict over the ordination of women, saw Allen's striving in terms of class, race, and personality. "He couldn't own power in the same way that a white male would. He has the maleness, but he doesn't have the race. He is a peaceful guy, often the mediator at the table. He is lively and enthusiastic when you know him one-on-one, but he doesn't carry that 'large energy.' He wasn't a big presence in a room. It wasn't his style."[504]

Judy and Bob Roussell characterize the Allen they remember from the 1960s in Dubuque in a way similar to Cearley's descriptions. They contrast him with the senior pastor, Dick Heydinger, who was a "big man, aggressive, loud." Allen came across as "calm, self-assured." He was likable, and they emphasize that he was always smiling.[505]

Over the decades, Allen's public persona is fairly constant. Even if he chose to be a "big presence in a room," as an Asian man he might have been shunned for assuming such a role. From the *Outlook* article describing Gwynn's surprising win of the moderator position, as well as Allen's reaction to him, Gwynn apparently conveyed the "large energy" expected of much of white male leadership when he spoke on the floor of the General Assembly.

This is the personality type often elected to leadership positions, characteristics Allen apparently chose not to or could not display. Angus's frustration when Allen practiced for his 1980 speech implies as much when his supporters urged, "Allen, get on fire!"

Allen's reaction: "I am on fire!"[506]

In all probability, Allen's "peaceful guy" style came across in both the 1980 and 1990 campaigns. This style also comes across in Cearley's representation of his preaching. It consists of "lots of stories, painting pictures of how you get from here to there, but they weren't great calls-to-arms sermons. I would say that about most of us who preached at Montview. It might be a function of the co-pastorate, that you end up with people who are not charismatic preachers, those who feel like they have to have center stage all the time. You can't have that in a co-pastor model. When Allen spoke, it was more intimate, more personal."[507]

Paired with the 1990 *Outlook* characterization of Allen as "soft-spoken," this "more intimate, more personal" style might imply a meek, retiring personality. This is not accurate. His rhetorical style might not convey the "large energy" of a white male, but it does not define him. One cannot lose sight of Allen's "go, go, go" (*issho kenmi*) temperament—all in, full throttle and nonstop. Nor can one forget Allen's characterization of how he maintained order during controversial session meetings: "I could be very stern."

A complex of characteristics emerges. Soft-spoken but stern. Energetic, but more in one-on-one situations. Willing to negotiate the shoals of the untried co-pastorate model. Cearley and others describe a specific attribute of all the team members that enabled the collegium. "I always say people in the co-pastor model have to have really high ego strength and not many ego needs. Allen didn't get credit for the credit due him. In that model you do a lot that people don't ever recognize because they don't know who did what."[508]

O'Keefe also observes that for the co-pastorate to work, it was necessary "to have three ministers willing to sacrifice their own egos." He speculates that that requirement set the general tone but that "Al was the balance, the moderator, between the other two [co-pastors]."

Allen mediated not only within the collegium. As a member of session, O'Keefe thought there were always divisions between liberals and conservatives, and the latter could be "quite vicious," but the co-pastors offered an alternative to handling difference. O'Keefe wonders if perhaps even the "vicious" people looked at the co-pastorate and concluded "screaming wouldn't get them anywhere."

At times, O'Keefe was frustrated with session meetings for yet other reasons. Members would "put in their two cents about the most ridiculous stuff." None of the three co-pastors during his time on session was authoritarian or stifled debate, though. Everyone could voice his or her opinion.[509]

Allen's perspective about the snags in session meetings is somewhat different than O'Keefe's. Allen did not necessarily find the issues under discussion frivolous but saw another problem, the size of the Montview session. It consisted of thirty-six members, so extraneous issues were bound to arise. The shared leadership model of the co-pastorate in which capable people trusted one another offered a solution that transferred to the unwieldy session meetings. The size could have been a barrier to moving forward, but just as screaming did not get members anywhere, neither did endless debate. When Allen moderated the meetings, what could have been another exercise in swimming upstream did not materialize.

"That's just absolutely too many people," Allen says. "But they realized, since the group was so big, they needed to limit discussion. We had four or five committees that met once a month before the session meeting. They would report. If there was controversy, it was usually within the committees, and it would be solved. The motion that would come to session would be a consensus of the committee. Session members might have questions, but the committee chair would explain the pros and cons. Usually the motion would pass."

Just as session could adjust its process and discover advantages to doing so, switching co-pastor committee assignments annually had its benefits. Allen says, "We would rotate committees so that over a three-year period each of us would have at least one of the three major committees. . . . Each rotation was almost like going to a new church. After we met with the committee chairperson and got to know the people in the committee, we could be pretty free in deciding what we wanted to do. Even if we may have preferred to stay with one committee, we agreed to switch it around so we could all have a part in all the programs of the church. We enjoyed working with new people and different programs."[510]

From O'Keefe's point of view, all the switching around had a downside. He concluded that the co-pastorate configuration was not the sort of "power center" to build the church into a "great institution."[511]

However, the combined dynamics of ministers who were not charismatic preachers, their non-authoritarian leadership style, and the fluid administrative pattern were the points of the co-pastorate. The co-pastorate modeled a shared ministry that was diffuse throughout the staff and lay membership, in lieu of a "power center." Just as electing the first Asian moderator might have taken some rethinking about leadership models, so would building a "great institution" around such a diffuse structure.

When Cearley reflects about Allen's reactions to his loss in 1990, that he respected Gwynn as an effective leader, she says, "That tells you something else about Allen. I know the loss was a disappointment for him, but it wasn't about him. In the final judgment it was about somebody doing a good job for the church. That was far more important to him than the fact he would be in the position or not."

Allen and Gwynn worked together effectively, but Allen's promotion of presbytery was not consistently reciprocated. The irony of Allen's enthusiasm for it and its lack of support for Montview and the co-pastorate is not lost on Cearley. Her memories of the decades-long correspondence between senior pastors and presbytery execs about the "three yo-yos" running the "cathedral church" of presbytery, "really hurtful things," still sting. She notes that "maybe the worst of it happened after Allen left, but there was an undercurrent all along. It must have been hard for Allen." If it was, it did not diminish his commitment to presbytery.

Allen confronted yet other difficulties as he approached retirement, these as a consequence of his cancer surgery and treatments. Cearley gives this example as one indicator of the toll of his illness: "The cancer treatments destroyed his salivary glands, so he didn't have any spit. That's terrible when you're speaking. He had to take these pills to manufacture moisture. The treatments just wore him out."

Surely for someone whose central professional activities require speaking, this was a high hurdle to overcome. Cearley also speculates that as a result of his "lowered energy level following the cancer" in 1985, he might not have invested himself with creating new programs when nearing retirement as he had in the past.[512]

Although Cearley highlights Allen's lower energy level as he neared retirement, Allen only alludes to the possibility that the treatments took their toll over the long term. Rather, he talks enthusiastically about his redirected emotional and intellectual engagement during this period. The "essential pattern" of Christian faith was evolving for him in significant ways as he explored new avenues of inquiry.

He says that as he was getting ready to retire and recovering from the cancer, he was drawn to "many theologians in the Catholic church who were mystics and known for their practices of meditation and spirituality. . . . They emphasized that their study of Buddhist leaders enabled them to find this deeper understanding. That, and being of Japanese descent myself, drew me to Buddhism. . . . Also, as I studied people like Matthew Fox and Thomas Merton, and then with authors who were digging into quantum physics, you get below the surface of much of your former understanding of the doctrines of the church and biblical narratives. That, and when the Dead Sea scrolls were unearthed and with discoveries in biblical archeology, all have caused a revolution in theology. I've really enjoyed that. I don't know what influence Buddhism had on my sermons at the time. All I remember is I was becoming more liberal."[513]

One of the books that intrigued him, in particular, was *Taking the Quantum Leap: The New Physics for Nonscientists* by Fred A. Wolf.[514] He characterizes it as asserting that "we've gone beyond Einstein into a science that's a spiritual engagement with the world."

He explains that "I realized all of my theological training and my neo-orthodoxy and my liberal theology was kind of passé. . . . The whole Garden of Eden story is simply a mythological story about creation that, according to Matthew Fox, has had a deadly influence upon the whole Christian religion. So much of the biblical narrative, when you look at all the customs that became religion, you understand that not only the Christian religion but every religion needs to be more deeply understood. So much of what people hold onto in their religion is all those customs. They're holding onto a culture rather than something spiritual." Allen remembers attending at least one week of Fox's summer workshops on Creation Spirituality, which was held at Denver's Iliff School of Theology in 1991.[515]

His attraction to Fox is not surprising, given that Fox is sometimes compared to Teilhard in that his work is inclusive of contemporary science and theology. The term "Cosmic Christ" is associated with Fox, and its nuance in his scheme is that nature is a sacrament, that is, creation is a divine expression of the Cosmic Christ. In addition to this creation spirituality, environmental, gender, and social justice concerns are Fox's central foci.[516]

Another phrase associated with Fox, as Allen notes, is "original blessing." Awareness of the goodness of creation, as represented in the Genesis story, should take precedence over the church's teaching about "original sin," Adam and Eve's disastrous, but assumed to be inevitable, decision to eat the forbidden fruit. Focusing on creation's goodness rather than the "fall" reorients one to its sacredness and one's place in it.

Just as Fox's theology pushed him to the fringe and then out of the Roman Catholic Church, Allen's unique ministry as a co-pastor seems to have positioned him at a slight remove professionally. The Denver Presbytery apparently never fully embraced the "collegium" model, and it was viewed sometimes with ambivalence by Montview members themselves.[517]

Perhaps the evolution of Allen's theology, taking on as it did flavors of Buddhist and creation spirituality, also set him apart. His interest in massage therapy definitely established him as a pastor on the fringe. In any case, Allen is not one to assume a posture of stasis, and the pathway he was taking to spiritual maturity prior to retirement certainly could be characterized as "swimming upstream."

On the other hand, he had been serving on committees and task forces at the very heart of the PC(USA) and was a constant presence in the life of the Denver Presbytery, even nominated by it to run again in 1990 for moderator of the General Assembly. Perhaps effective leaders often swim upstream as they continuously move between the center and the fringe. Quixote-like innovators do not stop pressing to realize their impossible dreams.

Chapter 31

Integration and Exploration

THE WORD "RETIREMENT" DOES not describe Allen's trajectory after he leaves Montview's employment. Based on his newfound commitment to integrate body, mind, and spirit, he is poised to begin another vocation and prepared to consolidate and share his theological perspectives in other congregations.

His gradual integration of Buddhism, creation spirituality, and scientific developments into an expanded theology was a process that he articulates in the present, but his awareness of it also emerges in contemporaneous documents near the time he left Montview. In March 1993, within a year of his June 1992 retirement, he completes a new Personal Information Form (PIF). Both the fact and content of the PIF signal that leaving Montview has not initiated a "post-work" period during which he will retreat from professional involvement in the church.

A PIF is circulated to churches in the denomination that are looking for pastors, both permanent and temporary. It serves as a resume and is an occasion for pastors to re-evaluate and articulate their beliefs as well as to update work experience. It functions as a professional identity statement.

On it, he lists the many steps he took in anticipation of this transition. Their number and the additional responsibilities they entailed could have contributed to the "lagging energy" Cearley observed prior to his retirement, perhaps as significant a contributor as his lengthy recovery from the cancer surgery.

The steps included two weeks of interim pastor training at Ghost Ranch, Abiquiú, New Mexico, in 1989 and 1990, as well as the 1991 workshop with

Matthew Fox. The most substantive commitment was his enrollment from September 1991 to October 1992 at the Massage Therapy Institute of Colorado, Denver. He studied anatomy and physiology and did clinical practice for 1020 hours, qualifying him as a certified massage therapist and for licensure in Colorado. In effect, he integrated yet another graduate degree as part of his professional repertoire in preparation for retirement.[518]

In the section of the PIF that asks for "Viewpoints," Allen notes that although he received his PhD in theology several decades ago, he has "kept up with the latest theological and biblical trends." His three years on the board of trustees at McCormick Theological Seminary have been "very helpful in realizing the new directions of theological inquiry."

He summarizes that liberation theology was only the beginning of a "new ecumenical thrust toward religious pluralism . . . that will challenge the survival of the Christian church." The challenge means this is "one of the most exciting ages to live," for we should "visualize a Christianity that will mature . . . and impact the future. . . . If we believe that Jesus Christ has created a new humanity after his own image, we need to allow the churches to proclaim and creatively implement these truths. The church has only begun to enable its members to realize the power of Christ to overcome anger, hate, fear, and so on." As indicated, these evolving beliefs will eventually reach, in his estimation, one of their best expressions in his 2002 sermon for Montview's hundredth anniversary.

A list under the 1993 form's category of "specific service to church or denomination" includes details that do not emerge elsewhere in interviews or biographical sketches in national church publications. In addition to serving on the General Assembly Nominating Committee (he will complete his term in 1994), he is "presently" chair of the Consulting Committee on Professional Development of the Church Vocation Unit, which is another national committee, and a member of Denver Presbytery's Permanent Judicial Commission. Since 1980, he has served at various times on the Vocation Agency (of the UPCUSA), the Council on Women and the Church, synod committees on Ministry and Mission Support, presbytery's Committee on Ministry, and Presbytery Council.

Under the section "Other Information," he indicates that "for fifteen years I have either chaired or served on the [General Assembly] Advisory Committee on Continuing Education. I am closely related to the Alban Institute, a group that has researched and assisted clergy of every denomination. Through the Vocation Agency and the Church Vocation Ministry Unit, I have been involved in Young Pastors' Seminars and Continuing Education events. I have taught at Dubuque Seminary and Iliff Seminary . . . and studied Buddhism on my sabbatical leave in Japan. This exposure has been an invaluable experience for growth in my Christian faith."

The quantity and variety of his commitments are impressive, but the significance of naming them lies in the meaning Allen assigns to them in this written representation of himself. His leadership in the national church has given him "insight into seeking and recognizing leadership in the local church . . . and an opportunity to grasp a national view of the church and a global view of ministry in the world."

These experiences lead him to an optimistic observation about the twenty-first century. "We [Christians] will be leaders in dramatizing the cooperation and world unity of nations, cultures, and religions. I believe that the next century will see a leap ahead of all humanity toward peace and human bondedness unknown before."

He had couched his fervor about the church's responsibility to carry out its commission as "God's own people" in similar terms in 1980 and again in 1990 in his candidating materials. On both occasions, he spoke in terms of unity, human rights, peace, and justice for all. In 1990 he visualized the church as God's instrument on earth, a leader in a complex world. Were he to have been elected as the first Asian-American moderator, he would have been an effective witness to Presbyterian inclusiveness and diversity. His is an expansive vision in which the church leads in drawing together humankind in its search for justice and peace.

A dreamer who visualizes humanity's leap toward unity and inclusiveness, Allen is simultaneously a practical person. He emphasizes on the form that his undergraduate degree in business management has given him the necessary foundation for effective church administration. At the time, this would have been an uncommon but welcome claim. Pastors are not necessarily noted for an interest in administrative matters or their competency in this area.

He also writes that his master's in Christian education has always been an asset in that he has monitored, resourced, and taught in the educational ministries of the churches he served, especially adult education programs. Again, while a number of pastors might have some background in education, Allen's training and degree in Christian education and his commitment to it would set him apart.

Although he has retired, he indicates for the benefit of anyone reading the form that he would relocate if a church position that interested him should present itself. "My wife is also retired and able to move with me as opportunities become available." Even though they are both retired, clearly such a status would not prohibit them from relocating for a church position.[519]

Three years later, in February 1996, Allen updates his PIF. The new form reflects that indeed he is not retired in the usual sense. The intervening years have been busy. He was hired for a six-month position as an interim pastor at Calvary Presbyterian Church in Denver, for which he did not have to relocate. He occasionally supplies (preaches at) various churches and serves as a parish associate at Wheat Ridge Presbyterian Church where his friend Rev. Larry Angus is pastor. He is having success in his new profession as a massage therapist in that he has grown his private practice and also teaches massage therapy.

Following through on his interest in education and using those skills, he describes teaching adult classes at various churches in Denver Presbytery. He makes his commitment to education more specific on the 1996 form and writes that one of his "keen interests since retirement is teaching adult classes . . . on the topics of theology, the future, and the integration of body, mind, and spirit."

His identifies his skills as open-mindedness and a belief "in the future as being open to God's new creation." His persistent orientation toward the future is paired with an explicit statement about the balance he achieves between religious tolerance and his own beliefs. While he thinks that "Christianity must capture the common thread of spirituality in all religions" and he has "become much more liberal" in his perspective toward other religions, he asserts that his "basic faith has not changed in the forty years since seminary."[520]

On first reading, this claim about an unchanging belief system seems to contradict his statement in the present that he realized around the time of his retirement from Montview that his neo-orthodoxy and liberal faith were somewhat "passé." However, the claim might also indicate that a broadening of perspective does not necessarily mean changing one's foundational beliefs or, alternatively, he might still be in the process of reintegrating his beliefs. Buddhism, Matthew Fox and other theologians, quantum physics, his commitment to the healing potential of massage therapy, going "below the surface" of his more traditional theological orientation—all are ingredients in his continued growth and post-retirement exploration.

What remains emphatically constant throughout Allen's life and ministry is the value he places on sociability. On the 1993 form he states, "I enjoy parties and seek to encourage creating greater fellowship through social gatherings," and he highlights "people-to-people relationships" as his greatest strength. In 1996 he repeats, "I enjoy fellowship occasions such as parties and receptions."

These affirmations actually downplay the energy Allen devotes to sociability. Cearley describes Allen as understated and a man of few words, but she says, "he was not understated when he was throwing a party!"[521]

Angus alludes to Allen's devotion to making parties memorable events when he remembers a stop they took en route to one of the General Assembly meetings. They drove out of the way to pass a particular "firecracker shop," perhaps in Kentucky. Angus says, "You know, you see these places, like, out in the middle of Wyoming, too. Allen could buy a hundred tons of firecrackers there. He's a pyromaniac! We loaded up the car. For years and years he used to have a Fourth of July party in his back yard." Any excuse for a party, the more spectacular, even explosive, the better![522]

Cearley attributes a large part of Allen's appeal to this sociability. She was initially hired as the assistant pastor for youth and children after Isbell left. As an ordained staff member, she was included in many of the co-pastorate's meetings and activities. She was eventually hired as a member of the co-pastorate to replace Barley, so she spent years as Allen's colleague. She describes him as an "incredible sort of gatherer of people in parties beyond work, a community-building person, making sure relationships were intact beyond work. He'd show up with bags of potato chips and hors d'oeuvres and lay everything out. . . . He embodied this servant role . . . and had a great sense of humor."

She tells any number of stories to support her perception about the value Allen places on sociability. "He was forever wanting to take us all on retreats and get the staff into hot tubs and go to the grocery store together and buy chips and put out snacks. For John Kuzma, our music director for years, this was pretty much the biggest nightmare. He would never sit in a hot tub. He thought chips were regressive. Many, many times, watching Allen trying to corral us, including John, and taking us on mountain retreats—Allen would just be in heaven, in his element, having the best time. John would be over [at one side], and we were all somewhere in the middle." Some were fine with Allen's enthusiasm; some were clearly more reserved but evidently tolerated it, perhaps more out of affection for him than their love for potato chips.

According to Cearley, another dimension of Allen's generosity was wanting to share the satisfaction he derived from integrating body, mind, and spirit through meditative practices, particularly massage. She says that Allen would sometimes go around the table at meetings and massage peoples' shoulders. From her perspective, some seemed uncomfortable with it. She speculates that their hesitancy might have been less pronounced if a clergywoman had been the one offering shoulder massages.[523]

The importance Allen places on social occasions as important for strengthening group bonds is emphasized by Montview member Shirley Burkhart. Allen promoted session retreats, which she found valuable because "you get to know your fellow elders and are much more able to discuss things there [than in a formal session meeting]." When she pictures Allen as sociable host, though, her more vivid memories are of post-session meeting gatherings at a nearby bar on Colfax Avenue. She describes him as "laughing a lot, . . . going through the crowd of elders [there were thirty-six on session, but probably not all stayed for the after-meeting "debrief"]. . . . He was a caregiver, . . . making sure everybody was okay." She adds that both Allen and Rose were "good hosts" who did "a lot of entertaining."[524]

Taylor, the pastor who followed Hutchison on Montview's team, also has vivid memories of the care Allen put into planning social occasions. She still laughs to the point of tears about a particular experience with Allen's sociability that she, Cearley, and Barley had with him at one of their staff retreats. Cearley also remembers it down to the minute details.

The event is so memorable to both women that they recall it at length, separately and unprompted. It took place at a mountain location. Cearley reminisces that "we [she and the three co-pastors] had lots of fun eating dinners out. On one retreat, . . . Ken [Barley] picked one restaurant for one of our meals, and Allen picked one for another meal. The restaurant Ken picked was white tablecloths, gorgeous windows, and views out into the mountains—this hoity-toity place.

"Allen picked out this restaurant that was like a cafeteria because, you know, the more food the better, the cheaper the better. The place did have entrees printed on the menu, and one of them was 'chicken bosoms.' Dusty [Taylor] and I looked at that, and finally one of us said, 'Oh, chicken breasts!' We got tickled and started laughing. We just laughed ourselves silly. Allen is taking the side of the restaurant [owners] and suggested, 'Maybe English isn't their first language. They probably thought "breast" and "bosom" are the same thing.' We're just laughing, tears running down our faces: the contrast of Allen being so pleased with the restaurant, and we could not get ourselves under control—like a *Saturday Night Live* skit."

A certain classist undertone again plays a part in memories of chips and cafeterias, but in Cearley and Taylor's characterizations of Allen as this "little guy from Las Animas" with "humble beginnings," his class origin takes on an endearing quality. Cearley's conclusion from the restaurant incident is nothing but positive. The memory of it leads her to point out that Allen is not pretentious. He even took the side of the restaurant owner for whom English was probably not a first language. Cearley admires him all the more because "Allen was who he was all the time. He didn't wear different personas. A lot of clergy paint on different personas for different places, and Allen never did that. And he always wore his clergy collar."[525]

John, Allen's son, would second not only Cearley's assessment about Allen being "who he was all the time" but also her remark about the ubiquitous clergy collar, even when being unpretentious did not put him in the best light. John says, "He never, ever put himself above anybody else. He was always one of the team."

Being one of the team included Allen's connections in the larger Denver community, in John's estimation, even though Allen represents his work at Montview as not being as attached to Denver as it was in Dubuque. Possibly father and son have differing definitions of "community" and differing ways of thinking about "connectedness." When Allen compares his numerous involvements in Dubuque to those in Denver, they are sparse, but John does not forget his father's advocacy when John needed to transfer universities in his senior year. He attributes his quick admission to the University of Denver to his father's connections.

A particularly treasured connection for both is to the Denver Broncos. John says, "He was definitely connected to the community, one example being the Broncos tickets. We started getting tickets in 1977. We got on the waiting list, and didn't come off until 2000—thirty-three years later! But Billy Van Heusen, a punter for the Broncos back in the '70s and a member at Montview, got my dad two tickets and transferred them to his name. Then we helped out Roger Peale, an avid Broncos fan who was disabled. Dad started taking him to games from '77 through, must have been, 2000. We'd go to the Broncos games every week and still do.

"One game Roger couldn't go, so my dad and I went straight from church. First quarter, the Broncos do something bad. Dad starts cussing. I looked over at him and said, 'Dad, take your collar off!' Because he was still wearing it. You can't have a minister yelling the profanities that he was yelling. . . . He was always calm except for football. I'd say, 'Dad, they're trying just as hard as the other team.'

"Football is such an emotional game. Maybe that's why I got into golf. It's one of the games where you need to keep a level head."[526]

Football, especially when the Broncos play, is undoubtedly Allen's passion, but on both the 1993 and 1996 PIFs he indicates he also loves golf—and fishing. Allen, John, and John's son Jonathan all enjoy golfing, and enjoyed doing it together. As for fishing, not only does Sam Calian have fond memories of fishing with Allen in Iowa. Rose remembered that Allen's real devotion to it began as far back as when her father bequeathed his tackle box to him.

She told a particularly memorable story about one of the many times Allen and Arthur Miller, the former pastor at Montview (1947–67), fished together in winter in the Rockies. They walked onto the frozen ice on "a little pond called Archer's Lake where Arthur and Lola had a cabin." The men carried an auger to the chosen spot, but Allen was too short to get the traction he needed to drill the hole, and Miller was by then too frail. After slipping around for a time, they gave up and fished out of a hole already drilled. Allen says they always caught something. "How can you help it? They stock the lake, and it's private!"[527]

The picture that emerges from these memory fragments is of someone who does not stop learning, exploring, or enjoying socializing with colleagues and friends. This openness and availability are also characteristic of Allen in terms of civic life. Even though he weighs the impact of his community involvements during his time at Montview as less than that of the ones in Dubuque, he lists a number of them in his 1996 PIF. He was an officer for the Denver Area Interfaith Clergy Conference, he served on the Governor's Prayer Breakfast Committee and the board/Ethics Committee of National Jewish Hospital, and he was active in the American-Israel Friendship League and the Interfaith Forum and Interfaith Consortium on Pluralism.

As reflected in the 1993 and 1996 PIFs, his sociable personality remains constant; his emerging theology revolves around what he perceives as a basically unchanged faith orientation. What does not emerge in the 1993 and 1996 documents are his feelings about his identity as a Japanese American, although his minority status was a primary motivation in both his candidacies for moderator of the General Assembly.

When he reflects in the present on his past, he does factor in race. He attributes some of his appointments in Denver to his status as the only Japanese-American pastor in the city. In contrast, in Dubuque, he had discovered "for the first time that it doesn't make any difference who you are in terms of your ethnic origin. What makes a difference is what you stand for and whether you can fight for those values. . . . I learned in Dubuque that being of a different racial origin can be a plus in white society where they value a person's brain and leadership ability more than they do your ethnic origin."[528]

If white society valued him at times, one group he joined in Denver that he felt never fully accepted him was the Japanese Association. He and Rose regularly attended their annual picnic. For about ten years, the association would invite him to offer the invocation, but he sensed he was on the fringe and attributed it to the fact that his wife was white.

This sense of having a "strike against him" because of having a white wife was something he also felt when he and Rose were in Japan. The other strike against him was the cultural marker of not speaking the language when he traveled there. He still remembers the moment of the taxi driver's confusion, perhaps his implied criticism, when he looked at Allen and said, "You have a Japanese face. Why don't you speak Japanese?"[529]

He gets similar mixed signals as a person of Japanese heritage in the United States. When Judy and Bob Roussell, whose wedding Allen helped officiate in Dubuque in the 1960s, sort out their perceptions of Allen's race, they come out in different places. Judy "didn't think of Allen as Japanese," but Bob says he was conscious of Allen's race. Perhaps Bob's sensitivity is due to his experience of various forms of discrimination in Dubuque during those years. There were no blacks that he can remember except for the African man he went to university with who had trouble finding someplace for a haircut.

The Roussells give a vivid picture of Dubuque as an "almost closed community." It was overwhelmingly Roman Catholic. Bob felt vulnerable at times as a student in his minority position as a Protestant, but they both remember that ecumenical efforts were a "big feature of the sixties." One of Bob's "scariest moments" was when their high school band went to the big ecumenical service at the newly constructed Wahlert High School gymnasium (a Roman Catholic school) and he had to play a solo. He didn't know what to expect, given all the hostility between the Catholic and Protestant students. Instead, when he finished, they gave him a standing ovation. He thinks everyone was just trying to be on their best behavior to be hospitable.[530]

Given these descriptions of Dubuque, it is somewhat remarkable that Allen says he learned in those years that his race was not necessarily a factor in how he was valued. The city was relatively closed to Protestants, and African Americans were as scarce as Asians were. Perhaps the success he enjoyed was based in part on his outgoing personality and how highly regarded he was in the Westminster congregation, a church that in turn is said to have enjoyed an exemplary reputation in the city.

These experiences fit into a larger pattern of ambivalent observations Allen makes regularly about his Japanese ancestry, which vary depending on the context and his age. The starting point is "the deep hatred I had about the Japanese race and the deep hatred I had of myself for being Japanese" during World War II. However, when he speaks at length about his Dubuque experience of being fully embraced because he was admired as "someone willing to take on the county commissioners and even go to an acid rock band concert and watch over the kids," he recognizes that race is not always a factor in how others value him.

Then again, Allen is quick to say that no person of color is completely accepted in US society. He offers as an example the "Spanish guy" who was chair of one of the General Assembly committees on which he served. Allen would fly into Newark, New Jersey, for many of the committee meetings because most of the other members lived on the East Coast. He doubted the committee members admired the chair for his leadership capacities, though, a conclusion Allen based on their behavior. They enthusiastically sought the committee leader's culinary expertise when it came to recommending "great Spanish restaurants in Newark" but were minimally responsive to him as chair of the committee's meetings.[531]

At times, Allen expresses regret about not more overtly claiming his Japanese heritage; at the same time, he sees himself as more American than Japanese American. If he had valued himself more as a Japanese American, he thinks he would have taken up meditative practices sooner in his ministry. He considers that a loss. "I didn't really have the experience that a lot of people do in the area of meditation/contemplation that goes along with the Asian and Buddhist spirituality." Instead, he describes himself in this way. "My physical make-up of being overly active and being a Type A personality [kept me from meditation/contemplation] until my cancer."[532]

His exploration of his sense of racial identity continues, an amorphous integrative task. In gatherings of persons of Japanese ancestry in the United States, he did not feel fully accepted, perhaps because his wife was white. In Japan, his face was recognized as Japanese, but he was not fully accepted because his culture is American and his wife was white. In the United States, although he considers himself more American than Japanese American, he postulates that, as a person of color, he will never be completely accepted by the majority white culture.

His investigation of various disciplines of contemplation started with Buddhism, but his inquiries soon ranged far and wide. They extended to the meditative practices of some Roman Catholic theologians such as Thomas Merton. They included indigenous and shamanistic disciplines. He says, "I went to several weekend workshops in the mountains sponsored by the international community of Shamanism in Boulder [the Foundation for Shamanic Studies]. They try to get you to understand meditation, deep spiritual knowledge, communicating with the creator. To really find out who you are and to be happy with who you are is something that happens a lot of times in periods of real aloneness.

"They practice healing by first getting the group together to dance to the beat of drums. We followed each other to the beat. It's that process of walking around, thinking about what ails you, and after maybe an hour you feel better. It's fascinating." He compares the benefits of walking in a group to the drumbeats and walking in "the European tradition. We simply say, walk regularly. If you want to keep your health, walk every day."

The workshops combined group and individual experience. "After their own kind of practice of silence and working together, during shamanic retreats they send you out for three hours. You are to wander around until you find a place that really appeals to you and gives you a sense that this is where you will find your spiritual center. Once you get there, you are to sit in silence and meditate on what surrounds you — flowers, trees, bugs, anything—and begin a conversation with them.

"The first hour you sit there and try to figure out what they're talking about and how to begin a conversation. Surprisingly, when you sit there long enough, you begin feeling the earth and the vegetation around you and begin talking with them—leaves, dirt, pebbles, rocks. If there are ants, you talk to the ants. You begin to have a sense of what nature is all about and how as human beings we've ignored the earth. Everything around us 'talks,' but we usually ignore it. You really begin to feel vibrations and that nature is speaking to you."

Sometimes when Allen describes this experience, he ends on a humorous note. "So, you can either go to sleep doing that or can concentrate until you go back to the group. They say, 'Tell about your experience.' I said, 'I have to be honest with you. On this little piece of ground, I said to the ants and pebbles, "Well, I hope you guys are happy down there. I don't know how you stand it. Seems kind of boring."' They answered me, 'Well, we can assure you that it won't be long before you're going to be down here yourself!'"

At other times in the telling, Allen concludes on a somber note. "Shamanism was very helpful because my whole lifetime, it's hard for me to sit quietly and talk to God. But I do feel I've overcome a lot of that and can communicate in my own way with God, Jesus, and the Holy Spirit. But it's a whole dimension of spirituality that I didn't learn in the church. And I learned [that spirituality] even more through massage workshops."[533]

As the 1993 and 1996 PIFs indicate, in Allen's preparations for retirement and during those first years he integrates an eclectic assortment of professional, intellectual, spiritual, and theological resources. Even the ants' message resonates. Everyone ends up back in the dirt, broken into indistinguishable molecular fragments, regardless of race.

In a 1992 "Personal Statement of Faith," Allen integrates his spiritual journey in these terms. "After a half century of ordained ministry in the PC(USA), my faith has grown deep and wide." He continues by observing that change is the overriding marker of those decades, with the 1960s as the watershed moment. No one is immune from the "hurricane force of a new age, a new era, a new creation," but he now thinks that most religions are reacting by seeking to change society in the opposite direction, by retreating to the past and advocating doctrines reflective of a world that no longer exists.

In his 2002 anniversary sermon for Montview's hundredth, he also evokes violent weather images that collide with the hurricane force of the new creation, that of "the cyclone, the tornado of conservatism." He commends Montview for withstanding this destructive conservatism that leaves disunity in its wake.

A decade earlier, in his PIF, Allen was optimistic that Christians would be leaders in dramatizing cooperation and world unity and that the twenty-first century would see a "leap ahead of all humanity toward peace and bondedness." By 2002, though, he sees Christianity as leading the resistance to change in the evolving cultural milieu, counter to the emphasis in the preaching of Jesus Christ. Jesus also lived in a changing world and proclaimed that God "was bringing God's kingdom in the midst of chaotic times," a message that Allen urges the church to recapture and articulate.[534]

Chapter 32

Connection

IN LIGHT OF ALLEN's devotion to seeking "peace and bondedness," Cearley emphasizes that Allen would do anything to support the rest of the staff in their ministries. "If someone needed to grab a broom, he would do that. If he needed to make the coffee, he would do that. He never felt above doing anything in an understated, humble way that made the church community work."

His supportive impulse included offering massage, his newly discovered dimension of spirituality. Cearley mentions this impulse in several contexts. She traces her awareness of Allen's enthusiasm about it to a time before his professional interest was widely known. "He was forever wanting to massage people and make them feel better and always into alternative methods of healing, maybe from his illness, to keep himself physically whole. . . . He wanted to touch people, in a positive way, to literally connect and touch people's lives. . . . He wasn't a man of many words. Allen was definitely the quietest of the group when it was Dusty, Ken, me, and Allen."[535]

Allen's self-awareness about connecting with people in supportive ways echoes Cearley's description. "Even before I went into the ministry, anytime someone at the university was having problems, I was one of the first to say, 'Is there anything I can do?' I would want to help them. That's a natural part of my being. I suppose being a pastor only enhanced the fact I could be more of a counselor. In Dubuque there was a Catholic hospital and a community hospital. I signed up with them to be available to do counseling. We had two, three workshops in which we had a professional counselor or teacher who worked with us. That was very helpful.

"But counseling was kind of separate from my idea about healing in those years. I had no idea. I was more interested in finding out what the person saw as their problem. I was always trying to let the person solve that problem themselves, whether it was marital problems or problems with their children, jobs, business, or friends."[536]

Perhaps distinguishing between counseling as problem-solving in contrast to counseling as healing could be seen as too subtle to be of consequence. However, Allen differentiates them. In his early years as a pastor, he thought of counseling as helping someone in emotional or relational distress to fix their problems, as in helping them repair something broken that is external to them.

Expecting that someone in distress is able to repair their problems implies a degree of physical, emotional, and mental fitness. Healing is a more basic task. Absent sufficient fitness, expecting a person in distress to fix his or her problems would be like assuming a person with a fractured leg can diagnose the injury, make the decision to get treatment, and then walk to the hospital for it.

Regardless of his approach to pastoral care in those years as one of fixing problems, not in the wider context of healing, colleagues and several Montview congregants describe Allen as the pastor on the team whom members sought out for it. Taylor, as a colleague, sums up comments from others. "He's a very, very compassionate person, and was always very popular at Montview." As if saying the word "compassionate" only once is not an adequate descriptor, Taylor goes on to say, "He was good to me, very caring about people and willing to help people. Very beloved by many people because of his compassion."[537]

Offering shoulder massages as a gesture of compassion was a gradual process for Allen. As he completed a course involving 1020 hours of anatomy and physiology and experienced the healing effects of massage himself, someone with his compassionate personality who is eager to comfort others would no doubt offer shoulder massages at meetings and church retreats.

Regarding hot tubs, anyone familiar with Japan or who has visited there and observed traditional customs would know about communal bath houses and relaxing together at day's end. Not only tourists seek out the *onsen*, which are the hot springs and the bathing facilities, hot tubs, and traditional inns near them. Min Mochizuki's treasured experience with colleagues from his older brother's university days took place at such a facility. Allen and Rose fondly remember being included in the church retreat at a similar location, invited as they were by his Tokyo friend from McCormick

Theological Seminary days. Hot tubs might have been the chic thing at Colorado mountain resorts in the 1980s, but Allen had even grown up with a small bath house on the farm. Naturally he would invite friends and colleagues to relax together in this most familial way.

More significantly, church members and staff might not have been aware of how fundamentally Allen's cancer diagnosis impacted him. "When my primary doctor said, 'You only have a year or two to live,' that was a radical change in my view of what my life was all about. Everything I had done to that point was with the church. I thought, 'I'm going to retire in a couple years. Maybe I should be doing something that helps people physically.' My shift was from spiritual health to physical health because it's very important that we maintain a healthy body if we're going to maintain a healthy mind and spirit.

"So when we went to Japan for my sabbatical, and I learned more about Buddhism, and we went to China, I sensed the importance of Asian health over against Western health care. That wore on me. It began to make a significant difference in my life."

He also observes that some aspects of life in Japan are not all that different from in the United States. Both in the East and in the West, tensions between generations, globalization, and the expanding influence of secularism are marking a transition. "I spent a little time with two Buddhist professors. . . . A funny thing they said, 'We have a hard time with our young people here because they just aren't into Buddhism. They don't even want to use chopsticks!'"

After this humorous observation, Allen returns to the subjects at hand: Asian views about physical and spiritual health and his exposure to Buddhism. "But in my conversations with the Buddhist professors, it was their spirituality I was impressed with, and with the life of Buddha. He was a very spiritual man, like Jesus in terms of his ability to love, to take care of the poor. Here he comes from a very rich family, gives that all up, wanders around on the streets, and gathers followers. He teaches loving your neighbor, bringing peace in the world."

His impressions about Buddhism and Asian health practices stayed with him after his return. "I continued what I was doing in the church, and my work in General Assembly was very, very important, but I was existing. I was preaching every third Sunday and involved in the regular activities of the church, but in my heart I was wondering . . ."[538]

To emphasize the centrality of his cancer diagnosis and treatments to his decision to focus on physical healing, he says, "I vowed at that time [of my cancer diagnosis] that after I retired I would do something for healing people. I wanted to go into acupuncture, but that was too expensive, maybe

$30,000, to attend a good acupuncture school. And acupuncture wasn't popular then like it is now. You can set up an office and make a living with acupuncture. I was trying to find something I could easily afford and would be able to practice [while] doing ministry as well. After a thousand hours of training for massage therapy, I really became interested in it."[539]

He represents his decision to run again for moderator, an interruption of these preparations, in this way. "Larry [Angus] said, 'I think you ought to run for moderator again.' I said, 'You're out of your mind!' But I started thinking, 'It would be good to see an Asian moderator. Maybe it's worth it. And I had so much support. Montview was very responsive. The group of supporters on my brochure was one I was really proud of—a former Colorado governor, Reagan's personal physician who became a friend, . . . seminaries, the Dubuque church and presbytery up in Iowa. At that point the conservatives at Dubuque Seminary who were against me in 1980 were gone. It looked very positive. We ran a really good campaign, and I had learned so much that first time."

Perhaps because he was satisfied that he had done all he could to win, he had no regrets and could be positive about Gwynn's victory. "Price Gwynn, who won, didn't run a campaign like that, or anything. People evidently thought, 'We haven't had a ruling elder recently.' And his speech—he did a really good job. I was so proud of him. I got to be a friend of his afterward, and then everything [in the church] started to draw to a close for me. My term was over on the [General Assembly] nominating committee, all that. It was very logical to say, when 1992 came, I could just wash my hands of the past and start a whole new career."

When Culver's 1992 *Denver Post* article about Allen and massage appeared on a Monday above the fold on the front page of the "Denver and the West" section six months prior to his retirement, what had been an evolving process for Allen was a shock for many. Culver, religion writer for the *Post* and also originally from Southeastern Colorado, had learned about Allen's interest over one of their regular lunches.

Her reaction to his massage training: "'You're kidding!' I said, 'No. I'm going to massage school now at nights and on weekends. It's wonderful, a way to relax and help your body regain or maintain its health.'"[540]

She interviewed him at length and asked for permission for a photographer to visit the school and take a picture of Allen doing massage. "The school thought it was wonderful. Great publicity. . . . I was expecting the article to be in the Sunday paper in a section people don't take very seriously. . . . Lo and behold, I get a telephone call from her on a Monday morning. 'Allen, do you have a paper yet?' I said, 'No.' And she said, 'Well, you're going to be shocked. When I saw it I went in screaming to the editor and asked how he could do this.' He said, 'Well, it will catch people's attention.'"[541]

The headline read, "Minister to retire, open massage parlor. New career in old profession."[542]

It did catch people's attention, in Denver and beyond. Perhaps the article was even an embarrassment for Denver Presbytery's "cathedral" church on the order of the publicity when Montview's study committee exposed Mafia activity along Colorado's front range in the 1970s. Even Sam Calian, president of Pittsburgh Theological Seminary and Allen's close friend, called and berated Allen with this greeting: "What the hell are you thinking?"

Those who were not shocked were amused. Allen reports that Taylor, his colleague, was attending a board of trustees meeting at Iliff School of Theology that Monday morning. "Dusty said that the topic of conversation was the question, 'Is Allen really going to be a massage therapist?' Finally one of them said, 'Wait a minute. Every pastor should know how to rub people the right way!' For my retirement, Dusty made a plaque for me with those words."[543]

The photo that accompanies the *Post* article shows Allen standing behind a massage table with his hands on a gentleman's bare back. The gentleman's goatee-groomed face is turned toward the camera, showing a contented expression, eyes closed. A large poster that diagrams the musculature of the human body, similar to ones seen in doctors' offices, front and back views, hangs on the wall behind them. Not only has Allen's clergy collar been replaced—by a short-sleeved polo shirt—but the empty massage tables lined up in the background give the impression of a row of church pews.

Having swum upstream most of his life, now he fought another current. Allen says, "A number of people are still not only shocked but disappointed that I became a massage therapist. They assumed I left the Presbyterian church. They said, 'You're in a secular vocation now.' I'd say, 'No, I didn't leave the Presbyterian church. I'm still a member of presbytery.' They responded that I'm in a secular vocation now and have nothing to do with the church. I shouldn't even be a member of presbytery as a minister. I challenged them. 'What proof do you have of that? I'm doing as much ministry as a massage therapist in terms of working with people as I did as a pastor.' . . . They backed off, but until then there were people in presbytery who wanted me out, even though I had retired."

When Calian called, after his outburst accusing Allen that he had left the ministry to become a massage therapist, Allen says he answered that, "'I never left the ministry. I retired, and this is a new vocation. There's nothing wrong with being a massage therapist, is there?' Sam had to pause and say,

'Well, I guess not.' Even Sam thought that massage therapy was some kind of a disrespectful . . ."

Rose interrupted. "Maybe it has something to do with an article I was reading: 'Go Slow to Go Fast.' Maybe you have to go slow in order for people to catch on."

Allen was quiet while he considered this possibility; then he disagreed. "I don't know of another pastor who became a massage therapist, do you?"

Rose did not respond immediately, so Allen challenged her, "Well, see?"

She did not give ground. "Maybe there'll be some now that you've led the way."

Allen seemed to yield to her argument. "I'd say within five years after I had been in massage therapy, it began to have reputable followers. People recognized that massage therapy was a decent vocation. . . . I think there are still some who don't understand because they've never had a massage. They still connect it with taking off your clothes and see it as . . ."

He stumbled to express himself, and ever-down-to-earth Rose said, "Prostitution is the word."

Her blunt comment prompted Allen to put his "coming out" as a massage therapist in historical context. "It's like physical therapy, or going to a chiropractor. In 1988 or so, in one of my couples groups that I used to sit in, we were talking about medicine, and one of the people said, 'Well, I go to a chiropractor all the time.' One of the wives says, 'You go to what?' She said chiropractors were just a bunch of quacks making money off people. You know, in the 1980s, people thought chiropractors were not doctors at all."[544]

Perhaps Rose's counsel to "go slow to go fast" in order for people catch on proved to be correct. Eventually, at least one other Presbyterian pastor found her way into massage therapy. Perhaps there are others, as well as pastors from various Christian traditions, who integrate massage into their ministry.

Teresa Eisenlohr, who has taught preaching and worship in seminary and written liturgy for the PC(USA) while serving in the national office in Louisville, offers twelve varieties of massage. She explicitly calls her practice in Cincinnati a ministry: Massage Ministration. She writes that, "What happens on the massage table is sacramental. You lay yourself bare before another to lay hands on you in hope of healing, which is as vulnerable as prayer." By using the word "ministration," she means to refer to "the hands-on approach of a minister who cares for you as if she were administering the sacraments."[545]

Allen had some support from colleagues when he began to consider massage therapy as a vocation. He traces the source of his initial interest to

Angie Bratt and her encouragement, a school teacher and spouse of Presbyterian pastor John Bratt. Given this Presbyterian source, and that his PIF (dossier) for the years immediately following his retirement indicate continued activity as a church professional, it seems misplaced that other church colleagues and friends dismissed or even got angry about this new aspect of his ministry. After retirement, he taught adult education classes throughout the presbytery, preached, and served as a parish associate while integrating physical healing with spiritual and mental health. As he emphasizes, he never felt that he left the ministry.

"I took massage very seriously," he says. "From some [massage] schools, you can graduate with as few as thirty-five hours of training. I had over a thousand. I went to the old Massage Therapy Institute in Denver, on Colfax Avenue, which is now the Colorado School of Traditional Chinese Medicine. In a thousand hours you learn only the basics, because there are over fifty types of massage: Swedish massage, foot massage, massage for athletes, deeper tissue massage, Trager massage. . . . You only get a taste of the varieties of techniques. Colorado doesn't require continuing education, but I went to at least a dozen continuing education classes.

"Around 1994 or 1995 I had continuing education on energy medicine called Reiki. I got very interested in it. I became a Reiki master. . . . I even spent two weekends [in Kansas City] learning Karuna Reiki, an advanced, more powerful Reiki."[546]

Allen's interest in Reiki was shared by increasing numbers of massage therapists in the United States. Other Reiki practitioners in Colorado indicate that its popularity surged in the early 1990s because its arrival on the US mainland corresponded with the decreasing cost of the training and less constriction on the time requirements to complete it.[547]

These developments correspond with the 1995 publication of Diane Stein's *Essential Reiki: A Complete Guide to an Ancient Healing Art*, a widely used text in the United States at the time. Her stated objective in writing the book was to make Reiki more accessible and available at a low cost. The traditional, expensive training method took many months to complete, but teachers began to move through the three training levels over a Friday through Sunday evening schedule.[548] This was Allen's teaching pattern when he became a Reiki master.

Some detail about Reiki and its history from Stein's book shed light on possible reasons for Reiki becoming Allen's focus. She summarizes the process of its migration to the US mainland from Japan, where it began with Mikao Usui (1865–1926). Although Usui's personal history and the sources for his philosophy are somewhat unclear, he was committed to spiritual healing as the basis for healing the body, mind, and emotions. He apparently combined the principle of Buddhist compassion for all living things with his "rediscovery" of what he called "universal life force energy." This energy, or "Ki," is a Japanese parallel to, for instance, the Chinese "Ch'i," or "Qi," and Hebrew "Ruach" (breath, spirit). The two kanji characters for the word Reiki translate as "spiritual energy."

Usui believed this energy lay behind various ancient healing practices, including those of Jesus. Usui's student and successor was Chujiro Hayashi (1880–1940), whose student, in turn, was Hawayo Takata from Hawai'i (1900–1980). Each taught many hundreds of practitioners. Takata's work in Hawai'i served as Reiki's springboard to the US mainland.[549]

Throughout her book, Stein is careful to clarify Reiki's position in relationship to religious and medical practices. When she notes the influence of Buddhism, she asserts that Buddhism is not a religion but a philosophy that accepts other cultures' deities. Neither is Reiki a religion. She also emphasizes that Reiki does not interfere with Western medical treatment. Rather, Reiki complements it. In fact, some cancer centers and other medical facilities presently make Reiki available to patients as part of supportive treatment regimens.[550]

In addition to compassion, basic to Reiki is its non-invasive character. It consists of gently placing the hands on or above the body. The receiver must give permission for the treatment. The practitioner is only a conduit of healing energy; the outcome depends on the acceptance of the one receiving it. Allen makes this comparison: "Reiki is like prayer healing. If you don't believe it, it's not going to do that much good."[551]

When Allen reflects on his professional life after seminary—the four decades of his pastoral ministry and the two decades during which he worked as a massage therapist and Reiki master—he values the latter two most highly. What he treasures is "teaching people in my classes, some who have never stepped into a church. Others were raised as a Christian or Buddhist or Muslim, or something, and most of them in massage therapy classes had 'lost' that faith. Essentially, . . . they were very good people, and you realize the truth about human beings, that it's a matter of life, of maturing, and relationships that have created either joy or sorrow."

These reflections lead him to articulate what sounds like his philosophy of life and its purpose. "Happiness is coming to yourself, understanding yourself, learning to love yourself, and to be some kind of help in the world, whether you're helping people or making somebody else happy or creating something that enables people to live better lives. . . . In any kind of profession you can make some kind of contribution to this earth and the environment, to the community in which you live."

The principles of Reiki and Karuna Reiki, the advanced Reiki Allen learned in Kansas City, reflect these values. Karuna is a Sanskrit word used in Hinduism and Buddhism that roughly translates as "compassionate action." More specifically, just as you want to heal your own wounds, you want to heal those of others.[552]

An observer could infer why these two decades of ministry after retirement were so significant for him, although Allen does not explicitly make the connection. He found tools for healing wounds that he attributed to his Japanese lineage. In turn, he made those tools available to others in his Western context.

To become a Reiki master and to attain the Karuna Reiki level, the practitioner will have first completed the three levels of Reiki training. Level I focuses on direct, physical self-healing and healing of others. Level II adds emotional, mental, and distance healing. Level III, which is the master's or teacher's degree, includes the capacity to convey energy, the Ki, to others receiving the training, a process called "attunement."

Attunement and the use of certain symbols are unique to Reiki. The practitioner learns three of the five Reiki symbols in Level II and learns the additional two symbols in Reiki III. The symbols, which have their origins in Sanskrit but are based in part on kanji characters, serve a focusing function. Reiki practitioners draw or visualize the symbols, which has the purpose of triggering their own intention.

The symbols are such a defining aspect of Reiki that they require further explanation. Perhaps their function can be better understood when they are compared to elements of the Japanese art of *Shodō*, Japanese calligraphy. Possibly, Usui's Japanese heritage connects use of the Reiki symbols to aesthetic principles underlying *Shodō*.

Also, Stein's detailed drawings of the figures that include diagrams with the proper direction of the strokes to be used is reminiscent of how the *Shodō* characters are taught. In Japan, the basic *Shodō* brush strokes and the direction the brush is to be moved for each kanji character are learned in elementary school, but apparently only those who practice the artistry of *Shodō* refine the techniques. The Reiki practitioner also learns the direction and sequence of the strokes that comprise the five symbols, whether they are actually drawn or just visualized.

To explain, *Shodō* is characterized as a Zen practice, similar to Japanese fencing (*Kendō*), other fighting arts (*Budō*), ikebana, and the tea ceremony. *Shodō* can even be used to enhance the artistry of ikebana and the tea ceremony. All these practices encompass the Zen aesthetic of simplicity paired with gracefulness. The execution of the composite movements, or, in the case of Reiki, of the five symbols, drawn or imagined, is as significant aesthetically as the outcome. Zen tradition has it that the kanji as drawn by *Shodō* masters transfer the wisdom of the traditional Chinese poems on which the *Shodō* content is typically based.[553]

This sounds similar to the Reiki practitioner's use of the Reiki symbols: the symbol connects the practitioner to the function, that is, to the content it represents. For example, the first symbol's function is to promote physical healing and is roughly translated as "bring power here." The second symbol promotes mental and emotional healing; the third promotes distance healing. The fourth functions as the enlightenment symbol and is used by Reiki masters when attuning initiates—a symbol that heals the healer. The practitioner uses the fifth symbol at the completion of a Reiki session.[554]

Just as the aesthetics of *Shodō* perhaps shed light on the use of the five Reiki symbols, the attunement process seems to have parallels. Allen does not explicitly connect the two, but the process of Reiki attunement, of passing healing energy to an acolyte, is reminiscent of part of the ritual in the service for the ordination of Presbyterian church leaders. They are similar in both gesture and outcome—a recognition of being set aside for a purpose, which is more likely to be effective if the person receiving it believes it will be, for themselves and for the people they will serve. Both ordination and attunement function as symbolic of validating a certain level of competency, as passing on a gift, and a responsibility.

At one moment in the ordination service, the person being ordained kneels, if able, and the other ordained church leaders present are invited forward. They place their hands on the ordinand while a prayer is offered. In ordination, "the church sets apart with prayer and the laying on of hands those who have been called by God through the voice of the church to serve."[555]

By the time Allen became a Reiki master, fully conversant with the use of the symbols and the process of attunement, he was not only qualified to offer both massage and Reiki treatments but also to teach them. Fortunately, these skills, as well as his skills as a teaching elder, were portable, because in 1996, Sarah and her husband needed Allen and Rose's help with their baby daughter. Allen and Rose were more than happy to relocate and moved to Olathe, Kansas, to be near Amanda and her parents.

Allen set up a massage room in their home, a "beautiful, ranch-style with three levels." As Rose noted, to say that Olathe, or anything about it, is "beautiful" is redundant. "Olathe" is the Shawnee word for "beautiful."[556]

Allen also had a portable table so he could "go out and do Reiki" when people called, and he worked part-time as a massage therapist "in a big salon where I would spend maybe six hours a week." As though he was not busy enough, he was on the staff of a massage school in Kansas City and taught Reiki classes for about six years there, "nights and weekends so they did not interfere with my [other] work."

Allen's particular joy was to teach Reiki I, II, and III. "I must have ended up with maybe two hundred to three hundred people who took Reiki, but only about twenty took all three Reiki steps. It surprised me that in the Reiki master's class, when we would practice [distance healing] together, and these people had relatives who were sick as far away as maybe even New York City, so many of them had responses. People in the class would say [about the ones willing to receive the distance healing], 'I can't believe it, but I got a letter, or a phone call, from my cousin or my aunt, for instance, and they say their illness improved all the time [I was doing the distance healing].'"

In the other [Level I and II] classes, there were "so many stories that the students would tell about the healing they did, whether it was with whooping cough or cancer, with MS, serious and simple illness. And all the Reiki work I myself have done with a number of people. I don't say I've cured them because I say Reiki is something you teach people, and they can heal themselves. It's energy, the energy from the sun, essentially. Reiki simply uses symbols that convey that energy toward healing in the body and mind."

When he describes his Reiki practice, he repeatedly emphasizes, "I don't do the healing. The energy does the healing." Allen, as are other Reiki practitioners, is careful to coordinate his treatments with Western medical practice. If he encounters something that seems to need that kind of attention, he "wants them to go to a doctor." Of course, when the doctor advises "there's really not a problem—you're just getting old!"—Allen offers Reiki.[557]

After they moved back to Denver, he says that "before Rose died [2017], I had a list of people I was doing it [Reiki distance healing] for, and I kind of ran out of energy myself. . . . I still do it every night when I remember them, but it's easy to get discouraged."[558]

When he and Rose moved to St. Andrew's in Aurora in 2013, he still had the energy and commitment to offer massage and Reiki comfort and healing in their new environment, a retirement home. They downsized in preparation for the move to St. Andrew's, but the one category of books and papers he kept were his Reiki materials, anticipating that it would be widely welcomed.

Several close friends were also residents there, including Bill Muldrow from University of Colorado days and his wife Betsy. As for Muldrow, "I didn't know his heart condition was so serious, but neither he nor his wife were very receptive to Reiki. He didn't really believe in ancient Asian healing."

The Muldrows' attitude toward Reiki was somewhat typical of that of other St. Andrew's residents. Because Allen is committed to Reiki's non-invasive approach and to the dynamic that it will not be all that effective if the receiver does not welcome it, he was not able to offer Reiki to the extent he had anticipated. Several people came to the first training class he offered, but when they realized all it entailed, they lost interest.

Muldrow has died, a death Allen experienced as somewhat sudden. Two other friends at St. Andrew's, one of whom Allen knew from Montview and golfed with on a course across the street from the retirement home, have also died. One of them was receptive to Reiki. Allen is grateful that he was able to be of help and that the man "lived a couple years more than the doctors expected."[559]

Allen's opportunities to offer Reiki as one of his supportive impulses that connected him with people was not received with the enthusiasm at St. Andrew's that he hoped, but that has not deterred him from finding ways to join with his new neighbors to enhance life together at St. Andrew's. As Cearley observes, he never feels above doing anything, however under-stated, that will "make community work."[560] Pre-COVID-19, he, sometimes accompanied by his acupuncturist college Lesley Shearer, offered massage to residents, joined study and exercise groups, and helped coordinate the weekly Sunday chapel services, among his many activities.

Chapter 33

Family and Vocation

HAPPILY FOR ALLEN, HIS vocations as massage therapist and pastor had come together in particularly satisfying ways in 1996 when family circumstances called for the move to Kansas. Allen and Rose had lived in Aurora for just over two decades.

The circumstances developed over a period of time. For several years, Sarah had tried to conceive, efforts that had included major surgery in 1993. When Sarah learned she was finally pregnant, a first thought was to "call my parents, but they were in the mountains in Colorado doing a wedding for a friend from Montview. We always told each other where we were going to be. Pre-cell phone, we'd also give a phone number. I called their motel and left a message. They called, and they were so excited!

"Amanda was a delight for all of us. The first grandbaby. Then I had the opportunity to go to Japan and work. My parents started flirting with the idea of moving. 'We'll sell our house and buy one there.' It was funny how certain things become a catalyst for some major change. They moved in January. I left for Japan the first week of March. Amanda turned one in April. They were so involved in her life."[561]

An undated letter from Rose to a young Amanda serves as another record of Allen and Rose's involvement in their granddaughter's life. It summarizes Rose's personal history and perspectives as she responds to Amanda's question about historical events during Rose's lifetime. Rose notes that she and Allen moved to Olathe, "to help take care of you so that your mom and dad could continue working."

In retirement, Rose and Allen finally had time to share the joy of grandparenting in ways they had not been able to share childrearing when they were young parents in Wisconsin and Iowa. Rose had characterized the Dubuque years, in particular, as a difficult period in their marriage. She said that Allen, with his community involvements and church and academic work, had little time for her and perhaps by extension for Sarah and John.[562]

Rose's letter to Amanda implies her devotion to her grandchildren throughout, and it also suggests that Allen's many Dubuque commitments had at least one positive outcome. They meant she consolidated her own professional identity as a teacher during those years. Rose's commitment and pride as an educator come through clearly in her letter when she emphasizes that she taught business classes for a total of twenty-nine years, in six different schools.

Even though Rose and Allen shared many interests, Rose's confidence about the value of her professional commitments carried forward from Dubuque to their move to Denver. Rose, along with Zoe Barley, Rev. Ken Barley's wife, was very clear from the outset about her choices regarding the role of a minister's wife. The two women accepted the invitation from "the women who wanted to meet with us. I remember us both saying that we had jobs and that we would not be attending their meetings. 'We're the wives, but don't count on us.' . . . They never bothered us."[563] Rose's choice about where and how much she would be involved in the church's life as Allen's wife was a bold declaration of independence in the early 1970s.

If controversies came up at Montview, Rose said, "I really stayed out of it. I went to church. I sang in the church choir. I listened to Allen when he wanted to talk. But I didn't talk to anyone [about controversial matters or personalities]. My mouth was shut. I [taught] and got involved in my own career, which was good."[564]

In Rose's eulogy, Cearley mentioned how important her work as an advisor to the Future Business Leaders of America was to her at the Gateway [Aurora] and Hempstead [Dubuque] high schools: "She was proud of the students she mentored and made a point to encourage kids who needed extra care." When Cearley follows those comments with "Rose embraced, loved, and lived beyond the role of pastor's wife," those listening to the words would not take exception. Rose could embrace and love the role of pastor's wife because she did indeed live beyond it.

In retirement, Rose and Allen invested themselves in their grandchildren. Rose begins one paragraph in her letter to Amanda with, "I love being a grandparent to you and Jonathan [John's son]." To underscore her feelings, she concludes the paragraph with, "It is a pleasure watching you and Jonathan as you mature and become more grown-up every day."

Sarah fills in details that give weight to the extent of Rose and Allen's devotion to their grandchildren by describing a particular scene. Their routine was to pick up Amanda from daycare, spend a few hours with her, then bring her over to Sarah's. They often arrived in time for Rose to prepare dinner for Sarah and Russ. One night Sarah walked into the kitchen, and all three were sitting on the floor, leaning against the wall, with their legs straight out in front of them.

"I'm like, 'What are you guys doing?' My parents just look at me and say, 'She wanted us to sit here.' I'm thinking, 'Okay, so the two-year-old says sit down, and they do what she tells them to do?' They would do anything for her."[565]

In Olathe, vocation and family were integrated in ways they were not at other times of Allen's life. Sarah and her brother John participated at Montview minimally, on the fringes as high school students and young adults. In the small Olathe congregation where Allen served for a time with a pastor Sarah remembers as "Ken," Sarah, Russ, and Amanda eventually immersed themselves completely. Rose was also quite involved in the Olathe congregation.

"Dad took a failing church, and at first we said to him, 'Oh, that's . . . wonderful.' He would tell us, 'You're welcome to come.' We were like, 'No, I don't think so,' because we thought it was weird. They were actually meeting in a strip mall. 'Really, Dad? You're in a church in a strip mall?' . . .

"Finally, for some reason, we decided to go. Maybe some special event or a little buffet dinner. Amanda was probably three or four. She liked it a lot, and we we liked it, too. Right around that time a family in the church donated a farm property close by, and it still had an old barn, a silo, and their farmhouse. The farmhouse, a brick, ranch-style home, became the new place of worship—Heritage Presbyterian Church. Another member was an architect . . . and they made one long area for worship, kept a couple of bedrooms and the bathroom, maybe the kitchen, and a sunroom off the back that maybe became the pastor's study. The bedrooms became the classrooms for the church school. There was still a big tree and rope swing out back.

"We were pretty involved. We liked it because it was so small. You got to know everybody. Amanda was in the Christmas play, and I started teaching Sunday school. I'd have to tell the kids to tiptoe through the back of the church to go outside. It was a fun time. I was a member of session, and Mom was too, I think. Mom was in the choir. Eventually they called a regular pastor so Dad could step away and just attend and enjoy it.

"It was so small that you had to give your time as well. They desperately needed that. We didn't have a custodial crew. Once we went to clean it, and Amanda thought that was really cool—to vacuum and clean the tables in the classrooms. We were all there together, and our lives were intertwined. It hadn't been a natural thing for Russ and me to be involved in church, so this was a great evolution.

"[When we moved back to Colorado], the church had a farewell for us. They said, 'You can't leave. We're going to have the highway patrol stop you at the border.' . . . We moved back when Amanda was seven."

Sarah's description of the Olathe congregation gives the impression that while serving there Allen had traveled full circle. He had come back to the size of congregation he describes as the place "where Christian community is developed very clearly." Rose had long ago indicated she had a similar emotional attachment to small churches in her notation beside the picture of the small Hogarty, Wisconsin, church, in her album celebrating the twenty-fifth anniversary of Allen's ordination: "The church with the truest Christian spirit of any church we have ever known."

It follows that a painful experience for Rose, "the most personal, terrible part of my life," would more likely occur in the context of a larger congregation where a degree of anonymity can disguise the development of unhealthy relationships. The experience was all the more painful because before their breakdown, the relationships had been so positive.

Allen says, "It all started with [a group of couples they gathered] going to Bronco's games, watching the games." From Rose's perspective, "We had so much fun together!"[566]

The combination of congenial couples and Allen's passion for football guaranteed good times. O'Keefe, who was part of the group, describes Allen as very "even-keeled," but "one thing that got Al excited, and I mean really excited—the Denver Broncos! He had virtually every Bronco game recorded and saved. About the Broncos, he would go absolutely bonkers."[567] Even in the present, Allen sports a Broncos case on his iPhone.

When Allen describes the couples' group, he says, "They became so close that they'd get together for birthdays, holidays, and when family members would visit they'd have a dinner together. Rose didn't see it developing, but I did—a chemistry happening between different couples. . . . The group fell apart. There were seven couples, and four of them got divorced and three of them stayed together."

Rose continued the sad account with, "I will tell you it was horrible. I was shook up. I just felt like, 'What's happening in our world? . . . Who can be trusted to maintain life and continue as it is?' . . . How could we have something terrible happen [from something that had been so enjoyable]? And the question was, 'How do we deal with this now? We have to be friends with everybody.' And we were. We tried to be with everybody. And we still are, I guess. . . . It shook me up more maybe than death, in a way. With death, it's over. You have memories. But with a break-up and a friendship, you have to walk on and look at both sides, try to understand everybody. It's still difficult for me."

When Allen reflects on the situation, he says he related to it "as a friend, more than anything. I didn't relate to it as a pastor. In a small congregation, you can't do that. You are the pastor. But in a large congregation, when you have that many pastors, you can."

Rose and Allen continued their reminiscences about the heartbreak by describing some of their continuing relationships with the individuals involved. One of the women who was traveling in Japan with her new husband at the time of Allen's sabbatical in 1986 met them in Kyoto for dinner.

The conversation moved to other dynamics in larger congregations, in particular, tensions between theologically conservative and liberal members. First, they reacted to O'Keefe's assessment that Montview's "extraordinary choir" held those factions together in that everyone took pride in it and could unite around it.

Allen thought that Montview's "overall program" was the more significant factor, "holding the congregation together until more recent times. It was pretty much middle of the road. It wasn't conservative; it wasn't liberal." Further back in Montview's history, Allen believes that Miller survived disputes between the conservative and liberal factions because he was a "man everybody just loved, and his sermons were moderate."

When Allen characterizes larger churches, regardless of their theological orientation, he sees them as being "socially liberal. Even theologically conservative large churches are pretty liberal socially—wine at weddings, things you wouldn't think conservative churches would allow. The bigger the church, the more liberal it is socially. Because they want money."

Rose did not hesitate. "I agree. I think you're right."[568]

Allen's realistic assessment about large churches and their financial interests does not make him a cynic. He is committed to the ministries of all sizes of congregations. During the six years in Kansas, he worked at the small new church development and also "taught adult education classes on Sunday mornings at a huge seven-thousand-member Presbyterian church where Dick Avery, a classmate, had a pastoral counseling office. . . . One class I taught was about massage and religion—body, mind, and spirit. How one takes care of one's body is part of Christianity. But I was also interested in Bible study and theology, so there was no end to the kind of classes I had. The classes were big, about thirty people in them. I taught at three different churches, and I served on the General Council of that presbytery. I was really busy going to presbytery meetings."[569]

When Allen says he values the twenty years following his retirement from Montview as the most fulfilling years of his ministry, that satisfaction includes more than the integration of his roles as a spiritual and physical healer in small and large congregations. While they were in Olathe and two decades after Allen's first run for moderator of the General Assembly, an Asian had yet to be elected. In 2000, Rev. Syngman Rhee stood for the position. Allen and Min and June Mochizuki all worked on his campaign committee. Allen was "very enthusiastic about the fact that an Asian was running for moderator." Allen traveled several times for campaign meetings to Richmond, Virginia, where Rhee worked for fifteen years as a visiting professor at Union Presbyterian Seminary. He thought Rhee had a good committee, "representative of all over the country."[570]

Rhee was a North Korean refugee who fled to South Korea in 1950 with his younger brother, leaving their father, who was a Presbyterian pastor, their mother, and their four sisters behind. Rhee had no contact with his family for twenty-eight years and never saw his parents again. He graduated from Louisville Theological Seminary in 1960 and served for twenty-five years on the staff of the national church under both its UPCUSA and PC(USA) iterations. He coordinated mission work in the Middle East and East Asia, eventually serving as the associate director for the Worldwide Ministries Division. During 1992–93, he was president of the National Council of Churches.[571]

Min and June recalled the context of their involvement in Rhee's run for moderator by comparing it to Allen's 1980 and 1990 campaigns. To recap, they speculated that when Allen ran, it was difficult for him to "reach out" to the "Asian-American picture" and the Asian caucus within the Presbyterian church, even though Allen says joining the Asian caucus was one of the first steps he took when he became involved in the national church's activities. June attributed Allen's fringe position to his minority status within the JaJA community in that "he tried to be non-Asian. He wanted to be American as he grew up." Min is quite direct in his assertion that although Allen is Japanese American, "he did not share the Japanese-American experience."

For Min and June, the defining experience for twentieth-century Issei and Nisei in the United States is the World War II incarceration of the majority of persons of Japanese ancestry who lived on the West Coast. That population was concentrated in the military zone declared in Roosevelt's Executive Order 9066 and was forcibly removed in its entirety to the incarceration camps in the interior.

It is the case that Allen's experiences during the war were different as a child growing up as a member of the small number of persons of Japanese lineage in Colorado. Min does grant that Allen "knew something of the Japanese-American experience, [but] he didn't know." In other words, Allen was certainly aware of the camps, lived only fifty miles from one, visited it, and even knew one of the incarcerated families. His sister-in-law had been incarcerated. But he was an outsider, external to the experience of being forcibly removed, losing everything, living behind barbed wire, and surveilled by soldiers in guard towers with guns. Min observes that as an outsider, Allen "had to run [for moderator] on his own."[572]

When June contrasted her World War II experiences with Min's, she marveled that "you can't find two people with the same stories [about those years]."[573] Even so, Allen's story evidently lay outside an indeterminate line of what the Mochizukis considered the JaJA norm. Perhaps Allen would have been more successful in his attempts if Presbyterian Japanese Americans like Min and June could have identified Allen first as Japanese American, second as Presbyterian, and only third as someone who did not share the trauma of incarceration.

On his part, Allen, as someone more assimilated at a young age, speaks about members of the Asian caucus as "these people." He also frankly admits that he would have been at a loss if he had had to minister to an ethnic congregation. He simply did not know what those communities were like. If Min and June were an indication, it seems some Asian Americans of a certain age did not see Allen as one of them, either, with which Allen would seemingly agree.

Otsuka, the Japanese-American doctor originally from Sedgwick, Colorado, has yet other observations about growing up in the interior of the United States that more completely frame Allen's relationship to the larger Japanese-American community. Sensei (third-generation) and born as the war ended, Otsuka experienced neither the incarceration nor the full force of the hatred heaped on Japanese Americans during the war years. Even so, he says he did not "come out," even to himself, as Japanese American until 2003, when he took back his Japanese first name. Before then, he thought of himself as part of white culture, but in retrospect, he can describe incidents of microaggression when he clearly was not seen that way. Also in 2003, he visited Japan for the first time. He did not feel at home there, but he no longer feels at home in white culture, either. Now in his retirement years, he says he is trying to sort out his place and come to peace with himself.[574]

In contrast to Otsuka's (Sansei) and Allen's (Nisei) sense of ambiguity with their standing in US society as Japanese Americans, Rhee's status was more clear. He was a first-generation Korean refugee. He escaped from the enemy (North Korea) and achieved remarkable professional success, an exemplary symbol of the American Dream.

However, his position as Korean in the Asian-American community revealed certain complexities in the dynamics of inclusion and exclusion. The lingering antipathy between Korea and Japan as a result of the Japanese occupation of Korea cannot be overstated. Min and June Mochizuki's close relationship with Rhee highlights these complexities. Min emphasizes the uniqueness of their friendship, which began when the two families started working together in the Presbyterian Asian caucus: Min and June, a Japanese-American couple, and Rhee and his Korean wife, Haesun. It made a consequential difference that the Mochizukis were American Christians, not Japanese Christians, because that "did not carry the emotional freight."

The magnitude of that "freight" between persons of Korean and Japanese heritage becomes more evident each time Min refers to it. It hung over the pan-Asian Christian youth conference sponsored by the World Council of Churches that he had attended in the Philippines during his 1964–65 sabbatical. As noted, students from various countries that had been or were at war were scheduled to meet for the purpose of reconciliation, the Japanese and Koreans among them.

The antipathy also dominated his visit to South Korea during that same time frame. Min tells the story of meeting with South Korean parents of a student he and June befriended when he was the assistant pastor in Dearborn in the 1950s, a relationship with the student and a friend of his that endured. When Min traveled to Seoul, as "an obligatory kind of response" for his friendship with their son, the young man's parents hosted Min, but housed him in a hotel, not their home. Also, they dared not speak Japanese with him in public, although he assumed they knew Japanese because they grew up during the occupation. An English-speaking nephew translated for them.

However, the last night of the visit, "they invited me to a fancy restaurant and arranged for us to dine in a detached room. No outside eyes other than the servers, at which point we are now speaking in Japanese." From Min's perspective, the Korean parents demonstrated an extraordinary generosity of spirit to interact with him as they did.[575]

Given this and innumerable other historical divisions represented in the Presbyterian Asian-American community, electing the "first Asian" moderator was no small feat. To Rhee's credit, he brought any number of qualifications to the position, including the force of his personality, to overcome these divisions and probable prejudice on the part of some members of the majority white PC(USA) denomination. June described Rhee as "an international figure," and Min goes on at length about Rhee's "outgoing" nature. Others who knew him are even more emphatic about the charisma

Rhee exuded, in that when Rhee was around, "the air buzzed with excitement and energy."[576]

Twenty years after Allen's first attempt in 1980 to become the first Asian moderator of the General Assembly, Rhee was elected to the position. Allen fully participated in the joy of that victory as a campaigner for Rhee and in his approval of Rhee's leadership capabilities. Not only did Allen realize that long sought-after goal during those Olathe years, but his family was fully engaged in his ministry in the Heritage congregation. In turn, he had time to devote to his wife, children, and grandchildren and to his teaching and healing ministries.

Chapter 34

Stories of Healing

WHEN SARAH, RUSS, AND Amanda returned to Colorado, so did Allen and Rose. During Allen's first decade of retirement, he had successfully combined his vocational shift to physical and spiritual healing in both Colorado and Kansas.

Back in Colorado, Allen and Rose bought a home in the suburb of Highlands Ranch, south of Denver and about one mile from Sarah and her family. Happily, this location also put them in close proximity to grandson Jonathan in Parker, a town further south of Denver. As Jonathan grew, he, Allen, and John golfed together—and went to Broncos games.

Rose and Allen were again involved in activities with their wide circle of friends in Denver. Allen regularly visited his decades-long Broncos games buddy, Roger Peale, at the Denver VA hospital (Department of Veterans Affairs) and was thankful he could bring Peale some relief from his multiple sclerosis by the means of Reiki treatments.

Allen sat up his massage table in their Highlands Ranch house, saw clients there, and visited clients in their homes. He worked part-time as a massage therapist in a large salon in the area. Because of his skills in massage therapy and Reiki, for a period of four to five years Allen was regularly called to augment patient treatment at the Craig Hospital, which specializes in rehabilitation and research for those with spinal and brain injuries. The Denver Presbytery put him back on its General Council, which Allen wryly attributes to their need for an Asian minority person.[577]

He attended workshops taught by his friend Lesley Shearer, and on occasion they see clients together. In addition to her work as an acupuncturist, Scheerer has devoted herself to homeopathic medicine and many other forms of energy healing, such as Qigong. Shearer defines Qi as "subtle life force energy" and Qigong as "energy cultivation." She describes Qigong as "very similar to" Reiki.[578]

She has lectured at conferences on these subjects in China and Europe and continues her teaching, research, and writing. In her search for "the nucleus of authenticity beneath [healing] traditions," she surmises that it survives "through rituals" that "evolved in support of the now forgotten truth" of their origins.[579] In her search for authentic origins, Shearer's approach to healing resembles Allen's reflections about Christian belief. Cultural accretions cloud the original core teachings of healing traditions, as they do those of Jesus.

Neither might explicitly connect their shared orientation about the importance of authentic origins as playing a part in their respect for one another, but they certainly admire each other's effectiveness and dedication to healing. Shearer's description of Allen's energy goes well beyond "go, go, go" (issho kenmi). "Allen's just power-packed, a person energetically organized, aligned with larger forces, surrounded by a healing field." Not only does she use the example of Allen's intrepid search for Mother Teresa's hospital in Kolkata as illustrative of his energy and resolve, but she emphasizes how much courage it took to have gotten into massage therapy, energy healing, and Reiki when it was not all that well known, and with the background of a Christian minister, no less.[580]

She thinks of him as an ally and help in that at difficult times he has served as guide and counselor. "Without knowing it, he is an aikido master. . . . With aikido, you just pull your opponent and let him topple by the energy of his own offense. You step out of the way, and that is what he suggested I do [in a situation in which she was professionally challenged]. It was elegant."

Shearer evokes his role as a healer with memories of two personal experiences. In one instance she was quite ill. He waited outside the Intensive Care Unit until they let the family—and Allen—see her. He "started doing Reiki and saved my life."

On another occasion, she invited him, "as the one clergyperson I trusted," to serve communion in the nursing home to her mother, who by then could not speak. However, Shearer sensed that the sacrament would be very meaningful for her mother, a conservative Lutheran. "He is one of those people through whom the sacred flows to transform the mundane. When he finished, my mother mouthed 'thank you' to me."[581]

The 1993 trip to Nepal and India was a formative experience for them both. It came about because they were intrigued by an invitation that Shearer unexpectedly received to attend the enthronement of the reincarnated Khyabje Dudjom Rinpoche, supreme head of the Nyingmapa school of Tibetan Buddhism, dated January 1, 1993. It was to be held at the Orgyen Do Ngak Choling Monastery in Boudhanath-Kathmandu, Nepal, "on the 15th of the 8th Tibetan month of the Water Bird Year—the Western date to be confirmed later when the Tibetan calendar is released."[582]

"What did I know about Tibetan Buddhism? Nothing," says Shearer. "But the price was right. I showed it to Dick [her husband]. Yeah, we could afford that. And then I showed it to Allen. 'Oh, yeah,' he said. 'We could do that.' Rose was, 'This is great.' And then Allen told me about Woody Strong."[583]

Allen and Rose's interests in Strong and his charitable connections with Nepal had been long-standing. That they would have occasion to visit the country they had heard so much about thrilled them both.

Strong's story is told by any number of people and in any number of publications and news releases. In the 1970s, Strong started responding to Nepalese need by gathering school and used medical supplies. Allen recalls that Strong, a member at Montview and on session, gathered the supplies "for years. He did it so often that he gained a reputation with the king of Nepal. Once he was up in Seattle with a whole bunch of medical equipment and couldn't get a plane to take it to Nepal. He called the king's office, and the king says, 'I'll get it for you.' He sent his private plane to Seattle" to transport the materials.

Shortly after Strong's wife died of cancer in 1982, he was diagnosed in his early seventies with an inoperable cancer. He was told he had one year to live, at most. He decided to spend his remaining days in Nepal.

Surprisingly, he returned to the United States soon thereafter. Allen tells how "Woody came to church one day and had a story to tell the pastors. . . . He said, 'You've got to hear this. It's about how I was healed in Nepal.'

"So we set up an appointment. We went into a room at Montview, and Woody said, 'I want to show you.' And he laid on a table and said, 'Before my recent visit, I saw the doctors here and they filled me with medicine. I went to Nepal and got sick. . . . The people there took me into their chapel. . . . All the priests they could gather came around [where they laid me] and said their prayers and chanted.' Suddenly he felt much better and later he came back to the States.

"The doctors tested him and said, 'The cancer is gone.' Woody said, 'What?' They said, 'There's no cancer.' He told them about his experience with the Buddhist priests, and, of course, the doctors just shook their heads and assumed that the treatments [they themselves had given] had taken it away. . . . So Woody said to us, 'I had to come to the church and tell you guys because I don't believe in faith healing, but evidently that's what [those Buddhist priests] did on me.'"[584]

Taylor was one of the co-pastors present at Strong's Montview demonstration of his Nepalese healing. As her daughter Kathy tells it, "He wandered into Montview one day and you asked where he'd been. And he said, 'Oh, I've got to tell you. I've been reincarnated. I was in Nepal and I got reborn.'"[585]

Allen told Strong's story to Shearer and described Strong's connections with the Montview pastors and congregation, so Shearer was not surprised that Rose was also enthused about making the trip and seeing Strong's work in Nepal. As Allen and Rose record in their report in the *Montview Messenger* upon their return, many times Strong had said to Allen, "'Come to Nepal and see [who] these wonderful people are and what we are doing [here].' . . . Woody is a man filled with passion for the Nepalese people and for his desire to give to them what he feels they have given to him—a life filled with love and compassion."[586]

From Shearer's perspective, Rose's reaction to the prospect of the trip was also characteristic of Rose and Allen's relationship. She says, Rose "mirrored Allen. . . . My relationship with my husband is similar to Allen's relationship with Rose—the opposition and yet also the support." She says Rose was Allen's counterpoint, the one who "held his string. Otherwise, he'd fly off into the cosmos. With all of us, we have to have partners who challenge us. That forces us to defend how we experience life, which makes us go deeper into ourselves. It's frustrating to have a partner like this because we feel like they're holding us back."[587] In this case, presented with the prospect of a trip to Nepal to see Woody's work, Rose was in full supportive mode.

In Rose and Allen's *Messenger* report, they write that the group they traveled with consisted of thirty-five people from throughout the United States, ten from the Denver area, several of whom were Montview members. Many in the group were Buddhists or had an interest in Buddhism. Rose and Allen emphasize in the article that, "for those of us who profess Christianity, this was an extraordinary experience and one that we approached with the dignity and respect other religions deserve."[588]

For Shearer, as a Westerner, the enthronement was "weird, because I knew nothing about it. . . . Now I understand the reasons and the purposes, but it was a very abrupt initiation for me."[589]

Rose included a clipping from *The Kathmandu Post* in her album of the trip. It matter-of-factly describes the first day of the three-day program from within its cultural context. The three-year-old "Tenzin Yeshe Dorje was enthroned as the 19th leader of the Nyingmapa sect, the oldest school of

Tibetan Buddhism, amid a traditional and colorful ceremony on Thursday [September 30]. He was welcomed with huge Tibetan trumpets, cymbals." A parade along a street to the monastery was "lined with thousands of followers" and the courtyard of the monastery "turned out to be too small for the thousands of monks and Lamas from all around the world." Rose, Allen, and the Shearers were among the thousands who lined the street.

The clipping explains that because he is so young, the boy will go back to his home "until he reaches an age when he should enter the monastic order," at which time he will be "detached" from his family and live in the monastery. The article concludes with some history of the Nyingmapa sect and explains it has "about" four monasteries in Nepal. An unobtrusive but poignant observation appears toward the end of the article: "There are also many Nyingmapa followers in Tibet, but they are not allowed to leave their homeland and their actual number is not known."[590]

Rose's album contains any number of pictures of Strong and his then wife, Penny. The Strongs entertained the Maruyamas, Shearers, and several others in the group and saw to it that they visited some of their many projects. Rose's pictures include schools, hospitals, an orphanage, and a carpet factory.

The enthronement ceremony and the visit with the Strongs were preliminary to the courageous side trip in the small plane to view Mount Everest and the stop in Kolkata, where Rose and Allen searched for Mother Teresa's hospital. The journey ended with a visit to Thailand.

They did not have the benefit of a Woody Strong to introduce them to life behind the Thai tourist scene, but Allen asked if a taxi driver could take him to a massage school. The driver explained the schools were attached to Buddhist temples. Of course he would take Rose and Allen to one. The people welcomed them and showed Allen a classroom. When Allen asked if they had a textbook in English, they supplied one. He noted that the instruction and text are no different from what he learned in Colorado, except Asians emphasize more energy work, such as touch healing, than Europeans. His conclusion? Massage is much the same the world over.[591]

Among the photos from the Thai portion of the trip, Rose included one of Allen's "thrilling adventure," a ride on the back of an elephant, and others of their visit to the Thai Rose Garden. Rose represented it as appropriately carrying her name and claimed it as her own space, captivated by its beauty and "entertaining show."

When Strong died, Allen was retired. In the intervening years, Montview and its members had participated regularly in Penny and Woody's mission projects. Taylor did the funeral in Nepal and believes she was around sixty-five years old at the time. Daughter Kathy remembers two details of the trip as relayed to her by her mother. First, Penny took Taylor to meet the royal family, and, second, Taylor was to fly in a helicopter to a ridge, "a little piece of ground," at around 12,000 feet on Mount Everest to deposit Strong's ashes.

Taylor takes up the story. "The storm was coming in, so we had just enough time to get out and drop his ashes. I was going to bury them, but there wasn't time."

Kathy offers this addendum. "You've said it was time just to say a prayer, and, of course, with the helicopter and the weather coming in, you know everything blows everywhere!"[592]

The disposition of Strong's ashes was fitting, scattered as they were throughout the land he cared about, inhabited by the people who restored his health and whom he served. His story of his near death and "rebirth" in Nepal influenced many who heard it—Allen and Rose, the other co-pastors at Montview, the congregation, and countless more. Not only was the story riveting, but Strong's enduring commitment to the Nepalese inspired others to support his efforts.

Allen's own stories of near death, rebirth, and commitment mark pivotal moments of his life, as well. In childhood, he came close to death consequent to the dog's bite. As a teenager, he confronted not physical death, but psychological death in the wake of the Pearl Harbor attack. His rebirth from his self-hatred and antipathy toward anything Japanese was a process that took place over a long period of time, and he describes its resolution in terms of "release" and "freedom."

He traces the healing process through the chronology of his personal history. After the Pearl Harbor attack, society indicted this all-American kid—captain of the elementary school patrol, winner of the American Legion award, athlete, and honor student—for his Japanese heritage.

"I developed such a complex. I saw myself as subhuman. Less than a person. In my early teenage years, I learned to really, really hate myself. Being in the military helped a little bit. When I got out, I began to see it wasn't that terrible a thing to be born Japanese in America. When I went to the University of Colorado, I was surrounded by veterans. Other veterans respect you and accept you for who you are. Just another human being like them. When you were in a [university] classroom it wasn't always that way. You didn't always feel accepted. But it didn't matter because you had this group of people that you lived with in your fraternity.

"And my church group. I went to church every Sunday with Bill Muldrow and that little group of Christians. In summer conference work, I felt the release of people accepting me for who I was, and I was able to provide leadership.

"Up in Wisconsin, in my churches I felt accepted, but in the wider community, I didn't. When I finally got to Dubuque, that's one place where it wasn't just the church community [that embraced me]. It was the whole city of Dubuque that seemed to accept me for who I was. I always ascribed that to getting my PhD. That was the time when I really felt that I was okay. To be Japanese was not something to be ashamed of, but to be proud of. You were of a different ethnic background, but you could be fully accepted in white society. That was the dawning of a new age for me, so that when I came to Denver after I'd gotten my PhD, I felt emancipated. I felt freed."[593]

This sense of emancipation and freedom varies, depending on his age and the context, as do the choices available to him and his family for iden-tifying racially and culturally. Culturally, he emphasizes the American, not the Japanese. Racially, he ran for moderator twice as an Asian. When the black girls spit water on Sarah at the Chicago museum, her parents referred to her, their biracial child, as white. When he compares his situation to the Mexican immigrants on the Maruyama farm and the Hispanic committee chair in Newark, he recognizes a hierarchy of exclusion. However, regard-less of how people of color perceive their status in that hierarchy, he con-tradicts himself and concludes that they are never fully accepted in white society in the United States. With a PhD in hand, though, he as a person of a "different" ethnic background had the self-confidence of his value in white society, if not full acceptance by it.

Otsuka's terms for self-reference also vary over time. He grew up thinking of himself as "part of white culture." He did not "come out," even to himself, as Japanese American until sometime in his adult years, but his subsequent travel to Japan confirmed it is not "home," either. He is trying to sort out his "place" and come to peace with himself as not quite Japanese but not fully accepted as white, either.[594]

That Allen expresses feelings of emancipation and freedom signals he is at peace with his Japanese-American identity more often than not. He can affirm his self-acceptance but recognizes that approval by the majority culture might not necessarily follow.

"All the work I did in Denver and in the denomination, I felt some persecution by those who didn't like Japanese people, whether it was in the church or in the Denver community. But it didn't affect me. There was [some] recognition in the larger community—when I was secretary-trea-surer of the Interfaith Council, and the president was an archbishop and the vice-president was an outstanding rabbi. You felt like you were really free."

Allen's rebirth, his journey from feeling subhuman to feeling free, was both an internal and external process, dependent on recognition by the larger communities of which he was a part, often as the sole Japanese

American. Only as they freed themselves of their prejudice and accepted him was his freedom more expansive. Self-acceptance alone is somewhat passive. Acceptance by the larger community invites active participation. In Allen's case, it opened the way for a particular level of participation. "I felt the release of people accepting me for who I was, and I was able to provide leadership."

Having leadership opportunities is central to Allen's feelings of worth. Accordingly, he has a clear definition of what that entails. "A good leader is a person who has a vision. He has a knowledgeable background, and if he doesn't he will find that knowledge. A leader has an open mind, always willing to listen to what other people think. You have a vision and a focus on where you think an organization should go, a country, a political party. It may not match the vision of other leaders, but you have your vision and you work toward that in every way you can. You use all your energy, and you focus on providing that leadership to reach that vision.

"But if you're wise enough to listen to those who differ from you and figure out why they differ, they may change your position. As a good leader, you're able to manipulate your own purposes and work to fit them with that new vision that has changed, maybe because of culture, or world, or national politics, or whatever. A good leader has to be flexible but still hold strong to their purpose, vision, and dream, and work toward that dream."[595]

In the context of leadership, having a vision, a dream, is crucial. Equally important, though, is flexibility. Shearer, who has observed Allen in many contexts—as fellow student in various workshops, pastor in hospital settings, partner in treating clients, as traveling companion—describes the quality of his flexibility more fully. She says he is "not judgmental." He is "very forward-looking." He has a "way of injecting fresh air" into what can be the "stifling community" of the church.[596]

A story Allen tells about Reiki and faith healing in the context of the Olathe storefront church's beginnings is one of many that illustrates the elements he considers basic to leadership: a person with expertise or the motivation to acquire it; a vision to which one devotes one's energy; and flexibility while not losing sight of one's purpose.

"We were trying to get new [church] members, and I was thinking, 'How can I attract people even to come in for a prayer meeting or anything else? Something new. I advertised a Reiki workshop. I had some people in the congregation come, half a dozen, and a couple of people who saw the signs about it outside the church. We had conversation and a half-day demonstration. I urged them to come back.

"Until then I didn't believe in faith healing, but one of the people who came to the workshop from the neighborhood called and said, 'Reverend,

I think you have to have prayer before that Reiki works.' I said, 'No. Reiki is separate from any kind of religion. You just work on rubbing your hands together, getting them warm, and sensing the power of that energy. Universal life energy is all around us.' . . . She said, 'You're wrong. If you don't have faith and you don't believe that God is doing this, it won't work.' I said, 'Okay. Do it your way.'

"But that made me study the way Jesus healed in the Bible. While I was doing that, I used to go to the home of one of the parishioners to give her a massage. Her sister was visiting, who was a faith healer. When I met her, she told me about the list of all the people she had healed with prayers. I asked her, 'You really did that and they got well?' She says, 'Oh, yes. When I go home, I'll probably have two or three phone calls from people who want to come over and have the experience of faith healing.'

"The more I studied the Bible, Jesus was teaching his disciples that in healing they were to use their hands and use prayer, too. I began realizing that when Reiki [practitioners] say you have to believe it, that is the same as saying you have to believe in faith healing.

"So I started using my faith in doing Reiki, and it was more effective than just saying the symbols, which is itself like faith. That language translates as 'Send energy here. . . . Total healing, all the senses of the body, and, finally, spiritual healing. That's all included in the symbols."

Allen continues to adjust his assumptions and explore various healing methods. He has purchased several devices that generate heat from laser technology and justifies using them with this rationale. "The source for Reiki [practitioners] is universal energy, and for me, that is the sun. . . . Now I've started using this laser energy [device] on myself because it is quicker and as effective as Reiki. Probably a true Reiki master person would say you shouldn't rely on it because it's not the same, but it's a matter of using energy, [whether] from the sun or from man-made lasers."[597]

To summarize Allen's leadership formula, he had a vision of growing a church in the environment in which he found himself, and he used his expertise as a pastor and a Reiki master to attract attention and invite people in. He listened to those who attended the workshop and came to understand Reiki in the context of faith, which led to recalibrating his own understanding of Reiki, a recalibration he continues as he is exposed to more information.

He easily compiles a list of people who have been examples of his definition of leadership. Not only were they flexible people with expertise, vision, and energy, but all of them were committed to developing and sharing leadership capabilities: Dick Heydinger, the pastor in Dubuque; Fay Hill at Montview, whom Allen admired but who was "just a man who fell into the wrong position at the wrong time"; Lois Stair, who appointed him to his first General Assembly position; Dr. Daniel A. Ruge, President Reagan's physician, "who helped me and was a very smart man"; Larry Angus, "who had a stronger vision of me . . . than I thought of myself and thought what I became was because of Rose"; Sam Calian, his closest friend in Dubuque; Art Cochran, "my advisor for my doctorate"; and a Catholic theologian in Dubuque who was "kicked out of the Catholic church, married a nun, and became an Episcopal professor at an Episcopal seminary.

"I forget his name, but he's the one who persuaded me to go on and get a doctor's degree. I told him, 'You're crazy! Why would I do that?' He said, 'You have to. You need to. You have the brains to do it.' I kept saying no and he kept after me and after me. . . . They weren't just friends but people who really believe in you and boost your ego and help you try to believe in yourself."

While he spoke, Rose was silently compiling her own list but did not offer names. "It's amazing that anyone like that would like me and would respect what I have to say or think. I'm impressed with that person if that person likes me! [Looking back now], every one of them helped me in some way that I didn't even realize was happening, as it happened."

In response to Rose, Allen expanded his thinking and about his vision and commitments. The quality of leadership that emerged was one of enabling and freeing others to realize their own capacities as people did for him. "I see myself as someone who guides people to find themselves. I see myself as a counselor who helps people find their own vision. I don't consider myself a healer but someone who tries to show people what they have, what they can do, and the power they have [to heal] themselves.

"When I was teaching Reiki, my greatest joy was to be able to make them a Reiki master, which was equivalent to what I was so they could go out and teach Reiki themselves. I was a conduit, if anything, for people.

"Probably even when I was a kid, that's what I was trying to do. It's a natural thing. In seminary, even in life generally, I think the whole purpose of friendship with people is not to try to get them to do what you want to do, but more to get them to do what they can do. I listened and sympathized with people, but I figured that's what all pastors did. The fact that a person becomes a pastor or priest automatically enables them, whether they try to or not, that people will get out of the confrontation they have [with pastors] an automatic feeling they have found some guidance. That's one of the charms of the pastoral ministry. The reason some pastors don't make it is that they've failed in the sense they have this gift that they don't know how to use, or they have closed their mind or personality from it."[598]

Shearer describes Allen's gifts as a counselor and guide in very much the same way. "One of my favorite expressions that Allen uses [is one] I need to use more often. You tell him a problem or your view of life or how you perceive a particular situation. He'll say, 'Is that right?' That can mean a whole lot of things. It can mean, 'I'm observing you. I'm not judging you. Is what you feel correct?' But it doesn't imply any kind of seeing it from his point of view. That is a masterful expression: 'Is that right?' . . . Or, 'Is that so?'"[599]

When Allen refers to one of the "charms" of pastoral ministry, he is referring to a nexus: capacity and training that has qualified one to heal/teach/counsel and whose skills are sought by others. From the perspective of many pastors, the charm or gift is reciprocated when people feel "they have found some guidance." The pastor might not be able to identify what exactly he or she did, or may not hear about the outcome for some time, but has met the expectations of the person who sought help.

Because of the pastoral role, parishioners give ministers extraordinary access, not only to the joy of their lives but also to their pain and suffering. Certainly it saddens and frustrates Allen that some pastors squander this gift, but the disappointment, even a sense of betrayal, on the part of people seeking help is acute if pastors fail to honor the trust placed in them by virtue of the pastoral role. Ministers fail to honor that trust when they do not seek training, do not remain current, or withhold the gift of listening and attending.

Allen had characterized this neglect vividly in his description of a colleague from his early years in ministry, the pastor who "carried his fishing pole and golf clubs around in his trunk. That's what he cared about, and his church knew it and suffered."[600]

While a person who uses this access to a pastor is giving a gift of trust, the gift does not come without potential hazards. As those in counseling professions know, when people are fragile—angry, addicted, fighting for survival, perhaps physically but also emotionally and mentally—they might blame and accuse even the most well-intentioned pastor of being the cause of or adding to their distress.

It takes courage to be exposed to the prospect of blame. Because of the skills required to be a counseling resource at times of such fragility, many pastors make clear to their congregations that, while they will certainly be available pastorally in such instances, they will refer parishioners to counselors specially trained in these areas when appropriate.

Allen's transition to include a ministry of physical healing might have been shocking to some of his colleagues, but it was a logical progression for him. He frames his 1992 retirement as a rebirth, as occurring in the context of his brush with mortality caused by his cancer. The transition was accompanied by another period of training, which gave him the skills and certification he needed to engage in "hands-on" physical healing. Both his pastoral skills and his skills as a masseuse are equally important gifts to share as indeed he does not separate the spiritual and the physical.

Sarah's characterization of her father is consistent with his stated commitments to spiritual and physical healing. She says he is "the most gracious person, giving and caring, a true servant person. . . . It's partly his Japanese culture and the fact that he is a man of faith. . . . You see all the time in the news stories about religious leaders who are very egotistical, but pastors who want to pastor in their churches are very caring and unselfish people. [My dad] was that. Generous. He'd come over to our house and say, 'Let me give you a foot massage.' Or we'd be traveling and he'd say, 'Let me give you a ride to the airport.' He calls me every day. He used to come by and bring Amanda breakfast, take her to school, pick her up from school, and take her to their house.

"We had two cats, and my parents used to take care of them when we'd go out of town or something. My dad would come over and feed them and play with them. We would laugh because he would put our cat Frankie on his chest, and she'd put her face right up to his. He would close his eyes and pet her. We used to joke that he was doing Reiki, and she was going to live forever."[601]

As she describes his personality, she makes the connection that "my dad and I are pretty much alike." Allen and Rose agreed that Sarah is like Allen in that they are quite "sociable," both "extroverts."[602]

The downside is that, as Sarah says, "When my dad and I have conflict, it is pretty intense." To illustrate this intensity, she tells a story about what she describes as "the worst of times." Russ became acutely ill in 2012 when the family was vacationing in California. Allen and members of Russ's side of the family traveled to Los Angeles to be supportive. Rose, who was not feeling well herself, stayed in Colorado.

"I was freaking out, saying to my dad, 'I don't know what I'm going to do. I've got to get back to work. I don't have the money to pay for hotels. I'm renting a car, and he's so sick, and now they're putting him in ICU, and I don't know what's going to happen.' My dad says, 'You go back to work and do your job. Take Amanda back. I'll stay here and take care of him.' I said, 'Dad, that doesn't work. He wants me here, and I have to make decisions.'"

The two of them might have proceeded to a resolution, had not Sarah continued, 'Dad, you're old. This is Los Angeles. It's hard to drive around in this town and not get mugged. I'm not comfortable with that.'

Inflammatory words: "You're old," implying he was no longer competent to take care of himself, much less his daughter.

"He starts yelling, and we're standing here yelling at each other. It was the intensity of the situation and the raw emotion, being upset about everything, both of us. He always wants to take over and fix it, but I want to take over and fix it."

Russ had been diagnosed with leukemia and was fighting pneumonia. Friends and family stepped forward to help in any number of ways. John gave Sarah two weeks' worth of hotel points. The hospital arranged with some of the hotels to give free rooms.

"My parents were wonderful. Amanda came home and they were around to help her. . . . I had my laptop and worked remotely [from the hospital]. They filled his body with so many fluids trying to fight the infection, but the chemotherapy could attack his organs and he could die from that. They checked his kidney function daily."

Amanda would fly out to California periodically. Finally Rose, Allen, and Amanda simply stayed there.

"When he died," Sarah says, "it was really sudden. I called my dad and said, 'I need you to bring Amanda to the hospital.' . . . [When we returned to Colorado], they were here through all the family events, and Dad participated in the memorial service."

The mutual assistance family members gave one another in this crisis grew out of their long history of caring. "I like that they lived just a mile away. Before Russ got sick, we could help each other. My dad had hip replacement surgery. One night he calls at ten o'clock and says, 'Your mom fell. The coffee table is broken. She can't get up and I can't help her.' I'm like, 'Do we need to call 911?' He says, 'No, she's okay. I put a pillow under her head.'

"Russ and I get all dressed, jump in the car, go one mile down to their house and walk in. The coffee table was a mess. . . . We helped her up because my dad just could not get down and do that. I think it happened another time. They started talking about moving to St. Andrew's. I said, 'I don't think you're ready for that.' They put it all on hold while Russ was sick. Within the year after that they decided to move. To this day, I tell people I'm so blessed that they chose to do it on their own, rather than having to be the daughter who says, 'I think you need to do this.'"[603]

Making the decision to give up their home, to radically downsize, and to move to a retirement community was difficult and played out over many months, but it also was healing. Moving to St. Andrew's provided innumerable close-at-hand resources for Allen and Rose, and their decision relieved their children of having to initiate uncomfortable conversations and force them into making choices that might have alienated parents and children.

Chapter 35

Adapting the Vision

MOVING TO AN APARTMENT in a senior living complex can signify loss of control. In Allen's case, it might have meant a compromised capacity to provide leadership and respond to need. This was not the case in Allen's early years at St. Andrew's. He did not compromise his leadership as much as adapt it.

When Rose and Allen downsized for their 2013 move and discarded papers and books, he did not part with his massage table or his Reiki materials, thinking Reiki treatments would be beneficial to residents at St. Andrew's. He also planned to interest them in the training.

Around a half dozen residents came to the information meeting Allen offered, but only three indicated they were interested in following through with Reiki training. However, when Allen described the time it would take and asked if they really wanted to continue, none followed through—a big disappointment.

He contacted his former massage school in Denver and offered to teach Reiki, but they said they were no longer offering it. Reiki was being taught in so many venues in the area that they had decided not to compete.

Not one to sit idly by, and still guided by his vision and commitment to ameliorate social need, Allen's interest was captivated by an article in *The Denver Post* about Fort Lyon, the former Veterans Administration facility in Southeastern Colorado located only several miles east of Las Animas. The VA had ceded its use as a psychiatric hospital. It was so isolated and expensive to maintain that the state legislature planned to shut it down, even though it had been variously repurposed, more recently as a minimum security prison.

When Allen read the article, Fort Lyon had been vacant for several years, and Governor John Hickenlooper had "decided to make it into a homeless rehabilitation center. . . . I started doing research on what was happening."[604]

Ken and Zoe Barley had never made the four-hour trip from Denver to Las Animas and had always been curious about Southeastern Colorado, the locale of Allen's origins. Neither Allen nor Barley recall who proposed the journey, but off the four of them went, Barley driving.

The Barleys' agenda was to explore. Who better to serve as tour guide than Allen? "He could show us around and point out stuff we'd not see otherwise. But Allen had another agenda—to get us involved with Fort Lyon and the homeless project. . . . He just moves forward when he sees something. I think he saw that he could get us involved in Fort Lyon.

"So he's got us all set up down there [for a visit]. . . . I don't know whether they thought we were important people or what. They had the director and the chairman of the board and they toured us through that whole facility, and then they sat us down. They were pleading with us to somehow get connected with Denver. . . . But I don't have the contacts anymore, and I just didn't feel I could do that."[605]

Allen responded differently. "I saw the great work they were doing. Of the first three hundred homeless people they had there, two-hundred fifty were put into jobs. The other fifty, they had to put out on the streets. The people didn't want to go back to Denver; they wanted to visit towns around because they said they felt much more at home walking around a little town because the people treated them so well. I'm sure some of them came back to Denver, though.

"The Coalition for the Homeless [sends] homeless veterans in Denver, really any person, young or old. But Fort Lyon can't house children, families. They've got teachers who come from the La Junta and Lamar junior colleges to teach those who are interested. They can get their high school diploma, and they have a big computer room, a huge library, and a beautiful dining room. They have two dormitories, one for men and one for women. They have about six dormitories in all where the VA used to keep patients.

"They set up a medical center in Las Animas right next to the nursing home. They have psychiatrists there and can take care of people with drug habits. . . .

"When we asked what we could do, they said, 'We don't need money. The state funds the program. We need support. We want people to visit us. We don't want the legislature to close us down.'"

Barley rightly assessed Allen's enthusiasm. Allen "moved forward." The Fort Lyon people had suggested getting the churches involved, so Allen's thought was to contact Adrian Miller, executive director of the Colorado

Council of Churches, who suggested names and gave him phone numbers. Allen says, "I started contacting all the executives of the denominations I'm familiar with: United Church of Christ, Methodist, Episcopal, Evangelical Lutheran, American Baptist. Some were very responsive. Some said, 'Send me a letter and I'll see about getting together with you.'

"I'm discovering that the best thing to do is find out when the pastors meet, get on their agenda, and make a presentation to them. I've found out that the cost per homeless person for the Coalition for the Homeless for the people in Fort Lyon is not any more than the cost per person in Denver."

Allen spoke about the Fort Lyon program to a meeting of the Pueblo Presbytery, which encompasses the churches in Southeastern Colorado, and to a meeting of the Denver Presbytery. He attended a day-long gathering about homelessness at Iliff Seminary sponsored by the Council of Churches and four other organizations.[606]

Shirley Burkhart, a member at Montview, says she has "never seen anybody promote anything as much as he's doing that [about Fort Lyon].... My goodness, he's everywhere promoting it. For a man his age, it's just a miracle that he's able to do that."[607]

He traces his interest in homelessness to Mother Teresa's visit to the General Assembly in 1988, which led to his determined search for her hospital in Kolkata during their 1993 trip. His concern about the homeless was renewed as he began to read articles about Pope Francis. "The more I read, ... the more I became convinced that the church has lost one of its primary missions. That mission should be to do whatever it can to take care of the homeless and the poor."

In the months following the Fort Lyon visit with the Barleys, Rose's capacities diminished and she increasingly needed Allen nearby. Once, she had a near panic attack and could not catch her breath. She cried out, "Allen! Allen!" He was immediately by her side, and they discovered her portable oxygen tank had shut off. She calmed down as soon as the problem was remedied.[608]

On the occasions when Allen had to leave their apartment, perhaps for a doctor's appointment, he asked others to keep Rose company. She had several falls over the span of their residence at St. Andrew's, some of which put her in the skilled nursing unit. Eventually, a fall resulted in a fatal head injury in 2017.

When an accident on a busy Denver freeway totaled his car, fortunately Allen emerged uninjured. There was no damage to the other vehicle. He transitioned to driving only short distances from home and during daylight hours and then to relying primarily on others for transportation.

Although the dimensions of his world narrowed, he fully occupied his space: coordinating the Sunday services at St. Andrew's, which were well attended; going to the book club and exercise classes and participating in other activities; and attending family functions, including birthday celebrations, anniversaries, and the mountain wedding of one of sister Virginia's grandsons. He maintains contact with friends near and far.

The Denver Broncos still try his patience, but come football season, the Broncos banner graces his doorway. Opposite is a square-shaped wall hanging that features *Shodō*. Following the Japanese custom of visitors and hosts exchanging these *Shodō* squares, Allen's pastor friend from McCormick days, Rev. Yoicho (perhaps also spelled Yoichiro) Saeki, had written it himself and presented it to Allen and Rose during their 1986 visit to Tokyo. He said, "This is my little gift to you for coming to see me in Japan." Allen remembers that Saeki had a number of similar squares arranged on the walls of his church office, given to him by friends and visitors. Had Allen's *Shodō* skills been up to the task, he could have presented Saeki with a reciprocal writing.[609]

As Min and June Mochizuki explained, it is customary for a host to invite the guest to write *Shodō* characters on a square piece of paper. Min was comfortable writing the word for "peace" but not much beyond that. June was sometimes invited to write on a square but she usually declined because she did not think her brush work was adequate.[610]

The phrase on the *Shodō* square from Saeki, hanging across from the Broncos banner, refers to Phil 3:20: "But our citizenship is in heaven, and it is from there that we are expecting a Savior, the Lord Jesus Christ."[611] The square includes Rose and Allen's names, the date of their visit, and Saeki's name.[612]

Biblical verses such as this and Eph 2:19 (God's household is comprised of fellow citizens, not strangers and aliens) pertain in particular ways to any number of Japanese-American and other Asian-Americans who feel the sting of alienation. Secretary Norman Mineta, former secretary of transportation under the George W. Bush administration, secretary of commerce under the Clinton administration, congressman, and the first Japanese-American mayor of San Jose, California, has this to say about citizenship. He wears a lapel American flag pin in public because "I still get treated like a foreigner."[613]

He remembers that when he was ten, he and his family returned from church on December 7, 1941, and his mother turned on the radio. The program was interrupted by the announcement about the Pearl Harbor attack. Placards soon appeared in his neighborhood calling for the detention of all those of Japanese ancestry, alien and non-alien. He asked his older brother what a non-alien was, and he was told, "You." Mineta retorted, "I'm not a non-alien! I'm a citizen!" He says that to this day he cherishes that word because his own government "was not willing to use the word 'citizen' to describe us."[614]

As Maruyama generations spiral toward the future, they pass familiar international and family touchstones in new contexts—Japan, Colorado University, and the Rocky Mountains. Sarah has remarried, and in 2019, she enjoyed showing husband Mike and Amanda some tourist highlights during a two-week vacation to Japan. For a while, Amanda stayed in the mountain condominium Allen has owned for years while she worked in the nearby resort town of Dillon before moving back to Denver. She attended the University of Colorado, Allen's alma mater.

John's job, based in Texas, involves travel throughout the western states and regular overnight visits with Allen. Those visits were more frequent throughout 2018 and 2019 when John faced a health crisis of his own and underwent treatments in Denver.

His son, Jonathan, studied Japanese as a college student and traveled to Japan with other students and several professors. "Oh, that boy!" Allen will say. "He's really something." Jonathan graduated from Metro State University in Denver with a degree in education and history and subsequently returned to Japan to teach English near Kyoto.

Church bodies, too, cycle through the historical accretions of political, social, and theological debates and challenges: poverty and homelessness, systemic racism and at-risk minority populations, the displacement of and discrimination against immigrants, ethnic churches and assimilation, stewardship of creation, regional and international conflicts (the list is endless), responsible use of the media and responsibilities of the media, just distribution of resources, the tension between emphasizing the church as an "ark of salvation" (evangelism) or as "God's agent for social change" (mission), anti-semitism and white supremacy, gender equality, nuclear disarmament, reproductive freedom, religious tolerance, . . .

Items on the agenda for the 2018 General Assembly in Saint Louis included resolutions on climate change, ending family separation at the southern border of the United States, and a moratorium on imposing the death penalty. The assembly celebrated the election of co-moderators, one of whom is a native of Puerto Rico for whom Spanish is her first language. The co-moderators elected in 2020 were Elona Street-Stewart, a descendent of the Delaware Nanticoke Tribe and the first Native American to serve as a moderator of the PC(USA), and Rev. Gregory Bentley, the African American pastor of Fellowship Presbyterian Church, Huntsville, Alabama.

In his 1992 "Personal Statement of Faith," Allen presses for a new Presbyterian confession of faith. In addition to recurring social, political, cultural, and environmental crises, he believes the church must address a rapidly approaching twenty-first-century context that is marked by change. The themes of his statement are expanded in his PIFs and his favorite 2002 Montview sermon.

He grieves that most religions are responding to change "by looking in the rearview mirror." They not only fear change but mistakenly "believe that if we only hold to an 'old' faith and 'ancient' doctrines of a world that no longer exists, all will be well." He writes that, sadly, Christianity has joined other religions in "seeking to maintain the status quo, believing that the new world will pass away and we can savor the old world and old culture as we did before."

In the statement, he notes that Jesus Christ lived in a century also marked by change and revolution. Jesus preached "the good news that God was bringing God's kingdom [realm] in the midst of the chaotic times in which he lived." That emphasis needs proclamation today; instead, the church holds more closely to its doctrines than to Christ's humanism. Christ proclaimed we are God's creation, made in God's image. Jesus was the first "new Adam," and we too can become that "new Adam." In the absence of a new confession, Allen proclaims "Teilhard de Chardin's Christo-genesis, by which our Lord Jesus Christ, the Savior of all the universe, will Christianize the universe."[615]

Almost as asides, Allen will refer to books oriented toward the future that "changed my life." *The End of Homo Sapiens and the Birth of a New Species* by Thomas E. Beck and Janet Colli is one. He characterizes its premise as "our bodies and minds are on the edge of an emancipation. They are changing, as well as our ability to work together."[616]

His characterization could be heard not so much as the book changing his life as reflecting his evolving thinking. Even in 1993, he had asserted on his PIF that "the next century will see a leap ahead of all humanity toward peace and human bondedness unknown before."

The 1992 "Statement of Faith" and the 2002 sermon sound similar, optimistic themes, unsurprising for someone whose orientation toward life is to move ahead toward a dream and a vision. Humanity might not be up to the challenge of the "leap ahead" that he envisions, at least not yet, but Allen's vision is resoundingly confident: following the pattern of "Christo-genesis," Jesus Christ will make the universe whole.

When he speaks about death, Allen says he does not fear it. He and Rose agreed years ago that, should either of them "become a burden to our families and to the society, then it's time to quit using the resources that our children need, and we ought to exit this life."

This is not a sad prospect for Allen. He speaks of a "whole change" in the way he views life and death, when he started studying Buddhism in the

1980s, changes that broadened to include a belief in reincarnation with his study of massage and Reiki. "It's so appealing to me to be a baby again and start life all over!"[617]

He envisions the essence of life in these terms. "You have to learn to accept your own life and all its suffering because you are what you are—and that's all you are. . . . When we die, our body, mind, and spirit die, but our soul never dies. Our soul, our essence, might come back as a cat, a dog, or a deer."

Allen had articulated this vision in a conversation eight months before Rose's death. At the time, she had inserted a bit of her practical, dry humor, perhaps to lighten the mood—too much existential speculation. "I want to be a cat!" she had said.

Allen had picked up what sounded like a playful response. "It's exciting that you can return to earth as some other kind of being. That's why I always used to play with the cats and imagine them as being someone that was a human being."

But Rose's humor in that moment had disguised a deeper issue, revealed when she had followed his comments about playing with the cats with a question: "How, at the end of this life, do we erase nagging self-doubt?"

After some back and forth between them, when it had became obvious her question had no easy answers, she had said, "Sorry I brought it up. . . . I still think this is something people struggle with."[618]

The conversation had moved on, but, while Rose's question raised a central personal issue for her, it also disclosed a dynamic between Allen and Rose that Shearer had described. Rose's question had pulled Allen's "string" and brought him back to earth from his cosmic, existential speculations about the soul and reincarnation to one of those nagging questions about self-worth, relationship, and purpose with which so many struggle.

Both Allen's existential musings and Rose's nagging question are part of a multitude of dilemmas with no easy answers. Allen's theology in his 1992 "Statement of Faith" reflects some of these unresolved conversations. Many of them take place under the umbrella of liberal and conservative disputes. Those controversies haunted Allen's 1980 candidacy, and they continue apace; they also predate his encounters with it by millennia. Allen was simply part of its stream as it manifested during his ministry.

The liberal/conservative friction had surfaced in O'Keefe's and Burkhart's comments about Montview, as it would in describing virtually any congregation, regardless of faith tradition and historical era, and it is a feature of nearly every General Assembly. The friction is endless because it revolves around contentious and irresolvable claims, in Langer's terms, about the "essential pattern of human life": humanity's search for purpose and meaning.

Examining a particularly contentious historical moment in the Presbyterian church at the turn of the nineteenth century gives perspective on these endless theological disputes in which Allen, too, was embroiled. From a historical remove, this "fundamentalist-modernist" fight over a century removed comes across as a nearly futile rehash of the same old friction, but any number of people were hurt in the process. Remnants of its viciousness linger institutionally in the present.

The fundamentalist-modernist controversy consumed a number of General Assemblies. Threatened and executed "defrockings," heresy trials (without the consequent burnings at the stake of earlier centuries!), expulsions, withdrawals, and church schisms characterize it. The flash point seems to have been a fight over biblical inerrancy. Charles A. Briggs, a biblical scholar at Union Theological Seminary in New York in the late 1880s, at the time a Presbyterian institution, advocated for a "more modern" method of biblical interpretation. "No," conservative scholars at Princeton Theological Seminary said, "The belief in biblical inerrancy must not be abandoned." A long heresy trial ensued, resulting in Briggs's defrocking. Union Theological Seminary rescinded its relationship with the Presbyterian Church and remains independent.[619]

William P. Merrill, an 1890 Union graduate, took up the modernist position in the battle. From the pulpits of Chicago's Sixth Presbyterian Church and New York's Brick Presbyterian Church, he preached and wrote in support of "modernist theology" until his 1936 retirement.

Many of Allen's positions are reflected in Merrill's. He and Merrill would agree that Jesus Christ is the "heart" of the Christian religion. Merrill wrote that "the Person and Character of Jesus of Nazareth" is the "one fact upon which all true Christian faith rests." He expanded the implications of this belief: if Jesus of Nazareth is that single fact, modernists (perhaps synonymous with liberals) do not focus on "details of creeds and doctrines" but "on ethics, on living as Jesus would live." The real gospel entails "walking in the way of Jesus." Allen's phrasing is, "To be a Christian is to follow in his footsteps."[620]

This emphasis on embracing Christianity as an ethical model and not on the basis of prescribed doctrines meant for Merrill that "the liberal Christian does not worry about the accuracy of the biblical accounts of, for example, the resurrection of Jesus." In fact, the doctrine regarding the resurrection of the body is "an outgrown fantasy, untrue for most thinking men and women. . . . That this body of ours shall rise and live we can neither believe nor desire." It is a mistake to believe that "Christ's resurrection, or ours, cannot be *real* unless it is *physical.*" He wrote that those who compiled the Apostles' Creed were simply affirming the resurrected body as "the continuity of personal existence," a "true and precious" conviction, a continuity that Allen affirms in his belief in the continuity of one's essence, one's soul.

Regarding Christianity and other religions, another "modernist" wrote that "'Christianity's uniqueness . . . lay not in any particular historical or doctrinal claims but rather in its selection of truths available in all religions, and in the simplicity of its central teachings.'" Conservatives countered that this "refusal to insist on the uniqueness of Christian faith" could not be tolerated: "Jesus Christ is the only Lord and Savior" and "complete and final truth lies in him alone."

Again, Allen would affirm that certain truths are available in all religions. In his 2002 sermon, he had asserted that Montview does not approach evangelism as a "fanatical drive" to convert the "heathen" but knows that other religions are "meaningful and redemptive" in their contexts.

Perhaps the most striking similarity between Allen and the modernists is their shared orientation toward the future. Modernists affirm that a "conception of God which is true for one time may be far from adequate for another." Accordingly, theology accommodates itself to "intellectual and cultural trends." In that way, liberal Christianity adapts to "modern thought" and is "the religious hope of the world."

Allen uses theological language from the second half of the twentieth century to say much the same thing about liberal Christianity's potential. He wrote on his 1993 PIF that liberation theology was only the beginning of a "new ecumenical thrust toward religious pluralism," which "challenged the survival of the Christian church" and made the current age one of the "most exciting." The challenge would press Christians to visualize a faith "that will mature . . . and impact the future."

Any number of battles were fought during the fundamentalist-modernist controversy. One of the more strident conservatives eventually left and established another denomination, the Orthodox Presbyterian Church. By the mid-1930s, the controversy came to a close with the exit of some of its main characters, but, as Allen's leadership headaches through subsequent decades and the discussions that are part of most General Assemblies indicate, the contours of the tensions between liberals and conservatives seem never to abate, regardless of the various terms used to describe them.[621]

Allen has lived at the center of most theological, political, cultural, intellectual, and technological movements of the second half of the twentieth century and the early decades of the twenty-first. He suffered anti-Japanese American discrimination in the 1940s, he served in the army during World War II, he was a seminary student during the heyday of neo-orthodoxy and a church leader during the many revolutions of the 1960s, he advocated for open housing and was stymied when he tried to leave his associate position

in Dubuque to more fully engage issues of redlining and other systemic inequities on a state-wide level, he immersed himself in the implications of
Marshall McLuhan's work, he modeled new patterns of church leadership
as a member of a co-pastorate, he twice ran to be the first Asian-American
moderator of the General Assembly, he promoted liberation theology and
feminist agendas and LBGTQ+ rights as they emerged, he recognized the
need and retrained himself to minister to both the spiritual and physical
dimensions of human life, he advocates for solutions to the homeless crisis,
and the list could be expanded.

As for his beliefs today, after sifting through Haroutunian, Teilhard,
Merton, Fox, Buddhism, Shamanism, and so much else, Allen says if he
were to write a statement of faith, it would be quite simple. Given its simplicity, perhaps Allen sidesteps some historical controversies. Then again,
even a simple statement might be interpreted differently by each reader because a person's faith expression, often inadvertently, incorporates various
iterations of these debates.

Themes from his favorite 2002 anniversary sermon echo in this spoken statement, in particular, his phrasing about evangelism's goal of keeping
Jesus Christ and what he taught and lived in the gospels at the center of
faith. His "quite simple" expression of belief is that "there's nothing else in
the Christian religion except Jesus Christ. If you follow in his footsteps, that
itself is life and death. . . . The spirit of Jesus is here. If you let that spirit enter
you, then you are beginning to fulfill what the Christian life is all about."

Apparently thinking this statement might be too brief, he adds, "To
be a Christian is to believe in the presence and humanity of Jesus Christ. To
try to understand as much as a person can about his life, his faith, his way
of treating people—taking care of the sick and the poor and the people that
others don't like. To love your enemies, to know God loves you and that you
should love God. Love is the greatest of all. Jesus Christ is the heart and essence of the Christian religion. To be a Christian is to follow in his footsteps,
everything Jesus did. That's my faith today."[622]

A simple statement, but achieving its goals is not feasible in any individual's lifetime, or perhaps on this earth. It is no surprise that the lyrics of
"The Impossible Dream" resonate with Allen. His statement is a theological
rephrasing of the quest to "fight for the right." A Nisei man whose character can be described by the phrase *issho kenmei*, "all in, full throttle and
nonstop," would doubtless be drawn to the action verbs in "The Impossible
Dream": run, love, strive, and reach—for that unreachable star. The aspira-
tion itself gives purpose to life. In terms of Allen's faith, the figure of Jesus
Christ sets the course toward that goal and animates the vision, one of human rights, peace, and justice.

Chapter Endnotes

1. Allen Maruyama, interview with author, Aurora, CO, Nov. 13, 2016.
2. Allen and Rose Maruyama, interview with author, Aurora, CO, Nov. 4, 2016.
3. Allen Maruyama, interview with author, Aurora, CO, Jan. 3, 2017.
4. *Bent County Democrat*, weekly issues from 1940–1942.
5. Allen Maruyama, interview with author, Aurora, CO, Nov. 13, 2016.
6. National Japanese American Memorial Foundation.
7. The War Relocation Authority and Office of Indian Affairs oversaw the Poston (Colorado River Relocation Center) and Gila River (Rivers Relocation Center) in Arizona as they were located on the Colorado River Indian Reservation and Gila River Indian Reservation—without those communities' consent. It can be said that "the Poston camp [and Gila River] was really an internment camp inside another internment camp" (Gingold, "Japanese Americans").
8. Allen and Rose Maruyama, interview with author, Aurora, CO, Jan. 3, 2017.
9. Allen Maruyama, interview with author, Aurora, CO, Nov. 13, 2016.
10. Niiya, "No-No Boys." See discussion of No-No Boys in Ch. 9.
11. Yamada and Inouye, "Letters to the Editor," 2.
12. The Presbyterian Church in the United States of America, the PC(USA), has undergone numerous splits and reunions during Allen's ministry, each involving a name change. Other than the historically accurate reference to the 1980 name above, it will be referred to as the PC(USA), the name used subsequent to the 1983 reunion of the northern and southern churches, a split that had reflected divisions during the Civil War. The numbering for the General Assemblies begins in 1789, with the first General Assembly that met in Philadelphia and launched the denomination.
13. General Assembly of the UPC, "One Hundred Ninety-Second."
14. Ruling elders are church members elected and ordained by their congregation to serve as its spiritual leaders on session, the governing body of a local church, and they are eligible to be commissioners to bodies of the church covering larger geographical regions—presbytery, synod, and General Assembly. Teaching elders are ministers of Word and Sacrament ordained by a presbytery. Their membership is in the presbytery where they serve, not a particular church, and they are also eligible to be elected as commissioners. Teaching elders are ordained by a presbytery after fulfilling certain educational, leadership and suitability criteria. The teaching elder(s) of a church serves as the moderator of session. Both teaching and ruling elders are eligible to moderate a presbytery, synod, or the General Assembly. See Office of the General Assembly, *Book of Order*, G–2.0301 and G–2.0501.

15. Allen and Rose Maruyama, interview with author, Aurora, CO, Apr. 17, 2017.

16. Joseph Maruyama, interview with author, Broomfield, CO, Nov. 28, 2016.

17. Allen Maruyama, interview with author, Aurora, CO, Mar. 6, 2017.

18. Samuel and Doris Calian, telephone interview with author, Feb. 27, 2017.

19. "Viewpoints on Specific Questions," 4.

20. Larry Angus, interview with author, Lakewood, CO, Mar. 9, 2017.

21. According to the *General Assembly Daily News*, June–July 1976, two African-American men, Rev. Edler Hawkins and Rev. Clinton Marsh, had been moderators in 1964 and 1973, respectively, and Dr. Thelma Davidson Adair was the first African-American woman to hold the office in 1976.

22. General Assembly of the UPC, "One Hundred Ninety-Second."

23. Socier, "Forty-Four Cats."

24. Allen Maruyama, interviews with author, Aurora, CO, Nov. 13, 2016, and Dec. 2, 2018.

25. Hildner, "GPSA Wildcats."

26. Allen Maruyama, interview with author, Aurora, CO, Nov. 13, 2016.

27. Allen and Rose Maruyama, interview with author, Aurora, CO, Mar. 6, 2017.

28. Brown, *I Thought*, 5, 7.

29. Wimberly, *Moving from Shame*, 66.

30. Brown, *I Thought*, 28.

31. JACL National, "JACL Initaties Series," 2.

32. Grace Kaori Suzuki, email to author, Apr. 26, 2019.

33. Johnston, "Farewell to Manzanar," 7.

34. "Congressman Dies," 1.

35. Allen and Rose Maruyama, interview with author Aurora, CO, Mar. 6, 2017.

36. Brown, *I Thought*, 13.

37. Allen and Rose Maruyama, interview with author, Aurora, CO, Mar. 6, 2017.

38. Brown, *I Thought*, 15.

39. Allen Maruyama, interview with author, Aurora, CO, May 29, 2019.

40. Allen and Rose Maruyama, interview with author, Aurora, CO, Mar. 6, 2017.

41. Allen Maruyama, interview with author, Aurora, CO, Apr. 25, 2017.

42. Allen and Rose Maruyama, interview with author, Aurora, CO, Oct. 12, 2016.

43. Judy and Robert Roussell, interview with author, Marion, IA, Oct. 24, 2019.

44. Allen and Rose Maruyama, interview with author, Aurora, CO, Jan. 3, 2017.

45. Allen and Rose Maruyama, interview with author, Aurora, CO, Mar. 2, 2017.

46. Allen's recollection is that the intent of the police was to protect the students.

47. John Maruyama, interview with author, Arvada, CO, Mar. 1, 2017.

48. Allen and Rose Maruyama, interview with author, Aurora, CO, Jan. 3, 2017.

49. Shirley Burkhart, interview with author, Denver, CO, Mar. 20, 2017.

50. Allen and Rose Maruyama, interview with author, Aurora, CO, Apr. 25, 2017.

51. Allen and Rose Maruyama, interviews with author, Aurora, CO, Jan. 3, 2017, and Apr. 25, 2017.

52. Special Committee on the Theology of Liberation and Renewal, *Report*. Liberation theology is an international theological movement initially identified with South America in the 1950s and 1960s. Primary concerns of those liberation theologians were poverty and social injustice. They believed the church, following the example of Jesus, was morally obligated to respond. They pointed out the many ways the church had failed in this responsibility.

53. General Assembly of the UPC, "One Hundred Ninety-Second."

54. Scripture is the foundational document of the PC(USA). Also authoritative is *The Constitution of the Presbyterian Church*, which consists of two parts, the *Book of*

Confessions and the *Book of Order*. As can be inferred, the *Book of Order* proscribes the underlying theology and the basics of the church's government, worship, and discipline. The *Book of Confessions* contains major statements of belief that the church has confessed through the centuries, based on the conviction that the church must speak to its historical context through time. The shorthand for this orientation is "Reformed, always reforming." In addition to the confessions named above, included in the *Book of Confessions* are the Apostles' and Nicene Creeds from the early centuries of the church; examples of later confessions are the Barmen Declaration and the Belhar Confession. The Barmen Declaration, much of whose text was drafted by Karl Barth, was adopted in Germany in 1934 in the face of Hitler's consolidation of power. It was a statement by German Lutheran, Reformed, and United churches of their opposition to pro-Nazi positions. The Belhar Confession, adopted by the Dutch Reformed Mission Church in South Africa in 1986 and by the PC(USA) in 2016, was motivated by a commitment to unity in response to apartheid. Belhar asserts that apartheid is a sin that leads to enmity and hatred, outcomes antithetical to Christian faith (Office of the General Assembly, *Book of Confessions*).

55. General Assembly of the UPC, "One Hundred Ninety-Second."
56. Lovelace, "Evangelicals and Pluralism."
57. Chapman, "Killing for Christ, 6.
58. Allen and Rose Maruyama, interview with author, Aurora, CO, Jan. 3, 2017.
59. General Assembly of the UPC, "One Hundred Ninety-Second."
60. Lebra, *We Chose Colorado*, 7.
61. Matsumoto, "Chinese Exclusion Act."
62. United States Department of State, "Chinese Immigration."
63. Matsumoto, "Chinese Exclusion Act."
64. Luck Young was the Chinese man who was beaten to death in the Denver 1880 anti-Chinese race riot (Asakawa, "Remembering Denver's Chinatown Roots").
65. Colorado Encyclopedia, "Timelines."
66. Densho Encyclopedia, "Timeline."
67. Matsumoto, "Chinese Exclusion Act."
68. Central Presbyterian, "Our History."
69. Lebra, *We Chose Colorado*, vii.
70. Asakawa and Yoshimura, "Asian American Journey."
71. Densho Encyclopedia, "Timeline."
72. Japanese aliens living in America for more than thirty years were permitted to become naturalized citizens. Non-citizens who served in World Wars I or II (Sept. 1, 1939–Dec. 31, 1946) were eligible for citizenship in 1948 with no residency requirement (Murata, *Images of America*, 43).
73. Lyon, "Alien Land Laws."
74. Densho Encyclopedia, "Timeline."
75. Lyon, "Alien Land Laws."
76. Lebra notes that the earliest Japanese agricultural workers were hired as farm laborers. As their situation improved, "they were able to sign contracts to work as share croppers or as renters" (Lebra, *We Chose Colorado*, 4).
77. Takahara, *Off the Fat*, 8.
78. Densho Encyclopedia, "Timeline."
79. Allen and Rose Maruyama, interview with author, Aurora, CO, Nov. 13, 2016. In Lebra's interviews with Japanese Americans in Colorado, the JAs note time and again that the values passed to them by their Issei parents were "work hard," and "be honest" (Lebra, *We Chose Colorado*).

80. Joeseph Maruyama, interview with author, Broomfield, CO, Nov. 28, 2016.

81. Virginia Maruyama Chapman, letter to author, Feb. 10, 2018. Lebra corroborates these perceptions. "The reputation of the Japanese as good workers spread wherever they settled [in Colorado]. They were known as industrious, hard working, diligent, honest, and faithful. Stories of their achievements meant that they readily found employment wherever they went" (Lebra, *We Chose Colorado*, 14).

82. Allen and Rose Maruyama, interview with author, Aurora, CO, Nov. 13, 2016.

83. At least one young Mexican man did attend Las Animas High School in the early 1940s, Fred Arguello. He was several years ahead of Allen and graduated in 1942. He says he was the first Mexican boy to receive a diploma from that school and describes how he learned to be virtually invisible to the other students by, for example, eating his lunch off the school grounds, embarrassed by the tortillas and beans, and by going to school dances but standing outside, under the window. Arguello enlisted after he graduated and served as a bombardier in Europe. He returned to Colorado, completed college on the GI Bill, and became an elementary school principal. His success was achieved against great odds (Fred Arguello, interview with author, Colorado Springs, CO, Dec. 7, 2012).

84. Allen and Rose Maruyama, interview with author, Aurora, CO, Nov. 13, 2016.

85. General Assembly of the UPC, "One Hundred Ninety-Second."

86. Lebra, *We Chose Colorado*, 39.

87. Seichi Otsuka, email, June 3, 2019.

88. Even in 2018, a student young enough to be Otsuka's or Allen's grandson writes, "I work hard at school and am proud of my grades, but I am respectful and modest when it comes to talking about my accomplishments." The excerpt comes from his essay written in competition for one of the Japanese American Citizens League's annual scholarships. He is addressing the question "What are the advantages and limitations of rallying around a single ethnic identity?" (Ishimoto, "Personal Statement," 11).

89. Seichi Otsuka, interview with author, Denver, Feb. 20, 2017.

90. Comments overheard by the author in the St. Andrew's Bistro, Aurora, CO, Sept. 2, 2018.

91. Allen and Rose Maruyama, interview with author, Aurora, CO, Nov. 13, 2016.

92. Along with working hard, education ranks among the top values of the other Nisei Japanese Americans in Colorado whom Lebra interviewed (Lebra, *We Chose Colorado*).

93. Allen and Rose Maruyama, interview with author, Aurora, CO, Nov. 13, 2018.

94. Lebra, *We Chose Colorado*, 3.

95. Allen Maruyama, interview with author, Aurora, CO, May 23, 2018.

96. Sarah Maruyama-Biles Brady, interview with author, Highlands Ranch, CO, Mar. 28, 2017.

97. Allen Maruyama, interview with author, Aurora, CO, Nov. 4, 2016.

98. Virginia Maruyama Chapman, letter to author, Feb. 10, 2018.

99. *Bent County Democrat*, 1940–1942.

100. Allen and Rose Maruyama, interview with author, Aurora, CO, Nov. 13, 2016.

101. That tradition continues at the Koshien Stadium outside Osaka (Lefton, "In Japan").

102. Joseph Maruyama, interview with author, Broomfield, CO, Nov. 28, 2016.

103. Allen Maruyama, interview with author, Aurora, CO, June 13, 2018.

104. Allen and Rose Maruyama, interview with author, Aurora, CO, Apr. 3, 2017.

105. General Assembly of the UPC, "One Hundred Ninety-Second."

106. Lebra, *We Chose Colorado*, 39.

107. Williams, *American Sutra*, 3, 35.

108. Williams, *American Sutra*, 52.

109. Williams, *American Sutra*, 22.

110. Sam and Doris Calian, telephone interview with author, Feb. 2, 2017.

111. Joseph Maruyama, interview with author, Broomfield, CO, Nov. 28, 2016. Military Intelligence Service personnel were attached to every Pacific unit and translated documents, interrogated prisoners, and deciphered enemy orders. Joe, a Nisei (second-generation), was one of more than six thousand other Nisei who received the training and served in the Pacific (Murata, *Images of America*, 43).

112. "Where It All Began."

113. Joseph Maruyama, interview with author, Broomfield, CO, Nov. 28, 2016.

114. Allen Maruyama, interview with author, Aurora, CO, June 13, 2018.

115. Virginia Maruyama Chapman, letter, Feb. 10, 2018.

116. Imai, "Immigration Act of 1924."

117. June and Minoru Mochizuki, interview with author, Denver, Apr. 25, 2017. During our conversations, June, Min, and I were careful to monitor June's stamina as she was not well. She died Oct. 29, 2017. She and Min were married sixty-eight years. I am at a loss as to how to express my gratitude for her openness and generous gift of time when she was struggling to get through each day.

118. Precedent for this type of arrangement had been set in *California v. Harada* in 1916. The case was settled in favor of the Harada family, who engaged in a similar property arrangement. In 1915, they had purchased their home in a transaction that placed ownership in the hands of the three youngest, minor children who were US citizens. In 1916, the state tried to seize the property. Theirs was an early constitutional test of the California Alien Land Law of 1913, which prevented foreigners ineligible for citizenship from owning property ("Harada House Foundation").

119. Johnston, "Aika Herzig-Yoshinaga."

120. June and Minoru Mochizuki, interview with author, Denver, Apr. 25, 2017.

121. "Minidoka Visitor Center."

122. Dallas, "After Internment."

123. Subsequent to learning about Indiana University's refusal to admit his grandmother during the war, Eric Langowski investigated and discovered this low admission rate. Langowski notes that the American Friends Service Committee and others formed the National Japanese American Student Relocation Council (NJASRC)—the primary placement office for Nisei during the war (Langowski, "Extending Redress").

124. June and Minoru Mochizuki, interview with author, Denver, Apr. 25, 2017.

125. Lewis Lubers, correspondence with Pauline Reyher, Nov., 1942.

126. June and Minoru Mochizuki, interview with author, Denver, Apr. 25, 2017.

127. Even after the war, many Japanese-American college students were given the same message. At school in Fort Collins, Frank Konishi's advisor told him, "'You'll never get a teaching job as a Japanese, so you'd better go back to the farm.'" (Lebra, *We Chose Colorado*, 49).

128. June's younger sister, Pat (Chiyoko) Suzuki, became a nationally known entertainer and star of the 1958 Broadway musical *The Flower Drum Song*. June and Minoru Mochizuki, interview with author, Denver, Apr. 25, 2017.

129. June and Minoru Mochizuki, interview with author, Denver, Apr. 25, 2017.

130. June and Minoru Mochizuki, interview with author, Denver, May 1, 2017. As Min's experience illustrates, "some were unable to secure [the necessary] military permission" to enroll in colleges and universities (Langowski, "Extending Redress").

131. Mochizuki, "Banished from California," unnumbered pages.

132. June and Minoru Mochizuki, interview with author, Denver, May 1, 2017.

133. See discussion of No-No Boys in Ch. 1.

134. Many were sent to federal prisons as a consequence, but President Truman eventually pardoned all the Nisei resistors (Muller, "Draft Resistance").

135. June and Minoru Mochizuki, interview with author, Denver, May 1, 2017. Several thousand Nisei in the Tule Lake Segregation Center renounced their US citizenship. Just days before their deportation was to begin in Nov. 1945, attorney Wayne Collins and others filed suits on behalf of nearly one thousand of them to stop it. "They were required to undergo a legal process spanning several decades to restore their American citizenship" (Williams, *American Sutra*, 246).

136. Johnston, "New Tome."

137. Mochizuki, "Two Worlds," unnumbered pages.

138. Mochizuki, "Banished from California," unnumbered pages.

139. June and Minoru Mochizuki, interview with author, Denver, Apr. 25, 2017.

140. Johnston, "New Tome."

141. Hiraga, "Dr. Michio Kaku," 7.

142. Johnston, "Japanese American Vets." The "model minority" designation opened a plethora of problems. David Inoue, Executive Director of the Japanese American Citizens League, notes one insidious side-effect. The term was coined during the civil rights movement to "pit Asian Americans as a contrast to the calls for fundamental human rights for African-Americans." The implication was, seemingly, that "as Asians had succeeded, why can't African-Americans?" Inoue's position is that the nation must recognize and honor the human value of every person. Equality is not a privilege to be conferred by those in power but a human right (Inoue, "We Can't Stand").

143. Pacific Citizen Staff, "San Diego JACL Reflects," 7.

144. Langowski, "Extending Redress." There are variations in the spelling of this expression, including *shikataga nai* and *shikata ga nai*.

145. Takahara, *Off the Fat*, 3, 13.

146. This might not be the correct spelling of the Fukimara name (Judy Petersen, email to author, Feb. 17, 2017).

147. Both Newman and Allen lived in the Denver metro area during their adult years and knew one another through their Presbyterian connections. Bruce Newman, telephone conversations with author, Feb. 17, 2017, and Dec. 14, 2018.

148. Judy Petersen, email to author, Feb. 17, 2017.

149. Allen and Rose Maruyama, interview with author, Aurora, CO, Nov. 13, 2016.

150. Takahara, *Off the Fat*, 17.

151. Allen and Rose Maruyama, interview with author, Aurora, CO, Nov. 13, 2016; and Judy Petersen, email to author, Feb. 17, 2017.

152. Allen and Rose Maruyama, interviews with author, Aurora, CO, Nov. 4, 2016 and Jan. 18, 2017.

153. Rose Maruyama, interview with author, Aurora, CO, Nov. 30, 2016.

154. General Assembly of the UPC, "One Hundred Ninety-Second."

155. Allen and Rose Maruyama, interview with author, Aurora, CO, Jan. 18, 2017.

156. Allen Maruyama, interview with author, Aurora, CO, July 2, 2018.

157. Allen Maruyama, interview with author, Aurora, CO, Nov. 13, 2016.

158. The 442nd RCT fought only in Europe. It returned July 15, 1946, and President Harry Truman greeted the soldiers on the South Lawn of the White House, following their march down Constitution Avenue.

159. Griego, "Special Honors."

160. Allen and Rose Maruyama, interview with author, Aurora, CO, Jan. 18, 2017.

161. John Maruyama, interview with author, Arvada, CO, Mar. 1, 2017.

162. Allen and Rose Maruyama, interview with author, Aurora, CO, Apr. 17, 2017.

163. Hite, *Spirit of Montview*, 26.

164. John Maruyama, interview with author, Arvada, CO, Mar. 1, 2017.

165. Allen and Rose Maruyama, interview with author, Aurora, CO, Nov. 13, 2016.

166. Allen and Rose Maruyama, interview with author, Aurora, CO, Jan. 18, 2017.

167. The term "neo-orthodox" comes up often in Allen's interviews. To explain, in a 1974 article, Voskuil traces neo-orthodoxy's development as a theological movement growing out of Karl Barth's work in Europe and identified in the United States, most notably, with Reinhold Niebuhr. It is sometimes represented as the cutting edge of theology in the 1930s and '40s on this side of the Atlantic. Neo-orthodox theologians were reacting to what they thought was the naïve approach of liberal Christianity, an orientation to theology dominant in the latter half of the nineteenth and early twentieth centuries. Neo-orthodox theologians criticized liberal Christianity foremost for what they characterized as its more anthropological (human-centered) than theological (God-centered) basis. They thought liberal Christianity's emphasis on God's immanence (nearness) resulted in humanizing the divine.

Rather, they emphasized the transcendence of God and believed that the gulf between God and humanity is so vast that it can be overcome only by divine grace. They attributed liberal Christianity's naïveté to its characterization of sin as mere ignorance of the right that can be eliminated through educational processes. Neo-orthodox theologians pointed, in particular, to the horrors of World War I as evidence of the basic nature of humankind as inherently sinful, both individually and in organizational structures. Accordingly, they urged the church to resist acculturation, especially to the "isms" of capitalism, nationalism, anthropocentrism, and humanism. They did not see their views as anti-modern, but they were "opposed to forms of modernism which relativized the demands of the gospel." These affirmations placed neo-orthodox theologians in the more conservative (hence, "orthodox") category.

However, conservative critics claimed neo-orthodoxy was just a new form of liberalism because it retained a concern for issues of social justice and peace. Also, conservatives were suspicious because, while they accepted an inerrant and infallible Bible, neo-orthodox theologians used forms of "modern" biblical interpretation that took the Bible's varied historical and cultural settings into account in their interpretations.

Voskuil asserts that Reformed and Presbyterian churches were especially influenced by neo-orthodoxy and notes that curriculum materials developed at the time by Presbyterian churches were "heavily flavored" by it (Voskuil, "Reformed Roots").

168. Allen and Rose Maruyama, interview with author, Aurora, CO, Jan. 18, 2017.

169. Because Allen's perspective dominates in this biography and he rarely describes his impact on others, his leadership qualities are somewhat muted. See *Bent County Democrat*, miscellaneous articles and announcements, 1940–42.

170. Allen and Rose Maruyama, interview with author, Aurora, CO, Jan. 18, 2017. Muldrow graduated and drew on his engineering skills to become a missionary in Ethiopia. He and his wife, Betsy, worked on community development efforts to improve access to clean water, health care, and education. When the political situation deteriorated, they returned and Muldrow obtained an anthropology degree. For twenty years, he was employed by the Colorado Civil Rights Comission in Denver and advocated, in particular, for social justice with Native Americans on the Pine Ridge Reservation in South Dakota. Betsy was the first woman ordained as a teaching elder (minister) in the Denver Presbytery, on Jan. 26, 1975.

In retirement they moved to Santa Fe, New Mexico, and volunteered with Waterlines, Inc., to bring clean water to communities in Latin America and Ethiopia. They returned to Denver in 2006. The Muldrows resided at St. Andrew's when Rose and

Allen moved there in 2013. Muldrow died a few years later, and Betsy is presently Allen's neighbor at their retirement facility.

171. General Assembly of the UPC, "One Hundred Ninety-Second."

172. Allen and Rose Maruyama, interview with author, Aurora, CO, Nov. 13, 2016.

173. One way to contextualize Allen's description of his convictions at this time in his life is to draw on Appiah's observations about avowals of faith (such as reciting creeds, confessions, and the Lord's Prayer). He notes that people repeat them as performance, for example, when the avowal is recited in worship as part of the liturgy. The recitation, the performance, comes to constitute the belief. As propositions, they are not necessarily believed or might not even be understood, but they are recited nonetheless. (Appiah, *Lies That Bind*, 38).

174. Allen and Rose Maruyama, interview with author, Aurora, CO, Jan. 18, 2017.

175. Allen Maruyama, interview with author, Aurora, CO, June 13, 2018.

176. Allen and Rose Maruyama, interview with author, Aurora, CO, Jan. 18, 2017.

177. Sittler, "Joseph Haroutunian."

178. Allen Maruyama, interview with author, June 13, 2018. One indication of how immersed Haroutunian was in Reformed theology and its "father," John Calvin, is Haroutunian's *Calvin: Commentaries* in collaboration with Louise Pettibone Smith, 1958.

179. Gepford, too, lived this devotion to "communion" with one's fellow. For example, in the 1980s he facilitated efforts to establish Muslim-Christian dialogue in Dearborn, Michigan, the location in those years of one of the largest Arab communities outside the Middle East.

180. Allen and Rose Maruyama, interview with author, Aurora, CO, Jan. 18, 2017.

181. Allen Maruyama, interview with author, Aurora, CO, July 2, 2018.

182. Allen Maruyama, interview with author, Aurora, CO, June 13, 2018.

183. Minoru and June Mochizuki, interview with author, Denver, May 1, 2017.

184. The United Auto Workers and the Farm Equipment Workers union were two of a number of workers' unions vying for members and influence in the post-war years. For example, the FE had called a strike at the Caterpillar tractor plant in Peoria, Illinois, in 1948, but other unions moved in, certain that the FE would not be eligible as it refused to sign the Taft-Hartley anti-communist oath. Joe arrived at a time of lively activity in his chosen field.

185. During the war years, there were so many unfilled positions that recruiters went to the JaJA incarceration camps begging for workers. Many responded because the fifty-five-dollar per week wage far exceeded the nineteen- or twenty-one-dollar wage in the camps. However, they faced a housing shortage in Chicago, made worse by the fact that many landlords would not rent to Japanese Americans (Murata, *Images of America*, ch. 6).

186. A church that meets Joe's description is Highland Park Presbyterian Church.

187. Joseph Maruyama, interview with author, Broomfield, CO, Nov. 28, 2016. Joe did not make this historical connection between Dorothy's arrival and the larger context, but it might be the case that she was part of the resettlement effort out of the camps. According to Johnston, by the fall of 1945, the incarceration sites were closing but many of those who had been confined had nowhere to go. They faced chronic housing shortages, and the government did not want those returning to settle in the same West Coast enclaves. Many were sent to Chicago. Its Japanese population grew from about four hundred to twenty thousand in just a few years. Dorothy might have been part of this group or part of the earlier recruitment efforts for scarce labor out of the camps during the war (Johnston, "New Tome").

188. General Assembly of the UPC, "One Hundred Ninety-Second."

189. Allen and Rose Maruyama, interview with author, Aurora, CO, Nov. 13, 2016.

190. Allen Maruyama, interview with author, Aurora, CO, Apr. 3, 2018.

191. Allen and Rose Maruyama, interview with author, Aurora, CO, Nov. 13, 2016.

192. Allen Maruyama, interview with author, Aurora, Colorado, Nov. 30, 2016.

193. To apply Appiah's observation to these kinds of disputes, religious faith consists not only of belief but also of practice and fellowship. "Correct actions" (orthopraxy) are as significant as "correct beliefs" (orthodoxy). In this light, rituals and architectural features (including the placement of communion tables) take on significance in that they are displays of "correct practices" of faith within a congregation (Appiah, *Lies That Bind*, 37).

194. Allen and Rose Maruyama, interview with author, Aurora, CO, Jan. 3, 2017.

195. Allen Maruyama, interview with author, Aurora, CO, Nov. 30, 2016.

196. Rose Maruyama, interview with author, Aurora, CO, Nov 30, 2016.

197. Judith Fischer, telephone interview with author, Jan. 28, 2017.

198. Allen and Rose Maruyama, interview with author, Aurora, CO, Apr. 10, 2017.

199. Judith Fischer, telephone interview with author, Jan. 28, 2017.

200. Allen Maruyama, telephone conversation with author, Aug. 10, 2020.

201. Allen Maruyama, interview with author, Aurora, CO, Nov. 30, 2016.

202. Allen and Rose Maruyama, interview with author, Aurora, CO, Jan. 3, 2017.

203. Allen Maruyama, interview with author, Aurora, CO, Nov. 30, 2016.

204. The Supreme Court case of *Loving v. Virginia*, in which state laws prohibiting mixed marriages were declared to be unconstitutional, was decided in 1967. Allen and Rose moved to Prairie du Sac in 1959. As late as 1958, two dozen states still prohibited mixed marriages, including nearby Nebraska. Allen's home state, Colorado, and Illinois, Rose's home, were not among the two dozen. Alabama did not overturn its ban until 2000, the last of the fifty states to do so.

205. Allen and Rose Maruyama, interview with author, Aurora, CO, Jan. 3, 2017.

206. Rose Maruyama, interview with author, Aurora, CO, Nov. 30, 2016.

207. Allen and Rose Maruyama, interview with author, Aurora, CO, Jan. 3, 2017.

208. Allen Maruyama, interview with author, Aurora, CO Nov. 30, 2016.

209. General Assembly of the UPC, "One Hundred Ninety-Second."

210. Allen Maruyama, interview with author, Aurora, CO, July 2, 2018.

211. Allen Maruyama, interview with author, Aurora, CO, Nov. 30, 2016.

212. Harriet Heitzman, interview with author, Dubuque, IA, Nov. 27, 2019.

213. Joseph Maruyama, interview with author, Broomfield, CO, Nov. 28, 2016.

214. Allen and Rose Maruyama, interview with author, Aurora, CO, Jan. 3, 2017.

215. Allen Maruyama, interview with author, Aurora, CO, Nov. 30, 2016.

216. Rose Maruyama, interview with author, Aurora, CO, Dec. 14, 2016.

217. Allen and Rose Maruyama, interview with author, Aurora, CO, Jan. 3, 2017.

218. Rose Maruyama, interview with author, Aurora, CO, Dec. 14, 2016.

219. Allen and Rose Maruyama, interview with author, Aurora, CO, Jan. 3, 2017.

220. Rose Maruyama, interview with author, Aurora, CO, Nov. 30, 2016.

221. "New Archbishop."

222. On Jan. 22, 1964, the United Presbyterian Commission on Religion and Race (CORAR) "sent fifty-two clergymen to participate in Freedom Day, a voter registration event" in Hattiesburg. Subsequently, "CORAR created the Hattiesburg Ministers' Project to coordinate clergy participation in picket lines, canvassing, and voter registration attempts." The participants were "met with bitterness and resentment." At one point, nine were arrested and charged with "disorderly conduct." Nevertheless, the project was judged "as successful and transferred to the National Council of the Churches of Christ, incorporated into the Mississippi Summer Project and later, into the Delta Ministry." As part of the ongoing Civil Rights struggles, Vernon Dahmer died in Hattiesburg in 1966,

as a result of the attack on his home by the Ku Klux Klan. Heydinger's participation apparently happened sometime over a span of these years ("Presbyterians," 3).

223. Allen and Rose Maruyama, interview with author, Aurora, CO, Jan. 3, 2017. Although he does not remember the specific date, he is possibly recalling the eight to one decision by the Supreme Court that upheld the constitutionality of the Voting Rights Act, decided on Mar. 7, 1966, in *South Carolina v. Katzenbach*.

224. Allen and Rose Maruyama, interview with author, Aurora, CO, Mar. 6, 2017.

225. Sarah Maruyama-Biles Brady, interview with author, Highlands Ranch, CO, Mar. 28, 2917.

226. Allen Maruyama, interview with author, Aurora, CO, July 2, 2018.

227. Motoko Rich discusses growing up "hafu," which in Japan comes from the English word "half." (Being of mixed race is described in other locales as being "hapa.") When a friend suggested dropping the descriptor "hafu," which communicates "less than," and replacing it with "double" to describe one's multiple racial/cultural/ethnic heritage, Rich happily agreed to the change of the label because of the effect of multiplying one's racial heritage in contrast to dividing it in halves (Rich, "Naomi Osaka").

228. Doris and Sam Calian, telephone interview with author, Feb. 27, 2017.

229. In his discussion of still "mostly white Iowa," Robert Leonard writes about the role of race in Deidre DeJear's 2018 candidacy for secretary of state. Although Iowa legalized interracial marriage in 1851 and granted African-American men the right to vote in 1868, two years before the Fifteenth Amendment, if elected, she would have been the first African American to hold statewide office in Iowa (Leonard, "Democrats Can Win").

230. Allen and Rose Maruyama, interview with author, Aurora, CO, Jan. 3, 2017. Failor's wife, Maurene, and Rose were particularly close. Maurene was the church's choir director.

231. Sam and Doris Calian, telephone interview with author, Feb. 27, 2017.

232. Allen and Rose Maruyama, interview with author, Aurora, CO, Jan. 3, 2017.

233. Maruyama, "Theological Critique."

234. Allen Maruyama, telephone conversation, June 24, 2020, and numerous other conversations.

235. Summaries of McLuhan's major arguments abound.

236. Maruyama, "Theological Critique," 254.

237. Marshall McLuhan, letter to Allen Maruyama, June 12, 1973. McLuhan's response to Allen is evidently not unusual in that he was difficult to pin down and saw his work as something always in progress. This enigmatic characteristic is memorialized in Woody Allen's 1977 movie *Annie Hall*, in which McLuhan makes a cameo appearance.

238. Pierre Teilhard de Chardin (1881–1955) was a Jesuit priest whose fields were human paleontology and geological research, particularly in China. To oversimplify, his work is admired by many as bringing together faith in Christ and a scientific approach to the world, and it is condemned by others as being inadequate scientifically and as being theologically outside Catholic doctrine. Redding, "The Jesuit Priest," and "Pierre Teilhard de Chardin" are two easily accessible online sources that summarize his life and thought, but any number are available.

239. Maruyama, "Theological Critique," 255.

240. Either John outgrew his allergies, or the move to arid Colorado helped. Perhaps both were factors, because the respiratory problems diminished (Allen and Rose Maruyama, interview with author, Aurora, CO, Jan. 3, 2017).

241. Allen and Rose Maruyama, interview with author, Aurora, CO, Jan. 26, 2017.

242. Allen and Rose Maruyama, interview with author, Aurora, CO, Dec. 14, 2016.

243. Perhaps this list, were it to be written in the present, would conclude with

words such as "gang rape" or "rape," not to be confused with "homosexuality."

244. Tighe, "Forum."

245. Allen Maruyama, telephone conversation with author, Oct. 21, 2019.

246. General Assembly of the UPC, "One Hundred Ninety-Second."

247. Allen and Rose Maruyama, interview with author, Aurora, CO, Dec. 14, 2016.

248. In a reflection he wrote in 2002 for the centennial celebration of the church, Allen remembers the vote was 250 for and 220 against.

249. Allen and Rose Maruyama, interview with author, Aurora, CO, Mar. 22, 2017.

250. Hite, *Spirit of Montview*, 30.

251. Montview Presbyterian Church, *Montview Messenger*, June 14, 1972.

252. Ed O'Keefe, telephone interview with author, Feb. 6, 2017.

253. Hite, *Spirit of Montview*, 14.

254. Allen and Rose Maruyama, interview with author, Aurora, CO, Mar. 22, 2017.

255. Hite, *Spirit of Montview*, 22.

256. Kenneth L. Barley, interview with author, Denver, CO, Mar. 27, 2017.

257. Devlin, "Memories of Amache."

258. Hite, *Spirit of Montview*, 25.

259. Hite, *Spirit of Montview*, 28–32.

260. Allen and Rose Maruyama, interview with author, Aurora, CO, Mar. 22, 2017.

261. Kenneth L. Barley, interview with author, Denver, Mar. 27, 2017.

262. Hite, *Spirit of Montview*, 20.

263. Hite, *Spirit of Montview*, 25.

264. Allen and Rose Maruyama, interview with author, Aurora, CO, Dec. 14, 2016.

265. Allen and Rose Maruyama, interview with author, Aurora, CO, Mar. 22, 2017.

266. Allen and Rose Maruyama, interview with author, Aurora, CO, Dec. 14, 2016.

267. Allen and Rose Maruyama, interview with author, Aurora, CO, Dec. 14, 2016 and Feb. 10, 2017.

268. Allen and Rose Maruyama, interview with author, Aurora, CO, Mar. 22, 2017.

269. Kenneth L. Barley, interview with author, Denver, Mar. 27, 2017.

270. Allen and Rose Maruyama, interview with author, Aurora, CO, Jan. 26, 2017.

271. Allen and Rose Maruyama, interview with author, Aurora, CO, Mar. 2, 2017.

272. Allen and Rose Maruyama, interview with author, Aurora, CO, Dec. 14, 2016.

273. Kenneth L. Barley, interview with author, Denver, CO, Mar. 27, 2017.

274. Allen and Rose Maruyama, interview with author, Aurora, CO, Dec. 14, 2016.

275. Ed O'Keefe, telephone interview with author, Feb. 6, 2017.

276. Allen and Rose Maruyama, interview with author, Aurora, CO, Mar. 22, 2017.

277. Shirley Burkhart, interview with author, Denver, Mar. 20, 2017.

278. As noted, even as far back as Miller's tenure, this leadership style was familiar. Responsibilities were shared among the pastors, so, while the staffing pattern was innovative at a structural level, the Montview congregation might not have experienced jarring changes with the co-pastor model.

279. Allen and Rose Maruyama, interview with author, Aurora, CO, Feb. 10, 2017.

280. Barley recalls the review period to be annually at first rather than the three-year period Hutchison had proposed. In any event, the arrangement was reviewed regularly, to the benefit of the co-pastors and the congregation (Kenneth L. Barley, interview with author, Denver, Mar. 27, 2017).

281. Hite, *Spirit of Montview*, 28.

282. Cearley, "The Co-Pastorate Model."

283. Hite, *Spirit of Montview*, 28.

284. Kenneth L. Barley, interview with author, Denver, Mar. 27, 2017.

285. Allen and Rose Maruyama, interview with author, Aurora, CO, Nov. 4, 2016.

286. Cynthia Ann Cearley, interview with author, Centennial, Colorado, May 24, 2017.

287. Kenneth L. Barley, interview with author, Denver, Colorado, Mar. 27, 2017.

288. Cynthia Ann Cearley, interview with author, Centennial, CO, May 24, 2017.

289. Harriet Isbell, interview with author, Boulder, CO, Mar. 14, 2017.

290. Kenneth L. Barley, interview with author, Denver, Mar. 27, 2017.

291. Shirley Burkhart, interview with author, Denver, Mar. 20, 2017.

292. Allen and Rose Maruyama, interview with author, Aurora, CO, Feb. 22, 2017.

293. Harriet Isbell, interview with author, Boulder, CO, Mar. 14, 2017.

294. These excerpts come from letters to session and were written by church members at the time of Hutchison's departure in 1980. They are held in Montview's archives. The sentiments reflect general attitudes toward the co-pastorate and Allen at the time he ran for moderator in 1980.

295. Kenneth L. Barley, interview with author, Denver, Mar. 27, 2017.

296. Larry Angus, interview with author, Lakewood, CO, Mar. 9, 2017.

297. Allen and Rose Maruyama, interview with author, Aurora, CO, Mar. 22, 2017.

298. Larry Angus, interview with author, Lakewood, CO, Mar. 9, 2017.

299. Allen and Rose Maruyama, interview with author, Aurora, CO, Mar. 6, 2017.

300. Allen Maruyama, *Campaign Brochure*.

301. Larry Angus, interview with author, Lakewood, CO, Mar. 9, 2017.

302. General Assembly of the UPC, "One Hundred Ninety-Second."

303. "New Testament," 386–87.

304. Allen and Rose Maruyama, interview with author, Aurora, CO, Jan. 18, 2017.

305. To put the dynamics Allen describes in Haroutunian's terms, "the miracle of the presence of our brother is one piece with the miracle of the presence of Christ with us, and the presence of Christ signifies, and is, the presence of God" (Sittler, "Joseph Haroutunian").

Allen's emphasis on the significance of these relationships would also fit into Appiah's scheme of religious faith as comprising not only matters of belief (Allen's commitment to Jesus Christ and the church's faithful transmission of Christ's message of justice and righteousness), but also practice (the mission he references) and fellowship (the relationships he values) (Appiah, *Lies that Bind*, 36).

306. Allen and Rose Maruyama, interview with author, Aurora, CO, Jan. 18, 2017.

307. For example, the Apostles' Creed is a foundational confession of faith. In addition to the Lord's Prayer and the Ten Commandments, the Apostles' Creed would be memorized by children in Presbyterian confirmation classes in those years. It summarizes the basic tenets of faith that Allen would have embraced at that time. The words of this confession, repeated regularly in worship services in congregations then and now, are: "I believe in God, the Father almighty, maker of heaven and earth, and in Jesus Christ, his only Son, our Lord; who was conceived by the Holy Ghost, born of the Virgin Mary, suffered under Pontius Pilate, was crucified, died, and was buried; he descended into hell; the third day he rose again from the dead; he ascended into heaven, and sitteth on the right hand of God the Father almighty; from thence he shall come to judge the quick and the dead. I believe in the Holy Ghost; the holy catholic church; the communion of saints; the forgiveness of sins; the resurrection of the body; and the life everlasting." Sources and varied wordings are numerous.

To put the regular recitation of this and other creeds in perspective, recall Appiah's comments that while believers will affirm their faith by corporate recitations of foundational statements such as creeds, they do not necessarily believe them or even know what they mean. If the creeds are identified with their particular faith, they affirm the formulations nonetheless (Appiah, *Lies That Bind*, 38).

308. Allen and Rose Maruyama, interview with author, Aurora, CO, Feb. 10, 2017.

309. Subsequent to Tillich's criticisms of the Nazi movement, he lost his position at the University of Frankfurt in the early 1930s. Reinhold Niebuhr, who was on the faculty of New York's Union Theological Seminary, persuaded Tillich to immigrate and join the faculty there.

310. Chapman, "Killing for Christ," 6.

311. "Candidates for UPCUSA Moderator."

312. The influence of liberation theology continues in the present. As a more contemporary example, in an Advent sermon on Dec. 9, 2018, Rev. Pedro Silva, First Congregational Church, United Church of Christ, Boulder, Colorado, speaks about liberation theology. To paraphrase, he says liberation theology orients one toward liberation from oppression as bringing about salvation. Liberation theology can locate us in the realm of God (Silva, "Advent Sermon").

313. Culver, "Liberation Theology."

314. Tighe, "Forum."

315. Culver, "Liberation Theology." In his 1979 *Presbyterian Layman* article, Chapman had clearly understood and articulated this economic threat from "poor non-whites," those "aggressively radical third-world Protestants, mostly from Africa and Asia," who "end up controlling the spending." However, Chapman did not dwell on what would surely have been an equally threatening element of liberation theology, that of pluralism, which Allen celebrates and names in his candidating speech. Pluralism had the potential to explode the confines of North American Protestantism with its roots in European history. For Chapman, the financial and racial threats that liberation theology posed were alarming enough (Chapman, "Killing for Christ").

316. General Assembly of the UPC, "One Hundred Ninety-Second."

317. "Denver Presbytery Dissolves Relation."

318. "Viewpoints on Specific Questions."

319. General Assembly of the UPC, "One Hundred Ninety-Second."

320. Allen Maruyama, interview with author, Aurora, CO, June 13, 2018.

321. General Assembly of the UPC, "One Hundred Ninety-Second."

322. June and Minoru Mochizuki, interview with author, Denver, May 1, 2017.

323. Allen and Rose Maruyama, interview with author, Aurora, CO, Mar. 29, 2017.

324. June and Minoru Mochizuki, interview with author, Denver, May 1, 2017.

325. To compensate for the lack of advocacy for and information about the JaJA experience, a number of organizations emerged. These four are examples, but many resources are available, including organizations restoring and providing educational services at each of the ten World War II incarceration sites. Densho is "a grassroots organization dedicated to preserving, educating, and sharing the story of World War II-era incarceration of Japanese Americans in order to deepen understandings of American history and inspire action for equity." The Japanese American National Museum's mission is "to promote understanding and appreciation of America's ethnic and cultural diversity by sharing the Japanese American experience." The Japanese American Citizen's League, established in 1929, exists "to secure and safeguard the civil and human rights of Asian and Pacific Islander Americans and all communities who are affected by injustice and bigotry." Its publication *Pacific Citizen* provides a wealth of contemporaneous documentation through the decades. The mission of Tsuru for Solidarity, a relative newcomer, is to "educate, advocate, and protest to close all U.S. concentration camps; build solidarity with other communities of color that have experienced forced removal, detention, deportation, separation of families and other forms of racial and state violence; [and] coordinate intergenerational, cross-community healing circles

addressing the trauma of our shared histories" (Densho, Japanese American National Museum, Japanese American Citizen's League, Tsuru for Solidarity).

326. Johnston, "Japanese American Vets," 6.

327. United Presbyterian Church in the United States of America, *Minutes, 1980.*

328. Tighe, "Forum."

329. Griepp, "Mass Media Witness."

330. Gregg Meister, "Mass Media Report Inadequate."

331. Anderson, "Work for Racial Justice." Jordan, the president of the National Urban League, had been shot and seriously wounded just days before, on May 29, 1980.

332. Griepp, "Young Stresses Church's Role."

333. In Jan. 1979, the Shah of Iran was deposed and fled to Egypt and Morocco. Khomeini returned to Iran and consolidated power, and militants overran the US embassy and held diplomats for several hours before they were released. However, on Oct. 21, 1979, President Jimmy Carter authorized that the shah could enter the United States for cancer treatment. On Nov. 4, militants overran the embassy again, stayed, and held hostages, some for 444 days. Two months prior to the Detroit Assembly, Apr. 1980, a military rescue failed, and the hostages were still being held captive. Information about these events is available from any number of sources. Summaries of these events are widely available.

334. SALT I and II were Strategic Arms Limitation Talks about arms control between the United States and the Soviet Union. President Carter and General Secretary Brezhnev signed SALT II in 1979. It was never ratified by the U.S. Senate, however, because the Soviets invaded Afghanistan six months after the signing and a Soviet combat brigade was discovered in Cuba. The Soviet invasion of Afghanistan would have begun only months prior to the 1980 General Assembly. This history is widely available.

335. General Assembly of the UPC, "One Hundred Ninety-Second."

336. Allen and Rose Maruyama, interview with author, Aurora, CO, Mar. 2, 2017.

337. "Outgoing Moderators."

338. Allen Maruyama, interview with author, Aurora, CO, July 2, 2018.

339. Maruyama, "Reflections."

340. Allen Maruyama, interview with author, Aurora, CO, Nov. 8, 2018.

341. Grant Ujifusa uses the phrase to describe Gracye Uyehara, a significant strategist in the movement to seek redress for the incarceration of JaJAs during World War II. In his tribute he refers to her as "a national Japanese American leader" (Ujifusa, "Gracye and Hiro Uyehara").

342. A paraphrase of Matt. 28:19–20, Mark 16:15, Luke 24:47, and the spirit of John 21:15–17.

343. Praying for the coming of God's realm is a central theme of the Lord's Prayer, recited routinely in Christian liturgy: "Our Father in heaven, hallowed be your name, your kingdom come, your will be done, on earth as in heaven. Give us today our daily bread. Forgive us our sins as we forgive those who sin against us. Save us from the time of trial and deliver us from evil. For the kingdom, the power, and the glory are yours now and forever. Amen." Sources and varied wordings are numerous.

344. Hite, *Spirit of Montview,* 22.

345. Maruyama, "People without a Vision."

346. Shirley Burkhart, interview with author, Denver, Mar. 20, 2017.

347. Founded in 1966, the World Future Society characterizes itself as "a gathering place for curious, open-minded citizens of the future as we come together to uncover new and exciting opportunities to impact our world" through discussions, conferences, publications, and monthly Q&As online and otherwise. The Institute of Noetic Sciences

was founded in 1973 by astronaut Edgar Mitchell and investor Paul N. Temple. As noted above in the discussion of Pierre Teilhard de Chardin, the word "noetic" has its source in the Greek *nous*, signifying a broad range of meanings that includes "awareness" and "mind." While reminiscent of Teilhard's noosphere, the Institute's appropriation of the Greek root is not necessarily equated with Teilhard's theological use of it. The Institute is described as engaging in parapsychological research about such phenomenon as meditation and alternative healing practices. More information is available on the two organizations' websites (Institute of Noetic Sciences and World Future Society).

348. Maruyama, "People without a Vision."

349. Hart, "Remarks."

350. Allen Maruyama, interview with author, Aurora, CO, Nov. 8, 2018.

351. Darion, "Impossible Dream."

352. Maruyama, "Theological Critique," 196.

353. Culver, "Liberation Theology."

354. Judy and Robert Roussell, interview with author, Marion, IA, Oct. 24, 2019.

355. This may not have been a policy during the entire time the Maruyamas lived in Dubuque, because Allen and Joe were quite the golfers. Various congregants enjoyed golfing with them, perhaps even at the country club (Harriet Heitzman, interview with author, Dubuque, IA, Nov. 27, 2019).

356. Allen and Rose Maruyama, interview with author, Aurora, CO, Nov. 13, 2016.

357. Allen and Rose Maruyama, interview with author, Aurora, CO, Mar. 22, 2017.

358. Maruyama, "Reflections."

359. Allen and Rose Maruyama, interview with author, Aurora, CO, Mar. 22, 2017.

360. Allen Maruyama, interview with author, Aurora, CO, Dec. 11, 2018.

361. Allen and Rose Maruyama, interview with author, Aurora, CO, Mar. 15, 2017.

362. Allen and Rose Maruyama, interview with author, Aurora, CO, Jan. 26, 2017.

363. Montview Boulevard Presbyterian Church, solicitation letter, Apr. 1978. In the archives of Montview Boulevard Presbyterian Church, Denver.

364. Allen and Rose Maruyama, interview with author, Aurora, CO, Mar. 2, 2017.

365. More than ten thousand Nisei (second-generation American citizens) lived in Japan at the start of the war, and approximately three thousand served in the Japanese Imperial Army or Navy (Williams, *American Sutra*, 167).

366. Mochizuki, "Banished from California," unnumbered pages.

367. Minoru and June Mochizuki, interview with author, Denver, Apr. 25, 2017.

368. The *Kyōdan* (United Church of Christ in Japan) was established in 1941, subsequent to government action in 1940 that forced all Protestant churches in Japan to merge. The 1940 law gave the government control over religious organizations. The law was repealed in 1945, and religious freedom was re-established by the Supreme Command of Allied Powers in 1946. Many groups left the *Kyōdan* and re-established their pre-war identities, but many stayed. The 1967 *Confession on the Responsibility during World War II* recovered the integrity of the *Kyōdan* by confessing complicity during the war. It remains the largest Japanese denomination (United Church).

369. Minoru and June Mochizuki, interview with author, Denver, May 1, 2017.

370. Joseph Maruyama, interview with author, Broomfield, CO, Nov. 28, 2016.

371. Lebra, *We Chose Colorado*, 95.

372. Mochizuki, "Two Worlds," unnumbered pages.

373. Minoru and June Mochizuki, interview with author, Denver, May 1, 2017.

374. Minoru and June Mochizuki, interview with author, Denver, Apr. 25, 2017.

375. "Eugene Carson Blake." For those interested in researching Blake further, the Presbyterian Historical Society has a trove of information; see https:/www.history.

pcusa.org/collections/research-tools/guides-archival-collections/rg-3.

376. Minoru and June Mochizuki, interview with author, Denver, May 1, 2017.

377. Synod of Wisconsin, "105th Annual Meeting."

378. Maruyama, "Christian Mission in Japan."

379. Allen and Rose Maruyama, interview with author, Aurora, CO, May 23, 2017.

380. Naropa University, accredited by the North Central Association of Colleges and Schools in 1988, promotes contemplative education. Activities include meditation, the Japanese tea ceremony, the Christian labyrinth, and ikebana, the art of flower arranging. It was founded by Tibetan Buddhist teacher Chögyam Trungpa in 1974 (Naropa University).

381. Allen and Rose Maruyama, interview with author, Aurora, CO, Apr. 10, 2017.

382. Allen Maruyama, interview with author, Aurora, CO, Jan. 15, 2019.

383. Allen and Rose Maruyama, interview with author, Aurora, CO, Apr. 10, 2017.

384. Sarah Maruyama-Biles Brady, interview with author, Highlands Ranch, CO, Feb. 28, 2017.

385. John Maruyama, interview with author, Arvada, CO, Mar. 1, 2017.

386. Allen and Rose Maruyama, interview with author, Aurora, CO, Mar. 2, 2017. In her later years, the family arrangement was for Mrs. Maruyama to periodically stay at each of her children's homes. Several of Allen and Rose's friends recall looking forward to her visits because she would prepare such delicious Japanese food. They regretted not knowing her better because she was not comfortable with her English, and their memory is that she characteristically stayed in the kitchen.

387. John Maruyama, interview with author, Arvada, CO, Mar. 1, 2017.

388. Sarah Maruyama-Biles Brady, interview with author, Highlands Ranch, CO, Feb. 28, 2017.

389. Maruyama, "Christian Mission in Japan," 25–26.

390. The first five hiragana and katakana symbols represent vowels; the next forty, initial consonants followed by a vowel; and the last symbol is a final "n," sometimes an "m." Additional sounds are variously signified by combining symbols and by tiny circles or two small strokes at the upper right-hand corner of the kana character. The information about the kanas combines an explanation from "Kanji" and Rev. Dr. Grace Kaori Suzuki, Christ United Presbyterian Church, San Francisco. Japanese is Suzuki's native language, and she too learned the poem as a child (Suzuki, email to author, June 4, 2019).

Additionally, one might use a Latin script (romaji) to write Japanese. One of the three main scripts, and the one most widely used, is the Hepburn romanization. It is named after the American Presbyterian medical missionary Dr. James Curtis Hepburn, who arrived in Japan in 1859. The Hepburn romaji text was published in 1867, a result of his years of Japanese language study ("James Curtis Hepburn" and "Romanization of Japanese").

391. Maruyama, "Christian Mission in Japan," 23.

392. Subsequent to his report, Allen would still affirm how integral Buddhist values, aesthetics, and cultural practices are to Japanese life, but he does not now think of Buddhism as a religion. He calls it a philosophy. Throughout his report and for the scholars he interviewed, however, it is assumed that Buddhism is a religion.

393. Ishikawa, Kokoro, in Maruyama, "Christian Mission in Japan," 24–25.

394. Mochizuki, "Two Worlds," unnumbered pages.

395. Details about Bushido/the Samurai code are available on many websites.

396. Maruyama, "Christian Mission in Japan," 27.

397. Maruyama, "Christian Mission in Japan," 14.

398. Maruyama, "Christian Mission in Japan," 18.

399. Doshisha University was founded in 1875 by Protestant educator Niijima Jō and is one of Japan's oldest private institutions of higher learning ("Doshisha University").

400. Maruyama, "Christian Mission in Japan," 29.

401. "Toyohiko Kagawa."

402. Maruyama, "Christian Mission in Japan," 29.

403. Minoru and June Mochizuki, interview with author, Denver, May 22, 2017.

404. Maruyama, "Christian Mission in Japan," 20.

405. Maruyama, "Christian Mission in Japan," 21.

406. In the article "Japan Wants Women in the Office. Housework Gets in the Way," Motoko Rich writes that Prime Minister Shinzo Abe has the goal of "energizing his nation's puttering economy by elevating women in the labor force," a goal he calls "womenomics." One of the biggest obstacles, though, is "the disproportionate burden women shoulder at home." The article describes in detail the "exacting domestic expectations and a [legacy of] rigid gender roles." Examples of these expectations include writing daily detailed journals for the children's preschools; cooking intricate, multiple small dishes for meals; and packing school lunches that are works of art (Rich, "Japan Wants").

407. Maruyama, "Christian Mission in Japan," 27, 23–24.

408. Maruyama, "Christian Mission in Japan," 19.

409. Maruyama, "Christian Mission in Japan," 35.

410. Maruyama, "Christian Mission in Japan," 36.

411. Maruyama, "Christian Mission in Japan," 37.

412. Maruyama, "Christian Mission in Japan," 7, 37.

413. Maruyama, "Christian Mission in Japan," 39.

414. Thorson-Smith et al., *Pornography*, 3.

415. Allen and Rose Maruyama, interview with author, Denver, Mar. 29, 2017.

416. Glendora ("Dusty") Taylor and her daughter Kathy, interview with author, Denver, May 23, 2017.

417. Allen and Rose Maruyama, interview with author, Aurora, CO, Mar. 22, 2017.

418. Glendora ("Dusty") Taylor and her daughter Kathy, interview with author, Denver, May 23, 2017.

419. Cynthia Ann Cearley, interview with author, Centennial, CO, May 24, 2017.

420. Allen and Rose Maruyama, interview with author, Aurora, CO, Mar. 22, 2017.

421. Cynthia Ann Cearley, interview with author, Centennial, CO, May 24, 2017.

422. Glendora ("Dusty") Taylor and her daughter Kathy, interview with author, Denver, May 23, 2017.

423. Allen and Rose Maruyama, interviews with author, Aurora, CO, Feb. 10, 2017, Mar. 29, 2017.

424. Allen and Rose Maruyama, interview with author, Aurora, CO, Mar. 29, 2017.

425. Thorson-Smith et al., *Pornography*, 71.

426. Thorson-Smith et al., *Pornography*, 7.

427. Thorson-Smith et al., *Pornography*, 25.

428. Thorson-Smith et al., *Pornography*, 78.

429. Kulish, Robles, and Mazzei, "Behind Illicit Massage Parlors."

430. Niiya, "Kazuo Masuda."

431. Any number of resources describe the process leading up to the Civil Liberties Act and its implementation. See also "Civil Liberties Act of 1988."

432. Allen and Rose Maruyama, interview with author, Aurora, CO, Apr. 10, 2017.

433. Lesley Shearer, interview with author, Littleton, CO, Apr. 14, 2917.

434. Allen and Rose Maruyama, interview with author, Aurora, CO, Apr. 10, 2017.

435. Allen and Rose Maruyama, interview with author, Aurora, CO, Mar. 6, 2017.

436. Killgore, "Rev. Benjamin M. Weir," 20.

437. Schaffer, "Ex-D.C. Area Pastor."
438. "Outgoing Moderators."
439. Anderson, "Assembly Affirms Commitment."
440. Allen Maruyama, interview with author, Aurora, CO, July 2, 2018.
441. Minoru and June Mochizuki, interview with author, Denver, May 1, 2017.
442. Tracy, "Welcome."
443. Minoru and June Mochizuki, interview with author, Denver, May 1, 2017.
444. Van Marter, "Confessions and Pensions."
445. Langer, *Philosophy*, 153.
446. Office of the General Assembly, *Book of Confessions*.
447. Youngs, "Textual Issues Addressed."
448. Cole and Cole, "Inclusive Language."
449. Youngs, "Textual Issues Addressed."
450. "Hopes for the Nineties."
451. "Cultural Pluralism in the Church."
452. Williams, "S. David Stoner."
453. Williams, "James E. Andrews."
454. Griepp, "Young Stresses Church's Role."
455. Hutcheson, "Presbyterian Polarization," 6.
456. Wuthnow, *The Struggle*.
457. Hutcheson, "Presbyterian Polarization."
458. Chapman, "Killing for Christ," 6.
459. Smith, "Two Hundred Second Assembly."
460. Rogers, "Alternative."
461. Poethig, "Two-Church Debate."
462. Aurelia Fule, numerous conversations with author, Santa Fe, NM, 2008, and Fule, *Minister Biographical Questionnaire*.
463. Fule, "For the Sake."
464. "Nominees for Moderator."
465. Williams, "Two More Endorsed."
466. Williams, "Major Structural Design Issues."
467. Van Marter, "Report on Environmental Peril."
468. "Nominees for Moderator."
469. Williams, "Charlotte Presbytery."
470. "Nominees for Moderator."
471. "Nominees for Moderator."
472. Williams, "Two More Endorsed."
473. "Nominees for Moderator."
474. "Nominees for Moderator."
475. Cynthia Ann Cearley, interview with author, Centennial, CO, May 24, 2017.
476. "Nominees for Moderator."
477. *Robert's Rules of Order* is said to be one of he most widely used manuals for conducting meetings in the United States. Its author was General Henry M. Robert, and it first appeared in 1876. Robert et al., *Robert's Rules*, and "Robert's Rules of Order."
478. Allen and Rose Maruyama, interview with author, Aurora, CO, Mar. 2, 2017.
479. "Nominees for Moderator."
480. "Nominees for Moderator."
481. The lyrics were written by John Oxenham (pseudonym for William A. Dunkerley) in 1908. The hymn is widely sung "throughout the whole wide earth" (Oxenham, "In Christ There Is No East or West").
482. "Nominees for Moderator."

483. "Hopes for the Nineties."

484. "Price H. Gwynn III."

485. Hirai, "Did You Know?"

486. Anderson, "Work for Racial Justice."

487. Grace Kaori Suzuki writes that the cultural shame component of the incarceration experience is still there in 2020. Only recently are people more open about speaking out about the internment. They would be even more unlikely to use it as an opportunity (Suzuki, email to author, Nov. 3, 2020).

488. "Price H. Gwynn III."

489. Allen Maruyama, interview with author, Aurora, CO, Sept. 5, 2019.

490. "Price H. Gwynn III."

491. Allen and Rose Maruyama, interviews with author, Aurora, CO, Mar. 6 and 15, 2017; and Allen Maruyama, interview with author, Aurora, CO, July 2, 2018.

492. *General Assembly Daily News*, June 7, 1990.

493. Ed O'Keefe, telephone interview with author, Feb. 6, 2017.

494. Allen and Rose Maruyama, interview with author, Aurora, CO, Mar. 6, 2017.

495. Allen and Rose Maruyama, interview with author, Aurora, CO, Mar. 15, 2017.

496. Allen and Rose Maruyama, interview with author, Aurora, CO, Nov. 4, 2016.

497. Cynthia Ann Cearley, interview with author, Centennial, CO, May 24, 2017.

498. Glendora ("Dusty") Taylor and her daughter Kathy, interview with author, Denver, May 23, 2017.

499. Allen Maruyama, interview with author, Aurora, CO, Nov. 13, 2016.

500. Allen and Rose Maruyama, interview with author, Aurora, CO, Jan. 26, 2017.

501. Allen Maruyama, interview with author, Aurora, CO, Nov. 13, 2018.

502. Rose Maruyama, interview with author, Aurora, CO, Nov. 30, 2016; and Allen and Rose Maruyama, interview with author, Aurora, CO, Apr. 10, 2017.

503. Allen Maruyama, interview with author, Aurora, CO, Nov. 8, 2018.

504. Cynthia Ann Cearley, interview with author, Centennial, CO, May 24, 2017.

505. Judy and Robert Roussell, interview with author, Marion, IA, Oct. 24, 2019.

506. Larry Angus, interview with author, Lakewood, CO, Mar. 9, 2017.

507. Cynthia Ann Cearley, interview with author, Centennial, CO, May 24, 2017.

508. Cynthia Ann Cearley, interview with author, Centennial, CO, May 24, 2017.

509. Ed O'Keefe, telephone interview with author, Feb. 6, 2017.

510. Allen and Rose Maruyama, interview with author, Aurora, CO, Feb. 10, 2017.

511. Ed O'Keefe, telephone interview with author, Feb. 6, 2017.

512. Cynthia Ann Cearley, interview with author, Centennial, CO, May 24, 2017, and Jan. 15, 2019.

513. Allen and Rose Maruyama, interview with author, Aurora, CO, Nov. 4, 2016, and Mar. 15, 2017.

514. Wolf, *Taking the Quantum Leap*.

515. Allen Maruyama, interview with author, Aurora, CO, Feb. 25, 2019.

516. Two of many sources for Fox's work are the books *Original Blessing* and *The Coming of the Cosmic Christ*. Quick summaries of his thought are found at http://www.matthewfox.org.

517. Coincidently, Fox, first a Dominican, also received one of his degrees at Dubuque's Aquinas School of Philosophy and Theology, prior to Allen's time there. In 1993, Fox became an Episcopal priest, following his expulsion from the Roman Catholic Church (Fox, Matthew Fox).

518. The dates Allen gives for his enrollment at the Massage Therapy Institute on his 1993 "Presbyterian Church (U.S.A.) Personal Information Form" and on a Feb. 15,

1996, form differ. Because an article in the *The Denver Post* from Jan. 1992 indicates he is currently enrolled, 1991–92 seems to be the accurate date (Culver, "Minister to Retire").

519. Maruyama, "Presbyterian Church (U.S.A.) Personal Information Form," 1993.

520. Maruyama, "Presbyterian Church (U.S.A.) Personal Information Form," 1996.

521. Cynthia Ann Cearley, interview with author, Centennial, CO, May 24, 2017.

522. Larry Angus, interview with author, Lakewood, CO, Mar. 9, 2017.

523. Cynthia Ann Cearley, interview with author, Centennial, CO, Jan. 15, 2019.

524. Shirley Burkhart, interview with author, Denver, Mar. 20, 2017.

525. Glendora ("Dusty") Taylor and her daughter Kathy, interview with author, Denver, May 23, 2017; and Cynthia Ann Cearley, interview with author, Centennial, CO, May 24, 2017.

526. John Maruyama, interview with author, Arvada, CO, Mar. 1, 2017.

527. Allen and Rose Maruyama, interview with author, Aurora, CO, Apr. 3, 2017.

528. Allen and Rose Maruyama, interview with author, Aurora, CO, Dec. 3, 2016.

529. Allen and Rose Maruyama, interview with author, Aurora, CO, Jan. 3, 2017; and Allen Maruyama, interview with author, Aurora, CO, Apr. 3, 2018.

530. Judy and Robert Roussell, interview with author, Marion, IA, Oct. 24, 2019.

531. Allen Maruyama, telephone conversation with author, Apr. 3, 2018.

532. Allen and Rose Maruyama, interview with author, Aurora, CO, Dec. 3, 2016.

533. Allen and Rose Maruyama, interviews with author, Aurora, CO, Nov. 4, 2016, and Jan. 3, 2017; and Allen Maruyama, interview with author, Aurora, CO, Feb. 25, 2019.

534. Maruyama, "Personal Statement of Faith."

535. Cynthia Ann Cearley, interview with author, Centennial, CO, May 24, 2017.

536. Allen and Rose Maruyama, interview with author, Aurora, CO, Mar. 15, 2017.

537. Glendora ("Dusty") Taylor and her daughter Kathy, interview with author, Denver, May 23, 2017.

538. Allen and Rose Maruyama, interview with author, Aurora, CO, Mar. 15, 2017.

539. Allen Maruyama, interview with author, Aurora, Colorado, Feb. 25, 2019.

540. Allen and Rose Maruyama, interview with author, Aurora, Colorado, Mar. 15, 2017.

541. Allen and Rose Maruyama, interview with author, Aurora, CO, Jan. 26, 2017.

542. Culver, "Minister to Retire."

543. Allen and Rose Maruyama, interview with author, Aurora, CO, Mar. 15, 2017.

544. Allen and Rose Maruyama, interview with author, Aurora, CO, Mar. 15, 2017.

545. Eisenlohr, *Massage Ministration.*

546. Allen Maruyama, interview with author, Aurora, CO, Jan. 26, 2017.

547. Ann Burdick, interview with author, Westminster, CO, Mar. 5, 2019.

548. Stein, *Essential Reiki.*

549. Stein, *Essential Reiki*, 9–13.

550. For example, see LifeSpark Cancer Resources and Reid, "Reiki in Denver."

551. Allen Maruyama, interview with author, Aurora, CO, Jan. 26, 2017.

552. The information about Karuna and Reiki is a composite from Allen and Ann Burdick (a Reiki practitioner), interview with author, Westminster, CO, Feb. 26, 2019; Sue Gill, who described her experiences with cancer treatment and Reiki to the author in a telephone conversation, Feb. 26, 2019; Stein's book; and a number of websites. Examples include Learn Religions and International Center for Reiki Training.

553. Japanese Calligraphy and Japan Visitor.

554. Stein, *Essential Reiki*, 145–47.

555. Office of the General Assembly, *Book of Order*, W-04.0401.

556. Rose Maruyama, Christmas letter, 1998.

557. Allen and Rose Maruyama, interview with author, Aurora, CO, Mar. 15, 2017.

558. Allen Maruyama, interview with author, Aurora, CO, Feb. 25, 2019.

559. Allen and Rose Maruyama, interview with author, Aurora, CO Jan. 26, 2017.

560. Cynthia Ann Cearley, interview with author, Centennial, CO, May 24, 2017.

561. Sarah Maruyama-Biles Brady, interview with author, Highlands Ranch, CO, Feb. 28, 2017.

562. Allen and Rose Maruyama, interview with author, Aurora, CO, Jan. 3, 2017.

563. Allen and Rose Maruyama, interview with author, Aurora, CO, Feb. 10, 2017.

564. Allen and Rose Maruyama, interview with author, Aurora, CO, Mar. 22, 2017.

565. Sarah Maruyama-Biles Brady, interview with author, Highlands Ranch, CO, Feb. 28, 2017.

566. Allen and Rose Maruyama, interview with author, Aurora, CO, Feb. 10, 2017.

567. Ed O'Keefe, email to author, Feb. 6, 2017.

568. Allen and Rose Maruyama, interview with author, Aurora, CO, Feb. 10, 2017.

569. Allen Maruyama, interview with author, Aurora, CO, Feb. 25, 2019.

570. Allen and Rose Maruyama, interview with author, Aurora, CO, Mar. 6, 2017.

571. "Remembering Syngman Rhee."

572. Minoru and June Mochizuki, interview with author, Denver, May 1, 2017.

573. Minoru and June Mochizuki, interview with author, Denver, May 22, 2017.

574. Seichi Otsuka, interview with author, Denver, Feb. 20, 2017.

575. Minoru and June Mochizuki, interview with author, Denver, May 22, 2017.

576. "Remembering Syngman Rhee."

577. Allen Maruyama, interview with author, Aurora, CO, Feb. 25, 2019.

578. Shearer, *Essays*, 3, 116.

579. Shearer, *Essays*, 175.

580. Lesley Shearer, interview with author, Littleton, CO, Feb. 25, 2019.

581. Lesley Shearer, interviews with author, Littleton, CO, Apr. 14, 2017, and Feb. 25, 2019.

582. The invitation is signed by Shenphen Dawa Rinpoche and Sangyum Rigdzin Wangmo with a French address and telephone number in the footer. The letterhead reads, "Ton Eminence Shenphen Rinpoche, Chef Supreme de la Ligne Tersar."

583. Lesley Shearer, interview with author, Littleton, CO, Feb. 25, 2019.

584. Allen and Rose Maruyama, interview with author, Aurora, CO, Mar. 29, 2017.

585. Glendora ("Dusty") Taylor and her daughter Kathy, interview with author, Denver, May 23, 2017.

586. Rose and Allen Maruyama, "Nepal."

587. Lesley Shearer, interview with author, Littleton, CO, Apr. 14, 2017.

588. Rose and Allen Maruyama, "Nepal."

589. Lesley Shearer, interview with author, Littleton, CO, Apr. 14, 2017.

590. Khanal, "Three-Year Boy."

591. Allen and Rose Maruyama, interview with author, Aurora, CO, Apr. 10, 2017.

592. Glendora ("Dusty") Taylor and her daughter Kathy, interview with author, Denver, May 23, 2017.

593. Allen and Rose Maruyama, interview with author, Aurora, CO, Apr. 17, 2017.

594. Seichi Otsuka, interview with author, Denver, Feb. 20, 2017.

595. Allen and Rose Maruyama, interview with author, Aurora, CO, Apr. 17, 2017.

596. Lesley Shearer, interview with author, Littleton, CO, Apr. 14, 2017.

597. Allen and Rose Maruyama, interview with author, Aurora, CO, Feb. 22, 2017.

598. Allen and Rose Maruyama, interview with author, Aurora, CO, Apr. 17, 2017.

599. Lesley Shearer, interview with author, Littleton, CO, Apr. 14, 2017.

600. Allen Maruyama, interview with author, Aurora, CO, Nov. 30, 2016.

601. Sarah Maruyama-Biles Brady, interview with author, Highlands Ranch, CO, Feb. 28, 2017.

602. Allen and Rose Maruyama, interview with author, Aurora, CO, Mar. 6, 2017.

603. Sarah Maruyama-Biles Brady, interview with author, Highlands Ranch, CO, Feb. 28, 2017.

604. Allen and Rose Maruyama, interview with author, Aurora, CO, Feb. 22, 2017.

605. Kenneth L. Barley, interview with author, Denver, Mar. 27, 2017.

606. Allen and Rose Maruyama, interviews with author, Aurora, CO, Feb. 22, 2017, and Mar. 29, 2017.

607. Shirley Burkhart, interview with author, Denver, Mar. 20, 2017.

608. Allen and Rose Maruyama, interview with author, Aurora, CO, Mar. 29, 2017.

609. Allen and Rose Maruyama, interview with author, Aurora, CO, May 23, 2017.

610. June and Minoru Mochizuki, interview with author, Denver, May 22, 2017.

611. Oremus Bible Browser, Phil 3:20.

612. Grace Kaori Suzuki, email to author, Dec. 11, 2020. Rev. Suzuki translated the *Shodō* and indicated the full spelling of Rev. Saeki's first name seems to be Yoichiro. See image on page 156.

613. Pacific Citizen Staff, "Norman Mineta's Legacy."

614. JACL National, "Setsuko's Secret."

615. Allen Maruyama, "Personal Statement of Faith."

616. Allen Maruyama, interview with author, Aurora, CO, Feb. 25, 2019.

617. Allen and Rose Maruyama, interviews with author, Aurora, CO, Nov. 4, 2016, and Nov. 13, 2016.

618. Allen and Rose Maruyama, interview with author, Aurora, CO, Apr. 17, 2017.

619. As has been noted, Reinhold Niebuhr, Paul Tillich, and Presbyterian pastor Aurelia Fule were among many notable theologians and cultural critics affiliated with Union Theological Seminary in the twentieth century.

620. Allen and Rose Maruyama, interview with author, Aurora, CO, Apr. 17, 2017.

621. Longfield, "William Merrill." The summation of the debate is taken from various portions of Longfield's article.

622. Allen and Rose Maruyama, interview with author, Aurora, CO, Apr. 17, 2017.

Epilogue

Resistance and Resilience

On June 12, 2019, Allen greeted me at his apartment door with, "I have bad news."[1]

He handed me a copy of a document on Denver Presbytery's letterhead dated and hand-delivered on June 7. Its title: "Conclusion of Investigation, Charges to be Filed, Alternate Forms of Resolution." The information had been compiled by a presbytery Investigative Committee (IC). It instructed Allen to respond within ten days. The "Conclusion" informs him that the IC is "prepared to move forward and file" six charges of sexual abuse that allegedly took place "on or about 1970 through 1992," while he was "Co-Pastor at Montview Presbyterian Church of Denver."[2]

The accusations were followed eight months later by the 2020 COVID-19 pandemic, another life-altering event. How Allen has met these threats illustrates that he continues to handle the vicissitudes of life based on his values. His reactions show that our responses can be redemptive if we have agency and/or the support of others.

In my discussion about the IC's decision, I focus primarily on two, public-facing documents and Allen's responses to them. The documents are the June 7 IC "Conclusion" letter and an August 30 letter written over the signatures of the Montview co-pastors and addressed to Montview church members.[3]

Allegations of sexual abuse must be taken seriously and thoroughly investigated. Those who come forward with their stories are to be listened to carefully and with respect. Institutions and individuals must be held

accountable. However, even a cursory reading of the IC's "Conclusion" letter raises questions about the merits of its evidence and the adequacy of its
process. Examining these questions is not straightforward due to the letter's
fragmentary organization and flawed logic.

In terms of the merits of its evidence, the overarching "on or about
1970 through 1992" time frame for each charge is too broad. This is a common expression to use when actual dates are unknown, but the breadth of
the IC's uncertainty is incongruous with the specificity of each of the six
charges. In addition to this lack of clarity, there are factual errors. Allen was
living in Iowa from 1970 through part of 1972, not Denver. Furthermore, he
did not serve as a co-pastor until 1975. He was initially an associate.

Since the events were alleged to have taken place thirty to fifty years
ago, neither the committee nor Allen can depend on the accuracy of witnesses' memories. In addition, Allen retired from Montview twenty-seven
years ago. So much time has elapsed that many who could speak on his
behalf are incapacitated, no longer at Montview, or have died. Rose is dead.
Three of the six charges concern a woman who is herself dead, compromis-
ing Allen's ability to cross-examine her if this matter were to go to trial.
The dynamic in her case goes beyond the typical "he said/she said" to a
convoluted "he said/they said that she said."

The evidence supporting each charge is also of questionable merit. The
first charge is made on behalf of the deceased. It claims that Allen forced
himself upon her by exposing himself and touching her inappropriately. The
IC puts forth six items to support this charge.

The first item consists of notes claimed to have been taken by the
deceased from a 2002 meeting between her and the stated clerk of the
presbytery. The notes were provided by one of the deceased's survivors. The
IC represents the notes as describing that the accused forcibly pulled the
woman "into a closet in his basement office," exposed himself, then forcibly
touched her inappropriately. The survivor's presentation of the notes simply
asserts their validity, an instance of "they said that she wrote."

Item two is testimony of the survivor who provided the notes. The survivor's testimony is about memories of conversations that reflect the notes'
content, in effect, an instance of "they said that she said." Memories are also
assertions, but evidence consists of a body of facts.

Item three of the IC's supporting evidence consists of two more survivor assertions. The survivor says that one of Allen's colleagues was present
at the 2002 meeting. The IC does not indicate that it verified this person's
presence, and merely asserting presence without verification of content is
not proof of the validity of the notes. The survivor's next assertion is that the
handwriting on the purported 2002 notes is that of the deceased, equivalent

to "they said that she wrote." The IC's "Conclusion" does not indicate that it independently verified this claim.

Item four concerns the presence of another of Allen's colleagues at the meeting. The IC represents only that the colleague confirmed being present at the 2002 meeting and hearing the complaint. The IC does not report whether the colleague confirmed or denied that the purported notes represent the complaint as it was put forth in 2002. Again, only confirming presence at a meeting does not confirm the validity of the notes.

Item five of the supporting evidence is short. The IC states it has testimony from the stated clerk who attended the meeting. The IC gives no indication that the stated clerk confirmed or denied the content of the notes. Item five only establishes that the stated clerk was also at the meeting. Once again, presence does not authenticate the content of the notes.

The sixth item of the IC's evidence is Allen's testimony that he counseled the deceased, had a basement office with a closet, and was "Co-Pastor at Montview Presbyterian church during 1970–1992."[4] Item six offers some facts, but that he counseled the deceased at one time and that his basement office had a closet does not confirm that the alleged events happened. As indicated, the facts about the dates of his employment and job title are incorrect.

As part of my research done before the IC report had become public knowledge, I had interviewed the colleague who confirmed being at the 2002 meeting and the one the survivor claims was there. Neither indicated to me that anything was ever improper about Allen's behavior, nor had they alluded to a 2002 meeting. I infer that they never mentioned this meeting because it did not establish that anything untoward happened.

Because Allen and Rose had both spoken at length about how negatively many people had reacted when Allen announced in 1992 that he was going into massage therapy, I was interested to hear the reactions of these two colleagues to his new vocation. One acknowledged some members and other colleagues were uncomfortable with it but emphasized having no knowledge of any instance when he violated boundaries.[5]

After he was confronted with the IC's "Conclusion" document, Allen frequently referred to it in trying to understand its content. When he reflected about the IC's report of the 2002 meeting, he said he remembered going to lunch with the stated clerk around the time he moved back from Kansas, perhaps in 2002 or 2003. He was asked if there was anything to a rumor about inappropriate behavior. He had answered no; nothing came of it. He did not give it another thought. He does point out that Denver Presbytery asked him to serve on its General Council at that time.[6]

The second and third charges also concern the deceased, and the IC's evidence again prompts questions about merit. The second charge relies once more on written documentation furnished by the survivor—one signed greeting card and one handwritten note. The survivor claims to have discovered them after the woman's death. The "Conclusion" makes no mention of dates on the card or note, which implies that there are none.

A troublesome aspect of the second charge is its representation that the survivor paid a handwriting expert to compare a May 2019 signature, purported to be Allen's, to the writing on the note and card. The expert concluded that all three were written by the same person, allegedly Allen Maruyama.[7]

Allen subsequently inquired about the intricacies of handwriting analysis. He learned that it is impossible to meaningfully compare writing from thirty to fifty years ago to a person's current penmanship. Samples from the same time period, known to be written by the person in question, would have to be used.[8]

Charge three follows with what the IC itself calls "circumstantial evidence" of a similar nature, again provided by the survivor. It consists of six more "sexually suggestive" cards, all unsigned and, presumably, undated, but also from the period "on or about 1970 through 1992." A "suggestive" phrase apparently typical of the handwritten note and cards is, "Have you ever thought of wearing a mini skirt?"[9]

When the IC showed Allen the cards and note, Allen says his reaction was that the phrases were "outlandish," things he would never express, much less think. He says he "never engaged in sexual insinuations." The cards struck him as a "sentimental type of greeting card," perhaps of a Hallmark nature. He says he never sent sentimental greeting cards to anyone in any church he served.[10]

According to the rules of discipline in the *Book of Order* of the PC(USA), an IC is responsible for conducting a thorough inquiry before deciding to file charges.[11] However, the IC accepted analysis about handwriting paid for by the survivor of the complainant as valid. There was no independent verification of the validity of any of the written material. The items that the IC puts forth in its "Conclusion" document as evidence to support the first charge are either not verified or fall into a category of hearsay. This does not meet the standard of a thorough inquiry. The IC's evidence only confirms that a meeting took place, that all but one of the named people were there, that Allen had counseled the woman, and that Allen had a basement office with a closet at some time during his employment at Montview.

Charges four and five concern a second woman whom Allen had allegedly tried to kiss on two occasions. The IC document asserts that on one occasion he pushed her against the wall at the door of her home after a meeting, and on the other occasion he pushed her against her car after a meeting at a restaurant and again tried to kiss her. Both times she claims that she slapped him and he left.[12]

These two charges are representative of "he said/she said" dilemmas. Allen thinks she might have served on one of the church boards. If the woman he remembers is the accuser, he says he was never in her home. Meetings of the board on which she served would have taken place at the church with a group of people. He does not remember, nor can he imagine, that he ever went to a restaurant with the person he thinks might be the accuser. He says he attempted to explain to the IC how these things simply could not have happened, particularly in the way they were described, and that he would never treat anyone that way. He felt his explanations were useless and that the IC had prejudged him.[13]

When he reflects on his behavior, he remembers that the only time he ever tried to kiss a woman who might not have welcomed it was an awkward interaction with a co-worker he dated when he was a teenager employed at the cantaloupe shed in Las Animas. "I didn't even date in college. The women my friends tried to get me to date were all too tall!"[14]

The sixth charge relates the experience of a third woman and is also a "he said/she said" conundrum. It describes one instance of inappropriate touching "on or about 1970 through 1992." Additionally, she says that she generally "felt discomfort in his presence."[15] Feelings of discomfort can be attributed to any number of factors, from worries about family to pressure to complete a work assignment. Discomfort is not evidence of sexual abuse. Allen's response to the charge is, "What [she] says just tears my heart out."[16]

In terms of the IC's process, as Allen and I discussed its "Conclusion" document on June 12, he gave the impression of being overwhelmed. He tried to piece together the sequence of the developments. He said that in February he had received a letter alluding to unspecified issues. He had not imagined what they might be.[17]

The IC's June 7 charging document mentions a letter dated February 21, 2019, apprising him of "an investigation into allegations of sexual abuse," which might be the letter Allen remembers receiving. If so, it appears he either did not understand it or did not give it proper attention.[18]

He explained that when he was told to attend his one meeting with the IC between the February letter and his receipt of its "Conclusion" document in June, he had only been advised that he "might want to bring some support." The IC confronted him at this meeting with the substance of the charges as they came to be represented in its "Conclusion." As a pastor, Allen translated "bring some support" into "bring a friend." He brought his friend Rev. Larry Angus. "Support" should have been specified as "bring legal representation" for what awaited him.

The process outlined in the rules of discipline indicates that, at the start of such a meeting, an IC must inform the person being accused of their rights. These include the right to remain silent, to be represented by counsel, and, if charges are later to be filed, to have counsel appointed if the person is unable to secure it.[19]

It will become evident from the IC's questioning at the meeting and from an event described below that Allen should have been told, perhaps also in writing, that he needed legal counsel for the meeting. When he and Angus met with the IC, according to item six of the evidence supporting the first charge, he confirmed "that he was Co-Pastor at Montview Presbyterian church during 1970 to 1992."[20] As discussed above, that information is incorrect. He of all people should have recognized that. Why would Allen testify to it?

According to Angus, the committee's questioning was "aggressive" and "mean," and Allen was treated "rudely." They "roasted" him and "kept piling it on until he didn't know what hit him."[21] Allen says he was stunned by the accusations, which he found to be "far out and ridiculous."[22] The IC failed to make an accurate assessment of his capacity to go through this process.

Because Allen was a leader in the denomination and the presbytery and is a retired co-pastor of a large urban church, those who do not know him might not notice his vulnerabilities. In the 1990s, he served on Denver Presbytery's Permanent Judicial Commission himself, a body that would have been involved in disciplinary matters such as this. If the committee assumed that someone with this background could have sufficient knowledge to prepare himself and interact with the IC, its assessment was insufficient.

Whether Allen could function at the same level as he has in the past was an evaluation anyone could have made who was at the October 23, 2018, Denver Presbytery meeting that occurred approximately four months before the IC's February letter. At issue was presbytery's decision to grant an exception so Montview could call a particular co-pastor. Allen was invested in the debate because it not only involved a Montview co-pastor, whom he supported, but also because he had served on the General Assembly committee that dealt decades ago with the very exception in question.

The presbytery assembly had determined that the vote to grant the exception would be taken by secret ballot. Allen stood and moved that a voice vote should be taken in the interest of time. A confusing sequence of events followed. When the pastor moderating the meeting indicated the vote would still be taken by secret ballot, Allen strongly objected. Awkward exchanges took place between him and the moderator.

After the meeting, Allen confided that he was afraid he had made a fool of himself. He thought the assembly had affirmed his motion to take a voice vote and the moderator was acting against its will. Only later had someone explained to Allen that the opposite had happened; the assembly had concurred in the preference for a secret ballot.

Several commissioners indicated to me as we left the meeting that they had felt very uncomfortable during Allen's back and forth with the moderator. No one knew what Allen was protesting, but each said something to the effect that they had wanted to rescue Allen.[23]

The incident revealed that Allen's energy level (his "go, go, go" personality) and his determination cloak his difficulty with functioning at the same level as when he was in elected leadership roles. The lesson: it was important to confirm how the ninety-two-year-old Allen manages information. The process issue is that the IC did not assess his hearing ability or his effectiveness in its meeting with him. Allen's failure to notice the incorrect dates and title and to function effectively on the floor of presbytery, and his inattention to the February letter, together with the adversarial nature of the investigation, all raise the question about process: Should the investigation have proceeded?

He did register that the IC's assertion about the basement office and the closet was inadequate. Allen says he tried to describe that the small, cramped closet was filled with supplies and that two people could not possibly fit into it, much less conduct themselves in the way described. Allen thinks it was clear that the committee would not go to the church to "even look at the closet."

Allen offered to meet with them again to give them his pastoral assessment about the counseling with the husband and the deceased and to explain that the counseling was prelude to a traumatic divorce. Allen summarizes the dynamic within the family as a "very sad and painful case." Allen did not think the IC took his offer to give them the details seriously. "They [the IC] had made up their minds."[24]

According to the rules of discipline, Allen had the right during the course of the investigation to ask for a review of the IC's procedures.[25] When Allen noted its apparent lack of curiosity about the closet and the counseling, he could have asked for such a review. He did not. With legal counsel present, he might have effectively questioned the IC's procedures.

After having had that single meeting with Allen and Angus, the IC states in its June 7 "Conclusion" document that it has sufficient evidence to determine probable cause. It is ready to move forward and file charges.[26]

The IC's process seems to have complied with the rules of discipline of the PC(USA) on the surface, but it apparently did not investigate the veracity of Allen's responses, nor did it prepare him properly for the one meeting it had with him. The merits of its evidence are questionable. They rely on inaccurate dates and hearsay, the memories of the survivor of an alleged victim, evidence provided by and paid for by that survivor, and circumstantial evidence also provided by the survivor, all without independent verification.

Regardless, the IC gives Allen two choices. He can initiate "Alternative Forms of Resolution" (AFR) and accept its censure before it files charges, or he can proceed to a full trial. If he chooses to "take advantage of this opportunity [the AFR]," the "Conclusion" document stipulates that he has to plead guilty to the charges. An advocate will be provided during the settlement process.

The IC's censure raises more questions of process. First, there are four degrees of censure in disciplinary cases: rebuke; rebuke with supervised rehabilitation; temporary exclusion from exercise of ordered ministry; and removal from ordered ministry.[27]

Although the IC's evidence is weak, the alleged events happened about thirty to fifty years ago, and Allen is ninety-two years of age and essentially confined to his apartment because he no longer drives, the IC chooses the third level, one of the more harsh choices. The censure reads as follows: "Temporary exclusion pursuant to D-12.0104 [of the rules of discipline] for a period of ten years, including acts of repentance: public acknowledgment of guilt, 60 hours of community service, and a contribution toward the documented psychological expenses incurred by each of the three victims. Further, during the period of ten years, temporary exclusion from the function of ordered ministry, and exclusion from membership."

What lesser forms of sexual assault would merit the level one and two censures? Sixty hours of community service for someone in Allen's circumstances? Even more perplexing, it is inconceivable that the censure stipulates ten years, which for a man of ninety-two is a life sentence. The IC had choices. The rules of discipline do not mandate ten years.

The enticement to take an AFR plea bargain is that charges will not be filed, nor will the accused have to pay for legal representation. The drawback is that the AFR offer assumes guilt. Pleading guilty is not a real option if a person is innocent. An innocent person cannot plead guilty with integrity.

Allen's other choice was a full ecclesiastical trial. If he chose a full trial, he would pay for his defense, and it is prescribed that his counsel be a member of the PC(USA). As he considered this option during our June 12 conversation, Allen said he had known plenty of attorneys when he served at Montview, but, of course, those relationships were well in the past.

As we talked, we noted that his deadline to respond was June 17. He had only five days to decide between the AFR and going to trial. He had not yet talked over his options with John and Sarah. He asked for suggestions about other people he might consult.[28]

Allen's assessment of the IC's "Conclusion" and how he eventually made his decision reveal his character. The decision he and his family reached was in part based on a practical consideration of the numbers. In terms of the AFR, those numbers were his age with its implications and his potential liability for contributing to the "documented psychological expenses incurred by each of the three victims." That provision seemed so open-ended as to imply that he would be liable for, perhaps, many thousands of dollars, given the 1970–92 span of years.

The trial option involved its own costs. He learned legal fees would likely be $5000 or more. Payment for a writing expert had to be added to the tally. He understood that charge could range from $350 to $1000 per hour. The unknown cost, if he lost, was still his contribution "toward the documented psychological expenses incurred by each of the three victims."[29]

Before reaching his decision, Allen spoke with the stated clerk of Denver Presbytery and an attorney to better understand his choices. He says he began to articulate for himself that "I'm ninety-two. My life has gone by. I've been very fortunate. After such a successful new vocation of being a massage therapist and a Reiki master, my life is over. As a Presbyterian pastor, I did what I could do. Even if I went to trial and said the accusations were not correct, that they were so far out, outlandish and ridiculous, that would have taken another month or more. It's not worth my time, my money, or Presbytery's time and money."[30]

He decided to demit the ministry, that is, to renounce his ordination, which would remove him from being subject to the charges and the censure. As his friend Lesley Shearer had observed, "Without knowing it, he is an aikido master. . . . With aikido, you . . . let [your opponent] topple by the energy of his own offense. You step out of the way."[31]

To demit was to step aside. From his perspective, his practice of ministry was over, regardless of the accusations, and demitting did not diminish his identity. "I'll always be a Presbyterian minister, ordained by Pueblo Presbytery."[32]

Allen felt, though, that he would be "sad if word got around. I'm so embarrassed."[33] Word did get around. The embarrassment, the shame, was made public. The charges were read, as required by the process, at the August 10, 2019, Denver Presbytery meeting. His demittal was also announced. Neither Allen, Angus, nor I attended.

From the outset of our conversations about his biography, Allen had given me permission to interview whomever I wanted and to pursue any research avenues I decided to explore. He repeated this carte blanche permission in various ways from time to time. No one and nothing was off limits, which implied that he had nothing to hide. He was willing to be exposed. Now, though, he was being exposed as someone he did not know himself to be.

Even more shaming awaited. Several Montview elders were among those at the presbytery meeting. Allen said the Montview co-pastors informed him that a letter of explanation to the entire membership, to be sent out over their signatures, was being considered. He understood that session would make the final decision.

Such a letter would only amplify his disgrace. The allegations predate his 1972 employment at Montview and surfaced only after his retirement almost thirty years ago. Because many of the members who knew him have died or moved, the letter would convey little meaning to the majority of current members for whom he is an unknown. Allen said John and Sarah were "adamant" that such a letter should not be distributed.[34]

However, it was. When I saw him in early September, Allen showed me his copy, dated August 30, 2019. He reported that representatives from the church had met with him and Sarah before it was mailed. They had showed Allen a draft, and his only suggested revision had been to include the words, "Allen has denied any improprieties during his time at Montview."[35]

Several aspects of the letter invite comment. The letter is quite formal, but throughout it refers to him as "Allen." The familiarity implied by using only his first name does not match the gravity of the subject and is curious because he is unknown to the majority of recipients. At the very least, the first name reference denies him respect, even if inadvertently.

Perhaps those who sent the letter were trying to avoid the title "Reverend" as he has demitted the ministry. However, he does retain the honors granted him by his PhD. By not referring to him as "Dr. Maruyama," the letter reduces his stature. In so doing, it suggests several interpretive possibilities: it demeans him; it is paternalistic, as a doddery, senile man is treated; or the first-name basis might communicate affection in spite of the letter's contents.

The overall sequence establishes him as persona non grata in relationship to the Montview congregation. It implies guilt in its first three paragraphs, even though the signatories are careful to write only that they are "deeply troubled" by allegations of sexual misconduct filed against Allen, and they take them "very seriously." They explain that the presbytery IC received the allegations and evidence from three different persons (adults) and found probable cause.

The third paragraph reads, "Allen was advised of these findings, presented with evidence, and was offered opportunity to plead guilty and enter into AFR, or to move forward with a Judicial Commission (i.e. ecclesiastical trial)." The Montview letter rightly represents Allen's choices: it rests with him to prove his innocence.

The fourth paragraph begins with his denial of improprieties. It continues, "After being presented with evidence and charges stemming from the investigation, and after being offered an opportunity to enter into AFR, Allen renounced his jurisdiction in the Presbyterian Church (USA). This effectively means he has surrendered his ministerial credentials and any authority to practice sacramental ministry in the denomination."

The order of the paragraph could imply that, although he denies any improprieties, his defense is weak. A person with a credible defense would not need to surrender his credentials. However, there could be alternate interpretations for Allen's demittal. For one, he does not have the physical and financial resources to mount a defense. Also, while the letter's first sentence establishes that Allen "served at Montview from 1972 to 1992," unlike the IC's erroneous 1970–1992 dates, the Montview letter neglects to note that one of the accusers is dead, nor does it call attention to the fact that the charges were brought almost thirty years after his retirement. If the letter had recognized these factors, a Montview member might consider yet other reasons for Allen to surrender his credentials. The accuracy of witnesses' memories has probably further deteriorated; some have died. Rose, his supportive spouse of sixty-three years, is dead.

The Montview letter moves from explaining the demittal to describing its consequences. When a clergy person renounces jurisdiction as part of a disciplinary process, the allegations must be "read aloud at a presbytery meeting." That happened on August 10. It concludes by noting that the "charges remain unadjudicated." Again, the order of the paragraph implies that Allen's guilt or innocence has not been, nor might it ever be, determined. The outcome is ambiguous, at best.

The letter then changes focus from Allen to Montview and a description of its "robust policies and procedures to prevent misconduct and abuse." The institution has twin responsibilities: to protect its members, as well as itself. This is reflected in the pastoral concern expressed in a later paragraph for "those for whom this news may trigger pain from previous abuse or trauma."

The intervening paragraph, though, returns to Allen's situation. It states that, in accordance with Montview's guidelines for former pastors, Allen "has agreed to move to another worshipping community, and is expected not to discuss this or other church matters with members of Montview."[36]

Indeed, general guidelines for departing pastors are that they make a clear break from the congregations they leave. Their primary worshipping community will be elsewhere, and they should not fulfill a pastoral role with former congregants. Montview has not been Allen's primary worshipping community for almost thirty years. Immediately following his retirement, he served in other churches in Denver Presbytery until he moved to Kansas in the mid-1990s, but Montview is expecting something more: that he not even talk with Montview members about "this or other church matters." Given that this letter is announcing charges of sexual abuse that remain "unadjudicated," the effect of this expectation is that of an old-fashioned shunning.

Contrary to the stipulation that Allen cannot speak with Montview members about any of this, unmentioned is the fact that none of them is refrained from speculating about and discussing these matters. Members will talk about and process this information, but Allen is denied that opportunity. His responses are suppressed, save for the short sentence indicating he has denied improprieties.

There is something particularly humiliating about this explicit statement about Allen's silence. It is an overreach because its practical effect is to isolate Allen from healing resources. It is an overreach because such a harsh expectation would be merited only if a person were guilty, but the overall effect of the letter is to imply just such guilt. The overreach is unwarranted in terms of Christian charity. From the perspective of those in the congregation who do remember Allen, and remember him fondly, the expectation about his silence does not recognize the depth of their love for him and their appreciation for his ministry.

Allen infrequently attended services or functions at Montview in recent years, but Rose's memorial service was held there January 6, 2018. He was happy to see those who attended from the congregation and eager to introduce me, implying his relationship with Montview was still emotionally significant for him. Now his relationship to it is that of an outcast. Absent contact with Montview, the only ongoing relationship he had pre-COVID with a worshipping community was with the St. Andrew's Sunday morning worship service. To emphasize, because he has demitted his ordination, he no longer has a voice in presbytery, either.

It is the case that because institutions controlled the narrative for all too long, those suffering abuse and trauma could not speak their truth. Their voices were suppressed, and the church must take corrective action. Ironically, Allen's is now the suppressed voice.

Allen, the pastor who spoke early and loudly on behalf of not only women suffering sexual abuse but also unequal employment opportunity, in the church and in the larger society.

Allen, who spoke, wrote, taught, and advocated not only for women but for other underrepresented groups, nationally and internationally, who suffer from any number of abuses stemming from such inequalities as those tied to race, ethnicity, gender identity, sexual orientation, poverty, and racism.

Allen, who was excoriated by conservative pastors for taking such stances.

Allen, whose formative young adult experience was one of shame as a Japanese American because he wore the face of the enemy but who found his voice because Presbyterians befriended him.

The PC(USA) now holds him at arm's length. His initial reactions are reflected in several titles he suggested for this biography after he received the IC's "Conclusion." All are variations on "How to Shatter/Destroy a Good Life."

Although Sarah and John were at first incensed by the whole "mess," as Allen refers to it, he tries to follow their evolving advice to let it go and move on. He is able to laugh when he quotes them as characterizing many of the people he knew at Montview, for whom all the "mess" would have significance, as "dead or too sick to care!"[37]

A series of crises and recoveries marks the aftermath of the accusations and his dimittal. Several months after the Montview letter was mailed, I asked in a phone call, "How are you doing?" He heard my question as "What have you been doing?" His answer was, "Nothing. I have been doing nothing. I take it easy. I read, do my exercises, and watch TV." Later in the call he said his children were concerned that he was in a "state of depression."[38]

Sarah and John were right to be concerned. For Allen, sitting around, save for exercising, was doing next to nothing. This represented a change. Prior to the IC's and Montview's ultimatums, Allen had continued his and Rose's hospitality by inviting friends for lunch or dinner at St. Andrew's. He and I had to schedule our interview times around such engagements, some with church and presbytery friends, some with people he knew from his years as a massage therapist. I know their conversations were lively and lengthy because sometimes I would arrive before his guests were ready to leave.

Allen had involved himself in any number of scheduled activities at St. Andrew's that took him out of the apartment, even after Rose's death, and he continued to strategize about how to support the homeless program at the Fort Lyon facility—another ironic outcome of the IC's proposed censure.

One of its provisions was to require "60 hours of community service." Subsequent to all the "mess," though, Allen withdrew from his active community participation and advocacy efforts. Not only does he no longer drive, his cachet and connections as an advocate derived from his position as an elder statesman of the church.[39]

He continued to attend exercise classes at St. Andrew's, though. In October, he missed the last step on his way to a session, fell, and hit his head. He needed about fourteen stitches, and the doctors said he had broken a bone. They were going to do surgery, which he declined. He was hospitalized for several days, and they only released him when he promised he would use a walker, for which he saw no need. Missing the step was simply "an accident."[40]

Certainly some of his discouragement was associated with his health, especially the difficulty he has with swallowing. The problem has plagued him for years but is getting worse. When he spent over an hour with his doctors at the VA hospital in late February to early March 2020, they told him nothing more could be done, other than continuing with his physical therapy. However, they noted that the therapy would stop in three to four months anyway, due to Medicare regulations.

The doctor he has seen at the VA for over a decade attributed his swallowing struggles to the cancer treatments he had in the 1980s, but he added that such difficulties are a common problem with aging. While this might be true, it is not unusual for physicians to attribute all sorts of health problems to "aging," as though they are intractable, and fail to offer appropriate treatment.[41]

Discontinuing the therapy sessions itself was a loss of something meaningful to Allen—the activity and interactions at the VA that came with an appointment. The forthcoming withdrawal of regular medical support seemed all the more poignant given its correspondence with the loss of the PC(USA)'s support subsequent to the IC's actions.

One might shrug off this progressive isolation as yet another aspect of aging, but the withdrawal of medical support and of the support of a significant community of faith seemed particularly heartless in that he had no control over either. The church's was the outcome of a process for which he did not have the social, physical, emotional, nor financial resources to engage effectively. The withdrawal of physical therapy was a medical decision that may or may not be premature and was dictated by medical professionals and insurance regulations.

Moreover, it is nearly impossible to avoid seeing Allen's later years and his feelings of sadness and embarrassment about the abuse charges in the context of the trauma of his adolescent shame. That shame was born in the ignominy of being a Japanese-American teenager at a time when even the president of the United States questioned the humanity of those who bore any trace of Japanese ancestry—to the point of ordering the mass incarceration of all of them living on the West Coast.

Allen could not hide that identity and felt "subhuman," as diligent as he was as a high school student athlete to prove himself worthy. Not until he earned the title of Doctor of Philosophy in 1972 and stood for Moderator at the 1980 and 1990 General Assemblies did he feel his striving had brought him close to the "unreachable star" of white-majority acceptance. He believed people were beginning to see him for who he was.[42]

From my perspective, Allen, now in his nineties, is again shunned. He bears the shame of accusations that represent him as someone other than he knows himself to be. Due to his choice to demit and Montview's strictures, he is prohibited from speaking his truth, even if he had the voice and energy to do so. The burden of this shame seems all the heavier because those not seeing him as he is are church professionals and members—friends and partners in ministry, representative of Presbyterians of his past who had befriended him and validated his existence as a teenager.

This is not Allen's perspective. He says he did not react to the accusations in the manner in which he "reacted as my teenage self" to the hatred heaped on Japanese Americans after the Pearl Harbor attack. "That's not how I felt."[43]

After the Montview letter was mailed, he said he received two letters of support from long-time members and one phone call. They meant a good deal to him, and he was convincing himself, as Sarah and John had assured him, that most people were already forgetting about all the "mess."[44]

When he reminisces, he maintains that while he may have discarded the external expressions of ministry in the PC(USA), his sense of calling and vocation is not something that he will ever lose. After the cancer scare, followed by the 1986 sabbatical and study of Buddhism, he had thought, "now I can do something to heal people. Jesus tried to get his disciples to heal people through touch, so I followed that pattern." The speciality that appealed to him most was Reiki, the laying on of hands. The 1990 moderator defeat and his 1992 retirement freed him for his vocational reconfiguration, when he felt he was doing God's work. He repeatedly says he is satisfied that he did more through healing touch to help people than he ever did as a pastor.

About his 1992 retirement, he is of the opinion that "I had fulfilled all my obligations to the church" and is satisfied that he had "done all I could do." Even though the first loss at the 1980 General Assembly was a disappointment, he sees it in the context of all the conservative attacks and the

departure of the Denver Presbyterian churches that left in spite of his conversations with the departing pastors. He emphasizes that those churches
who supported only their friends with mission money did so to the detri-
ment of the mission of the larger church. Denver Presbytery was right to
confront them.

He points out that in spite of the subsequent attacks directed at him
personally about their departures, a significant number of 1980 General Assembly commissioners still gave him their votes on the early ballots, and
Montview continued to embrace him after his defeat. They "gave that big
party on my return. Forty to fifty people were there, and a band! I was able
to take that loss."

He also cherishes all the enthusiasm for his 1990 run, including from a
number of Montview members, especially the support of President Reagan's
personal physician, Dr. Daniel A. Ruge. Although Allen does not mention
it, this connection to Ronald Reagan, the US president who apologized for
the World War II incarcerations and signed the 1988 Civil Liberties Act
that paid camp survivors or their descendants reparations, seems particularly significant. Ruge's affirmation could be seen as ameliorating the official
shame visited on JaJAs during World War II.

Also, because he thought Vice Moderator Herbert Meza was his real
competition in 1990, as did many General Assembly observers, that Gwynn
came out of nowhere and surprised everyone blunted that loss. He consistently expresses his admiration for Gwynn. "I don't know of any other moderator than Price Gwynn who did so much for the church. I had completed
my work."[45]

As he and Rose had pointed out, though, the negative reaction to his
new commitment to massage therapy when he announced it in 1992 underscored the potential toxicity of touch. Typical reactions included that of
Rev. Dr. C. Samuel Calian, his close friend from Dubuque days: "What the
hell are you thinking?"[46]

Even so, Allen forged ahead in his new vocation, committed to his
vision to integrate spiritual and physical healing. When he looks back on
those post-Montview decades, he feels he successfully accomplished that
integration during his seven years in Kansas City.

Presbyterians there still connected his name to General Assembly activities, so he was immediately taken into that presbytery and had "plenty of
opportunities to preach." A caucus of seven to eight liberal pastors invited
him to be part of their group. He taught classes at a large church with several
thousand members. He and the half-time clerk of the presbytery started a
new church (the one of which Sarah and her family were so fond), "something I always wanted to do."

Balancing the ministries of preaching and healing was sometimes a juggling act, though. Concurrently, he practiced massage and Reiki at a large salon and taught Reiki. "Because I was doing both [preaching and healing], I was burning the candle at both ends."[47]

Even when he returned to Colorado, his healing and preaching ministries continued, but with less intensity. Denver Presbytery invited him to serve on General Council. He re-established his Colorado massage and Reiki practices and responded to Craig Hospital's regular requests for his skills as a massage therapist and Reiki master. He was pleasantly surprised when he looked up "massage therapists in Denver" on his computer and saw his name near the top of the list as one of just a few who were recommended. Only when he and Rose moved to the St. Andrew's facility in 2013, both at the age of eighty-six, did those ministries further diminish.

Allen reviews these details with satisfaction. He can no longer affirm unequivocally, as he did in front of the 1980 General Assembly commissioners assembled in Cobo Hall, that while his larger community looked at him with suspicion and distrust during World War II, Presbyterians befriended him. However, he often repeats the theme that "as a Presbyterian pastor I had accomplished all I could . . . . My ministry is over, but I'll always be a Presbyterian minister."[48]

The COVID-19 pandemic imposed yet more layers of physical and social isolation on Allen's daily routines in March 2020. St. Andrew's residents were confined to their rooms with meals delivered to their doors. All educational, social, and exercise activities were canceled, including the Sunday worship services. Outside visitors were prohibited. "Sociable" Allen and Sarah continued their daily phone calls, and occasionally met and walked together in the parking lot, all the while keeping physical distance and wearing masks.

Sarah thought Allen looked like he was losing weight, and he complained of stomach pain from time to time. The increased isolation seemed to be taking its toll.

On Memorial Day, she decided she should take him to her home for a little family gathering. The social contact was worth the risk, and everyone would follow the proper protocols. He called that morning to say he felt so bad that he "didn't want to come." Still, she went to pick him up and learned he had fallen. He had been sitting on a bench in front of St. Andrew's, getting some sun, but a gust of wind blew a piece of mail across the parking lot. He chased it. He had quite a scrape on his head from the tumble.

For Sarah, the call and the parking lot fall were reasons enough to get him to the emergency room. A blood test revealed massive infection. Further tests showed its source—a blocked bile duct needing immediate surgery. But that required general anesthesia, not recommended for a man in his 90s. The doctor said the sepsis meant he would be dead in days without surgery. His Do Not Resuscitate order prompted a family discussion about whether to operate or not. Did the DNR apply in this instance?

It was decided to proceed with surgery. By the following weekend, Allen was headed back to St. Andrew's, and son John planned to stay with him in isolation for the next seven days.

Instead, Allen was transferred to the skilled nursing unit where he had the benefit of regular interactions with staff. His health status was more closely monitored, unlike when it was declining in the isolation of his fourth floor apartment with the accumulating infection from the blocked bile duct. His nursing unit room was on the first floor, so Sarah and other family members could wave to him from outside his window.[49]

The process of growing old will eventually entail indignity and loss, and Allen has suffered his share in the past several years—his separation from the PC(USA) and the isolation of COVID-19, his diminishing health and recent falls, and Rose's death. In addition, he has lost his two brothers—ninety-nine-year-old George, following an unexpected fall while gardening, and Joe, his ninety-five-year-old brother, after a six-month decline precipitated by an accidental fall while volunteering at his golf club. Joe died just before his retirement community had to impose the isolation demanded by the COVID-19 pandemic. Thankfully, Joe's children could be with him during his final week.[50]

A particularly tragic loss was that of his sister-in-law, Florence, brother Ted's widow. Her health had been in decline from her struggles with Parkinson's disease, and Allen wanted to visit her in the nursing home in Las Animas, which was the summer of 2020. Such a visit required a four-hour drive. He had hoped that Sarah could take him. Of course, COVID-19 dashed that hope. Florence died from COVID complications before Christmas 2020.[51]

In one of my first conversations with Allen and Rose about writing his biography, Allen told a story about a president of New York's Union Theological Seminary "way back in the 1960s, when he and his wife, at about age 70, took their own lives together. It was publicized because they wrote ahead of time that they felt their lives had been complete. They did all they could do in this world, and rather than become a burden to their families, they decided it was time for them to go. They were both very active, very alive, very prominent. People said, 'How could he do that?' I thought, 'That is so wise.'

"Another thing that impressed me was Governor Lamb [Colorado, 1975–1987], who insisted that . . . our nursing homes are burdened with people no longer able to even understand who they are. . . . With the overpopulation of the world, we're going to have to learn that when you reach a certain age, it's time to quit using the resources that our children need and that we ought to exit this life."[52]

At the time, I found Allen's viewpoint disturbing. How could that couple have denied their children and grandchildren or society, for that matter, the companionship of an older generation and the gifts that elders have to offer from their life experiences? It is not that they would have taken resources from their children so much as they would have been resources to them.

Now I wonder. If a long life means increasing decline and loss, where along that path would one, or can one, resolve to, as Allen says, exit this life?

In October 2019, just months after he demitted the ministry, my husband and I had invited him to visit us in Iowa, where Terry was working temporarily. Perhaps we could drive him over to Dubuque, and he could revisit places that figured so prominently in his development as a pastor. He immediately answered the email invitation by writing that his traveling days were over. He would need someone to drive him to the airport because "even a cab would be hard for me, and Sarah and Mike are so busy." He added that he didn't think he would be of much help to Terry.

His objections assumed that he could not consider such a trip because getting to the airport would be an imposition, and he would not be a contributor once he got to Iowa. If it is the case that "resilient people have a social support system, and they support others," Allen has been a model of resilience. Always the team player, always encouraging his colleagues, always the one offering rides to the airport. I read between the email's lines that if he had to impose, if he could not contribute, what was the point of a visit? I was concerned we were losing the resilient Allen.

Between receiving the June 2019 IC document and his May 2020 bile duct surgery—in his isolation from Montview and presbytery, and his COVID-19 isolation from his family and activities within St. Andrew's as a widower—he was more alone than at any time in his life. For sociable Allen, the period was deadly. "Very few [resilient] people go it alone."[53]

In the context of his description several years ago of the Union Theological Seminary president's death by suicide, Allen had said, "In reincarnation, you understand that when this life ends, you return and start over. It is so appealing to me to be able to be a baby and start life all over again."[54]

He was still hospitalized when I spoke with him by phone four days after his bile duct surgery. He said, "I'm really upset. I just had a big fight with the doctor. He wouldn't give me a pill."[55]

Only after Sarah and I talked did I understand the significance of his reference to a pill. Oh, that pill. His understanding of physician-assisted suicide. Seen from one perspective, it would end this life; seen from the perspective of reincarnation, it would initiate his new one.

But everything can change in a matter of weeks. When I next reached Allen after the surgery, he was comfortably situated in St. Andrew's rehabilitation center. After the first few words, our conversation fell into a familiar pattern. He described how he had sat in rehab for days with very few staff appearing for any sort of therapeutic treatments. He complained to the supervisor, who explained that, due to COVID-19, they were limiting the number of patient-staff interactions. When Allen insisted on more therapy, the supervisor responded he could provide that, but only if Allen requested. Allen did and said he was kept busy all day with therapists, including one who helped with his swallowing. He hoped to be back in his apartment in several weeks.

He initiated the last topic of that conversation, an article he wanted to write about the intersection of McLuhan's "the medium is the message" with the converging crises of COVID-19 and the widespread 2020 protests against systemic injustice so eloquently brought to the fore by the Black Lives Matter movement. He thought the cultural milieu would have to be demolished before it will be receptive to minority groups, but how do you change culture? Perhaps if "culture" can be equated with McLuhan's "message," a "medium" can be found that will be the tool that brings about the transformation. But what is "culture" if thought of in this way, and what would be the tool(s)?

I find McLuhan to be complex, and the questions Allen was asking were way beyond my ken. It is even possible I have misrepresented them. He thought that perhaps he would write the article when he got back to his apartment and sorted out the "bugs" in his computer. He seemed to be himself, a year after facing the IC's charges and still enduring the isolation imposed by COVID-19.[56]

Whether as adolescent or elder, Allen places himself or finds himself at the center of historical, theological, social, cultural, and ethical conundrums: in 2019, feeling ensnared by the #MeToo movement; in 2020, the subject of controversies swirling around aging, DNRs, assisted suicide, and the impact of COVID-19, particularly in retirement communities; and his attentiveness to how entire societies might reckon with the urgency of systemic injustice. Even now, Allen serves as teacher and guide in the manner that he fully engages life—and death.

Epilogue Endnotes

1. Allen Maruyama, interview with author, Aurora, CO, June 12, 2019.
2. Investigative Committee, *Conclusion of Investigation*, 1–5.
3. Montview Presbyterian Church, "Letter to Church Members."
4. Investigative Committee, *Conclusion of Investigation*, 2.
5. Glendora ("Dusty") Taylor and her daughter Kathy, interview with author, Denver, May 23, 2017; and Cynthia Ann Cearley, interviews with author, Centennial, CO, May 24, 2017, and Jan. 15, 2019.
6. Allen Maruyama, interview with author, Aurora, CO, July 10, 2019.
7. Investigative Committee, *Conclusion of Investigation*, 2–3.
8. Allen Maruyama, interviews with author, Aurora, CO, July 10, 2019, and Sept. 13, 2020.
9. Investigative Committee, *Conclusion of Investigation*, 2–3.
10. Allen Maruyama, interview with author, Aurora, CO, July 10, 2019.
11. Office of the General Assembly, *Book of Order*, D–10.0203(c).
12. Investigative Committee, *Conclusion of Investigation*, 3–4.
13. Allen Maruyama, interview with author, Aurora, CO, June 12, 2019.
14. Allen Maruyama, interview with author, Aurora, CO, Sept. 5, 2019.
15. Investigative Committee, *Conclusion of Investigation*, 3.
16. Allen Maruyama, interview with author, Aurora, CO, July 10, 2019.
17. Allen Maruyama, interview with author, Aurora, CO, June 12, 2019.
18. Investigative Committee, *Conclusion of Investigation*, 1.
19. Office of the General Assembly, *Book of Order*, D–10.0203(c).
20. Investigative Committee, *Conclusion of Investigation*, 2.
21. Larry Angus, telephone conversations with author, week of Aug. 3, 2020, and Dec. 28, 2020.
22. Allen Maruyama, telephone conversation with author, Sept. 13, 2020.
23. Allen Maruyama and various presbyters, conversations with author, Lakewood, CO, Oct. 23, 2018.
24. Allen Maruyama, interview with author, Aurora, CO, July 10, 2019, and telephone conversation with author, Sept. 13, 2020.
25. Office of the General Assembly, *Book of Order*, D–10.0204.
26. Investigative Committee, *Conclusion of Investigation*, 1.
27. Office of the General Assembly, *Book of Order*, D–12.0100.
28. Allen Maruyama, interview with author, Aurora, CO, June 12, 2019.
29. Investigative Committee, *Conclusion of Investigation*, 5.

30. Allen Maruyama, telephone conversation with author, Sept. 13, 2020.

31. Lesley Shearer, interview with author, Littleton, CO, Apr. 14, 2017.

32. Allen Maruyama, telephone conversation with author, Sept. 13, 2020.

33. Allen Maruyama, interview with author, Aurora, CO, July 10, 2019.

34. Allen Maruyama, telephone conversation with author, Aug. 11, 2019.

35. Allen Maruyama, interview with author, Aurora, CO, Sept. 5, 2019.

36. Montview Presbyterian Church, "Letter to Church Members."

37. Allen Maruyama, interview with author, Aurora, CO, Sept. 5, 2019.

38. Allen Maruyama, telephone conversation with author, Oct. 2, 2019.

39. Allen Maruyama, telephone conversation with author, Oct. 2, 2019.

40. Allen Maruyama, telephone conversation with author, Oct. 23, 2019.

41. Allen Maruyama, telephone conversation with author, Mar. 9, 2020.

42. Allen and Rose Maruyama, interview with author, Aurora, CO, Apr. 17, 2017.

43. Allen Maruyama, telephone conversation with author, Sept. 13, 2020.

44. Allen Maruyama, telephone conversation with author, Oct. 2, 2019.

45. Allen Maruyama, interview with author, Aurora, CO, Sept. 5, 2019.

46. Allen and Rose Maruyama, interview with author, Aurora, CO, Mar. 15, 2917.

47. Allen Maruyama, interview with author, Aurora, CO, Sept. 5, 2019.

48. Allen Maruyama, telephone conversation with author, Sept. 13, 2020.

49. Sarah Maruyama-Biles Brady, telephone conversation with author, May 29, 2020.

50. Allen Maruyama, telephone conversation with author, Mar. 10, 2020.

51. Allen Maruyama, telephone conversation with author, Jan. 4, 2021.

52. Allen and Rose Maruyama, interviews with author, Aurora, CO, Nov. 4, 2016, and Nov. 13, 2016.

53. Zimmerman, "Build Your Resilience Toolbox."

54. Allen and Rose Maruyama, interview with author, Aurora, CO, Nov. 13, 2016.

55. Allen Maruyama, telephone conversation with author, May 29, 2020.

56. Allen Maruyama, telephone conversation with author, June 24, 2020.

Bibliography

Amache. "Amache and Japanese American Timeline." https://amache.org/timeline/.

Amache Preservation Society. https://amache.org/amache-preservation-society/.

Anderson, Ann. "Assembly Affirms Commitment to Racial Justice, Opposes Racist Groups." *General Assembly News,* June 18, 1987.

———. "Work for Racial Justice Urged." *General Assembly Daily News,* June 3, 1980.

Appiah, Anthony Kwame. *The Lies That Bind: Rethinking Identity, Creed, Country, Color, Class, Culture.* New York: Liveright, 2018.

Asakawa, Gil. *Being Japanese in America: A JA Sourcebook for Nikkei, Hapa . . . and Their Friends.* 2nd ed. Berkeley, CA: Stone Bridge, 2015.

———. "Remembering Denver's Chinatown Roots in the Midst of Renewed Anti-Asian Hate." *Pacific Citizen* 172, no. 4. (Mar. 5–18, 2021) 3. https://pacificcitizen.org/wp-content/uploads/archives-menu/Vol.172_%2304_Mar_05_2021.pdf.

Asakawa, Gil, and Erin Yoshimura. "The Asian American Journey, and the Brains and the Bias." Workshop given at the White Privilege Symposium, Denver, Nov. 2–3, 2018.

Beck, Thomas E., and Janet Colli. *The End of Homo Sapiens and the Birth of a New Species.* N.p.: CreateSpace, 2015.

Bent County Democrat. Jan. 1940–Mar. 1942.

Bent County Historical Society. "Boggsville Historic Site." https://www.bentcountyheritage.org/boggsville/.

"Brief Statement of Faith." https://en.wikipedia.org/wiki/Brief_Statement_of_Faith.

Brown, Brené. *I Thought It Was Just Me: Women Reclaiming Power and Courage in a Culture of Shame.* New York: Gotham, 2007.

Burney, Christian. "Could Amache Become a National Park?" *Bent County Democrat,* Oct. 1, 2020.

"Candidates for UPCUSA Moderator." *Presbyterian Outlook,* May 26, 1980.

Cearley, Cynthia Ann. "The Co-Pastorate Model: A Viable Model for Pastoral Staff Relationships in the Now and Future Church." DD diss., San Francisco Theological Seminary, 1995.

———. "Homily for Rose Maruyama." Montview Boulevard Presbyterian Church, Denver, Jan. 6, 2018.

Central Presbyterian Church. "Our History: Since 1860." https://www.centraldenver.com/history/.

Chapman, Stephen. "Killing for Christ." *Presbyterian Layman* (Dec. 1978–Jan. 1979) 6–8.

"Civil Liberties Act of 1988." https://en.wikipedia.org/wiki/Civil_Liberties_Act_of_1988.

Cole, Richard C., and Florence M. Cole. "'Inclusive Language' and the new *Presbyterian Hymnal*." *Presbyterian Outlook*, May 14, 1990.

Colorado Encyclopedia. "Timelines." https://www.coloradoencyclopedia.org.

"Congressman Dies." *Bent County Democrat*, Mar. 6, 1942.

"Cultural Pluralism in the Church." *Presbyterian Outlook*, Feb. 12, 1990.

Culver, Virginia. "Liberation Theology No Popular Fad." *Denver Post*, Nov. 25, 1977.

———. "Minister to Retire, Open Massage Parlor: New Career in Old Profession." *Denver Post*, Jan. 27, 1992.

Dallas, Sandra. "After Internment." *Denver Post*, May 28, 2009. https://www.denverpost.com/2009/05/28/after-internment/.

Darion, Joe. "The Impossible Dream" (song). In *Man of La Mancha* (musical). 1965.

Densho. https://www.densho.org.

Densho Encyclopedia. "Timeline." https://encyclopedia.densho.org/timeline/.

"Denver Presbytery Dissolves Relation with a Church." *Presbyterian Outlook*, May 26, 1980.

Devlin, Neil H. "Memories of Amache." *Denver Post*, Nov. 13, 2003.

"Doshisha University." https://en.wikipedia.org/wiki/Doshisha_University.

Eisenlohr, Teresa Lockhart. Massage Ministration (website). https://www.massageministration.com.

"Eugene Carson Blake." https://en.wikipedia.org/wiki/Eugene_Carson_Blake.

Frishman, Richard. "Hidden in Plain Sight: The Ghosts of Segregation." *New York Times*, Nov. 30, 2020, updated Dec. 1, 2020. https://nyti.ms/2VelH2m.

Fox, Matthew. *The Coming of the Cosmic Christ: The Healing of Mother Earth and the Birth of a Global Renaissance*. San Francisco: HarperOne, 1988.

———. Matthew Fox (website). https://www.matthewfox.org.

———. *Original Blessing: A Primer in Creation Spirituality*. Rochester, VT: Bear & Co., 1983.

Fule, Aurelia T. "For the Sake of Creation." *Presbyterian Outlook*, Apr. 30, 1990.

———. *Minister Biographical Questionnaire*. Philadelphia: Office of the General Assembly, n.d.

General Assembly Daily News, June–July, 1976.

General Assembly Daily News, June 4, 1980.

General Assembly Daily News, June 7, 1990.

General Assembly of the United Presbyterian Church. "One Hundred Ninety-Second General Assembly." General Assembly: Detroit, 1980. Cassette recordings. In the archives of the Presbyterian Historical Society, Philadelphia.

Gingold, Naomi. "Japanese Americans Weren't the Only US Citizens Housed in Camps." *World*, Oct. 18, 2017. https://www.pri.org/stories/2017-10-18/japanese-americans-werent-only-us-citizens-kept-camps.

Gregg Meister, J. W. "Mass Media Report Inadequate." *Presbyterian Outlook*, May 26, 1980.

Griego, Tina. "Special Honors." *The Denver Post*, Nov. 5, 2011. https://www.denverpost.com/2011/11/05/griego-special-honors-for-japanese-american-wwii-veterans-two-fronted-battle-against-discrimination/.

Griepp, Virgil. "Mass Media Witness Re-Established." *General Assembly Daily News*, June 3, 1980.

———. "Young Stresses Church's Role in Human Rights." *General Assembly Daily News*, June 3, 1980.

"Harada House Foundation Receives Grant." *Pacific Citizen* 168, no. 11 (June 28–July 11, 2019) 12. https://pacificcitizen.org/wp-content/uploads/archives-menu/Vol.168 _%2311_Jun_28_2019.pdf.

Haroutunian, Joseph, ed. *Calvin: Commentaries.* Library of Christian Classics 23. London: SCM, 1958.

Hart, Ruth. "Remarks." Personal remarks delivered at retirement tribute. Montview Boulevard Presbyterian Church, Denver, May 17, 1992. In author's possession.

Hildner, Judy. "GPSA [Greater Pueblo Sports Association] Wildcats Rule Gridiron." *Pueblo Chieftain*, July 12, 2009. https://www.chieftain.com/article/20090712/ SPORTS/307129881.

Hiraga, Alissa. "Dr. Michio Kaku and What's Next for Humanity." *Pacific Citizen* 166, no. 5 (Mar. 23–Apr. 5, 2018) 6–7. https://pacificcitizen.org/wp-content/uploads/ archives-menu/Vol.166_%2305_Mar_23_2018.pdf.

Hirai, Alex. "Did You Know? Everything About JA History in Utah." *Pacific Citizen* 168, no. 5 (Mar. 22–Apr. 4, 2019) 8. https://pacificcitizen.org/wp-content/uploads/ archives-menu/Vol.168_%2305_Mar_22_2019.pdf.

History Colorado. "One Hundred Sixty-Seven Years Ago the U.S. and Mexico Signed the Treaty of Guadalupe Hidalgo." https://www.historycolorado.org/press-release /2015/02/02/167-years-ago-us-and-mexico-signed-treaty-guadalupe-hidalgo.

Hite, Sarah. *The Spirit of Montview, 1902–2002: A History of Montview Boulevard Presbyterian Church, Denver, Colorado.* Denver: Walsworth, 2001.

"Hopes for the Nineties." *Presbyterian Outlook*, Jan. 1–8, 1990.

Hosokawa, Bill. *Colorado's Japanese Americans: From 1886 to the Present.* Boulder, CO: University Press of Colorado, 2005.

Hutcheson, Richard G., Jr. "Presbyterian Polarization and the 'Two-Church' Hypothesis." *Presbyterian Outlook*, May 28, 1990.

Imai, Shiho. "Immigration Act of 1924." https://encyclopedia.densho.org/Immigration_ Act_of_1924/.

Inoue, David. "We Can't Stand on the Shoulders of Others without Reaching Back to Help Everyone Up." *Pacific Citizen* 170, no. 7 (Apr. 24–May 7, 2020) 5. https://pacificcitizen.org/wp-content/uploads/archives-menu/Vol.170_%2307_ Apr_24_2020.pdf.

Institute of Noetic Sciences. https://www.noetic.org.

The International Center for Reiki Training. https://www.reiki.org.

Investigative Committee. *Conclusion of Investigation, Charges to Be Filed, Alternate Forms of Resolution.* Presbytery of Denver, June 7, 2019.

Ishikawa, Takashi. *Kokoro: The Soul of Japan.* Tokyo: East, 1986.

Ishimoto, Zachary. "Personal Statement." *Pacific Citizen* 167, no. 6 (Sept. 28–Oct. 11, 2018) 11. https://www.pacificcitizen.org/wp-content/uploads/archives-menu/ Vol.167_%2306_Sep_28_2018.pdf. Site discontinued.

JACL National. "JACL Initiates Series on Sexual Assault." *Pacific Citizen.* 166, no. 1 (Jan. 26–Feb. 8, 2018) 2. https://pacificcitizen.org/wp-content/uploads/archives-menu/ Vol.166_%2301_Jan_26_2018.pdf.

———. "Setsuko's Secret: Friendships Forged in Times of Trial." Dec. 8, 2020. https:// www.youtube.com/watch?v=-W8cRoRHutU.

"James Curtis Hepburn." https://en.wikipedia.org/wiki/James_Curtis_Hepburn.

Japan Visitor. https://www.japanvisitor.com.

Japanese American Citizen's League. https://www.jacl.org.

Japanese American National Museum. https://www.janm.org.

Japanese Calligraphy. https://www.japancalligraphy.eu.

Johnston, George Toshio. "Aika Herzig-Yoshinaga Dies at Ninety-Three." *Pacific Citizen* 167, no. 3 (Aug. 3–23, 2018) 13. https://pacificcitizen.org/wp-content/uploads/archives-menu/Vol.167_%2303_Aug_03_2018.pdf.

———. "'Farewell to Manzanar' at Forty-Five: Homecoming for Houston." *Pacific Citizen* 166, no. 09 (May 18, 2018) 7. https://www.pacificcitizen.org/farewell-to-manzanar-at-45-homecoming-for-houston/.

———. "Japanese American Vets Still Ponder the Vietnam War." *Pacific Citizen* 165, no. 9 (Nov. 3–16, 2017) 6. https://pacificcitizen.org/wp-content/uploads/archives-menu/Vol.165_%2309_Nov_03_2017.pdf.

———. "New Tome Tells of 'Life After Manzanar.'" *Pacific Citizen* 166, no. 7 (Apr. 20–May 3, 2018) 8. https://pacificcitizen.org/wp-content/uploads/archives-menu/Vol.166_%2307_Apr_20_2018.pdf.

"Kanji: Japanese Writing." https://www.britannica.com/topic/kanji.

Khanal, Ajaya Bhadra. "Three-Year [*sic*] Boy Enthroned as New Rinpoche." *Kathmandu Post*, Sept. 30, 1993.

Killgore, Andrew I. "The Rev. Benjamin M. Weir." *Washington Report on Middle East Affairs* (Dec. 1986) 20. https://www.wrmea.org/1986-december/personality-the-rev.-benjamin-m.-weir.html.

Kulish, Nicholas, Frances Robles, and Patricia Mazzei. "Behind Illicit Massage Parlors Lie a Vast Crime Network and Modern Indentured Servitude." *New York Times,* Mar. 2, 2019. https://www.nytimes.com/2019/03/02/us/massage-parlors-human-trafficking.html.

Langer, Susanne K. *Philosophy in a New Key: A Study in the Symbols of Reason, Rite, and Art.* Cambridge, MA: Harvard University Press, 1942.

Langowski, Eric. "Extending Redress: My University, My Ancestors." *Pacific Citizen* 167, no. 11 (Dec. 14, 2018–Jan. 24, 2019) 47. https://pacificcitizen.org/wp-content/uploads/archives-menu/Vol.167_%2311_Dec_14_2018.pdf.

Learn Religions. https://www.learnreligions.com.

Lebra, Joyce. *We Chose Colorado: Japanese American Voices.* Palm Springs, CA: Old John, 2016.

Lefton, Brad. "In Japan, One Hundred Years of Glory Days for High School Baseball." *New York Times,* Aug. 16, 2018. https://www.nytimes.com/2018/08/16/sports/japan-high-school-baseball.html?searchResultPosition=1.

Leonard, Robert. "Democrats Can Win in Farm Country" (print), "How Democrats Should Talk to People in Farm Country" (online). *New York Times,* Sept. 21, 2018. https://www.nytimes.com/2018/09/20/opinion/democrats-women-iowa-obama.html?searchResultPosition=1.

LifeSpark Cancer Resources. https://www.lifesparknow.org.

Longfield, Bradley J. "William Merrill, the Brick Church, and the Fundamentalist-Modernist Conflict." *Journal of Presbyterian History,* 97, no. 2 (Fall–Winter 2019) 60–72.

Lovelace, Richard F. "Evangelicals and Pluralism." *Presbyterian Layman* (Dec. 1978–Jan. 1979) 4–5.

Lyon, Cherstin M. "Alien Land Laws." https://encyclopedia.densho.org/Alien_land_laws/.

Mails, Thomas E. *Fools Crow: Wisdom and Power.* Tulsa, OK: Council Oak Books, 1991.

Maruyama, Allen. *Campaign Brochure for Moderator of 192nd General Assembly.* 1980.

———. "The Christian Mission in Japan: A Sabbatical Study." Unpublished manuscript, 1986.

———. "People without a Vision Shall Perish." Sermon given at Montview Boulevard Presbyterian Church, Denver, Apr. 14, 2002.

———. "Personal Statement of Faith." 1992. In author's possession.

———. "Presbyterian Church (U.S.A.) Personal Information Form." Mar. 5, 1993. Partial copy in author's possession.

———. "Presbyterian Church (U.S.A.) Personal Information Form." Feb. 15, 1996. Partial copy in author's possession.

———. "Reflections, 1972–1992." For the one hundredth anniversary of Montview Boulevard Presbyterian Church, Denver, 2002.

———. "A Theological Critique of Marshall McLuhan's New Man of the Electric Age." PhD diss., Aquinas School of Philosophy and Theology, 1972.

Maruyama, Rose and Allen. "Nepal." *Montview Messenger,* 1993.

Matsumoto, Mieko. "Chinese Exclusion Act." https://encyclopedia.densho.org/Chinese _Exclusion_Act/.

"Minidoka Visitor Center Officially Opens." *Pacific Citizen* 170, no. 5 (Mar. 20–Apr. 2, 2020) 8. https://pacificcitizen.org/wp-content/uploads/archives-menu/Vol.170 _%2305_Mar_20_2020.pdf.

Mochizuki, Minoru. "Banished from California: Discovered a World." Unpublished manuscript.

———. "The Two Worlds of Shigeaki Mochizuki, 1919–1944." Unpublished manuscript, 1993.

Montview Presbyterian Church. "Letter to Church Members." Aug. 30, 2019. In author's possession.

———. *Montview Messenger,* June 14, 1972.

Muller, Eric L. "Draft Resistance." Densho. https://encyclopedia.densho.org/Draft_ resistance/.

Murata, Alice. *Images of America: Japanese Americans in Chicago.* Chicago: Arcadia, 2002.

Naropa University. https://www.naropa.edu.

National Japanese American Memorial Foundation. https://www.njamemorial.org/about.

"New Archbishop." *Telegraph Herald,* May 8, 1962.

"The New Testament, First Peter, Chapter Two." *Westminster Study Bible: The Holy Bible (Revised Standard Version Containing Old and New Testaments).* New York: Collins' Clear-Type, 1965.

Niiya, Brian. "Kazuo Masuda." https://encyclopedia.densho.org/Kazuo_Masuda/.

———."No-No Boys." https://encyclopedia.densho.org/No-no_boys/.

"The Nominees for Moderator and Their Views." *Presbyterian Outlook,* May 21, 1990.

Office of the General Assembly. *Book of Confessions.* The Constitution of the Presbyterian Church (U.S.A.), Part 1. Office of the General Assembly: Louisville, 2016. https://oga.pcusa.org/section/mid-council-ministries/constitutional-services/ constitution/#confessions.

———. *Book of Order, 2019–2023.* The Constitution of the Presbyterian Church (U.S.A.), Part 2. Office of the General Assembly: Louisville, 2019. https://oga.pcusa.org/ section/mid-council-ministries/constitutional-services/constitution/#confessions.

Oremus Bible Browser. https://www.bible.oremus.org.

"Outgoing Moderators of UPC and PC Reflect." *Presbyterian Outlook*, May 5, 1980.

Oxenham, John. "In Christ There Is No East or West." https://www.hymnary.org.

Pacific Citizen Staff. "Norman Mineta's Legacy Chronicled on PBS." *Pacific Citizen* 168, no. 8 (May 10–May 30, 2019) 4. https://pacificcitizen.org/wp-content/uploads/archives-menu/Vol.168_%2308_May_10_2019.pdf.

———. "San Diego JACL Reflects, Remembers on Thirtieth Anniversary of Redress," *Pacific Citizen* 167, no. 7 (Oct. 12–26, 2018) 6–8. https://pacificcitizen.org/wp-content/uploads/archives-menu/Vol.167_%2307_Oct_12_2018.pdf.

"Pierre Teilhard de Chardin." https://en.wikipedia.org/wiki/Pierre_Teilhard_de_Chardin.

Poethig, Eunice Blanchard. "Two-Church Debate Continues." *Presbyterian Outlook*, June 4, 1990.

"Presbyterians and the Civil Rights Movement." Presbyterian Historical Society. https://www.history.pcusa.org/content/presbyterians-and-civil-rights-movement.

"Price H. Gwynn III Elected Moderator of the Two Hundred Second General Assembly on the Second Ballot." *Presbyterian Outlook*, June 11, 1990.

Purvis-Smith, V. L. *Greenwood Riven*. Self-published, 2016.

Redding, Micah. "The Jesuit Priest Who Believed in God and the Singularity." *VICE*, Mar. 8, 2016. https://www.vice.com/en/article/nz7z7q/the-priest-who-believed-in-god-and-the-singularity-pierre-teilhard-de-chardin.

Reid, T. R. "Reiki in Denver—A Drug-Free Treatment for Pain, Insomnia, Arthritis." *Denver Post*, Aug. 12, 2019. https://yourhub.denverpost.com/blog/2019/08/reiki-in-denver-a-drug-free-treatment-for-pain-insomnia-arthritis/248034/.

"Remembering Syngman Rhee." *Presbyterian Outlook*, Jan. 19, 2015. https://pres-outlook.org/2015/01/remembering-syngman-rhee/.

Rich, Motoko. "Naomi Osaka, a New Governor and Me." *New York Times*, Oct. 7, 2018.

———. "Japan Wants Women in the Office. Housework Gets in the Way." *New York Times*, Feb. 3, 2019.

Ricoeur, Paul. *A Ricoeur Reader: Reflection and Imagination*. Edited by Mario J. Valdés. Toronto: University of Toronto Press, 1991.

Robert, Henry M., III, et al. *Robert's Rules of Order Newly Revised*. 11th ed. Boston: Da Capo, 2011.

"Robert's Rules of Order." https://en.wikipedia.org/wiki/Robert's_Rules_of_Order.

Rogers, Jack. "An Alternative to the 'Two-Church' Hypothesis." *Presbyterian Outlook*, May 14, 1990.

"Romanization of Japanese." https://en.wikipedia.org/wiki/Romanization_of_Japanese.

Rooks, Curtiss Takada. "Reflections on Being Mixed, but Not Mixed Up." *Discover Nikkei: Japanese Migrants and Their Descendants,* July 6, 2020. http://www.discovernikkei.org/en/journal/2020/7/6/reflections-on-being-mixed/.

Schaffer, Michael D. "Ex-D.C. Area Pastor to Lead Presbyterians." *Washington Post*, June 10, 1989.

Shearer, Lesley E. *Essays on Energy I—Eternal Blueprints, Essays on Energy II—Kaleidoscopes*. Englewood, CO: Omega, 2006.

Silva, Pedro. "Advent Sermon." First Congregational Church, Boulder, CO, Dec. 9, 2018.

Sittler, Joseph. "Joseph Haroutunian: Total Theologian." *Journal of Religion* 50, no. 3 (July 1970) 215–28.

Smith, Alexa. "Two Hundred Second Assembly to Tackle Chapter Nine Issues." *Presbyterian Outlook*, June 4, 1990.

Socier, David. "Forty-Four Cats Were Football Champs." *Pueblo Chieftain*, July 10, 1994.

Special Committee on the Theology of Liberation and Renewal. *Report of the Special Committee on the Theology of Liberation and Renewal.* In *Minutes of the 1977 General Assembly of the United Presbyterian Church in the United States of America: Part 1*, 260–97. New York: Office of the General Assembly, 1977.

Stein, Diane. *Essential Reiki: A Complete Guide to an Ancient Healing Art.* Berkeley, CA: Crossing, 1995.

Synod of Wisconsin. "105th Annual Meeting, June 12–14, 1956." In *Minutes of the Synod of Wisconsin, 1956–1958.* In the archives of the Presbyterian Historical Society, Philadelphia.

Takahara, Kumiko. *Off the Fat of the Land: The Denver Post's Story of the Japanese American Internment during World War II.* Powell, WY: Western History, 2003.

Thorson-Smith, Sylvia, et al. *Pornography: Far from the Song of Songs: A Study Paper Adopted by the Two Hundredth General Assembly (1988).* Edited by Wayne Cowan et al. Office of the General Assembly: Louisville, 1988. https://www.pcusa.org/site_media/media/uploads/_resolutions/pornography-far-from-song-of-songs.pdf.

Tighe, Mike. "Forum with the Reverend Maruyama." *Telegraph Herald*, July 3, 1972.

"Toyohiko Kagawa." https://en.wikipedia.org/wiki/Toyohiko_Kagawa.

Tracy, E. Kenneth. "Welcome to Salt Lake City." *Presbyterian Outlook*, June 4, 1990.

Tsuru for Solidarity. https://www.tsuruforsolidarity.org.

Ujifusa, Grant. "Gracye and Hiro Uyehara: In Memoriam after Five Years." *Pacific Citizen* 168, no. 3 (Feb. 22–Mar. 7, 2019) 11. https://pacificcitizen.org/wp-content/uploads/archives-menu/Vol.168_%2303_Feb_22_2019.pdf.

The United Church of Christ in Japan. https://uccj-e.org.

United Presbyterian Church in the United States of America. *Minutes of the General Assembly of the United Presbyterian Church in the United States of America, 1980: Part 1.*

United States Department of State, Foreign Service Institute, Office of the Historian. "Chinese Immigration and the Chinese Exclusion Acts." https://history.state.gov/milestones/1866-1898/chinese-immigration.

Van Marter, Jerry L. "Confessions and Pensions Expected to Dominate Two Hundred Second GA." *Presbyterian Outlook*, May 14, 1990.

———. "Report on Environmental Peril Readied." *Presbyterian Outlook*, May 14, 1990.

"Viewpoints on Specific Questions." *Presbyterian Outlook*, May 26, 1980.

Voskuil, Dennis. "The Reformed Roots of American Neo-Orthodoxy." *Journal of Theological Studies* 25, no. 2 (Oct. 1974) 271–80.

"Where It All Began . . . at the Presidio of San Franciso." Advertisement. *Pacific Citizen* 169, no. 9 (Nov. 8–21 2019) 7. https://pacificcitizen.org/wp-content/uploads/archives-menu/Vol.169_%2309_Nov_08_2019.pdf.

Williams, Duncan Ryūken. *American Sutra: A Story of Faith and Freedom in the Second World War.* Cambridge, MA: Harvard University Press, 2019.

Williams, Gene. "Charlotte Presbytery Endorses Price H. Gwynn III for Moderator of the Two Hundred Second General Assembly." *Presbyterian Outlook*, Feb. 19, 1990.

———. "James E. Andrews Sees Dramatic Changes Coming in the Nineties." *Presbyterian Outlook*, Feb. 26, 1990.

———. "Major Structural Design Issues Still Unresolved." *Presbyterian Outlook*, June 4, 1990.

———. "S. David Stoner Looks at the Nineties." *Presbyterian Outlook*, Feb. 19, 1990.

————. "Two More Endorsed for Moderator of the Two Hundred Second General Assembly." *Presbyterian Outlook*, Feb. 26, 1990.

Wimberly, Edward P. *Moving from Shame to Self-Worth: Preaching and Pastoral Care.* Nashville: Abingdon, 1999.

Wolf, Fred Alan. *Taking the Quantum Leap: The New Physics for Nonscientists.* New York: Harper Perennial, 1981.

World Future Society. https://www.worldfuture.org.

Wuthnow, Robert. *The Struggle for America's Soul: Evangelicals, Liberals, and Secularism.* Grand Rapids: Eerdmans, 1989.

Yamada, Gerald, and David Inouye. "Letters to the Editor." *Pacific Citizen* 169, no. 7 (Oct. 11–24, 2019) 2, 8. https://pacificcitizen.org/wp-content/uploads/archives-menu/Vol.169_%2307_Oct_11_2019.pdf.

Youngs, Sharon K. "Textual Issues Addressed by the Hymnbook Committee." *Presbyterian Outlook*, June 4, 1990.

Zimmerman, Eilene. "Build Your Resilience Toolbox." *New York Times*, June 21, 2010.

Index

www.ingramcontent.com/pod-product-compliance
Lightning Source LLC
Chambersburg PA
CBHW060134280326
41932CB00012B/1516